Brad Dayley

Sams **Teach Yourself**
Django

in **24**
Hours

SAMS   800 East 96th Street, Indianapolis, Indiana, 46240 USA

Sams Teach Yourself Django in 24 Hours

ISBN-13: 9780672329593
ISBN-10: 067232959X

Library of Congress Cataloging-in-Publication Data:

Dayley, Brad.

  Sams teach yourself Django in 24 hours / Brad Dayley.

    p. cm.

  ISBN 978-0-672-32959-3 (pbk.)

  1. Web site development. 2. Django (Electronic resource) 3. Python (Computer program language) I. Title.

  TK5105.888.D397 2008

  006.7'6—dc22

                             2008001956

005.72
Django
Dayley

Printed in the United States of America

Second Printing April 2008

Trademarks

All terms mentioned in this book that are known to be trademarks or service marks have been appropriately capitalized. Sams Publishing cannot attest to the accuracy of this information. Use of a term in this book should not be regarded as affecting the validity of any trademark or service mark.

Warning and Disclaimer

Every effort has been made to make this book as complete and accurate as possible, but no warranty or fitness is implied. The information provided is on an "as is" basis. The author and the publisher shall have neither liability nor responsibility to any person or entity with respect to any loss or damages arising from the information contained in this book or from the use of the CD or programs accompanying it.

Bulk Sales

Sams Publishing offers excellent discounts on this book when ordered in quantity for bulk purchases or special sales. For more information, please contact

    U.S. Corporate and Government Sales
    1-800-382-3419
    corpsales@pearsontechgroup.com

For sales outside of the U.S., please contact

    International Sales
    international@pearsoned.com

This Book Is Safari Enabled

The Safari® Enabled icon on the cover of your favorite technology book means the book is available through Safari Bookshelf. When you buy this book, you get free access to the online edition for 45 days.

Safari Bookshelf is an electronic reference library that lets you easily search thousands of technical books, find code samples, download chapters, and access technical information whenever and wherever you need it.

To gain 45-day Safari Enabled access to this book:

▶ Go to http://www.informit.com/onlineedition.
▶ Complete the brief registration form.
▶ Enter the coupon code ERBC-2QCB-ZL1W-YDBJ-YZ42.

If you have difficulty registering on Safari Bookshelf or accessing the online edition, please email customer-service@safaribooksonline.com.

Editor-in-Chief
Mark Taub

Development Editor
Songlin Qiu

Managing Editor
Gina Kanouse

Project Editor
Jovana San Nicolas-Shirley

Copy Editor
Gayle Johnson

Indexer
Cheryl Lenser

Proofreader
Anne Goebel

Technical Editor
Timothy Boronczyk

Publishing Coordinator
Vanessa Evans

Book Designer
Gary Adair

Compositor
Nonie Ratcliff

Contents at a Glance

Table of Contents

Sams Teach Yourself Django in 24 Hours

About the Author

Brad Dayley is a senior software engineer in Novell's Product Development Group. He has 16 years of experience in designing, developing, and implementing software from the kernel level through web development. He is the author of several books on server and network management as well as programming languages. When he is not developing software or writing books, he can be found biking, hiking, and/or Jeeping somewhere in the remote regions of the western United States with his wife, DaNae, and four sons.

Dedication

For D, A & F!

Acknowledgments

My sincere gratitude goes out to the following persons, without whom this book could not have happened:

My wife, who provides the inspiration and strength behind everything I do. Thank you for being everything for me.

My friends, who force me to be more intelligent and creative than I necessarily would like to be.

My editors, who made the book readable, technically accurate, and kept me on track. It seems that nothing gets by you. Thanks to Songlin Qiu for all your hard work in keeping me on the right track and ensuring the quality of the book is the best. Thanks to Gayle Johnson for making it appear as though I can actually write. Thanks to Tim Boronczyk for making sure the book is technically useful as well as technically accurate. Thanks to Jovana San Nicolas-Shirley and Gina Kanouse for seeing me through to the end. Last but not least, thanks to Mark Taber for getting the book off the ground and making it happen. All of you are the best.

We Want to Hear from You!

As the reader of this book, *you* are our most important critic and commentator. We value your opinion, and we want to know what we're doing right, what we could do better, what areas you'd like to see us publish in, and any other words of wisdom you're willing to pass our way.

You can email or write us directly to let us know what you did or didn't like about this book—as well as what we can do to make our books stronger.

Please note that we cannot help you with technical problems related to the topic of this book, and that we might not be able to reply to every message.

When you write, please be sure to include this book's title and author, as well as your name and phone number or email address.

E-mail: feedback@samspublishing.com

Mail: Sams Publishing
800 East 96th Street
Indianapolis, IN 46240 USA

Reader Services

Visit our website and register this book at informit.com/register for convenient access to any updates, downloads, or errata that might be available for this book.

Introduction

I have been working with the Django framework for about a year and a half, and I love it. Every so often you run into ideas that make absolute, complete sense, and Django is one of those. The folks at Django seem to be bent on making it the most elegant web framework available, and so far they are doing a great job.

This was a tough book to write. The Django framework is simple to implement, but you can accomplish so much with it. The format of this book is Teach Yourself in 24 Hours. The idea is that after spending 24 hours with this book and a Django installation, you should have a pretty good idea of how to use Django to build a full-featured production website.

Throughout this book, I use a fictitious website project called iFriends to illustrate the building blocks of a Django-powered website. The book has several "Try It Yourself" sections that take you through specific tasks of building the iFriends website. Actually *do* the "Try It Yourself" sections. They will help everything else make a lot more sense. They build on each other, so if you skip one, future "Try It Yourself" sections may not work properly.

When you have finished the "Try It Yourself" sections, you will have a mostly functional website. You should easily have enough skills by then that you could tweak and finish the website on your own in only a few hours if you wanted to. There just wasn't enough room in the book to finish every component. I felt it was much more important to cover the topics that I did.

I do have one disclaimer: There is absolutely no CSS code in my HTML template examples. I would much rather have used CSS code to format my HTML templates than the classic HTML tags (some of them deprecated) that I used. I chose not to include CSS for two important reasons. The first reason is room. Adding CSS files to all the examples would have taken quite a bit more room, which I didn't have. The second reason is that this book is designed for Python programmers as well as HTML programmers. Using CSS for someone who is not as familiar with it could provide a distraction. This book is about learning to implement the Django framework. CSS programming techniques belong in a different book.

When designing the content for this book, I tried to come up with the most relevant way to present the Django framework that will actually help programmers develop websites that are pertinent to real-world needs. I know that a few components and concepts have been left out. I welcome your comments and any suggestions on things that you feel need to be added to this book. If I get a chance, I will try to incorporate them into future revisions of the book. You can email any queries or suggestions to dayleybooks@yahoo.com.

I hope you enjoy the Django framework as much as I have and that the concepts in this book prove useful to you.

Who Should Read This Book

This book should be read by anyone who is developing or even considering developing websites. The Django framework saves web developers a lot of time and headaches. This book is designed for website developers who have at least some familiarity with the Python programming language. Don't worry if you are not very familiar with Python. You should be able to pick up on what is going on with a few visits to www.python.org.

How This Book Is Organized

This book is organized into four parts that help you quickly navigate the Django framework so that you will have the knowledge necessary to leverage the framework to build production websites. I tried to design the book to start slowly so that you will be able to build a good foundation for the Django framework. Then, as the hours (chapters) progress, the book delves deeper into different aspects of the Django framework.

▶ Part I, "Creating the Website Framework," covers the basics of installing, configuring, and using the Django framework to build basic websites. You are introduced to the model, template, and view concepts that Django uses to implement websites.

▶ Part II, "Implementing the Website Interface," covers building templates and views to build web pages. You will learn how to use templates and views to store, access, and retrieve data that is stored in the website's database.

▶ Part III, "Implementing a Full-Featured Website," covers adding authentication, cookie handling, and other features necessary to implement a full production website. You will learn how to create users and groups and how to assign permissions to specific data.

▶ Part IV, "Implementing Advanced Website Components," covers some of the advanced features of the Django framework that you will likely want to implement in production websites. You will learn how to implement middleware to enable advanced request and response handlers. You will also learn how to implement localized strings to add multiple-language capability to the website, implement caching to improve website performance, and deploy a Django website.

How to Use This Book

The *Teach Yourself in 24 Hours* series has several unique elements that will help you as you are trying to learn the Django framework. Throughout the book, I use the following elements to draw attention to specific concepts:

This element provides information about slightly off-topic tangents that may be beneficial to you but that are not necessarily directly related to the current section.

This element provides information that is directly related to the current section but that does not necessarily flow with the text. It discusses what is happening in the background or points that you may not easily pick up on but that are important.

This element notes important things that you need to know before proceeding through the book. It is important to read these sections to avoid problems with your website.

The "Try It Yourself" sections are designed to take you through the steps of actually performing the tasks that you have been reading about. Do not skip these sections. They usually provide additional information about the topic and are a great chance to practice the concepts.

At the end of each hour, you will find the following sections that are designed to help you solidify what you have read:

▶ The "Q&A" section poses questions and gives answers on concepts that are related to the hour but that fall outside what is covered in the book.

▶ The "Quiz" section provides questions and answers about the topics covered in each hour.

▶ The "Exercises" section lists activities that you can do to practice what you have learned during the hour. These exercises are a great way to strike out on your own a bit and get more confident with Django.

PART I

Creating the Website Framework

HOUR 1

Understanding Django

What You'll Learn in This Hour:

▶ What the Django framework is, and why you should use it
▶ How Django uses models to define data
▶ How Django uses Python functions to build views
▶ How Django implements templates
▶ Where to configure Django projects
▶ How to use the `manage.py` utility
▶ What views are available in the admin interface
▶ How to install Django

Designing and implementing websites can be fun and rewarding; however, it can also be stressful and demanding. Django is one of the best frameworks available to quickly develop full-featured production websites. Django is flexible and makes it easy to design a website that can be easily updated and expanded. As soon as you have learned the Django framework, you will be able to speed up design, implementation, and maintenance of your websites.

The purpose of this hour is to introduce you to the Django framework and give you a basic understanding of the architecture. The rest of the hours in this book provide the in-depth details you need to implement a full-featured production website using Django.

This hour is a basic overview of the Django framework, including models, views, and templates. We will also cover the utilities that you will use to configure and manage your Django projects. Then we will give you a brief overview of the admin interface that you can use to create and modify objects in your Django projects. Finally, we discuss how to install Django.

What Is Django?

Django is a high-level web framework that simplifies website development. As a high-level web framework, Django abstracts much of the web development process, allowing developers to quickly implement database-backed websites using dynamic web pages.

> Django is pronounced "JAN-go" with the "D" silent.

By dynamic, we mean web pages that are built on-the-fly using data from the browser request, URL, and a database. Dynamic pages solve several different problems. The biggest problem they solve is trying to maintain numerous static pages scattered all over a classic website.

Django implements a Model View Controller (MVC) architecture to separate the data, logic, and view layers in website development. This has two major advantages. One is that it's easy to have some developers develop the database and others develop the web pages. Another is that code and URLs become much cleaner, easier to maintain, and more elegant.

Why Use Django?

The biggest reason to use Django is that it's easy to set up a production website in no time at all. As soon as you have learned how to use Django to build websites, you will be able to implement basic websites in a matter of hours.

Another reason to use Django is that components or even entire websites are portable and can be used in other websites. Only minimal reconfiguration is needed to port the views.

Understanding Models

Django implements a Python class, `django.db.models.Model`, to define data models that will be used in a website. A data model is a set of definitions that define the attributes of objects that will be stored in the database. When you build your website, you create a subclass of the `Model` class and add `Field` members to that class to define specific data. Django's model interface provides a full-featured selection of field types that make it easy to define each model.

The models you define in your project are synchronized to an SQL database backend as tables. Django also provides a nice database interface that lets you access data in the database from views and templates. We will discuss models more in Hour 3, "Adding Models and Objects to Your Website," and Hour 5, "Using Data from the Database in Views."

Understanding Views

Rendering a view from an URL request is a multistep process in Django. When a Django server receives an URL request, it parses the URL and, using a set of previously defined patterns, determines which Python code should render the view.

The way it works is that as you design your website, you write Python functions that will build and render web pages. For each Python function, you define at least one URL pattern that will link a specific URL to that view function. The Django framework receives the URL request, handing the request to the view function and then sending the dynamically built response back to the web browser. We will discuss the URL configuration more in Hour 4, "Creating the Initial Views."

Understanding Templates

Django also provides a robust template parser that allows you to build templates that the view functions can use to build response web pages. This allows your Python developers to focus on building the data that should be displayed and allows your HTML programmers to focus on designing the web pages. We will discuss templates much more starting in Hour 7, "Implementing Django Templates to Create Custom Views."

Configuring the `settings.py` File

Most of the website configuration that you need to implement is done in the `settings.py` file. When you create a new project, Django automatically adds the `settings.py` file to the project's root directory. The `settings.py` file contains the configuration for databases, installed applications, and numerous other configuration settings. The Django framework relies heavily on the `settings.py` file to define all kinds of behavior.

You can also use the `settings.py` file to set your own global settings for the website. You can access this file as an object from within Python code in your projects. To access the `settings.py` file, import the settings object, as shown in the following example:

```
from django.conf import settings.py
if settings.MY_CUSTOM_SETTING:
    #perform custom work
```

Do not try to modify settings in the `settings.py` file on-the-fly from Python code in your project. This can have unexpected (bad) results.

Throughout this book, we will discuss several different settings that you need to make in the `settings.py` file. You can find more information about the `settings.py` options at `http://www.djangoproject.com/documentation/settings`.

Using the `manage.py` Utility

Another file that is automatically installed in each project you create is the `manage.py` utility. The `manage.py` utility is actually a wrapper to an application called django-admin.py that needs to be located somewhere in the `PYTHONPATH`.

The `manage.py` utility is used to perform all kinds of development, administration, and testing tasks. The best way to describe the `manage.py` utility is to list some of the commands you can implement:

- ▶ `startproject` creates a new Django project. A directory is created for the project that includes the initial files.

- ▶ `startapp` creates a new application in a Django project. A directory is created for the application that includes the initial files.

- ▶ `syncdb` synchronizes data from project models to the SQL database.

- ▶ `runserver` starts the development server.

- ▶ `shell` launches a Python interpreter shell that has access to the Django project, including the database.

- ▶ `dbshell` launches an SQL command-line client for the database.

Usually the `manage.py` utility should be used from the root of your Django project. We will discuss using the `manage.py` utility for various tasks throughout this book. You can find more information about the `manage.py` utility at `http://www.djangoproject.com/documentation/django-admin`.

Understanding the Django Development Server

Django comes with a lightweight development HTTP server that you can use to test your website while you are developing it. The great thing about the development server is that it is just there. After you install Django, you don't need to spend time trying to hook it into some other web server to test your code.

The development server works well for testing and uses few system resources. It should give you all the functionality you need to test your website.

Start the development server using the following command at the root of your Django project:

```
python manage.py runserver
```

You can stop the development server by pressing Ctrl+Break or Ctrl+C.

By the Way

Understanding the Admin Interface

One of the best features of Django is that it comes with a full-featured, attractive admin interface that you can use to maintain websites. The admin interface lets you create, view, and modify data in your database models from an administrator perspective.

The three main views that you deal with in the admin interface are the main or model view, the change list view, and the form view. The following sections briefly describe each of these views to give you an initial feel for the admin interface. We will discuss the admin interface more in Hours 2, 3, 17, and 18.

Admin Model View

The admin model view is the main view that is displayed when you access the admin interface. You can see the model view by typing the URL /admin/ into a browser:

```
http://127.0.0.1:8000/admin/
```

The model view displays a list of the models that are currently installed in the admin interface for the project. From the model view, click the Add or Change link to the right of each model, as shown in Figure 1.1, to access the add form or change list view.

FIGURE 1.1
The model view
in the admin
interface.

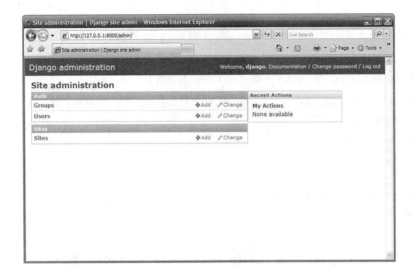

Admin Change List View

The admin change list view displays a list of objects that currently exist in a specific
model. You can access the change list view for a model by clicking the Change link
next to the model in the model view, as shown in Figure 1.1. You can see the change
list view by typing the URL /admin/*application*/*model* into a browser:

```
http://127.0.0.1:8000/admin/auth/user
```

From the change list view, you can filter the list of objects using items in the filter
list or by typing text into the search box. You can also sort the items in the list in
ascending or descending order by clicking one of the headings in the list. You can
add new objects to the list and, subsequently, the database as well by clicking the
Add user link in the upper right corner of the change list view, as shown in
Figure 1.2.

Admin Form View

There are two different admin form views: the change form and the add form. The
change form view, shown in Figure 1.3, displays the details of an object that currently exists in the database. You can access the change form by clicking one of the
objects displayed in the change list, shown in Figure 1.2. You can see the change
form for a specific object by typing the URL /admin/*application*/*model*/*object-id* into
a browser:

```
http://127.0.0.1:8000/admin/auth/user/1/
```

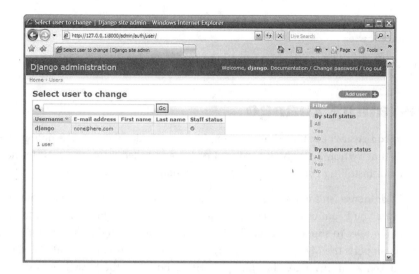

FIGURE 1.2
The change list view in the admin interface.

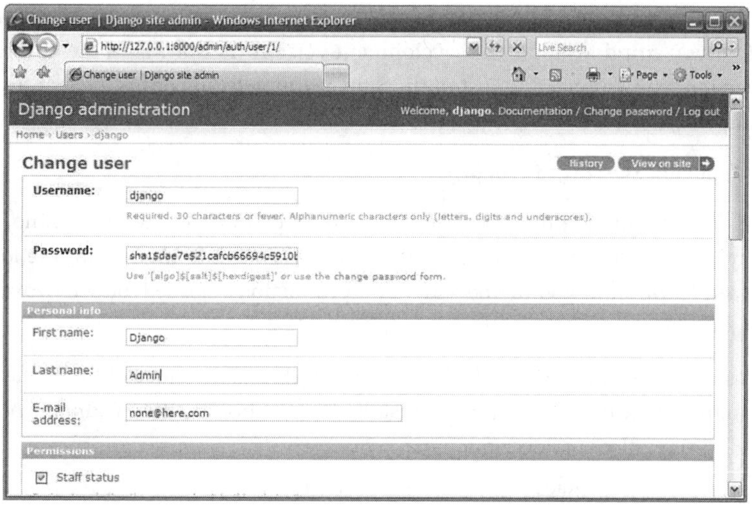

FIGURE 1.3
The change form view in the admin interface.

Any changes you make in the change form are saved to the database when you click the Save button.

The add form is basically the same as the change form, except that it represents a new object that doesn't exist in the database. You can add data to the form, and then a new object is created.

You can get to the add form by clicking the Add link in the model view, shown in Figure 1.1, or the Add user link in the change list view, shown in Figure 1.2. You can see the add form for a specific object by typing the URL /admin/*application*/*model*/ add in a browser:

```
http://127.0.0.1:8000/admin/auth/user/add/
```

Installing Django

Django can easily be installed on a Linux, Mac, or Windows server. The only prerequisite is that Python 2.3 or higher must already be installed. You can find information about installing Python at `http://www.python.org/download/`.

An SQL database isn't required to install Django. However, you will want to install one before you begin creating Django projects. You may need to install additional Python modules to support the database, depending on which database you choose. Django supports the MySQL, Postgre SQL, SQLite3, Oracle, and Microsoft SQL database backends. In this book, the examples will be based on the MySQL database.

At this time, you can install Django in two different ways. You can install an official release, or you can download the development version. To download the development version, you will need to install the Subversion version control system from the following website:

```
http://subversion.tigris.org/
```

The folks at the Django project are making a lot of great changes all the time, so you may want to use the development version if you want to implement the latest feature set. However, if you are developing a production website, you will want to use the released version.

Django should typically be installed in the site-packages directory of the Python installation. For example, if Python is installed in /Python25, then Django would be installed in the following location:

```
/Python25/Lib/site-packages/django
```

The following "Try It Yourself" sections take you through the steps of installing Django using each of these methods.

Some Linux distributions now provide versions of Django integrated with their package management system. You can find a list of those third parties at the following URL:

```
http://www.djangoproject.com/documentation/distributions/
```

Try It Yourself

Install the Released Version of Django

This section describes the steps to install the released version of Django. Follow these steps to download and install the Django tarball file:

1. Install Python 2.3 or later.

2. Download the Django tarball from the following location:

   ```
   http://www.djangoproject.com/download
   ```

3. Use the following command to extract the tarball:

   ```
   tar xzvf Django-version.tar.gz
   ```

4. Change the directory to the Django directory created by extracting the tarball:

   ```
   cd Django-version
   ```

5. Use the following command to install Django (you need to use the sudo command on Linux so that Django gets installed as the super user):

   ```
   python setup.py install
   sudo python setup.py install (linux)
   ```

6. Start a Python interpreter.

7. Use the following command to verify that Django is installed:

   ```
   import django
   django.VERSION
   ```

Try It Yourself

Install the Development Version of Django

This section describes the steps to install the development version of Django. Follow these steps to download and install the Django tarball file:

1. Install Python 2.3 or later.

2. Install Subversion.

3. Check out the Django trunk using the following Subversion command:

   ```
   svn co http://code.djangoproject.com/svn/django/trunk django_src
   ```

4. Either copy the django_src/django directory, or create a symbolic link to that directory in the Python site-packages directory to place Django in the Python path.

5. Copy django/bin/django-admin.py somewhere in the system path.

By the
Way

> You don't need to run `setup.py` because it does what was done in steps 4 and 5.

   6. Start a Python interpreter.

   7. Use the following command to verify that Django is installed:

```
import django
django.VERSION
```

Summary

This hour discussed the basic architecture of the Django framework, including models, views, and templates. Then we discussed configuring Django in the `settings.py` file and some of the project commands you can run using the `manage.py` utility.

Then we briefly covered the admin interface that you can use to create and modify objects in your Django projects. We ended the hour by discussing what you need to do to get Django installed and running.

Q&A

   Q. *Does Django have to be placed in the site-packages directory?*

   A. No. It just needs to be somewhere in the Python path. You could also manually add the Django directory to the Python path by editing the `PYTHONPATH` environment setting.

   Q. *Where can I find information about backward-compatibility issues?*

   A. Go to `http://code.djangoproject.com/wiki/`
   `BackwardsIncompatibleChanges`.

Workshop

The workshop consists of a set of questions and answers designed to solidify your understanding of the material covered in this hour. Try answering the questions before looking at the answers.

Quiz

1. Which file is used to configure Django projects?

2. Which utility would you use to install new applications to a Django project?

3. Where can you go to create new objects in your website?

Quiz Answers

1. The `settings.py` file.

2. The `manage.py` utility.

3. The Django admin interface for the website.

Exercises

1. Install Python 2.3 or higher. Verify that you can access the python interpreter from a console prompt by issuing the following command:

```
python
```

2. Install a Django supported SQL database. The examples in this book use the MySQL database, however, Postgre or any of the others will work as well. Appendix A, "Django Resources," lists links that you can use to get download and installation instructions for each database.

3. Download Django and install it. Make certain that you can import the Django framework into a Python interpreter using the following command in the Python interpreter:

```
import django
```

HOUR 2

Creating Your First Website

What You'll Learn in This Hour:

▶ How to begin creating a Django project
▶ How to start and stop the built-in web server
▶ The steps to configure Django to access the database
▶ How to create and install an application
▶ The steps to apply a model to an application
▶ The steps to activate a model in Django
▶ How to configure Django to accept specific URL requests
▶ How to create a simple view for a web browser

In Hour 1, "Understanding Django," you learned some of the basics about the Django framework. This hour guides you through the steps of creating a functional website called iFriends. Although this website will be basic, it will be the basis for future hours to build on as you are guided through the various aspects of the Django framework.

Creating a Django Project

Let's begin the process of creating a working website by creating a Django project. A Django project is a collection of settings that define a specific instance of Django. These settings include things such as database configuration, URL configuration, and other options that you will learn about as the hours tick by.

▼ Try It Yourself

Create Your First Django Project

Creating a Django project is relatively simple to do from the command prompt. In this section, you create a project called iFriends.

1. From a command prompt, change to the directory where you want to store the code for the iFriends project.

2. Create a directory called iFriends. This will be the root directory for the iFriends project.

3. Change to the iFriends directory.

4. Type the following command to create the iFriends project:

```
python django-admin.py startproject iFriends
```

Watch Out!

> Because the project will act as a Python package, avoid using a project name that conflicts with any existing built-in Python packages. The documentation for built-in Python packages can be found at http://www.python.org.

By the Way

> There is no need to put your project code in a directory in the web server's document base. The Django framework will be responsible for executing the code. In fact, it is a much better idea to store the code somewhere outside the web server's root. That way your code will be protected from being accessed directly from a web browser.

The startproject command first creates a directory called iFriends, and then it stores the basic set of Python files that are needed to begin the project in the iFriends directory. The startproject command creates the following files:

▶ __init__.py is an empty file that tells Python that the website directory should be treated as a Python package.

▶ manage.py is the command-line utility that allows the administrator to start and manage the Django project.

▶ settings.py is the configuration file that controls the behavior of the Django project.

▶ urls.py is a Python file that defines the syntax and configures the behavior of the URLs that will be used to access the website.

▼

The basic purpose of these files is to set up a Python package that Django can use to define the website's structure and behavior. We will discuss these files a bit more in this hour and in subsequent hours as the website gets increasingly complex.

Starting the Development Server

After you have created the Django project, you should be able to start the development server to test it. The development server is a lightweight web server that is included with the Django project. It lets you develop and test your website without having to deal with all the configuration and management issues of a production web server.

Try It Yourself

Start the Development Server

In this section, you learn how to start the development server.

1. From a command prompt, change to the root directory for the iFriends project.

2. Enter the following command to start the development server, as shown in Figure 2.1:

   ```
   python manage.py runserver
   ```

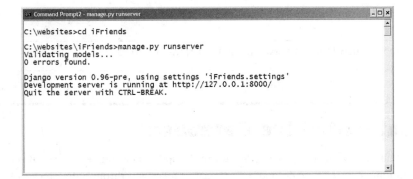

FIGURE 2.1
Starting the development server from a command line.

> The manage.py utility is copied into the root of your project by the createproject command discussed earlier in this hour. The manage.py utility first validates the project and reports any errors. If no critical errors are encountered, you are notified that the development sever is running at http://127.0.0.1:8000/.

By the Way

3. Verify that the development server is working properly by opening a web browser and entering the following address:

```
http://127.0.0.1:8000/
```

If the development server starts properly (and you haven't changed the debug setting), you should see a page similar to the one shown in Figure 2.2.

FIGURE 2.2
Initial browser
view of a Django
website.

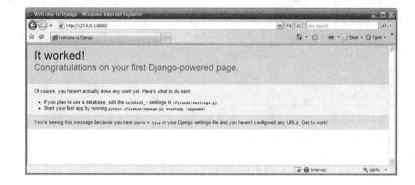

You can tell the development server to use a different port than 8000 if that port is already being used by adding the port to the command line. The following example shows the syntax for configuring the development server to run on port 8008:

```
manage.py runserver 8008
```

To stop the development server, press Ctrl+Break or Ctrl+C.

Configuring the Database

After you have verified that you can start and stop the development server, it is time to configure access to the database. This section takes you through the process of creating and configuring access to the database that will be used in the sample project.

Django can dynamically serve web pages without using a database to store information. However, one of the best aspects of Django is its ability to implement database-backed websites.

Configuring the database involves three major steps. The first is to create the database and assign rights. The second is to modify the `settings.py` file to specify the database type, name, location, and access credentials. The third step is to synchronize the Django project with the database to create the initial tables necessary for the Django engine.

Django supports several different types of database engines. The project used in this book uses a MySQL database. This section assumes that you have already installed, configured, and started a database engine and that it is accessible from the development server.

The MySQL database does not allow you to use case sensitive names when creating tables. If you want to define objects in your project that have uppercase characters, then you will need to turn off case sensitivity in the Django framework by using the following setting in the `<django installation path>/django/db/backends/__init__.py` file:

```
uses_case_insensitive_names = True
```

Watch Out!

Try It Yourself

Create the Database and Grant Rights

This section takes you through the steps of creating the database, creating an admin user, and granting rights from your SQL database command console. You will also modify the uses_case_insensitive_names setting in the Django framework so that you can name objects with uppercase characters. This step will be critical for some of the other Try it Yourself sections.

1. From your SQL database command console, enter the following command to create a database called iFriends:

   ```
   CREATE DATABASE iFriendsDB;
   ```

2. Enter the following command to begin using the iFriends database:

   ```
   USE iFriendsDB;
   ```

3. Enter the following command to create an administrative user named dAdmin with a password called test:

   ```
   CREATE USER 'dAdmin'@'localhost' IDENTIFIED BY 'test';
   ```

4. Enter the following command to grant all rights on the iFriends database to the dAdmin user:

```
GRANT ALL ON *.* TO 'dAdmin'@'localhost';
```

> If your database engine has a graphical interface that allows you to manage databases and users, you can use that interface as well to create the database and admin user and to assign rights.

5. Open the `<django installation path>/django/db/backends/__init__.py` file in an editor.

6. Add the following setting to the file to disable case sensitivity for the MySQL database:

```
uses_case_insensitive_names = True
```

7. Save the `__init__.py` file.

Configuring Database Access in `settings.py`

After the database has been created and a user account set up for Django, you need to configure the `settings.py` file in your Django project to access that database. Each Django project has its own `settings.py` file. The `settings.py` file is a Python script that configures various project settings.

Django uses the following settings in the `settings.py` file to control access to the database:

▶ DATABASE_ENGINE is the type of database engine. Django accepts `postgresql_psycopg2`, `postgresql`, `mysql`, `mysql_old`, `sqlite3`, and `ado_mssql`.

▶ DATABASE_NAME is the name of the database. For SQLite, you need to specify the full path.

▶ DATABASE_USER is the user account to use when connecting to the database. No user is used with SQLite.

▶ DATABASE_PASSWORD is the password for DATABASE_USER. No password is used with SQLite.

▶ DATABASE_HOST is the host on which the database is stored. This can be left empty for localhost. No host is specified with SQLite.

▶ DATABASE_PORT is the port to use when connecting to the database. This can be left empty for the default port. No port is specified with SQLite.

Try It Yourself ▼

Configure Django to Access the iFriends Database

The following section takes you through the steps to modify the settings in the set-tings.py file for the database and user created in the preceding section (a MySQL database named iFriendsDB, and a username of dAdmin with a password of test running on the localhost and default port). Open the iFriends\settings.py file in a text editor.

1. Find the DATABASE_ENGINE setting, and change the value to the following:

   ```
   DATABASE_ENGINE = 'mysql'
   ```

If you have elected to use an SQL database other than MySQL, you need to use that database type here instead of mysql.

By the Way

---

2. Change the value of the DATABASE_NAME setting to the following:

   ```
   DATABASE_NAME = 'iFriendsDB'
   ```

3. Change the value of the DATABASE_USER setting to the following:

   ```
   DATABASE_USER = 'dAdmin'
   ```

4. Change the value of the DATABASE_PASSWORD setting to the following:

   ```
   DATABASE_PASSWORD = 'test'
   ```

5. Verify that the DATABASE_HOST and DATABASE_PORT settings have no value:

   ```
   DATABASE_HOST = ''
   DATABASE_PORT = ''
   ```

When the DATABASE_HOST and DATABASE_PORT settings are left blank, they default to the localhost and default port. If the database is on a remote server or is running on a nondefault port, these options need to be set accordingly.

By the Way

▲

Synchronizing the Project to the Database

After you have configured access to the database in the `settings.py` file, you can synchronize your project to the database. Django's synchronization process creates the tables necessary in the database to support your project.

The tables are created based on what applications are specified in the INSTALLED_ APPS setting of the `settings.py` file. The following are the default settings already specified in the INSTALLED_APPS setting:

```
INSTALLED_APPS = (
    'django.contrib.auth',
    'django.contrib.contenttypes',
    'django.contrib.sessions',
    'django.contrib.sites',
)
```

The following list describes the default applications that get installed in the Django project:

▶ django.contrib.auth is the default authentication system included with Django.

▶ django.contrib.contenttypes is the framework of types of content.

▶ django.contrib.sessions is the framework used to manage sessions.

▶ django.contrib.sites is the framework used to manage multiple sites using a single Django installation.

Try It Yourself

Synchronize the iFriends Project to the iFriends Database

This section guides you through the steps to synchronize the Django project to the database. During the process, Django creates the default tables and prompts you to input the name, email address, and password for a website administration account. The username and password you specify allow you to access the Django authentication system.

1. Make certain that the development server has stopped by pressing Ctrl+Break from the console prompt.

2. Change to the root directory of the iFriends project.

3. Enter the following command at the console prompt to begin the synchronization, as shown in Figure 2.3:

```
python manage.py syncdb
```

```
C:\websites\iFriends>python manage.py syncdb
Creating table auth_message
Creating table auth_group
Creating table auth_user
Creating table auth_permission
Creating table django_content_type
Creating table django_session
Creating table django_site

You just installed Django's auth system, which means you don't have any superuse
rs defined.
Would you like to create one now? (yes/no): y
Please enter either "yes" or "no": yes
Username: django
E-mail address: django@iFriends.com
Password:
Password (again):
Superuser created successfully.
Installing index for auth.Message model
Installing index for auth.Permission model
Loading 'initial_data' fixtures...
No fixtures found.
```

FIGURE 2.3
Synchronizing the initial Django project with the database from a command line.

4. At the prompt, enter a username for the website administrator's account.
5. At the prompt, enter a password for the website administrator's account.

The database now has the appropriate tables configured to allow Django to use its authentication, content, session, and site frameworks correctly.

Installing an Application

After you have configured and synchronized the database, you can begin installing applications in it. Installing applications is simply a matter of creating an application directory, defining a model, and then activating the application so that Django can access it in the database.

Try It Yourself

Create Your First Application

The first application you will create is an application called People, which will be used to keep track of the individuals who use the website.

1. From a console prompt, change to the root directory of the iFriends project.
2. Enter the following command to create a blank application called People:

```
python manage.py startapp People
```

The startapp command creates a People directory within the iFriends directory and then populates it with the following files:

▶ __init__.py is a necessary file for the application to be used as a Python package.

▶ models.py contains the Python code that defines the model.

▶ views.py contains the Python code that defines the views for the model.

The files in the application directory define how information for the application will be stored and accessed in the database. They also define how information in the model will be viewed when accessed from the website.

Creating a Model

After the application has been created, you need to create a model for the data that will be stored in the application. A model is simply a definition of the classes, attributes, and relationships of objects in the application.

To create a model, you need to modify the models.py file located in the application directory. The models.py file is a Python script that is used to define the tables that will be added to the database to store objects in the model.

The models.py file initially has only one line, which imports the models object from the django.db package. To define the model, you need to define one or more classes. Each class represents an object type in the database.

▼   **Try It Yourself**

Create a Model for the People Application

In this section, you create the class Person in the People model by modifying the Python script, models.py, for the People application. Initially, the script is blank. This section takes you through adding the Python code to define classes in the model.

1. Open the iFriends\People\models.py file in an editor.

2. Add the following line of code to the file to import the Django models package into the application:

```
from django.db import models
```

3. Add the following code snippet to define the Person class with name, email, headshot, and text attributes:

```
class Person(models.Model):
    name = models.CharField('name', maxlength=200)
    email = models.EmailField('Email', blank=True)
    headshot = models.ImageField(upload_to='img', blank=True)
    text = models.TextField('Desc', maxlength=500, blank=True)
    def __str__(self):
        return '%s' % (self.name)
```

4. Save the file.

Listing 2.1 shows the complete code for the iFriends\People\models.py file.

LISTING 2.1   Full Contents of the iFriends\People\models.py File

```
from django.db import models

class Person(models.Model):
    name = models.CharField('name', max_length=200)
    text = models.TextField('Desc', max_length=500, blank=True)

    def __str__(self):
        return '%s' % (self.name)
```

The definition for __str__ defines a string representation of the object that can be used in views or other Python scripts. Django uses the __str__ method in several places to display objects as well.

By the Way

Try It Yourself

Activate the Person Model

This section takes you through the process of activating the Person model by adding it to the INSTALLED_APPS setting in the settings.py file and then synchronizing the database.

1. Open the iFriends\settings.py file in an editor.

2. Find the INSTALLED_APPS setting, and add the iFriends.People application to it, as shown in the following snippet:

```
INSTALLED_APPS = (
    'django.contrib.auth',
    'django.contrib.contenttypes',
    'django.contrib.sessions',
    'django.contrib.sites',
    'iFriends.People',
)
```

3. Save the file.

4. Synchronize the People application into the iFriends database by using the following command from the root of the iFriends project, as shown in Figure 2.4:

```
python manage.py syncdb
```

FIGURE 2.4
Synchronizing the new People application with the database from a command line.

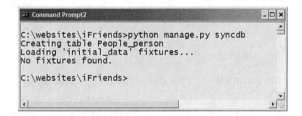

The syncdb command creates the necessary tables in the iFriends database for the People application. The model is now active, and data can be added to and retrieved from the database using Django at this point.

Adding Data Using the API

This section briefly describes how to use the Django shell interface and database API to quickly add a single Person object to the People table. The Django shell is a Python shell that gives you access to the database API included with Django. The database API is a set of Python methods that allow you to access the project database from the data model.

Try It Yourself

Add a Person Object to the iFriends Database

Open the Django shell, and follow these steps to add yourself as a Person object in the People model of the iFriends database.

1. From a console prompt, change to the root directory of the iFriends project.

2. Enter the following command to invoke the Django shell:

```
python manage.py shell
```

3. From the shell prompt, enter the following to import the Person class from the
   People package:

   ```
   from iFriends.People.models import Person
   ```

4. Enter the following command to create a Person object named p:

   ```
   p = Person(name="<your name>", email="<your eMail>")
   ```

5. Save the Person object you just created using the following command:

   ```
   p.save()
   ```

6. Verify that the object was created by using the Person.objects.all() function, which returns a list of all Person objects, and then print the list:

   ```
   lst = Person.objects.all()
   print lst
   ```

Figure 2.5 shows these commands.

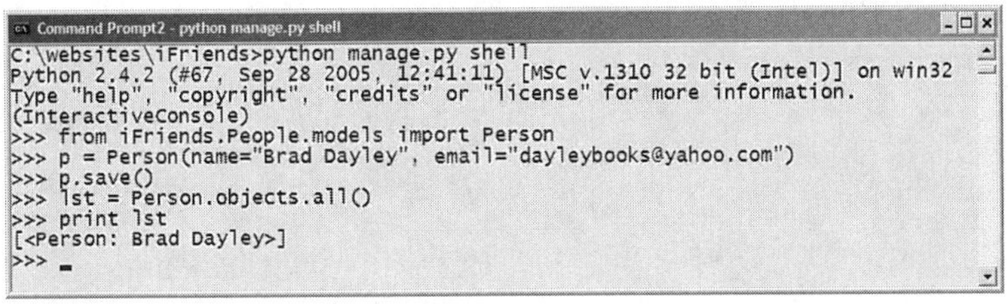

FIGURE 2.5
Using the
Python shell to
add an object to
the database.

A Person object has now been created in the iFriends database. We will discuss
accessing the database and using the database API in more depth later.

Setting Up the URLConf File

This section discusses configuring the URLConf file to define how installed applications are accessed from the web. The URLConf file is a Python script that allows you
to define specific views that are accessed based on the URL that is sent by the web
browser. When the Django server receives an URL request, it parses the request
based on the patterns that are contained in the URLConf file. The parsed request is
translated into a specific Python function that is executed in the views.py file, discussed in a moment.

The location of the URLConf file is defined by the ROOT_URLCONF setting in the settings.py file. The default location is the name of the project's root directory. In the case of the iFriends project, the value of ROOT_URLCONF would be set to the following value, where 'iFriends.urls' equates to iFriends/urls.py:

```
ROOT_URLCONF = 'iFriends.urls'
```

▼   **Try It Yourself**

Add an URL Pattern to Use for a People View

In this example, you set up a simple URL pattern for the People application by modifying the urlpatterns setting in the iFriends/urls.py file.

1. Open the iFriends\urls.py file in an editor.

2. Find the urlpatterns setting, and add the iFriends.People.views.index pattern to it:

   ```
   urlpatterns = patterns('',
       (r'^People/$', 'iFriends.People.views.index')
   )
   ```

3. Save the file.

By the Way

▲   In the preceding code snippet, iFriends.People.views.index refers to the index() function located in the iFriends/People/views.py file, which is discussed next.

Creating a Simple View

After you have configured the URLConf file, you need to add the views to the application. The application's views are stored as functions in the views.py file in the application directory. When the Django server receives an URL request, it parses the request based on the patterns that are contained in the URLConf file and determines which function to execute to generate the web view.

Try It Yourself ▼

Create the Index View for the People Application

This section guides you through the steps of creating an index view stub for the People application in the iFriends project. After the view is created, you start the development server and view the web page that is generated.

1. Open the iFriends/People/views.py file in an editor. The views.py file is empty at first.

2. Use the editor to add the following code snippet to the file:

```
from django.shortcuts import HttpResponse
from iFriends.People.models import Person

def index(request):
    html = "<H1>People</H1><HR>"
    return HttpResponse(html)
```

3. Save the file.

4. From a command prompt, change to the root directory for the iFriends project.

5. Enter the following command to start the development server:

```
python manage.py runserver
```

6. Access the http://127.0.0.1:8000/People URL. You should see a web page similar to the one shown in Figure 2.6.

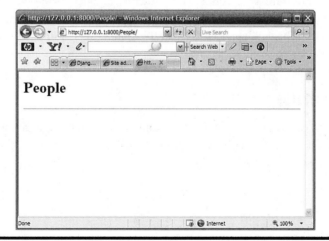

FIGURE 2.6
Accessing a custom index view in the Django project from a web browser.

Summary

In this hour, you created a Django project called iFriends. You configured access to a MySQL database for the project. You created an application called People, added a Person class, and populated the database with one Person object. You then configured the URL behavior to support an index view and added the necessary code in that view to display a list of objects in the Person class.

The steps you took during this hour helped demonstrate how easy it is to set up a website using the Django framework. Subsequent hours will build on this framework to implement a full-featured website.

Q&A

Q. *How do I modify a model after it has been synced to the database?*

A. Currently, Django cannot update models reliably. The safest and easiest method to modify an existing model is to make changes to the model and then delete all tables related to the model in the database using the SQL drop command. Finally, use the syncdb command to sync the model with the database.

Q. *Is there a way to check for errors in my model before trying to sync to the database?*

A. Django has a utility to validate the contents of models before syncing to the database. From the root directory of the project, enter python manage.py validate. The validate utility checks the model's syntax and logic and reports any problems.

Workshop

The workshop consists of a set of questions and answers designed to solidify your understanding of the material covered in this hour. Try answering the questions before looking at the answers.

Quiz

1. What file contains the information that Django uses to connect to the database?

2. What default file contains the configuration that Django uses to parse the location URLs?

3. What file contains the code that implements an index view for the `People` application in the iFriends project?

Quiz Answers

1. `settings.py`

2. `urls.py`

3. `iFriends/People/views.py`

Exercises

Try your hand at creating and activating a simple application. Create an application called Comments. Add a class to the model called `Note`, with two `CharField` attributes called `Title` and `Text`. Then activate the model by adding it to the `INSTALLED_APPS` setting in the `settings.py` file. Synchronize the model to the database. Test your application by adding an object to the database using the Django shell.

HOUR 3

Adding Models and Objects to Your Website

What You'll Learn in This Hour:

▶ How to install the Django admin interface model application
▶ How to configure the URLconf file to allow web browsers to see the admin interface
▶ How to activate a model in the admin interface
▶ How to add, delete, view, and modify objects using the admin interface
▶ How to add fields to data models
▶ How to change the behavior of fields in a data model
▶ How to create relationships between classes in data models

In Hour 2, "Creating Your First Website," you went through the steps to create a basic Django website. As part of that process, you created a simple application and model. In this hour, you will activate and install Django's admin interface so that you will be able to manage the data in the models from the web. This hour also provides more details on creating and managing models, including some of the different types of fields that you can add to a model and which options are available to control the behavior of those fields.

Installing the Admin Interface Model

Django's admin interface is actually a Django application. Therefore, it must be installed just like any other application you create. Installing Django's admin interface is a simple process of adding the application to the list of installed applications in the settings.py file and then synching the database. This process creates new tables in the database to support the admin interface.

Install the Admin Interface as an Application

In this section, you install the admin interface in your iFriends project.

1. Make certain that the development server has stopped by pressing Ctrl+Break from the console.

2. Open the iFriends\settings.py file in an editor.

3. Find the INSTALLED_APPS setting, and add the django.contrib.admin application to it, as shown in the following snippet:

```
INSTALLED_APPS = (
    'django.contrib.auth',
    'django.contrib.contenttypes',
    'django.contrib.sessions',
    'django.contrib.sites',
    'iFriends.People',
    'django.contrib.admin',
)
```

4. Save the file.

5. Synchronize the Django admin application into the iFriends database by using the following command from the root of the iFriends project:

```
python manage.py syncdb
```

By the Way

> The first time you run the syncdb utility, you are asked to create a superuser, which is required to access the Django admin site. If you don't create a superuser at that point, you can create one at any time by running the following utility:
>
> ```
> djanngo/contrib/auth/bin/create_superuser.py
> ```

Updating the URLconf File to Allow Admin Access

The Django admin interface must be added to the URLconf file so that you can access it from a web browser. Django automatically puts the following line in the urls.py file. However, it is initially commented out and therefore is inactive:

```
(r'^admin/', include('django.contrib.admin.urls'))
```

▼

You don't have to use the default value of admin as the web location for the admin interface. You can specify any name you want. For example:

```
(r'^WebMaster/', include('django.contrib.admin.urls'))
```

Did you Know?

Try It Yourself

Add Admin Access to the URLconf File

In this section, you enable access to the admin interface for a web browser by adding the default entry for the admin application to the urls.py file.

1. From a console prompt, change to the root directory of the iFriends project.

2. Open the iFriends\urls.py file in an editor.

3. Find the urlpatterns setting, and uncomment the (r'^admin/', include('django.contrib.admin.urls')), pattern, as shown in the following snippet:

```
urlpatterns = patterns('',
    (r'^People/$', 'iFriends.People.views.index')
# Uncomment this for admin:
    (r'^admin/', include('django.contrib.admin.urls')),
)
```

4. Save the file.

5. Enter the following command to start the development server:

```
python manage.py runserver
```

6. Access the http://127.0.0.1:8000/admin URL. You should see a web page similar to the one shown in Figure 3.1.

7. Log in to the admin site using the superuser name and password that you set up in Hour 2. You should see a web page similar to the one shown in Figure 3.2.

From the main page in Django's admin interface, you can add users, groups, and sites and manage any objects that have had the admin interface activated.

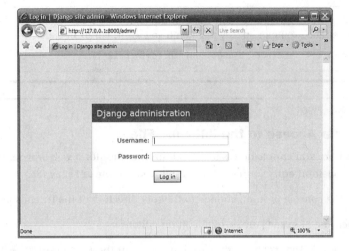

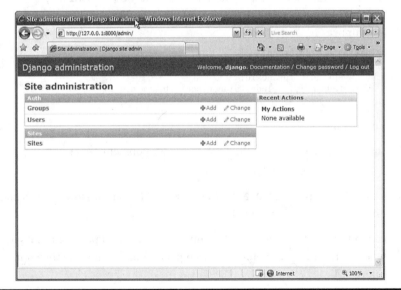

Activating the Model in the Admin Interface

Models are not visible in Django's admin interface automatically. You must activate a model for it to be accessible from the admin interface. The admin interface provides an easy way to add and edit objects in the model. However, it is not necessary to activate all or any models for Django to function.

The Admin class must be added to the model to activate the model in the admin interface. Only a simple Admin class is required:

```
class Admin:
    pass
```

Specific items that can be defined in the Admin class will be discussed in Hour 17, "Customizing Models in the Admin Interface."

Try It Yourself ▼

Activate the People Model in the Admin Interface

In this section, you activate the People application you created in Hour 2 to make it accessible in the admin interface.

1. Open the iFriends\People\models.py file in an editor.

2. Add the Admin class to the Person class, as shown in Listing 3.1, to activate the Person model in the admin interface.

LISTING 3.1 Full Contents of the iFriends\People\models.py File with the Admin Interface Activated

```
from django.db import models

class Person(models.Model):
    name = models.CharField('name', max_length=200)
    desc = models.TextField('Desc', max_length=500)

    def __str__(self):
        return '%s' % (self.name)

    class Admin:
        pass
```

3. Save the file.

4. Refresh your web browser. The People application should be available, as shown in Figure 3.3.

▼

FIGURE 3.3
Main page for
Django's admin
interface, show-
ing the People
application.

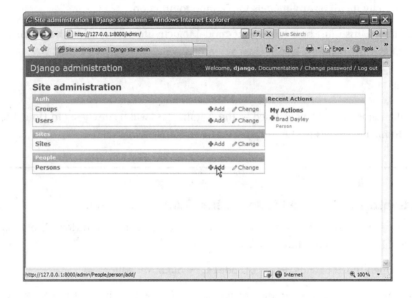

You don't have to stop the Django server and log in again to the admin interface
to allow the Django admin to access a model that has been activated. All you
need to do is refresh the web browser within the admin interface.

Adding, Modifying, and Viewing Objects in the Admin Interface

Django's admin interface provides a versatile and dynamic method of administering
objects on your website. You can add, modify, and delete objects from the admin
interface.

Typically, most objects are added programmatically through a series of web forms
and application code. However, often it is useful to be able to quickly view, add, or
modify an object from the admin interface.

The admin interface contains a number of predefined views. The main page, shown
in Figure 3.3, has three main parts: the title bar, the site administration table, and
the Recent Actions list. The title bar at the top displays the site name, a login welcome message, and links to change the password and log out. The Recent Actions
list is a history of events that have taken place on the admin interface.

The admin interface is easy to navigate. The Add link allows you to add objects, and the Change link allows you to modify existing objects.

Most of the work is done from the site administration table. In the Auth section, you can enter users and groups. These users are tied into Django's authentication system. In the Sites section, you can enter domain names that the Django server will service. Applications that are enabled in the admin interface appear below Sites.

Try It Yourself ▼

Add and Modify an Object Using the Admin Interface

In the preceding section, you enabled the `People` model in the admin interface, and it appeared on the main page of the admin interface. In this section, you will use the admin interface to add a `Person` object to the database.

Follow these steps to open the admin interface and add a `Person` object and then modify it:

1. Start the development server.

2. Log in to the admin interface using a web browser.

3. From the admin interface (refer to Figure 3.3), click the Add link next to Persons to bring up the add form, shown in Figure 3.4.

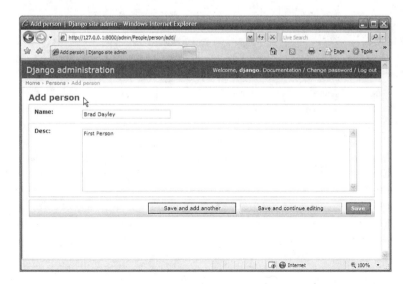

FIGURE 3.4
Add form for a Person object in Django's admin interface.

4. Enter a name and description, and click the Save button. The new object should appear in the Person list, as shown in Figure 3.5.

FIGURE 3.5
Object list of
Person objects
in Django's
admin interface.

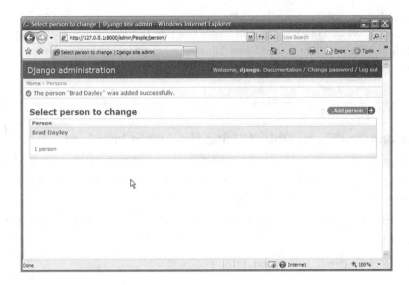

5. Click the name link under Person that you just created to bring up the edit form, as shown in Figure 3.6.

FIGURE 3.6
Update form for
a Person object
in Django's
admin interface.

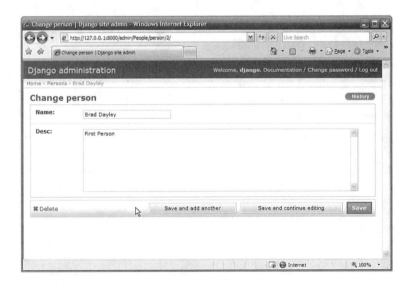

The edit form looks similar to the add form, but notice that it has two additional links. The Delete link at the bottom left is used to delete the object. The History link at the upper right lists changes that have been made to the object.

By the Way

6. Change the description, and click the Save button.

7. Click the name link under Person again to bring up the edit form (see Figure 3.6). Click the History link to see the history of changes to the object, as shown in Figure 3.7.

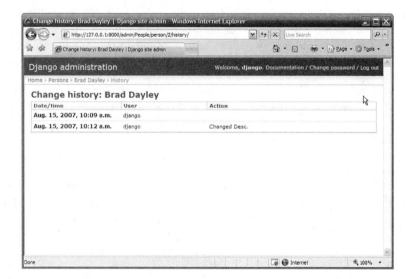

FIGURE 3.7
History list for a Person object in Django's admin interface.

Notice the navigation links, Home > Persons > Brad Dayley > History, below the title bar in Figure 3.7. These are quick links back to previous pages that you navigated. These are almost always present in the admin interface and can speed up navigation.

Did you Know?

Defining Data Models

Hour 2 mentioned that Django uses data models to define classes of data objects that belong to a particular application. Each application has its own `models.py` file that contains the Python code that defines that application's data model.

Django has an extensive package, `models.django.db`, that contains several predefined class field types that help you define data objects as well as a set of options to manage the behavior of those fields.

Django has a backend engine that runs SQL commands to create tables for each object and relationship.

Understanding Field Types

You can add several different types of fields to your data model. The benefit of having different types of fields is that the Django engine can understand what type of data should be in the field. Django has built-in validation that simplifies the process of verifying that the right type of data is being added to an object in the model. Django also can use the field type to display the field properly in predefined and admin views.

The following sections describe some of the field types that you will use the most.

Text Fields

You will use two main field types for simple text fields.

The `CharField` type is designed for smaller strings with specific length limitations, such as names or titles. `CharField` tells Django that the field is expecting text data. It requires that a maximum length be specified using the `max_length` argument:

```
name = models.CharField('Name', max_length=100)
```

The `TextField` type is designed for larger strings of text, such as a description. `TextField` tells Django that the field is expecting a variable amount of text. You can specify a maximum size for `TextField` using the `max_length` argument, as shown here, but this is not required:

```
desc = models.TextField('Desc', max_length=1000)
```

Date and Time Fields

You can use three different types of fields when adding date and time fields to your models. `DateField`, `TimeField`, and `DateTimeField` are designed to accept a date, time, and date with time of day value, respectively:

```
bday = models.DateField('Birthday')
alarm = models.TimeField('Alarm')
appnt = models.DateTimeField('Appointment')
```

All three date and time field types accept the following two optional arguments:

▶ auto_now tells Django to automatically set the value of this field to the current time each time the object is saved. This is useful for last-saved time stamps.

▶ auto_now_add tells Django to automatically set the value of this field to the current time when it is initially created. This is useful for creation time stamps.

EmailField

EmailField is similar to CharField, with two notable differences. Django verifies that the value entered into this field is a valid email address. Also, this field does not accept the max_length argument. The maximum length is automatically set to 75 characters.

File Fields

You will use two types of file fields. The first is the standard FileField, which is used to upload files to the website. FileField requires an upload_to argument that specifies a path, relative to MEDIA_ROOT, on the local file system of the web server to store the file, as shown here:

```
doc = models.FileField('File', upload_to='documents')
```

The MEDIA_ROOT path is specified in the settings.py file. No path is defined by default, so you must define one.

By the Way

The path you specify in upload_to can contain Python's strftime formatting, which is replaced by the data and time of the file upload. This can be useful if you want to control file uploads.

Did you Know?

The second type of field is the ImageField. The ImageField is very similar to the FileField except that in validation, the ImageField will validate the file as a valid image file. The ImageField also includes two extra optional arguments, height_field and width_field that contain height and width of the image. These fields are autopopulated when the object is saved.

URLField

URLField is similar to TextField. It also accepts the max_length argument. URLField also accepts the verify_exists argument. If this argument is set to True (the default), Django checks the URL to verify that it exists before accepting it:

```
location = models.URLField('WebPage', verify_exists=True, max_length=100)
```

▼ **Try It Yourself**

Add Fields to a Model

The previous sections have discussed several different types of fields that can be applied to a model for specific purposes. In this section, you apply that knowledge to extend the Person class by adding fields to it.

Follow these steps to add a DateField, EmailField, and URLField to the Person class in the iFriends database:

1. Make certain that the development server has stopped by pressing Ctrl+Break from the console.

2. Open the iFriends\People\models.py file in an editor.

3. Add the following code line to the models.py file to import the User class from Django's authentication model:

    ```
    from django.contrib.auth.models import User
    ```

4. Add the code shown in Listing 3.2 to the Person class to add a birthday DateField, an email EmailField, and a favorite URL URLField.

LISTING 3.2 Full Contents of the iFriends\People\models.py File Showing the New Fields in the Person Model

```
from django.db import models
from django.contrib.auth.models import User

class Person(models.Model):
    name = models.CharField('name', max_length=200)
    birthday = models.DateField('Birthday')
    email = models.EmailField('Email')
    favoriteURL = models.URLField('myURL')
    desc = models.TextField('Desc', max_length=500)

    def __str__(self):
        return '%s' % (self.name)

    class Admin:
        pass
```

5. Save the file.

6. Clear the old Person table in the database by using the following SQL command:

```
drop table people_person;
```

> You need to remove the Person table in the database because, currently, Django doesn't have a good way to update the data. Any objects that were created in the Person table will be deleted.

Watch Out!

7. Sync the model to the database using the following command from the root directory of the iFriends project:

```
python manage.py syncdb
```

8. Enter the following command to start the development server:

```
python manage.py runserver
```

9. Access the Django admin interface at http://127.0.0.1:8000/admin, and log in as the superuser.

10. Click the Add button next to Persons in the People section, as shown in Figure 3.8.

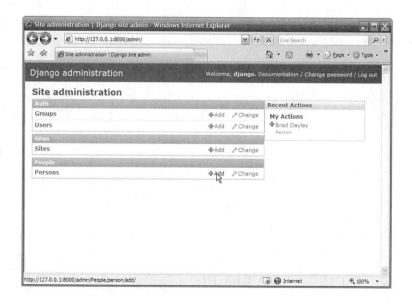

FIGURE 3.8
Add link for Persons on the main page for Django's admin interface.

11. Figure 3.9 shows that the new fields were added to the `Person` object.

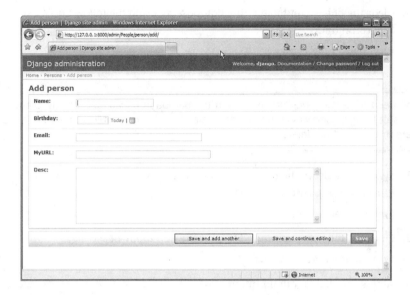

Adding Field Options to a Field Type

Django provides several options that can be applied to fields to control their behavior in the SQL database as well as Django's admin interface. The following sections discuss some of the most common options that can be passed as arguments to field definitions. These arguments are all optional and are available to all Django field types.

`null` and `blank` Field Options

Django provides two different options that allow you to leave fields blank when adding new objects. The `null` option tells Django to store any fields left blank as the NULL in the database:

```
count = models.Integer('count', null=True)
```

The `blank` option tells Django's validation engine to allow the field to be left blank:

```
count = models.Integer('count', blank=True)
```

There is a big difference between the `null` and `blank` options. The `null` option is strictly at the database level. The `blank` option is used by the validation engine on the Django admin site. This means that if you want to allow null values to be stored in the database and accessed in your code, you will need to set both the `null` and `blank` options to True.

Use the `null=True` argument on only nonstring-type fields such as dates, files, and integers. When you use the `blank=True` option, Django stores the empty string as the value of the field.

Watch Out!

Both the `blank` and `null` options are set to `False` by default. If you want to allow fields to be left blank in web forms and in the database, you must set these options to `True`.

Did you Know?

`default` **Field Option**

The `default` option allows you to specify a value that will be applied to the field by default:

```
title = models.Integer('Title', default='<no title>')
```

`choices` **Field Option**

The `choices` field option allows you to specify a list of two tuples to use as viable values in the field. Django's model validation accepts only values specified in the `choices` field option when validating form entry. When this option is used, the Django admin interface provides a selection box for you to make your choice.

The value of `choices` doesn't necessarily need to be a list or tuple. It can be any Python iterable object.

By the Way

This code snippet shows how to add a list of choices to a field definition:

```
gender_list = (('M', 'Male'), ('F', 'Female' ))
. . .
    gender = models.CharField(max_length=1, choices=gender_list)
```

`core` **Field Option**

The `core` field option is used when you relate objects to another object in the model. The Django admin interface lets you specify that multiple objects that are related to each other can be edited inline together.

Fields that have `core=True` set are treated as required fields in the object. When all the fields that have `core=True` set are cleared in the admin interface, the object is deleted.

editable **Field Option**

The editable field can be useful if you have a field, such as the modified time stamp shown here, that you do not want to be edited by the admin interface or Django's default forms. Fields are editable by default. However, if you specify editable=False, they cannot be changed in Django's admin interface:

```
last_modified = models.DateTimeField('Last Modified', auto_now_add=True,
   editable=False)
```

primary_key **Field Option**

The primary_key field option allows you to specify which field will be used for the primary key in the database. If you set primary_key=True for a field, blank=False, null=False, and unique=True are implied for the field. Only one primary key is allowed per object.

If you don't specify a primary key for an object, Django adds the following field behind the scenes:

```
id=models.AutoField('ID', primary_key=True)
```

unique **Field Options**

The unique field option allows you to specify if you want the field's value to be unique throughout the table in the database. When unique=True is set, values are not allowed if they already exist for that field in another object in the database. The unique option is enforced at both the Django admin validation level and the database level.

Django also provides the following field options that allow you to specify uniqueness of objects based on date:

▶ unique_for_date: When this option is set to True for a DateField or DateTimeField, Django enforces uniqueness in the date of that field.

▶ unique_for_month: When this option is set to True for a DateField or DateTimeField, Django enforces uniqueness in the month of that field.

▶ unique_for_year: When this option is set to True for a DateField or DateTimeField, Django enforces uniqueness in the year of that field.

> The unique_for_date, unique_for_month, and unique_for_year options are enforced only at the Django admin validation level.

Try It Yourself

Add Options to Fields in a Model

The previous sections have discussed several different options that can be applied to fields that control the behavior of the fields in the admin interface and also in the database. In this section, you apply that knowledge to modify the Person class by adding options to fields.

Follow these steps to force the email field to be unique, to allow the birthday and desc fields to be blank in the admin interface and the database, and to add a gender choice field to the class:

1. Make certain that the development server has stopped by pressing Ctrl+Break from the console.

2. Open the iFriends\People\models.py file in an editor.

3. Modify the email field to make certain that it is unique in the table:

   ```
   email = models.EmailField('Email', max_length=100, unique=True)
   ```

4. Modify the birthday and desc fields to allow them to be left blank in the admin interface and NULL in the database:

   ```
   birthday = models.DateField('Birthday', blank=True, null=True)
   desc = models.TextField('Desc', max_length=500, null=True)
   ```

5. Add the following code snippet to add a gender choice field to the Person class:

   ```
   gender_list = (('M', 'Male'), ('F', 'Female' ))
   . . .
       gender = models.CharField(max_length=1, choices=gender_list)
   ```

6. Save the file. Listing 3.3 shows the results.

LISTING 3.3   Full Contents of the iFriends\People\models.py File with New Options in the Fields

```
from django.db import models
from django.contrib.auth.models import User

gender_list = (('M', 'Male'), ('F', 'Female' ))

class Person(models.Model):
    name = models.CharField('name', max_length=200)
    birthday = models.DateField('Birthday', blank=True, null=True)
```

LISTING 3.3   Continued

```
gender = models.CharField(max_length=1, choices=gender_list)
email = models.EmailField('Email', max_length=100, unique=True)
favoriteURL = models.URLField('myURL')
desc = models.TextField('Desc', max_length=500, null=True)

def __str__(self):
    return '%s' % (self.name)

class Admin:
    pass
```

7. Clear the old Person table in the database by using the following SQL command:

```
drop table people_person;
```

Watch Out!

You need to remove the Person table in the database because currently Django doesn't have a good way to update the data. Any objects that were created in the table will be lost.

8. Sync the model to the database using the following command from the root directory of the iFriends project:

```
python manage.py syncdb
```

9. Enter the following command to start the development server:

```
python manage.py runserver
```

10. Access the Django admin interface at http://127.0.0.1:8000/admin, and log in as the superuser.

11. Click the Add button next to Persons in the People section (see Figure 3.8).

12. Figure 3.10 shows that the new fields were added to the Person object.

You should see the Gender field now available in the admin interface. Also, the Birthday field label is no longer bold, which means that this field may be left blank. The Desc field is bold because the blank option was not set to True. Remember that you don't need to set the blank option for CharField, because Django allows a zero-length string.

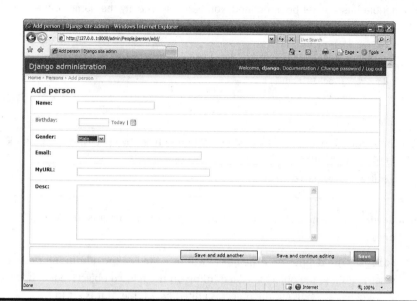

FIGURE 3.10
Add page for a
Person object in
Django's admin
interface, with
new fields
added.

Adding Relationships to Models

As you begin to develop more complex websites using Django, you will find it necessary to link classes within models and also link classes in other models. Django provides a simple but effective means of accomplishing class relationships. The
following sections discuss how to define class relationships within models.

Many-to-One Relationships

Arguably the most common type of relationship you will deal with is the many-to-
one relationship, in which one object can be related to several others.

Many-to-one relationships are defined by adding a ForeignKey field to a class and
specifying a second class as the key. For example, our sample website currently has
a Person class defined. If we were to add a Hometown class, several people might
come from the same hometown. The code used to define the many-to-one relationship would be similar to the following:

```
class Hometown(models.model):
. . .
class Person(models.Model):
    hometown = models.ForeignKey(Hometown)
```

If a module has not yet been defined, you can also specify the name of the object instead of the object itself as the argument to ForeignKey. For example:

```
class Person(models.Model):
    hometown = models.ForeignKey('Hometown')
. . .
class Hometown(models.model):
```

You can create a recursive relationship within an object by specifying self as the argument to ForeignKey:

```
. . . models.ForeignKey('self')
```

The following are some of the more common optional arguments that you will use with ForeignKey:

▶ edit_inline defines how the object will be edited in the admin interface. If it is set to False, the object is edited inline on the related object's page. If it is set to models.TABULAR, the object is edited as a table. If it is set to models.STACKED, the fields for each object are displayed as stacked on top of each other.

▶ related_name can be set to the name to be used from the related object back to this one.

▶ to_field specifies the field in the related object this field relates to. This defaults to the primary key of the related object.

Many-to-Many Relationships

Many-to-many relationships are defined by adding a ManyToMany field to a class and specifying a second class as the key. For example, our sample website currently has a Person class defined. If we were to add a Blog class, we might have several persons who belong to several blogs and several blogs that have several people using them. The code used to define the many-to-many relationship would be similar to the following:

```
class Blog(models.model):
. . .
class Person(models.Model):
    blogs = models.ManyToManyField(Blog)
```

> You can create a recursive relationship within an object by specifying `self` as the argument to ManyToMany:
>
> ```
> friends = models.ManyToManyField('self')
> ```

The following are some of the more common optional arguments you will use with ManyToManyField:

- ▶ `filter_interface` can be set to `models.VERTICAL` or `models.HORIZONTAL` to tell Django to use a built-in JavaScript interface to display the field in the admin form.

- ▶ `related_name` can be set to the name to be used from the related object back to this one.

- ▶ `symmetrical` is used when you use `self` as the object for the relationship. Setting `symmetrical=True` tells Django that the relationship between the two objects is reciprocal. In other words, if it exists in one, it also exists in the other.

One-to-One Relationships

Quoted from djangoproject.com: "The semantics of one-to-one relationships will be changing soon, so we don't recommend that you use them."

One-to-one relationships are defined by adding a `OneToOne` field to a class and specifying a second class as the key. For example, our sample website currently has a `Person` class defined. If we were to add an Alias class that limits each person to have only one Alias, the code used to define the one-to-one relationship would be similar to the following:

```
class Alias(models.model):
. . .
class Person(models.Model):
```

Try It Yourself ▼

Add Many-to-One and Many-to-Many Relationships to a Model

The preceding section discussed the different types of relationships that you can add between objects. This section takes you through the steps of adding some relationships to the `People` model in your iFriends application.

In this section, you will add a many-to-one relationship between the `Person` class and the `User` class in Django's authentication system. You also will create a recursive relationship between the `Person` class and itself, as well as a many-to-many relationship between the `Person` class and a new `Blog` class.

1. Make certain that the development server has stopped by pressing Ctrl+Break from the console.

2. Open the `iFriends\People\models.py` file in an editor.

3. Add the following code snippet to the `models.py` file to import the `User` class from Django's authentication model:

```
from django.contrib.auth.models import User
```

4. Add the following code to the `Person` class to add a many-to-one relationship to the `User` class in Django's authentication model:

```
userID = models.ForeignKey(User, unique=True)
```

5. Add the following code to the `Person` class to add a many-to-many recursive relationship between the `Person` class and itself:

```
friends = models.ManyToManyField('self', blank=True)
```

6. Add the code shown in Listing 3.4 to the `People` model to add a many-to-many relationship between the `Person` class and a new `Blog` class.

LISTING 3.4   Full Contents of the `iFriends\People\models.py` File Adding Many-to-One and Many-to-Many Relationships to a Model

```
from django.db import models
from django.contrib.auth.models import User

gender_list = (('M', 'Male'), ('F', 'Female' ))

class Blog(models.Model):
    title = models.CharField('Title', maxlength=200)
    text = models.TextField('Text', maxlength=2048)

class Person(models.Model):
    userID = models.ForeignKey(User, unique=True)
    name = models.CharField('name', maxlength=200)
    birthday = models.DateField('Birthday', blank=True, null=True)
    gender = models.CharField(maxlength=1, choices=gender_list)
    email = models.EmailField('Email', maxlength=100, unique=True)
    favoriteURL = models.URLField('myURL')
    desc = models.TextField('Desc', maxlength=500, null=True)
    friends = models.ManyToManyField('self', blank=True)
    blogs = models.ManyToManyField(Blog, blank=True)

    def __str__(self):
        return '%s' % (self.name)

    class Admin:
        pass
```

7. Save the file.

8. Clear the old Person table in the database by using the following SQL command:

```
drop table people_person;
```

9. Sync the model to the database using the following command from the root directory of the iFriends project:

```
python manage.py syncdb
```

10. Enter the following command to start the development server:

```
python manage.py runserver
```

11. Access the Django admin interface at http://127.0.0.1:8000/admin, and log in as the superuser.

12. Click the Add button next to Persons in the People section, as shown in Figure 3.11.

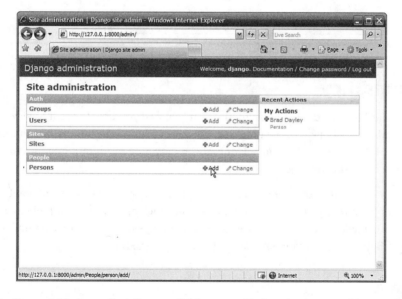

FIGURE 3.11
Add link for Persons on the main page for Django's admin interface.

13. Figure 3.12 shows that the new fields were added to the Person object.

In this example, you imported the User class from django.contrib.auth.models so that you can use it as the ForeignKey field. Using the ForeignKey field in this way allows you to access the Django User object from a Person object. You will see this in action later in the book.

FIGURE 3.12
Add page for a
Person object in
Django's admin
interface, with
more fields
added.

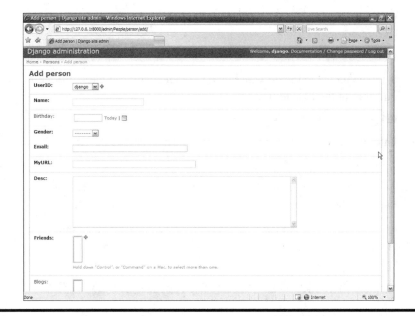

Summary

This hour introduced the admin interface and showed you how to use it to view, create, and modify objects in the database. We covered how to install the admin interface, how to activate it in a model, and how to navigate the admin interface to create and modify an object.

We also discussed creating models in more depth. You saw some of the different types of fields that you can add to a model and which options are available to control the behavior of those fields. We also covered the relationships between different classes both within the same model and in different models.

Q&A

Q. *Is it possible to change how object forms appear in Django's admin interface?*

A. Yes. When you activate the admin interface, you add the Admin class to the model with a simple pass as the code for the class. You can add code to the Admin class that you add to the model to change its appearance.

Q. *Is it possible to add metadata to a class in a model?*

A. Yes. Django provides a subclass called `Meta` that you can add to a class to define metadata for the class.

Workshop

The workshop consists of a set of questions and answers designed to solidify your understanding of the material covered in this hour. Try answering the questions before looking at the answers.

Quiz

1. What type of field would you use to add a long textual description to a model?

2. What type of field would you use to add a relationship between a person and an address class where more than one person can live at that address?

3. What file should you change to activate a model in the admin interface?

Quiz Answers

1. `TextField`

2. `ForeignKey`

3. That application's `models.py` file

Exercises

1. Activate the `Blog` class in the admin interface, and create some blog entries.

2. Create a new user using the Add link on the Users line in the Auth table.

3. Add some more `Person` objects to the database, and link them using the many-to-many `friends` field.

HOUR 4

Creating the Initial Views

What You'll Learn in This Hour:

▶ How to configure the initial URLconf file

▶ How to handle HTTP requests

▶ How to display web pages using the HttpResponse object

▶ How to configure URL patterns to enable a view

▶ How to add URL-based arguments to a view

This hour shows you how to create and configure the initial views for your projects. Django requires some initial configuration to enable views. As soon as views are enabled through the URLconf file, they are simple to use and powerful.

This hour also shows you how to handle HTTP requests and send HTTP responses directly from your views.

Setting Up the URLconf File

URL configuration of a Django website begins with the ROOT_URLCONF setting in the settings.py file. The ROOT_URLCONF setting points to a file that contains a series of URL patterns that define how the website will respond to various addresses.

The value of the ROOT_URLCONF setting in the iFriends projects initially is set to the following:

```
ROOT_URLCONF = 'iFriends.urls'
```

The syntax for the ROOT_URLCONF setting is as follows:

```
sitename.location.(URLConf filename without the .py extension)
```

The best way to illustrate the syntax is to use some examples. Let's say we want to set the root location of the URLconf file to the People directory in our iFriends project and that we want the name of the URLconf file to be PeopleURLS.py. We would use the following value for ROOT_URLCONF to point to that location:

```
ROOT_URLCONF = 'iFriends.People.PeopleURLS'
```

Understanding the `HttpRequest` and `HttpResponse` Classes

Later in this hour, we will discuss how to use the URLconf file to control how Django displays information. You need to understand the basics of Django's HttpRequest and HttpResponse classes. These two classes are simple to use. They allow you to quickly create dynamic code that helps you manage data that gets passed from the web browser through your view code and back out to the web browser.

The HttpRequest object is actually passed into your view function by Django. You use this view to gather and process information about the request in the view function. When you are finished handling the request, the view function is required to return an HttpResponse object.

Retrieving Information from a Web Request Using the `HttpRequest` Object

The HttpRequest object is a Python class that contains metadata about an HTTP request. The HttpRequest object is passed as the first argument to the view function that is called when the view is activated by a web browser. When you define a view in a views.py file, you must specify a name for the HttpRequest object, just as you did when you edited the people/views.py file in Hour 2, "Creating Your First Website":

```
def index(request):
```

When the index function is initiated, you can use the request object to acquire the metadata about the request. The following are some of the most common HttpRequest object attributes you will likely use:

▶ path contains a string representation of the path of the HTTP request.

▶ method contains a string representation of the HTTP method, typically GET or POST.

▶ GET contains a Python dictionary-like object that contains the
   HTTP GET parameters.

▶ POST contains a Python dictionary-like object that contains the
   HTTP POST parameters.

> The POST attribute does not contain the file information if the POST request contains a file upload. See the description of the FILES attribute.

By the Way

▶ REQUEST contains a Python dictionary-like object that searches POST first and
   then GET to find all parameters.

> Although this feature is provided in Django, it is much better to use the method attribute to determine if the request is a GET or POST and then use the GET and POST attributes accordingly:
>
> ```
> if request.method == "GET":
>     name = request.GET["name"]
> elif request.method == "POST":
>     name = request.POST["name"]
> ```

Watch Out!

▶ FILES contains a Python dictionary-like object that includes any files that are
   uploaded using an HTTP POST request.

> Each value in the FILES attribute is a dictionary object that contains three keys named filename, content-type, and content.

By the Way

▶ META contains a Python dictionary that includes all available headers in the
   HTTP request, such as CONTENT_TYPE, REMOTE_ADDRESS, and HTTP_HOST.

▶ user contains a Django User object for the currently logged-in user.

> You can tell if the request comes from an authenticated user by using the is_authenticated() method of the User object:
>
> ```
> if request.user.is_authenticated():
>     #Handle authenticated users
> else:
>     #Handle anonymous users
> ```

Did you Know?

Did you Know?

You can tell if the request comes from a secured connection by using the is_secure() method of the HttpRequest object:

```
if request.is_secure():
    #Handle secure users
else:
    #Handle unsecured users
```

Displaying a Web Page Using the HttpResponse Object

The HttpResponse class in Django's http package allows you to generate a web page as a response to an HTTP request directly from your Python code. Unlike the HttpRequest object, which is created automatically by Django and passed into the view function, you must create your own HttpResponse object. The simplest way to create an HttpResponse object is to import the class from the django.http package using the following code snippet:

```
from django.http import HttpResponse
```

There are several ways to build an HTTP response using the HttpResponse object. The simplest method is to create an HTML string and pass it as an argument to the HttpResponse object, as shown in the following code snippet, to generate a web page similar to the one shown in Figure 4.1.

```
def view_index(request):
    colors = ("BLUE","RED","GREEN")
    html = "<HTML><BODY>\n"
    html += "<H1>Colors Index</H1><HR>\n"
    for c in colors:
        html += "<FONT COLOR=%s><LI>%s</LI></FONT>\n" % (c, c)
    html += "</HTML></BODY>"
    return HttpResponse(html)
```

FIGURE 4.1
Web page generated by the view_index code.

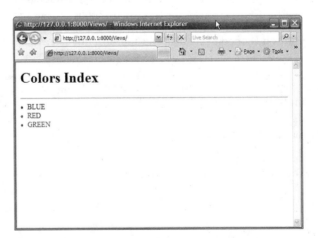

You can also treat an `HttpResponse` object like a file. First, create an `HttpResponse` object, and then use the `write()` function to write the HTML code to the object. When you are through writing to the `HttpResponse` object, use it as a return value for the `view` function. The following code snippet shows how to use an `HttpResponse` object as a file to generate the web page shown in Figure 4.2:

```
def view_calendar(request):
    week week_days = ('Sunday','Monday','Tuesday',\
                      'Wednesday','Thursday','Friday',\
                      'Saturday')
    weeks = 5
    response = HttpResponse()
    response.write("<HTML><BODY>\n")
    response.write("Calendar<HR>\n")
    response.write("<TABLE BORDER=1><TR>\n")
    for d in week_days:
        response.write("<TD>%s</TD>\n" % d)
    response.write("</TR>\n")
    for w in range(1,weeks):
        response.write("<TR>\n")
        for d in week_days:
            response.write("<TD> </TD>\n")
        response.write("</TR>\n")
    response.write("</BODY></HTML>")
    return response
```

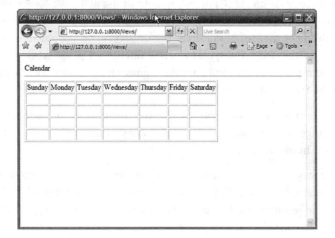

FIGURE 4.2
Web page generated by the `view_calendar` code.

You can also add and change the HTTP response headers by treating the `HttpResponse` object like a Python dictionary. The following code snippet sets the mimetype of the HTTP response:

```
def view index(request):
    response = HttpResponse("<HTML><BODY>Index</BODY></HTML>")
    response['mimetype'] = "text/plain"
    return response
```

> You do not need to check for the key before deleting the header. Using the Python
> del function to delete a header from the HttpResponse object, as shown here,
> does not raise an exception if the key you specify doesn't exist:
>
> ```
> del response['mimetype']
> ```

Configuring the URL Patterns

One of Django's best features is its ability to allow developers to define an elegant
URL scheme. Having a good URL scheme will make your code much cleaner and
simpler to administer. It will also be easier for web users to access applications on
the website in a clean, professional way.

URL processing is done by Django's URL dispatcher. At first glance, Django's URL dispatcher algorithm may seem complex and difficult. However, after you get used to
it, you will be able to quickly implement and change URL behavior with only a few
keystrokes.

Here's how it works:

When Django receives an HTTP request, it looks at the ROOT_URLCONF setting in the
settings.py file and finds the name of the URLconf file. It then opens the URLconf
file and finds the urlpatterns variable. The urlpatterns variable is a list of user-
defined URL patterns that correspond to view functions. Django scans the list of URL
patterns until it finds one that matches the request. It then calls the view function,
passing in the request object as the first argument.

Each URL pattern entry is also a Python list. The first element of each list is the pattern that Django tries to match to the HTTP request. The second element is the view
function that should be called.

The simplest way to illustrate this is with some examples. Consider the iFriends
website. We defined a view called index that should be called if the URL /People
is accessed. The resulting entry in the patterns variable of the URLconf file is
as follows:

```
r'^People/$', 'iFriends.People.views.index'),
```

Using this URL pattern, when a web browser sends an HTTP request to access the
URL /People, the index function in the iFriends/People/views.py file is called.

Add a New URL Pattern to the URLconf File

The index view was configured in Hour 2. In this section, you will prepare another view named details() that will eventually display detailed information about a specific person.

Follow these steps to create the details() view and then add a pattern to handle the view in the URLconf file:

1. From a console prompt, change to the root directory of the iFriends project.

2. Open the iFriends/urls.py file in an editor.

3. Find the urlpatterns setting. Add a new entry for a view called details() that is called when the URL /Info is accessed by a web browser as shown in the following snippet from Listing 4.1:

   ```
   (r'^People/Info/$', 'iFriends.People.views.details'),
   ```

4. Save the iFriends/urls.py file.

5. Open the iFriends/People/views.py file in an editor. Create a view with a simple HttpResponse that generates a web page with a details heading as shown in the following code snippet from Listing 4.2:

   ```
   def details(request):
       html = "<HTML><BODY><H1>Person Details Index</H1><HR></BODY></HTML>"
       return HttpResponse(html)
   ```

6. Save the iFriends/urls.py file.

7. Verify that the URL pattern works correctly by accessing the http://127.0.0.1:8000/Info URL. You should see a web page similar to the one shown in Figure 4.3.

The Django URL dispatcher is case-sensitive. Make certain that the case matches between the patterns in the URLconf file and the views.py file.

Watch Out! ▼

FIGURE 4.3
details() view
for the People
application.

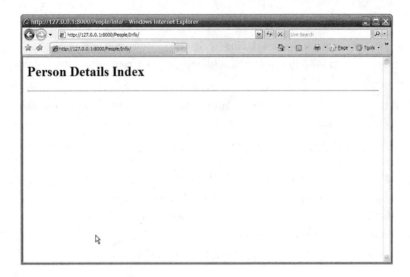

Listing 4.1 shows the complete urls.py file.

LISTING 4.1   Full Contents of the iFriends\urls.py File with the New
details() Entry

```
from django.conf.urls.defaults import *

urlpatterns = patterns('',
    (r'^People/$', 'iFriends.People.views.index'),
    (r'^People/Info/$', 'iFriends.People.views.details'),

    # Uncomment this for admin:
    (r'^admin/', include('django.contrib.admin.urls')),
)
```

Listing 4.2 shows the complete views.py file.

LISTING 4.2   Full Contents of the iFriends\People\views.py File
Including the details() view

```
from django.http import HttpResponse

def index(request):
    html = "<H1>People</H1><HR>"
    return HttpResponse(html)

def details(request):
    html = "<HTML><BODY><H1>Info</H1><HR></BODY></HTML>"
    return HttpResponse(html)
```

Adding URL-Based Arguments to the Views

So far, we have created only simple URL patterns in the URLconf file. Django's URL dispatcher can handle much more complicated URLs by adding more complicated URL patterns to the URLconf file. These patterns will help you define the behavior of your website with regard to the URLs that are being accessed.

This section discusses how to add expressions to URL patters that will allow you to control what type of data will be allowed in URLs. It also covers assigning names to expressions that correlate to arguments that can be passed into your views when they are called by the URL dispatcher.

Adding Expressions to URL Patterns

In the previous section, you defined an URL pattern for the URL /People/Info. This is the most basic type of URL pattern—a simple name. Django also allows you to include expressions in the URL patterns, giving you much more flexibility.

> **By the Way**
>
> Each expression you define in the view is passed to the view function as an argument, so you need to modify the definition of the view function in the views.py file to handle the additional arguments.

The following are some of the more common expressions that can be used to define URL patterns:

▶ . (dot) matches any character. The following pattern matches the URL /People/Info1/:

```
(r'^People/Info./$', 'iFriends.People.views.details'),
```

▶ \d matches any digit. The following pattern matches the URL /People/Info/1/:

```
(r'^People/Info/\d/$', 'iFriends.People.views.details'),
```

▶ [A-Z] matches any character from A to Z, uppercase. The following pattern matches the URL /People/Info/A/ but not /People/Info/a/:

```
(r'^People/Info/[A-Z]/$', 'iFriends.People.views.details'),
```

▶ [a-z] matches any character from a to z, lowercase. The following pattern matches the URL /People/Info/a/ but not /People/Info/A/:

```
(r'^People/Info/[a-z]/$', 'iFriends.People.views.details'),
```

▶ [A-Za-z] matches any character from a to z, uppercase or lowercase. The following pattern matches the URLs /People/Info/a/ and /People/Info/A/:

```
(r'^People/Info/[A-Za-z]/$', 'iFriends.People.views.details'),
```

▶ [^/]+ matches all characters until a slash is encountered. The following pattern matches the URL /People/Info/123abc***/:

```
(r'^People/Info/[^/]+/$', 'iFriends.People.views.details'),
```

▶ + matches one or more of the previous characters. The following pattern matches the URLs /People/Info/Person1, /People/Info/Person12/, and /People/Info/Person123/:

```
(r'^People/Info/Person\d+/$', 'iFriends.People.views.details'),
```

▶ ? matches zero or more of the previous characters. The following pattern matches the URLs /People/Info/, /People/Info1/, and /People/Info12/:

```
(r'^People/Info/\d?/$', 'iFriends.People.views.details'),
```

▶ {n1,n2} matches a number of the previous characters between n1 and n2, inclusive. The following pattern matches the URLs /People/Info/1/ through /People/Info/99/:

```
(r'^People/Info/\d{1,2}/$', 'iFriends.People.views.details'),
```

Using the Expression Values in the View

After you have added an expression to a pattern in the URLconf file, you can pass it to the view function as an argument. This allows you to use passed arguments to define the behavior of the view instead of having to access data from GET and POST data. The result is that your URLs have a much more elegant design than if you used PHP or CGI scripts.

By the Way

> The values of expressions that Django passes as arguments to the view function are string format even if the pattern specifies digits using \d. If you need to use those values as a number, you must convert them first.

You need to assign an argument to the view function definition for each expression that you add to the URL pattern for the view.

To show this, we will look at an example of an URL pattern for a search application that provides a view function doc_search() that queries a database of documents by document number. In the example, we want to define an URL pattern for a view that searches only one document at a time. The following URL pattern is designed to collect the document number and pass it to the doc_search() function:

```
(r'^docSearch/\d{1,3}/$', 'iHistory.docSearch.views.doc_search'),
```

The URL to access this pattern is as follows, where # can be any document number between 1 and 9999:

```
". . ./docSearch/#"
```

The corresponding view definition in the views.py file would look something like this:

```
def doc_search(request, doc_number):
```

We can add a second expression to another pattern to also provide a specific page number argument by modifying the URL pattern, as shown here:

```
(r'^pageSearch/\d{1,3}/\d{1,4}/$', 'iHistory.docSearch.views.page_search'),
```

The URL to access this pattern is as follows, where #a can be any document number between 1 and 9999, and #b can be any page number between 1 and 999:

```
". . ./docSearch/#a/#b"
```

The corresponding view definition in the views.py file would look something like this:

```
def page_search(request, doc_number, page_number):
```

Adding Argument Names to Expressions

In the examples in the preceding section, the arguments that were captured were passed to the view function as positional arguments. As the URLconf file grows and more patterns are defined, this can become confusing.

Assigning an argument name to each expression allows you to keep your URLconf file much less confusing. The arguments are then passed to the view function as keyword arguments that do not require a specific order.

The syntax to assign an argument name to an expression is as follows, where name is the name of the argument in the view function, and pattern is the matching pattern:

```
(?P<name>pattern)
```

The following example modifies the examples from the previous section to use named expressions:

```
(r'^pageSearch/(?P<page_number>\d{1,4})/(?P<doc_number>\d{1,3}/$',
  'iHistory.docSearch.views.page_search'),
  (r'^pageSearch/(?P<doc_number>\d{1,3}/(?P<page_number>\d{1,4})/$',
  'iHistory.docSearch.views.page_search'),
```

Both of these examples work exactly the same way, because the doc_number and page_number arguments are passed to the page_search() function as a keyword dictionary.

Did you Know?

Django allows you to have multiple patterns point to the same view, as long as you can define initial values to the view's arguments. For example, consider the following view function:

```
def view_page(request, pgnum="1"):
```

Both of the following URL patterns could be added to the URLconf file:

```
(r'^viewPage/$', 'iBooks.views.view_page'),
(r'^viewPage/\d{1,4}/$', 'iBooks.views.view_page'),
```

▼ **Try It Yourself**

Add a Named Expression to an URL Pattern

In the preceding "Try It Yourself" section, you added a details() view to the URLconf file. The details() view appears in the web browser when you access the http://127.0.0.1:8000/Info URL. In this section, you modify the URLconf file to also allow an argument named pID (person ID) to be specified in the URL.

You will modify the URLconf file to have two different URL patterns that both point to the details() view. The first will not pass a parameter to the view, and the second one will.

Follow these steps to add an URL pattern with a named expression URLconf file and update the details() view:

1. Open the iFriends/urls.py file in an editor.

2. Find the urlpatterns setting. Add a new entry for a view called details() that will be called when the URL /Info/# is accessed by a web browser as shown in the following snippet from Listing 4.3:

   ```
   (r'^People/Info/(?P<pID>\d+)/$', 'iFriends.People.views.details'),
   ```

3. Save the iFriends/urls.py file.

4. Open the iFriends/People/views.py file in an editor, and modify the details() view that will accept a pID argument, as shown in the following code snippet from Listing 4.4:

```python
def details(request, pID='0'):
    response = HttpResponse()
    response.write("<HTML><BODY>\n")
    if (pID == '0'):
        response.write("<H1>Person Details Index</H1><HR>\n")
    else:
        response.write("<H1>Details for Person%s</H1><HR>\n" % pID)
        response.write("(details go here)")
    response.write("</BODY></HTML>")
    return response
```

Notice that the sample code sets an initial value for pID. If you don't do this, the URL http://127.0.0.1:8000/Info generates an error, because no pID argument is added when details() is called.

5. Save the iFriends/People/views.py file.

6. Verify that the details() view now accepts the pID argument in the URL by accessing the http://127.0.0.1:8000/Info/5 URL. You should see a web page similar to the one shown in Figure 4.4.

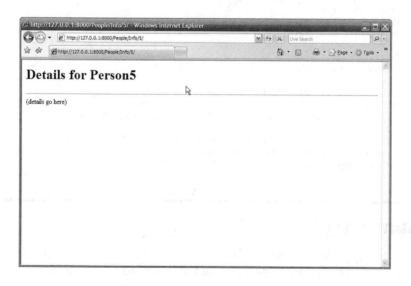

FIGURE 4.4
Individual details() view for the People application based on the person ID.

Watch Out!

The Django URL dispatcher is case-sensitive. Make certain that the case matches between the patterns in the URLconf file and the views.py file.

Listing 4.3 shows the complete urls.py file.

LISTING 4.3   Full Contents of the iFriends\urls.py File with an Entry that Passes the pID to the details() View Function

```
from django.conf.urls.defaults import *

urlpatterns = patterns('',
    (r'^People/$', 'iFriends.People.views.index'),
    (r'^People/Info/$', 'iFriends.People.views.details'),
    (r'^People/Info/(?P<pID>\d+)/$', 'iFriends.People.views.details'),

    # Uncomment this for admin:
    (r'^admin/', include('django.contrib.admin.urls')),
)
```

Listing 4.4 shows the complete urls.py file.

LISTING 4.4   Full Contents of the iFriends\People\views.py File with Additional pID Argument Code

```
from django.http import HttpResponse

def index(request):
    html = "<H1>People</H1><HR>"
    return HttpResponse(html)

def details(request, pID='0'):
    response = HttpResponse()

    response.write("<HTML><BODY>\n")
    if (pID == '0'):
        response.write("<H1>Person Details Index</H1><HR>\n")
    else:
        response.write("<H1>Details for Person%s</H1><HR>\n" % pID)
        response.write("(details go here)")
    response.write("</BODY></HTML>")
```

Summary

In this hour, we discussed the HttpRequest and HttpResponse objects. You learned how to access information in the HttpRequest object and how to use the HttpResponse object to build and generate a response web page.

We also discussed how the URL patterns in the URLconf file enable the views. You learned how to define different types of patterns to handle different URLs and even collect arguments from the URLs to pass to the view function.

We also covered how to write views using the HttpRequest and HttpResponse objects to handle HTTP requests that get parsed by Django's URL dispatcher.

Q&A

Q. *The URL dispatcher allows me to send arguments to the view function directly in the URL. Can I still send additional GET and POST information in the HTTP request?*

A. Yes. The ability to parse the URL and obtain arguments to pass the view function is a powerful feature of Django. However, you still can retrieve data that is passed as part of a GET and POST request.

Q. *Is the HttpResponse object the only way to generate web pages in Django?*

A. No. Several subclasses of the HttpResponse object can be used. For example, you can use HttpResponseRedirect to redirect pages to a different URL or HttpResponseNotFound to automatically return a 404 error. Also, as you will learn in future hours, you can use the render_to_response object to use a template to generate the web page.

Q. *As I create more and more applications, I can see that the URLconf file could get cumbersome. Is there a way to break URLconf into separate files?*

A. Yes. In fact, that is what is happening with the admin interface you have already enabled. Look at the line of code for that admin interface in the URLconf file:

```
(r'^admin/', include('django.contrib.admin.urls')),
```

Instead of pointing to a view in your urls.py file, it includes an urls.py file that is located in the django/contrib/admin/ directory. You can also create separate urls.py files for your applications and store them in the application directory. Then have the URLconf file include each urls.py file based on the URL pattern for the application.

Workshop

The workshop consists of a set of questions and answers designed to solidify your understanding of the material covered in this hour. Try answering the questions before looking at the answers.

Quiz

1. Which Django object class is used to generate web pages?

2. Which Django object class would contain the user object ID for a user who initiated an HTTP request?

3. What is a valid value after `/Info/` in the following URL pattern?

   ```
   (r'^People/Info/\d{1,2}/$', 'iFriends.People.views.details'),
   ```

Quiz Answers

1. `HttpResponse`

2. `HttpRequest`

3. A number between 1 and 99

Exercises

1. Create an additional view for the `People` object that accepts the person's name instead of the `pID`.

2. Create an URL pattern in the `URLconf` file that collects the person's name from the URL request and passes it to the view you created in Exercise 1.

3. Use the `META` attribute of the `HttpRequest` object that is passed to the view you created in Exercise 1 to add metadata about the request to the web page the view generates.

PART II

Implementing the Website Interface

Using Data from the Database in Views

What You'll Learn in This Hour:

- ▶ How to add objects to the SQL database
- ▶ How to access objects in the SQL database
- ▶ How to modify objects and update the SQL database
- ▶ How to perform complex queries on the SQL database
- ▶ How to apply data from the database in views

Django provides a valuable database-abstraction application programming interface (API) that allows you to create, retrieve, update, and delete objects in the database using Python code rather than SQL requests.

The database-abstraction API is automatically added to the models you create in the models.py file. As you will see in the following sections, you can access the API methods used to create, modify, and query objects in the SQL database directly from the model object.

In this hour, we will explore using this API to add, modify, and access objects in the database using the model object defined in the models.py file.

Adding Data to the Database

Adding entries to the SQL database using the Django database-abstraction API is a simple process. The basic steps involve importing the object class from the model, creating a new object, and then using the database-abstraction function save() to save the object to the database.

Although the process itself is rather simple, the amount of work necessary depends on how complex your objects are. Simple objects with only a few text type fields are easy to create. For example, consider adding an object for the Blog class in the models.py file:

```
class Blog(models.Model):
    title = models.CharField('Title', max_length=200)
    text = models.TextField('Text', max_length=2048)
```

The first step in adding an object to the database is to import the object class from the model using the following line of code in the Django shell:

```
from iFriends.People.models import Blog
```

After the object class has been imported, you can use the class constructor to create a new Blog object using the following line of code:

```
b = Blog(title='MyBlog1', text = 'My Blog Entry')
```

A new Blog object is created and assigned to b. Then you can use the save() function to save the new object in the SQL database, as shown in the following line of code:

```
b.save()
```

Django provides a create() function in the database-abstraction API that automatically creates the object in the database without you having to use the save() function. In the preceding example, we could have saved a step by using the following single line of code:

```
b = Blog.create(title='MyBlog1', text = 'My Blog Entry')
```

Now let's look at creating a new object for a more complex class listed in the following code snippet:

```
class Blog(models.Model):
    userID = models.ForeignKey(User, unique=True)
    title = models.CharField('title', max_length=200)
    date = models.DateField('Date', blank=True, null=True)
    text = models.TextField('Text', max_length=2048)
```

This example contains a couple different problems. The first is that there are too many fields to reasonably create the object using a single line of code. The second is that the userID field requires a django.contrib.auth.models.User object, not a string or number. The third is that the date field requires a Python datetime object.

To overcome these problems, you would first create a blank object:

```
b = Blog()
```

A new blank `Blog` object is created and assigned to b. You would use the following code snippet to add the `title` and `text` fields to the `Blog` object:

```
b.title='MyBlog1'
b.text = 'My Blog Entry'
```

Then you would use the following Python code to access the first `django.contrib.auth.models.User` object and assign it to the `userID` field:

```
from django.contrib.auth.models import User
b.userID = User.objects.get(id=1)
```

Finally, you would use the following code to assign the current time to the `date` field:

```
from datetime import datetime
b.date = datetime.now()
```

After you have added all the fields to the object, you can add the object to the database using the following line of code:

```
b.save()
```

If you set the primary key value when creating a new object, you must make certain that it doesn't already exist in the database. If the key already exists, the existing object is overwritten with the new one.

**Watch
Out!**

Try It Yourself   ▼

Add an Object to the SQL Database

In this section, you will use the Django shell to add a `Person` object to the People table in the SQL database.

Follow these steps to create a `Person` object, populate the data in the `Person` object's fields, and then save the object in the database:

1. Because we will add a `Person` object, we need to use the Django admin interface to create a new user object first. Access the admin interface at the following web address:

```
http://127.0.0.1:8000/admin/
```

▼

2. Click the Add link next to Users to bring up the dialog box shown in Figure 5.1.

FIGURE 5.1
The Add user
page in the
Django admin
interface.

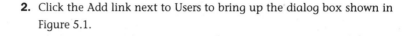
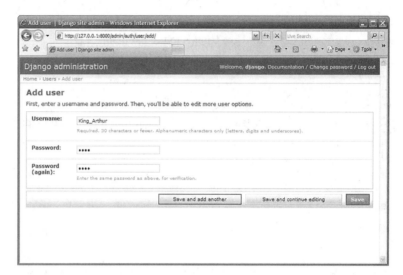

3. Add a new user object with the username King_Arthur, and give it the password test.

4. Save the user by clicking the Save button.

5. Now we are ready to create the new `Person` object using the Django shell. From a command prompt, navigate to the root of the iFriends project.

6. Open the Django shell using the following command:

```
python manage.py shell
```

7. From the Django shell, import the `Person` class using the following command:

```
from iFriends.People.models import Person
```

8. Create a blank `Person` object using the following command:

```
p = Person()
```

9. Use the following commands to assign the `userID` field of the `Person` object to the `King_Arthur` object you created in step 3:

```
from django.contrib.auth.models import User
p.userID = User.objects.get(username='King_Arthur')
```

10. Use the following commands to assign the `birthday` field of the `Person` object to a proper date:

```
from datetime import datetime
p.birthday = datetime(2000, 1, 1)
```

11. Assign the rest of the necessary fields, shown in Listing 5.1, using the following commands:

```
p.name = 'King Arthur'
p.gender = 'M'
p.email = 'kingofthebrits@camelot.com'
p.favoriteURL = 'http://www.camelot.com'
p.desc = 'King of the Brits'
```

12. Save the new `Person` object to the SQL database using the following command:

```
p.save()
```

Listing 5.1 shows the complete `models.py` file.

LISTING 5.1   Full Contents of the `iFriends\People\models.py` File

```
from django.db import models
from django.contrib.auth.models import User

gender_list = (('M', 'Male'), ('F', 'Female' ))

class Blog(models.Model):
    title = models.CharField('Title', max_length=200)
    text = models.TextField('Text', max_length=2048)

class Person(models.Model):
    userID = models.ForeignKey(User, unique=True)
    name = models.CharField('name', max_length=200)
    birthday = models.DateField('Birthday', blank=True, null=True)
    gender = models.CharField(max_length=1, choices=gender_list)
    email = models.EmailField('Email', max_length=100, unique=True)
    favoriteURL = models.URLField('myURL')
    desc = models.TextField('Desc', max_length=500, null=True)
    friends = models.ManyToManyField('self', blank=True)
    blogs = models.ManyToManyField(Blog, blank=True)

    def __str__(self):
        return '%s' % (self.name)

    class Admin:
        pass
```

Accessing Data in the Database

The preceding section discussed how to add objects to the database. This section discusses how to retrieve those objects from the database. The Django database-abstraction API provides several methods for retrieving objects from the SQL database. Like the `save()` function, these methods are automatically built into each class you define in your `models.py` file.

The database-abstraction layer provides an object manager that gives you access to objects in the database. Each model you define will have at least one manager called `objects`. For example, if you have a model called `Blog`, you can access the objects manager using `Blog.objects`.

The following sections describe two of the more common ways to retrieve objects from the database using the object manager `objects`. We will cover more complex queries later in this hour.

Retrieving All Objects

The simplest way to retrieve objects from the SQL database is to use the `all()` function that is built into the object manager in each model. The `all()` function returns a QuerySet that represents a collection of objects from the database. For example, to retrieve all `Blog` entries from the database, you would use the following code:

```
from iFriends.People.models import Blog
blogs = Blog.objects.all()
```

A QuerySet is basically a Python array that can be indexed, iterated in for loops, and sliced. For example, to iterate through all the entries in `Blog` and print the title, you would use the following code:

```
from iFriends.People.models import Blog
blogs = Blog.objects.all()
for b in blogs:
    print b.title
```

QuerySets do not actually access the database until they are evaluated in some way. In the preceding example, the database does not actually get accessed until `b.title` is accessed. This is useful, because the entire contents of the database do not need to be read in at first.

You can also use the Python `len()` and `list()` functions on the QuerySet. For example, to print the title of the last entry in `Blog`, you would use the following code to evaluate the number of entries and then index the last entry:

```
from iFriends.People.models import Blog
blogs = Blog.objects.all()
blog_list = list(blogs)
b = blogs[len(blogs)-1]
print b.title
```

When you use the list() function to convert the QuerySet into a Python list, all objects are read into memory from the database and are added as entries in the list. If the database is large, it can take a large amount of memory and make the list difficult to manage.	**Watch Out!**

Retrieving One Object

The preceding section showed you how to retrieve all objects from the database. In this section, you will learn how to retrieve only one object from the database using the get() function. The get() function does not return a QuerySet, as the all() function does. Instead, the get() function returns a single object if it is found. For example, to print the title field of the Blog entry with an id of 1, you would use the following code:

```
from iFriends.People.models import Blog
b = Blog.objects.get(id=1)
print b.title
```

The get() function accepts a list of arguments that can be any number of the fields in the object's model. For example, if you want to get the Blog object with a specific value in the title field, you would use the following code:

```
from iFriends.People.models import Blog
b = Blog.objects.get(title='MyBlog')
print b.title
```

The most useful feature of the get() function is that it raises exceptions if no object or multiple objects are found. If the get() function does not find an object, a DoesNotExist exception is raised. If more than one entry is found, an AssertionError exception is raised. These exceptions are useful if you need to be able to add code to handle conditions where the specific objects were not found. For example, the following code snippet handles conditions when the object wasn't found:

```
from iFriends.People.models import Blog
try:
    b = Blog.objects.get(title='MyBlog')
    print b.title
except Blog.DoesNotExist:
    print 'Object Not Found'
```

Did you *Know?*

> The DoesNotExist exception inherits from the django.core.exceptions.
> ObjectDoesNotExist class. You can import that class and then use
> ObjectDoesNotExist instead of DoesNotExist so that you can handle
> all ObjectDoesNotExist types of exceptions.

Try It Yourself

Retrieve Objects from the Database

In this section, you will apply the all() and get() functions to retrieve Person objects from the People table in the SQL database.

Follow these steps in the Django shell to access the object manager for the People class, and use it to retrieve objects from the database:

1. From the Django shell, import the Person class using the following command:

   ```
   from iFriends.People.models import Person
   ```

2. Retrieve all the Person entries from the database, and assign them to the variable persons using the all() function:

   ```
   persons = Person.objects.all()
   ```

3. Iterate through the persons QuerySet, and print the name and userID of each entry using the following code, as shown in Figure 5.2:

   ```
   for p in persons:
       print 'Name: %s' % p.name
       print 'UserID:%s\n' % p.userID
   ```

FIGURE 5.2
Using the all()
function in the
Python shell
to retrieve
objects from
the database.

4. Use the `get()` function to retrieve the `Person` object that you created in the preceding Try It Yourself section using the following code snippet, also shown in Figure 5.3:

```
p = Person.objects.get(name='King Arthur')
print 'Name: %s' % p.name
print 'UserID: %s' % p.userID
```

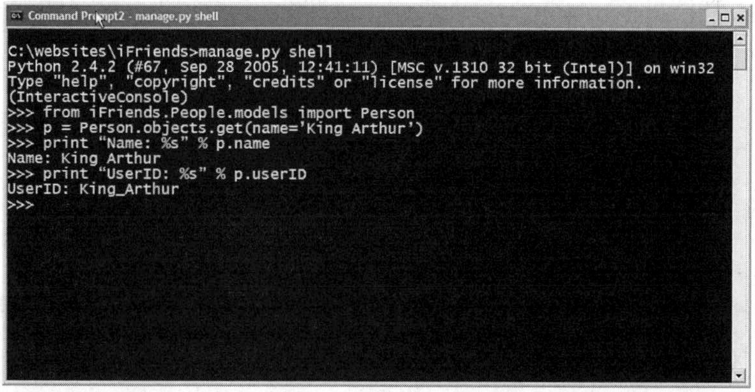

FIGURE 5.3
Using the `get()` function in the Python shell to retrieve a specific object from the database.

Modifying Data in the Database

Now that you know how to use the `get()` and `all()` functions of the database object manager, it is worth discussing how to modify objects that already exist in the database. The two most common functions that you will use are `save()` and `delete()`. The `save()` and `delete()` functions are part of the database-abstraction API and are accessible through each object in the model.

Earlier in this hour, we used the `save()` function to create a new object in the database. The `save()` function can also be used to update objects that exist in the database. When you retrieve an object from the database and modify it, those modifications exist only in the instance of the object in your Python code, not in the database. To update the database with the new values, use the `save()` function on the object. The following code snippet shows an example of updating an existing object:

```
from iFriends.People.models import Person
from datetime import datetime
p = Person.objects.get(name='King Arthur')
p.birthday = datetime(934, 8, 3)
p.save()
```

If you modify an object's primary key and then use the save() function, the original object with that key is not modified in the database. Either a new object is created, because the new key doesn't exist in the database yet, or the object that does have that key is updated with the new values. This can be useful to quickly clone objects in the database.

The delete() function is used to delete objects that already exist in the database. All you have to do is retrieve the object from the database and then use the delete() function on the object, and it is deleted from the database. The following code snippet shows an example of deleting objects from the database:

```
from iFriends.People.models import Person
p = Person.objects.get(name='Brad Dayley')
p.delete()
```

The delete() function also works on a QuerySet. This can be useful to delete several objects at the same time. For example, the following code deletes all the Blog objects:

```
from iFriends.People.models import Blog
Blog.objects.all().delete()
```

Performing Queries in the Database

The Django database-abstraction API provides a rich set of objects and functions that allow you to perform complex queries on the database. We touched on this earlier in this hour when we discussed the all() and get() functions. This section discusses how to use the filter() and exclude() functions to retrieve QuerySets from the database.

Using the filter() Function

The filter(**kwargs) function accepts any number of lookup parameters to use when querying the database. The lookups are field-based. Only entries whose fields match those in the lookups are returned in the QuerySet. For example, the following code snippet shows using one filter to query for Blog objects by the name field and another filter to query for Blog objects by the name and text fields:

```
from iFriends.People.models import Blog
blogs = Blog.objects.filter(title='MyBlog')
blogs = Blog.objects.filter(title='MyBlog', text='Some Text')
```

Using the `exclude()` Function

The `exclude(**kwargs)` function accepts any number of lookup parameters to use when querying the database. The lookups are field-based. All entries whose fields *do not* match those in the lookups are returned in the `QuerySet`. For example, the following code snippet shows using one filter to query for `Blog` objects by the `name` field and another filter to query for `Blog` objects by the `name` and `text` fields:

```
from iFriends.People.models import Blog
blogs = Blog.objects.exclude(title='MyBlog')
blogs = Blog.objects.exclude(title='MyBlog', text='Some Text')
```

Understanding Field Lookups

So far, we have done only simple field lookups that look for exact matches using the syntax *field=value*. However, the database-abstraction API provides numerous types of field lookups that allow you to create complex queries.

These field lookup types are applied by attaching them to the end of the field name using a double underscore. For example, the following line of code performs a query using the `iexact` field lookup type on the `title` field of the `Blog` object:

```
blogs = Blog.objects.filter(title__iexact='MyBlog')
```

The information in the field lookup is translated behind the scenes into an SQL query by the Django database-abstraction layer so that the database can be queried. For instance, in the preceding example, the case-insensitive `iexact` search would be translated into the following SQL statement:

```
SELECT ... WHERE title ILIKE 'MyBlog';
```

The following is a list of the different types of field lookups that you can use in `filter()`, `exclude()`, and `get()` functions:

▶ exact finds an exact match. This is the default if no lookup type is specified:

```
blogs = Blog.objects.filter(name__exact='MyBlog')
```

> If you specify None as the value for the exact lookup type, it is translated into NULL for the SQL query. This is a good way to find entries that have NULL field values.

By the Way

▶ iexact finds a case-insensitive exact match:

```
blogs = Blog.objects.filter(title__iexact='myblog')
```

▶ `contains` finds entries that contain the specified text:

```
blogs = Blog.objects.filter(title__contains='Blog')
```

▶ `icontains` finds entries that contain the specified case-insensitive text:

```
blogs = Blog.objects.filter(title__icontains='blog')
```

▶ `search` is similar to the `contains` lookup type, except that it takes advantage of the full-text search available in MySQL.

> You must configure MySQL to add the full-text index before you can use the `search` lookup type. Also, this is currently available only on MySQL, so you may not want to use it if you plan to port the site to another database engine.

▶ `gt` finds entries that are greater than the specified value:

```
blogs = Blog.objects.filter(id__gt=9)
```

▶ `gte` finds entries that are greater than or equal to the specified value:

```
blogs = Blog.objects.filter(id__gte=10)
```

▶ `lt` finds entries that are less than the specified value:

```
blogs = Blog.objects.filter(id__lt=10)
```

▶ `lte` finds entries that are less than or equal to the specified value:

```
blogs = Blog.objects.filter(id__lte=9)
```

▶ `in` finds entries that are contained in the specified set:

```
blogs = Blog.objects.filter(id__in=[2,4,6,8])
```

▶ `startswith` finds entries that start with the specified string:

```
blogs = Blog.objects.filter(title__startswith='Test')
```

▶ `istartswith` finds entries that start with the specified case-insensitive string:

```
blogs = Blog.objects.filter(title__istartswith='test')
```

▶ `endswith` finds entries that end with the specified string:

```
blogs = Blog.objects.filter(title__endswith='Test')
```

▶ `iendswith` finds entries that end with the specified case-insensitive string:

```
blogs = Blog.objects.filter(title__iendswith='test')
```

▶ range finds entries whose values fall inclusively between a list of two specified values:

```
dateA = datetime.date(2000, 1, 1)
dateB = datetime.datetime.now()
blogs = Blog.objects.filter(postDate__range=(dateA, dateB))
```

▶ year finds date entries whose year value matches the specified year:

```
blogs = Blog.objects.filter(postDate__year=2008)
```

▶ month finds date entries whose month value matches the specified month:

```
blogs = Blog.objects.filter(postDate__month=12)
```

▶ day finds date entries whose day value matches the specified day:

```
blogs = Blog.objects.filter(postDate__day=24)
```

▶ ISNULL accepts either True or False as the value and then finds entries that are either NULL or not NULL, respectively:

```
blogs = Blog.objects.filter(text__ISNULL=True)
```

▶ regex accepts a regular expression statement for the SQL backend and then uses that expression in the SQL query:

```
blogs = Blog.objects.filter(title__regex=r'^(An?¦The) +')
```

▶ iregex accepts a regular expression statement for the SQL backend and then uses that expression in the case-insensitive SQL query:

```
blogs = Blog.objects.filter(title__iregex=r'^(An?¦The) +')
```

Chaining `QuerySets`

Now it's time to put together all the pieces we have discussed in this section. The `all()`, `get()`, `filter()`, and `exclude()` functions are all part of the `QuerySet` class of objects that is attached to each object in the model. The `all()`, `filter()`, and `exclude()` functions all return `QuerySet` objects. You can also use the `all()`, `get()`, `filter()`, and `exclude()` functions on each new `QuerySet` object that is returned. For example, consider the following code snippet:

```
qs1 = Blog.objects.filter(title__icontains='test')
testBlogs = qs1.exclude(postDate__year=2008)
```

The first `QuerySet` object, `qs1`, contains all `Blog` entries whose title field contains the text `test`. The second `QuerySet` object, `testBlogs`, refines the initial `QuerySet` to exclude any `Blog` entries posted in the year 2008. By joining the `QuerySets` in this manner, you can create complex lookups in your code to handle the most complex types of database queries.

Django also provides another object, django.db.models.Q, that helps immensely with difficult queries. The Q object allows you to encapsulate a collection of field lookup arguments. For example, the following code snippet encapsulates a contains field lookup in a Q object and assigns it to variable q1:

```
from django.db.models import Q
q1 = Q(title__contains='test')
```

The filter(), exclude(), and get() functions accept the Q objects as their arguments. You can also use the ¦ and & operators to define SQL OR and AND behavior in the queries. For example, the following code snippet shows how to define two Q objects and then use them with OR and AND logic in the filter() function:

```
from django.db.models import Q
q1 = Q(title__contains='test')
q2 = Q(title__contains='obsolete')
oldBlogs = Blog.objects.filter(q1 ¦ q2)
oldTestBlogs = Blog.objects.filter(q1 & q2)
```

To illustrate this further, let's look at a slightly more complex query that involves using Q objects and QuerySets:

```
from django.db.models import Q
qs1 = Blog.objects.filter(uName__exact='Admin')
qs2 = qs1.exclude(postDate__year=2008)
q1 = Q(title__contains='SPAM')
q2 = Q(title__contains='obsolete')
oldBlogs = qs2.filter(q1 ¦ q2 )
```

Ordering Objects in a QuerySet

Another valuable function that is available through QuerySet objects is the order_by() function. The order_by() function accepts one or more field names as its arguments and then returns a new QuerySet that is ordered based on the field name you specify.

For example, the following code creates two QuerySets, qs1 and qs2. qs1 is ordered by the title, and qs2 is ordered by the postDate:

```
qs1 = Blog.objects.all().orderby('title')
qs2 = Blog.objects.all().orderby('postDate')
```

Django does not have case sensitivity built into the order_by() function. Therefore, the order is determined by the database backend.

Django orders the list by default in ascending order. You can also order the objects in descending order by specifying a – before the field name:

```
qs1 = Blog.objects.all().orderby('-postDate')
```

Django provides a handy tool to randomize QuerySets. If you specify a ? as the only argument to order_by(), as in the following code, order_by() returns a randomly ordered QuerySet.

```
qs1 = Blog.objects.all().orderby('?')
```

Did you Know?

Try It Yourself ▼

Perform Queries on the Database

In this section, you will use the Django shell to add some Blog entries to the database. Then you will perform queries on them to get a feel for how the queries work and how to include them in your code later.

Follow these steps from the Django shell to create some Blog entries, and then perform queries on them:

1. Import the Blog object using the following command at the shell prompt:

```
from iFriends.People.models import Blog
```

2. Add some Blog entries by entering the following commands at the shell prompt, as shown in Figure 5.4:

```
b = Blog(title='BlogA', text='Text in BlogA')
b.save()
b = Blog(title='BlogB', text='More text in BlogB')
b.save()
b = Blog(title='BlogC', text='Even more text in BlogC')
b.save()
```

```
Command Prompt2 - manage.py shell

C:\websites\iFriends>manage.py shell
Python 2.4.2 (#67, Sep 28 2005, 12:41:11) [MSC v.1310 32 bit (Intel)] on win32
Type "help", "copyright", "credits" or "license" for more information.
(InteractiveConsole)
>>> from iFriends.People.models import Blog
>>> b = Blog(title='BlogA', text='Text in BlogA')
>>> b.save()
>>> b = Blog(title='BlogB', text='More text in BlogB')
>>> b.save()
>>> b = Blog(title='BlogC', text='Even more text in BlogC')
>>> b.save()
>>>
```

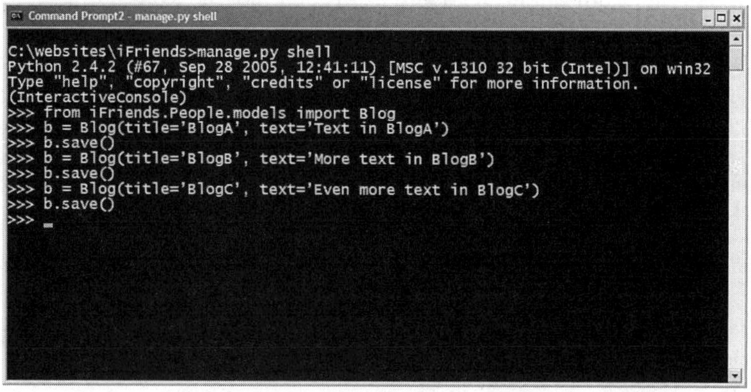

FIGURE 5.4
Using the save() function in the Python shell to add Blog objects to the database.

▼

3. Get the entry with the `title` BlogC, and print the `text` field using the following commands at the shell prompt, as shown in Figure 5.5:

```
e = Blog.objects.get(title='BlogC')
print e.text
```

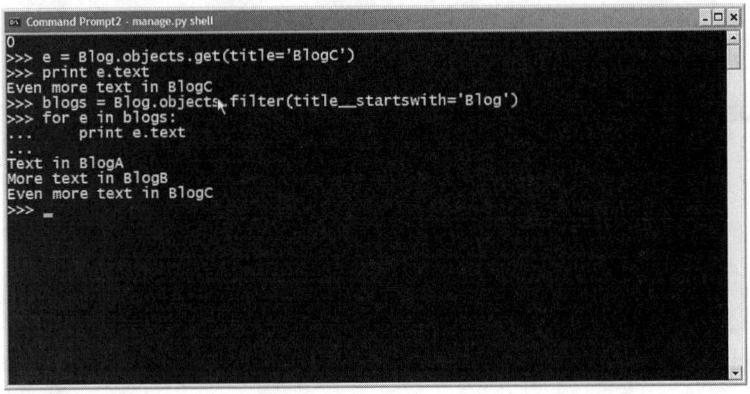

FIGURE 5.5
Using the
`filter()` func-
tion in the
Python shell
to query the
database.

```
Command Prompt2 - manage.py shell
0
>>> e = Blog.objects.get(title='BlogC')
>>> print e.text
Even more text in BlogC
>>> blogs = Blog.objects.filter(title__startswith='Blog')
>>> for e in blogs:
...     print e.text
...
Text in BlogA
More text in BlogB
Even more text in BlogC
>>>
```

4. Retrieve all entries whose `title` field begins with Blog, and print the `text`
fields using the following commands at the shell prompt, as shown in
Figure 5.5:

```
blogs = Blog.objects.filter(title__startswith='Blog')
for e in blogs:
    print e.text
```

5. Retrieve all entries whose `title` field begins with Blog and whose text fields
contain the word "more" (case-insensitive) but not the word "even" (case-
insensitive). Then print the `text` field using the following commands at the
shell prompt, as shown in Figure 5.6.

```
from django.db.models import Q
q1 = Q(text__icontains='more')
q2 = Q(text__icontains='even')
qs1 = Blog.objects.filter(title__startswith='Blog')
qs2 = qs1.filter(q1)
blogs = qs2.exclude(q2)
for e in blogs:
    print e.text
```

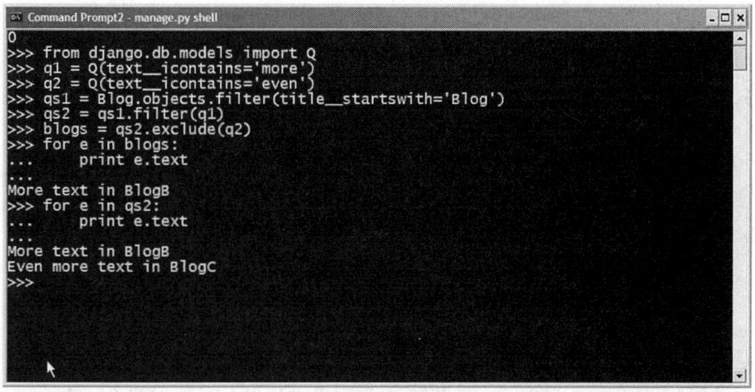

FIGURE 5.6
Using the Q
object and the
filter() and
exclude() func-
tions in the
Python shell
to query the
database.

Adding Data in a Model to a View

So far in this hour, you have used the Django shell to access the database. This section switches to creating web pages. Ultimately, most of the database queries that you will perform on the database will be done from the view functions in the views.py file and will be used to generate web pages.

Using the database-abstraction API that we have covered so far in this hour, you can retrieve data from the database in your views and then use that data to build web pages that contain meaningful content. Adding data from the database to a web page is simple. You add the Python code in the view necessary to retrieve the data from the database and then use that data when constructing the web page.

Try It Yourself ▼

Display Data from the Database in Views

In the past hours, you have had a chance to generate some web pages using HttpResponse objects in views. However, the web pages that were generated had simple headings as the content.

In this section, you will use the database-abstraction API in the views to add content from the database to web pages in the iFriends project. ▼

Follow these steps to modify the index() and details() view so that the index() view displays a list of Person objects in the database and the details() view displays detailed information about a specific version:

1. Open the iFriends/People/views.py file in an editor.

2. Add the following code to the index() function, shown in Listing 5.2, to create an HttpResponse object and begin generating the HTTP response:

```
response = HttpResponse()
response.write("<html><body>\n")
response.write("<h1>People</h1><hr>")
```

3. Use the all() function to retrieve all Person objects from the database:

```
pList = Person.objects.all()
```

4. Add the following code snippet to iterate through the QuerySet that was generated in step 3, and generate a list of links for each Person object:

```
for p in pList:
    link = "<a href=\"Info/%d\">" % (p.id)
    response.write("<li>%s%s</a></li>" % (link, p.name))
```

5. Add the following code snippet to finish and return the HTTP response:

```
response.write("</body></html>")
return response
```

6. Verify that the URL pattern works correctly by accessing the URL http://127.0.0.1:8000/People. You should see a web page similar to the one shown in Figure 5.7.

FIGURE 5.7
index() view for the People application.

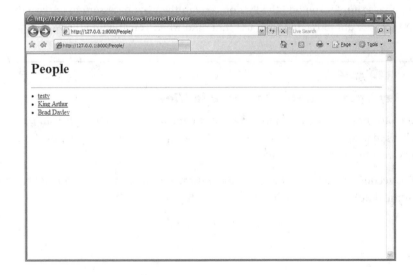

7. Add the following code to the `details()` function, shown in Listing 5.2, to query the database and find the `Person` object with an `id` field that matches the `pID` parameter passed into the function and handle cases where no object is found:

```
try:
    p = Person.objects.get(id=pID)
    . . .
except Person.DoesNotExist:
    response.write("Person Not Found")
```

8. Add the following code snippet to display detailed information about the `Person` object:

```
response.write("<h1>Details for Person %s</h1><hr>\n" % p.name)
response.write("<li>Birthday: %s</li>" % p.birthday)
response.write("<li>Email: %s</li>" % p.email)
response.write("<li>Favorite URL: %s</li>" % p.favoriteURL)
response.write("<li>Desc: %s</li>" % p.desc)
```

9. Add the following code snippet to finish and return the HTTP response:

```
response.write("</body></html>")
return response
```

10. Verify that the URL pattern works correctly by clicking one of the links on the details view, as shown in Figure 5.7. You should see a web page similar to the one shown in Figure 5.8.

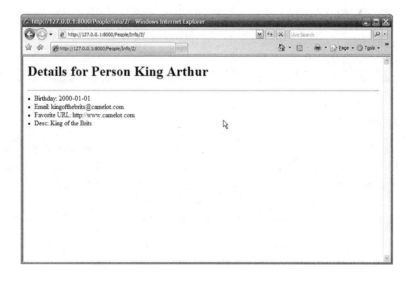

FIGURE 5.8
Details for a
Person object.

Listing 5.2 shows the complete views.py file.

LISTING 5.2   **Full Contents of the** iFriends\People\views.py **File**

```python
from django.http import HttpResponse
from iFriends.People.models import Person

def index(request):
    response = HttpResponse()

    response.write("<html><body>\n")
    response.write("<h1>People</h1><hr>")
    pList = Person.objects.all()
    for p in pList:
        link = "<a href=\"Info/%d\">" % (p.id)
        response.write("<li>%s%s</a></li>" % (link, p.name))
    response.write("</body></html>")

    return response

def details(request, pID='0'):
    response = HttpResponse()

    response.write("<html><body>\n")
    try:
        p = Person.objects.get(id=pID)
        response.write("<h1>Details for Person %s</h1><hr>\n" % p.name)
        response.write("<li>Birthday: %s</li>" % p.birthday)
        response.write("<li>Email: %s</li>" % p.email)
        response.write("<li>Favorite URL: %s</li>" % p.favoriteURL)
        response.write("<li>Desc: %s</li>" % p.desc)
    except Person.DoesNotExist:
        response.write("Person Not Found")
    response.write("</body></html>")

    return response
```

Summary

The focus of this hour was to familiarize you with the Django database-abstraction API. You got a chance to create some objects in the database. Then you learned how to access the objects through the database abstraction API using the get() and all() functions. You also learned about QuerySet and how to use the filter() and exclude() functions to perform queries on objects.

Throughout the rest of the book, you will get more experience accessing the database as more complex views are created.

Q&A

Q. *We used the Blog.objects.all() function to create a QuerySet of all objects. Couldn't I just use the* `Blog.object` `QuerySet` *object?*

A. No. `objects` QuerySet is a special-case QuerySet object that acts as a "root" object that cannot be evaluated.

Q. *Is there any way to limit the size of a* `QuerySet`*?*

A. Yes. Because the QuerySet is basically a Python array, you can use the Python array slicing syntax to limit the size of the QuerySet:

```
first10 = Blog.objects.all()[:10]
second10 = Blog.objects.all()[10:20]
```

Workshop

The workshop consists of a set of questions and answers designed to solidify your understanding of the material covered in this hour. Try answering the questions before looking at the answers.

Quiz

1. What happens if you modify an object's primary key and then use the object's function?

2. If you use the `filter()` function to create a `QuerySet`, when is the database actually accessed?

3. Which lookup type would you use if you needed to search for `userID` numbers between 1 and 10?

Quiz Answers

1. If another object exists with that primary key, it is overwritten by the new object. Otherwise, a new object is created.

2. When the filter object is evaluated in some way.

3. A range lookup.

Exercises

In this hour, you got a chance to use the database-abstraction API to build the index() and details() views in the iFriends application. Use the following exercises to expand the site a bit further and add views for the Blog objects:

1. Add entries to the URLconf file to handle web access to a blog_index() and blog_details() view for Blogs.

2. Create a blog_index() view that displays links to all Blog entries in the database.

3. Create a blog_details() view that displays the title and text of a single Blog entry.

HOUR 6

Configuring Web Page Views

What You'll Learn in This Hour:

▶ How to pass extra options to a view function
▶ How to implement view prefixes
▶ How to create URLconf files for each application
▶ How to use a callable object instead of a string in an URL pattern

In Hour 4, "Creating the Initial Views," you learned how to set up the initial views in the URLconf file. In this hour, we will expand on that topic to include more advanced configuration options for views. When designing your website, the more complete your URLconf file configuration for web page views is, the easier it is to keep your code in the view cohesive and clean.

The following sections describe some advanced configuration options that you can make in the URLconf and views.py files.

Passing Extra Options to a View

The syntax for URL patterns in the URLconf file allows you to add additional options that will be passed as additional arguments to the view function. This is different from capturing arguments inside the URL, which we have already discussed.

Django allows you to specify a Python dictionary containing arguments that will be passed to the view function by the URL dispatcher. For example, the following URL pattern passes a simple dictionary:

```
(r'^People/BlogArchive/$', 'iFriends.Blogs.views.index', {'label':'Archive'}),
```

When this URL pattern is accessed, the URL dispatcher calls the index() view function:

```
index(request, label='Archive')
```

By the Way

Just as with arguments captured from the URL, you need to add the arguments to the view function definition in the `views.py` file.

You can also capture arguments from the URL along with passing extra options in a dictionary. For example, the following URL pattern captures the year argument and passes a simple dictionary containing a `label` argument:

```
(r'^People/BlogArchive/(?P<year>\d{4})/$', 'iFriends.Blogs.views.index',
{'label':'Archive'}),
```

When this URL pattern is accessed, the URL dispatcher calls the `index()` view function:

```
index(request, year='2008', label='Archive')
```

Watch Out!

It is possible to specify the same argument name in both the captured arguments and the extra options dictionary. If this occurs, the value in the extra options dictionary is used instead of the value that was captured from the URL.

The ability to pass options to view functions provides much more control over the views from the URLconf file. This gives you much more flexibility in the URL patterns that your website will handle. The captured arguments and the extra options dictionary also make the website easier to design and manage, because much of the control is contained in the URLconf file.

▼ **Try It Yourself**

Pass Extra Options to the View Function from the URLconf File

The best way to help you understand how useful the extra options dictionary can be is to apply it to the iFriends website that we have been working with. Currently, we have two views—an `index()` view that displays a list of `Person` objects, and a `details()` view that displays details of a specific `Person` object.

In this section, you will add functionality to the `details()` view that will make it possible to use the URLconf file to determine what details will be displayed. Follow these steps to modify the `views.py` and `urls.py` files of the iFriends project:

1. Open the iFriends/urls.py file in an editor.

2. Add the following dictionary definitions to the `urls.py` file, as shown in Listing 6.1, to define what items of the `Person` object to display in the details view:

▼

```
details1 = {'opts':('name','email')}
details2 = {'opts':('name','birthday')}
details3 = {'opts':('name','desc','favoriteURL')}
```

3. Add the following URL patterns to the urls.py file, shown in Listing 6.1. The Contact, Birthday, and Details URL patterns pass the details1, details2, and details3 extra options dictionaries to the details() view function, respectively:

```
(r'^People/Contact/(?P<pID>\d+)/$', 'iFriends.People.views.details',
➥details1),
(r'^People/Birthday/(?P<pID>\d+)/$', 'iFriends.People.views.details',
➥details2),
(r'^People/Details/(?P<pID>\d+)/$', 'iFriends.People.views.details',
➥details3),
```

4. Save the iFriends/urls.py file.

5. Open the iFriends/People/views.py file in an editor.

6. Add the following change to the definition of the details() view function, shown in Listing 6.2, to allow the opts argument to be passed in:

```
def details(request, pID='0', opts=()):
```

7. Replace the code that currently writes all the Person object details to the response object with the following code, shown in Listing 6.2. This code iterates through the opts list and writes the details specified by the URLconf file to the HTTP response:

```
for d in opts:
    response.write("<li>%s: %s</li>" % (d, p.__dict__[d]))
```

The sample code here uses the __dict__ member of the Person class to find the field names specified in the opts list. The __dict__ is built into all Python objects.

 By the Way

---

8. Save the iFriends/People/views.py file.

9. Access the People/Contact/1 URL to verify the Contact version of the details() view, as shown in Figure 6.1.

10. Access the People/Birthday/1 URL to verify the Birthday version of the details() view, as shown in Figure 6.2.

FIGURE 6.1
The Contact
version of
the details()
view in a web
browser.

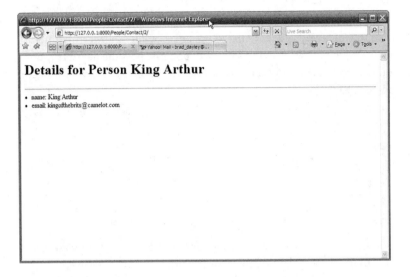

FIGURE 6.2
The Birthday
version of the
details() view
in a web
browser.

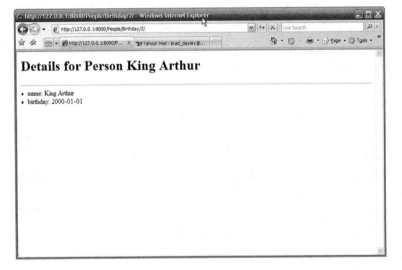

11. Access the People/Details/1 URL to verify the Details version of the details()
view, as shown in Figure 6.3.

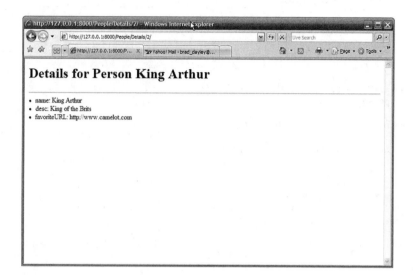

FIGURE 6.3
The Details version of the details() view in a web browser.

LISTING 6.1   Full Contents of the iFriends\urls.py File

```
from django.conf.urls.defaults import *
details1 = {'opts':('name','email')}
details2 = {'opts':('name','birthday')}
details3 = {'opts':('name','desc','favoriteURL')}

urlpatterns = patterns('',
    (r'^People/$', 'iFriends.People.views.index'),
    (r'^People/Info/$', 'iFriends.People.views.details'),
    (r'^People/Info/(?P<pID>\d+)/$', 'iFriends.People.views.details'),
    (r'^People/Contact/(?P<pID>\d+)/$', 'iFriends.People.views.details',
    details1),
    (r'^People/Birthday/(?P<pID>\d+)/$', 'iFriends.People.views.details',
    details2),
    (r'^People/Details/(?P<pID>\d+)/$', 'iFriends.People.views.details',
    details3),

    # Uncomment this for admin:
    (r'^admin/', include('django.contrib.admin.urls')),
)
```

LISTING 6.2   Full Contents of the iFriends\People\views.py File

```
from django.http import HttpResponse
from iFriends.People.models import Person

def index(request):
    response = HttpResponse()

    response.write("<h1>People</h1><hr>")
    pList = Person.objects.all()
```

LISTING 6.2   Continued

```
    for p in pList:
        link = "<a href=\"Info/%d\">" % (p.id)
        response.write("<li>%s%s</a></li>" % (link, p.name))

    return response

def details(request, pID='0', opts=()):
    response = HttpResponse()

    response.write("<html><body>\n")
    try:
        p = Person.objects.get(id=pID)
        response.write("<h1>Details for Person %s</h1><hr>\n" % p.name)
        for d in opts:
            response.write("<li>%s: %s</li>" % (d, p.__dict__[d]))
    except Person.DoesNotExist:
        response.write("Person Not Found")
    response.write("</body></html>")

    return response
```

Using View Prefixes

In the preceding section, you added three new URL patterns to your URLconf file. In each pattern, you specified the same view, iFriends.People.views.details. This is a lot of redundant code. This also can be problematic if you change the project's name, because you would need to change every URL pattern.

Django solves this problem by allowing you to specify a view prefix as the first argument to the patterns() function in the URLconf file. This can be used if all URL patterns being defined are located in the same view file. When a view prefix is added, you need to specify the view function in only the URL pattern. For example, if all URL patterns are located in the iFriends.Blogs.views file, you could use the following code to define the URL patterns for the index() and details() view functions:

```
urlpatterns = patterns('iFriends.Blogs.views',
    (r'^Blogs/$', 'index'),
    (r'^Blogs/Details/$', 'details'),
)
```

Sometimes you may need to have more than one prefix defined in the same URLconf file. You can use more than one prefix in the same URLconf file by calling the patterns() function multiple times and appending them to one another using the += operator, as shown in the following code snippet:

```
urlpatterns = patterns('iFriends.Blogs.views',
    (r'^Blogs/$', 'index'),
```

```
        (r'^Blogs/Details/$', 'details'),
)

urlpatterns += patterns('iFriends.People.views',
    (r'^People/$', 'index'),
    (r'^People/Details/$', 'details'),
)
```

Try It Yourself ▼

Add a View Prefix to an URLconf File

In this section you will modify the URLconf file for the iFriends project to separate all the URL patterns that use the iFriends.People.views prefix to use a view prefix.

Follow these steps to open the iFriends/urls.py file and move the iFriends.People. views entries to their own patterns() function and specify a view prefix for them:

1. Open the iFriends/urls.py file in an editor.

2. Add the following code to append another patterns() function, as shown in Listing 6.3, specifying the iFriends.People.views prefix:

   ```
   urlpatterns += patterns('iFriends.People.views',
       )
   ```

3. Move the URL patterns that use iFriends.People.views from the main patterns() function to the new patterns() function created in step 2:

   ```
   (r'^People/$', 'iFriends.People.views.index'),
   (r'^People/Info/$', 'iFriends.People.views.details'),
   (r'^People/Info/(?P<pID>\d+)/$', 'iFriends.People.views.details'),
   (r'^People/Contact/(?P<pID>\d+)/$', 'iFriends.People.views.details',
       details1),
   (r'^People/Birthday/(?P<pID>\d+)/$', 'iFriends.People.views.details',
       details2),
   (r'^People/Details/(?P<pID>\d+)/$', 'iFriends.People.views.details',
       details3),
   ```

4. Modify the URL patterns to remove the iFriends.Blogs.views prefix to streamline the URLconf file, as shown in Listing 6.3:

   ```
   (r'^People/$', 'index'),
   (r'^People/Info/$', 'details'),
   (r'^People/Info/(?P<pID>\d+)/$', 'details'),
   (r'^People/Contact/(?P<pID>\d+)/$', 'details', details1),
   (r'^People/Birthday/(?P<pID>\d+)/$', 'details', details2),
   (r'^People/Details/(?P<pID>\d+)/$', 'details', details3),
   ```

▼

5. Save the iFriends/urls.py file.

6. Test the URLConf file by accessing the following URL from a web browser:

http://127.0.0.1:8000/People/Info/1/

LISTING 6.3   Full Contents of the iFriends\urls.py **File**

```
from django.conf.urls.defaults import *

urlpatterns = patterns('',
    # Uncomment this for admin:
    (r'^admin/', include('django.contrib.admin.urls')),
)

details1 = {'opts':('name','email')}
details2 = {'opts':('name','birthday')}
details3 = {'opts':('name', 'desc', 'favoriteURL')}

urlpatterns += patterns('iFriends.People.views',
    (r'^People/$', 'index'),
    (r'^People/Info/$', 'details'),
    (r'^People/Info/(?P<pID>\d+)/$', 'details'),
    (r'^People/Contact/(?P<pID>\d+)/$', 'details', details1),
    (r'^People/Birthday/(?P<pID>\d+)/$', 'details', details2),
    (r'^People/Details/(?P<pID>\d+)/$', 'details', details3),
)
```

Using Additional URLconf Files

As you add more applications to your website, your URLconf file can become congested with all the URL patterns for the different applications. The best way to avoid this is to create an URLconf file for each application.

Django provides the include() function to add URLconf files to the URLconf file. The include() function accepts the location of the URLconf file using . (dot) syntax and takes the place of the view function in the URL pattern. For example, to include a new URLconf file, iFriends/Blog/urls.py, to be used when the /Blog/ URL is accessed, you would specify the following URL pattern:

```
(r'^Blog/', include('iFriends.Blog.urls')),
```

By the Way

Notice that the r'^Blog/' pattern doesn't include the $ character. This is because the URL dispatcher deletes the portion of the URL that is read before executing the include and passes only the remaining string. For example, if the preceding URL were Blog/index, only index would be passed in as the URL to the new URLconf file. The new URLconf file needs to have the trailing $ character specified in the pattern.

Django passes captured parameters through the include() function to other URLconf files. For example, if your root URLconf file contained the following pattern:

```
(r'^(?P<pID>\d+)/Blog/', include('iFriends.Blog.urls')),
```

the pID argument would still be captured and passed to the display() view function in the following pattern in the iFriends/Blog/urls.py URLconf file:

```
(r'^', 'iFriends.Blog.views.display'),
```

Django also allows you to pass a dictionary of extra options as an argument after the include() function. This passes the extra options to other URLconf files, which pass them to the view functions they invoke. For example, if your root URLconf file contains the following pattern:

```
(r'^Blog/', include('iFriends.Blog.urls'), {'pID':0}),
```

the dictionary containing the pID argument is still passed to the display() view function in the following pattern in the iFriends/Blog/urls.py URLconf file:

```
(r'^', 'iFriends.Blog.views.display'),
```

Try It Yourself   ▼

Add an URLconf File to Your Django Project

In this section, you will add a new URLconf file to the People application of the iFriends project. Follow these steps to create the new URLconf file and modify the root URLconf file to include the new one:

1. Use an editor to create a file called iFriends/People/urls.py.

2. Add the following code to the new urls.py file to handle the URL requests to People, as shown in Listing 6.4:

```
from django.conf.urls.defaults import *

details1 = {'opts':('name','email')}
details2 = {'opts':('name','birthday')}
details3 = {'opts':('name','desc','favoriteURL')}

urlpatterns = patterns('iFriends.People.views',
    (r'^$', 'index'),
    (r'^Info/$', 'details'),
    (r'^Info/(?P<pID>\d+)/$', 'details'),
    (r'^Contact/(?P<pID>\d+)/$', 'details', details1),
    (r'^Birthday/(?P<pID>\d+)/$', 'details', details2),
    (r'^Details/(?P<pID>\d+)/$', 'details', details3),
)
```

▼

> The code in the new URLconf file is similar to the code that was in the original URLconf file. However, remember that you need to remove the People/ portion of the pattern, because it is deleted before the `include()` function sends the URL to this file.

3. Save the iFriends/People/urls.py file.

4. Open the iFriends/urls.py file in an editor.

5. Remove the following code that is used for the People/ URLs:

```
details1 = {'opts':('name','email')}
details2 = {'opts':('name','birthday')}
details3 = {'opts':('name','desc','favoriteURL')}

urlpatterns += patterns('iFriends.People.views',
    (r'^People/$', 'index'),
    (r'^People/Info/$', 'details'),
    (r'^People/Info/(?P<pID>\d+)/$', 'details'),
    (r'^People/Contact/(?P<pID>\d+)/$', 'details', details1),
    (r'^People/Birthday/(?P<pID>\d+)/$', 'details', details2),
    (r'^People/Details/(?P<pID>\d+)/$', 'details', details3),
)
```

6. Add the following pattern, as shown in Listing 6.5, to point People/ URLs to the iFriends/People/urls.py URLconf file:

```
(r'^People/', include('iFriends.People.urls')),
```

7. Save the iFriends/urls.py file.

8. Test the new URLConf file by accessing the following URL from a web browser:

```
http://127.0.0.1:8000/People/Info/1/
```

LISTING 6.4   Full Contents of the iFriends\People\urls.py **File**

```
from django.conf.urls.defaults import *

details1 = {'opts':('name','email')}
details2 = {'opts':('name','birthday')}
details3 = {'opts':('name','desc','favoriteURL')}

urlpatterns = patterns('iFriends.People.views',
    (r'^$', 'index'),
    (r'^Info/$', 'details'),
    (r'^Info/(?P<pID>\d+)/$', 'details'),
    (r'^Contact/(?P<pID>\d+)/$', 'details', details1),
    (r'^Birthday/(?P<pID>\d+)/$', 'details', details2),
    (r'^Details/(?P<pID>\d+)/$', 'details', details3),
)
```

LISTING 6.5   Full Contents of the `iFriends\urls.py` File

```
from django.conf.urls.defaults import *

urlpatterns = patterns('',
    (r'^People/', include('iFriends.People.urls')),

    # Uncomment this for admin:
    (r'^admin/', include('django.contrib.admin.urls')),
)
```

Calling the View Functions Directly

Django supports an alternative method of calling the view functions from the URLconf file. Instead of pointing to the location of the view function using a .-based syntax string, you can import the function into the URLconf file and then use the function name instead. For example, if your current view file contains the following URL patterns that point to an `index()` and `display()` view functions:

```
(r'^Blog/List/$', 'iFriends.Blog.views.index'),
(r'^Blog/Display/$', 'iFriends.Blog.views.display'),
```

you could import the `index()` and `display()` view functions in the URLconf file using the following line of code:

```
from iFriends.Blog.views import index, display
```

and then you could pass callable function objects directly using the following code:

```
(r'^Blog/List/$', index),
(r'^Blog/Display/$', display),
```

Summary

In this hour, you learned how to create dictionaries of arguments and pass them to the view functions from the URLconf file. You also learned how to keep your URLconf files cleaner by using view prefixes and separating application URL patterns into their own URLconf files. We also covered how to specify the view function directly in the URL pattern.

Q&A

Q. *If I need to include only one extra variable, can I just specify the variable as a parameter after the view location in the URL pattern?*

A. The extra options must be contained in a dictionary. You can add the dictionary to the URL pattern as follows:

```
(r'^Blogs/', 'mySite.Blogs.views.index', {'maxSize':10}),
```

Q. *Is there a way to get the absolute URL for a view in my Python code?*

A. Yes, Django provides the `django.core.urlresolvers.reverse(viewname, urlconf=None, args=None, kwargs=None)` function that will return the absolute URL for a view function. The `reverse()` function accepts either a function reference or a string version of the name as the `viewname` argument. The `reverse()` function also accepts optional arguments that allow you to specify which Urlconf file to use and the args and kwargs that should be passed to the view in the absolute URL. For example, consider the following URL:

```
(r'^People/Details/(?P<pID>\d+)/$', 'details'),
```

The following code allows you to retrieve the absolute URL for the `iFriends.People.views.details` view for a specific `userID`:

```
from django.core.urlresolvers import reverse
from iFriends.People.views import details
def getURL(userID):
    absoluteURL = reverse(details, args=[userID])
```

Workshop

The workshop consists of a set of questions and answers designed to solidify your understanding of the material covered in this hour. Try answering the questions before looking at the answers.

Quiz

1. What is the relative path of the URLconf file for the following URL pattern?

```
(r'^Blogs/', include('mySite.Blogs.urls')),
```

2. If a variable is captured in the URL pattern and also is specified in an extra options dictionary, which value is passed to the view function?

3. If the URL Blogs/display/10 is passed into the following URL pattern, what URL is passed into the URLconf file called by the `include()` function?

```
(r'^Blogs/', include('mySite.Blogs.urls')),
```

Quiz Answers

1. mySite/Blogs/urls.py

2. The value in the dictionary

3. `display/10`

Exercises

1. Create an additional view for the `People` object that displays the `Blog` contents for a specific person.

2. Create an URL pattern in the `URLconf` file that collects the person's ID from the URL request and passes it to the view function you created in Exercise 1.

HOUR 7

Implementing Django Templates to Create Custom Views

What You'll Learn in This Hour:

▶ How to configure the template directory for a project
▶ How to create templates in the Django shell
▶ How to render views using templates
▶ How to extend templates
▶ How to embed templates in other templates

So far, all the examples of web pages that you have created in your views have been hard-coded by Python code that generates an HTML web page. This has worked well because the web pages that you have created have been basic.

As you create more advanced web pages, you will want to begin using the Django template system. The Django template system allows you to write template files that define the presentation of the web page independent of the data. This means that you can write generic web pages and then use the Python code in the views to generate dynamic content inside them.

Using the template system has several benefits. For example, an HTML developer could be working on the web page views, and a Python developer could be working on processing the data at exactly the same time.

In this hour, you will get a chance to create some HTML templates and use them to render the data in your views.

Configuring the Template Directory

The first step in adding templates to your website is to create and configure a directory to store them in. You will want to create at least one directory to store the templates in and then add that directory to the TEMPLATE_DIRS setting in the project's settings.py file.

Django's template engine will read the TEMPLATE_DIRS setting and use the directories that are configured there to process the relative paths you will specify for the template.

▼ **Try It Yourself**

Create and Configure a Template Directory for a Project

In this section, you will create a template directory in the root of the iFriends project and then configure Django to search that directory when trying to find templates.

 Did you Know?

> The Django admin interface uses templates extensively to display the admin web pages. The admin template directory is built into the template search path and doesn't need to be specified in the TEMPLATE_DIRS setting in the settings.py file. The admin template directory is located in the following path relative to where Django is installed:
>
> django/contrib/admin/templates

Follow these steps to create the directory and modify the settings.py file:

1. Create a new directory named templates in the iFriends/ directory.

2. Open the settings.py file in an editor.

3. Add the full path of the templates directory created in step 1 to the TEMPLATE_DIRS setting:

```
TEMPLATE_DIRS = (
    # Put strings here, like "/home/html/django_templates" or
    # "C:/www/django/templates".
    # Always use forward slashes, even on Windows.
    # Don't forget to use absolute paths, not relative paths.
    "C:/websites/iFriends/templates",
)
```

▲ 4. Save the settings.py file.

Creating a Template

Django templates can combine a Django placeholder and just about any type of raw text code that displays a web page. Django placeholders are designated by encapsulating them in double braces:

```
{{ person_name }}
```

The raw text portion of the file can contain various types of information. The best way to explain this is with some examples. The following sections take you through some different methods of creating and using Django templates.

Creating Templates in the Django Shell

The first example we will look at is using Django templates in the Django shell to format text output. You probably won't use templates in the shell. However, the shell is a great place to learn about them and try them out.

To create a template in the Django shell, first import the `Template` object class from the `django.template` project using the following command:

```
from django.template import Template
```

> You can use the following command from the root of your project to start the Django shell:
>
> ```
> python manage.py
> ```

By the Way

You create a template by calling the constructor of the `Template` class and passing in a string containing a placeholder. For example, the following line of code defines a Template object t that contains a variable placeholder `emotion`:

```
t = Template("I feel {{emotion}}.")
```

Next, you create some `Context` objects by calling the `Context()` constructor and passing it a dictionary that contains the `emotion` key:

```
from django.template import Context
c1 = Context({'emotion': 'happy'})
c2 = Context({'emotion': 'fine'})
c3 = Context({'emotion': 'good'})
```

You can change the contents of `Context` by treating it as a Python dictionary. For example, to change the emotion of the `c1` `Context` object in the preceding example, you could use the following line of code:

```
c1['emotion'] = 'cool'
```

After you have created the `Template` and `Context` objects, you can render the template to text by calling the `render()` function of the `Template` object and passing the appropriate context, as shown in Figure 7.1.

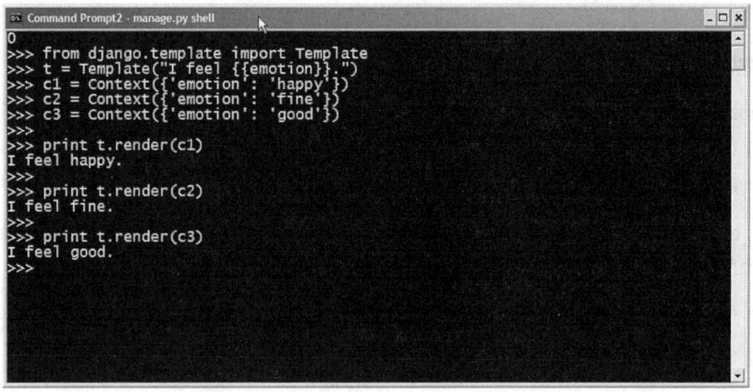

FIGURE 7.1
Creating and
rendering a
template in the
Django shell.

The `render()` function reads the dictionary in the context and replaces variable placeholders in the template that match keys in the dictionary with the key's value.

Did you Know?

If you have a lot of text that needs to be processed as a template, you can store the template text as a text file and then use Python's file functions to read in the contents of the template as a string. This also works when you use the Django shell to test your HTML templates. For example, to read the contents of a `myTemplate.html` file into a `Template` object, you could use the following line of code:

```
myT = Template(open('myTemplate.html', 'rU').read())
```

Creating HTML Templates

Most of the templates you will work with in your Django website will be HTML templates. HTML templates are text files that contain mostly HTML code but do contain some variable placeholders. You will be able to render the HTML template, using custom contexts, as a response to an HTTP request. Using this method, you can write your web pages using basic HTML tags but still can programmatically control the variable content.

The best way to create an HTML template is to first create an HTML file with the look and feel that you like and test it in a web browser. Then add the variable placeholders for data that needs to be dynamic. For example, `test.html`, shown in Listing 7.1, displays the simple web page shown in Figure 7.2.

LISTING 7.1   Full Contents of the `test.html` File

```
<html xmlns="http://www.w3.org/1999/xhtml" lang="en-us" xml:lang="en-us" >
<head>
<title>Title</title>
</head>
<body>
<table width=100%>
<tr bgcolor="aabbcc"><td colspan="2">
<font size="12" color="white">Title</font>
</td></tr>
<tr valign="top"><td width=70% bgcolor="aaaaaa"><font color="white" size="5">
    <H2>Headline</H2>
    data
</font></td>
<td width=30%>
    <h3>Current Time</h3>
    time
</td></tr>
</table>
</body>
</html>
```

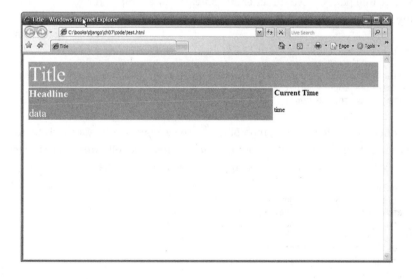

FIGURE 7.2
Web page generated by `test.html`.

To turn test.html into a Django template, you would replace the dynamic items Title, Headline, data, and time with the following variable placeholders, as shown in Listing 7.2:

{{ title}}, {{ headline }}, {{ data }} and {{time}}

LISTING 7.2   Full Contents of the Modified test.html File

```
<html xmlns="http://www.w3.org/1999/xhtml" lang="en-us" xml:lang="en-us" >
<head>
<title>{{ title }}</title>
</head>
<body>
<table width=100%>
<tr bgcolor="aabbcc"><td colspan="2">
<font size="12" color="white">{{ title }}</font>
</td></tr>
<tr valign="top"><td width=70% bgcolor="aaaaaa"><font color="white" size="5">
    <H2>{{ headline }}</H2>
    {{ data }}
</font></td>
<td width=30%>
    <h3>Current Time</h3>
    {{ time }}
</td></tr>
</table>
</body>
</html>
```

With the variable placeholders in the test.html file, Django enables you to deliver dynamic web pages based on different contexts. For example, the following code snippet creates a context that generates the web page shown in Figure 7.3:

```
c = Context()
c['title'] = 'My Log'
c['headline'] = 'Entry #5'
c['data'] = 'Found errors in subroutines 2, 5 and 8.'
from datetime import datetime
c['time'] = datetime.now()
```

To change the content that Django places in the web page, all that needs to happen is for the data in the context to change. For example, the following code snippet creates a context that generates the web page shown in Figure 7.4:

```
c = Context()
c['title'] = 'Corporate Memos'
c['headline'] = 'Company Party'
c['data'] = 'There will be a company Party on Friday. '
c['data'] += 'Families are invited.'
from datetime import datetime
c['time'] = datetime.now()
```

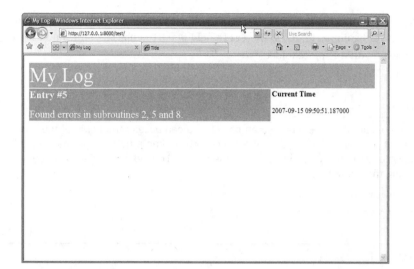

FIGURE 7.3
Web page generated by context using the My Log code snippet.

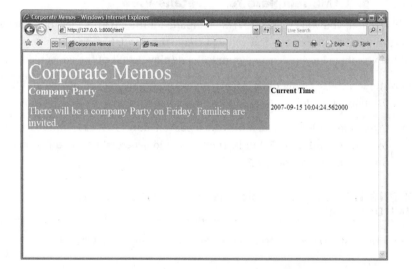

FIGURE 7.4
Web page generated by context using the Corporate Memos code snippet.

Accessing Objects Using HTML Templates

Django's template parser allows you to access object fields directly from the template. This is a major advantage, because most of the data you will display in the web pages will be in the form of objects that were queried from the database. Instead of having to add each field as an entry in the Context dictionary, you only need to add the object.

Django uses the . (dot) syntax in the variable placeholder to access fields in the object. For example, to access the title field of a Blog object, you would use the following variable placeholder:

```
{{ blog.title }}
```

By the
~~Way~~

> If the value of the field is also an object, you can access the fields of the sub-object as well. For example, if the Person object has a field blogs that refers to a list of Blog objects, you could access the title field of the first Blog object using the following syntax:
>
> ```
> {{ person.blogs[0].name }}
> ```

▼

Try It Yourself

Create an HTML Template for a Details View

In this section, you will create an HTML template for the details view of a Person object in the iFriends project. You will first create the HTML file, and then you will add the variable placeholders to dynamically display details of the Person object.

Follow these steps to create an HTML document to display Person details and turn it into a Django template:

1. Using a text editor, create a file called person_details.html, and place the code shown in Listing 7.3 in it. The file should generate a web page similar to the one shown in Figure 7.5.

LISTING 7.3   Full Contents of the person_details.html HTML Document

```
<!DOCTYPE html>
<html xmlns="http://www.w3.org/1999/xhtml" lang="en-us" xml:lang="en-us" >
<head>
<title>Test Page</title>
</head>
<body>
<table width=100%>
<tr bgcolor="aabbcc"><td colspan="3">
<font size="12" color="white">Personal Information</font>
</td></tr>
<tr valign="top"><td width=30% bgcolor="aaaaaa"><font color="white" size="5">
    <li>Name: name</li>
    <li>Birthday: birthday</li>
    <li>Gender: gender</li>
    <li>Desc: desc</li>
</font></td>
<td width=40% bgcolor="aa99aa"><font color="white" size="4">
```

▼

LISTING 7.3   Continued

```
    <p align="center">Comments</p>
    <p align="center">None.
</font></td>
<td width=30%>
    <h3>Contact Info</h3>
    <li>Email: email</li>
    <li>Website: website</li>
</td></tr>
</table>
</body>
</html>
```

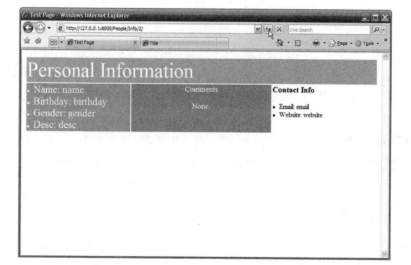

FIGURE 7.5
Web page
generated by
person_details.
html.

2. Modify the following line from Listing 7.3 to match Listing 7.4 to display the
   person's name in the title bar of the web browser:

   ```
   <title>Test Page</title>
   ```
   It becomes

   ```
   <title>{{ p.name }}</title>
   ```

3. Modify the following lines from Listing 7.3 to match Listing 7.4 to display the
   person's details in the details section of the web browser:

   ```
   <li>Name: name</li>
   <li>Birthday: birthday</li>
   <li>Gender: gender</li>
   <li>Desc: desc</li>
   ```

They become

```
<li>Name: {{p.name}}</li>
<li>Birthday: {{ p.birthday }}</li>
<li>Gender: {{ p.gender }}</li>
<li>Desc: {{ p.desc }} </li>
```

4. Modify the following lines from Listing 7.3 to match Listing 7.4 to display the person's contact information in the contact section of the web browser:

```
<li>Email: email</li>
<li>Website: website</li>
```

They become

```
<li>Email: {{ p.email }}</li>
<li>Website: {{ p.favoriteURL }}</li>
```

5. Save the new file. (It is shown in Listing 7.4.)

6. Copy the person_details.html file to the iFriends/templates/People template directory for the People application of the iFriends project.

LISTING 7.4 **Full Contents of the Modified** person_details.html **Django Template**

```
<!DOCTYPE html>
<html xmlns="http://www.w3.org/1999/xhtml" lang="en-us" xml:lang="en-us" >
<head>
<title>{{ p.name }}</title>
</head>
<body>
<table width=100%>
<tr bgcolor="aabbcc"><td colspan="3">
<font size="12" color="white">Personal Information</font>
</td></tr>
<tr valign="top"><td width=30% bgcolor="aaaaaa"><font color="white" size="5">
    <li>Name: {{p.name}}</li>
    <li>Birthday: {{ p.birthday }}</li>
    <li>Gender: {{ p.gender }}</li>
    <li>Desc: {{ p.desc }} </li>
</font></td>
<td width=40% bgcolor="aa99aa"><font color="white" size="4">
    <p align="center">Comments</p>
    <p align="center">None.
</font></td>
<td width=30%>
    <h3>Contact Info</h3>
    <li>Email: {{ p.email }}</li>
    <li>Website: {{ p.favoriteURL }}</li>
</td></tr>
</table>
</body>
</html>
```

Rendering a Template as an HTTP Response

In the preceding section, you learned how to create a Django template from an HTTP document. This section covers how to display it using the `render_to_response()` shortcut function. The `render_to_response()` function accepts the name of a template file and a dictionary as its only two arguments, as shown in the following example:

```
render_to_response('person_detail.html', {'p': person})
```

When you call `render_to_response()`, it opens the template file, reads the contents into a `Template` object, creates a `Context` object using the `dictionary` argument, renders the `Template` object based on the `Context` object, and outputs the results as an `HttpResponse`.

You can use the `locals()` Python function to generate a dictionary containing all the locals in the current function context. Instead of building your own dictionary, you can just specify the `locals()` function in the `render_to_response` call:

```
render_to_response('person_detail.html', locals())
```

Did you Know?

Try It Yourself ▼

Render a Web Page from a Template

In this section, you will modify the `details()` view function for the `People` application to use `render_to_response()` to display the `Person` details using the `person_details.html` template file you created in the preceding "Try It Yourself" section.

Follow these steps to modify the `details()` view to use the `person_details.html` template:

1. Open the `iFriends/People/views.py` file in an editor.

2. Import the `render_to_response()` function using the following line of code from Listing 7.5:

   ```
   from django.shortcuts import render_to_response, get_object_or_404
   ```

3. Remove the current contents of the `details()` function.

4. Add the following line of code to the `details()` function to get the `Person` object specified by the `pID` argument, as shown in Listing 7.5:

   ```
   p = get_object_or_404(Person, pk=pID)
   ```

▼

5. Add the following line of code to the `details()` function to render the view using the `person_details.html` template, as shown in Listing 7.5:

```
return render_to_response('people/person_details.html', {'p': p})
```

6. Save the `views.py` file.

7. Access the following URL in a web browser to verify that the view is working correctly, as shown in Figure 7.6:

```
http://127.0.0.1:8000/People/Info/2/
```

FIGURE 7.6
Web page generated by the `details()` view of the People application.

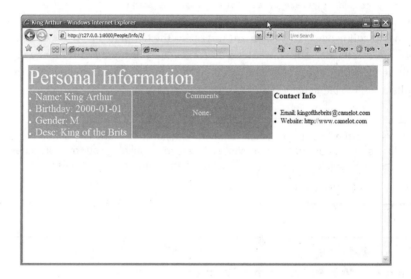

LISTING 7.5   Full Contents of `iFriends/People/views.py`

```python
from django.http import HttpResponse
from iFriends.People.models import Person
from django.shortcuts import render_to_response, get_object_or_404

def index(request):
    response = HttpResponse()

    response.write("<h1>People</h1><hr>")
    pList = Person.objects.all()
    for p in pList:
        link = "<a href=\"Info/%d\">" % (p.id)
        response.write("<li>%s%s</a></li>" % (link, p.name))

    return response

def details(request, pID='0', opts=()):
    p = get_object_or_404(Person, pk=pID)
    return render_to_response('people/person_details.html', {'p': p})
```

Extending Templates

As you build your website, you will need to create several different template files for different applications and views. This can result in a lot of redundant HTML code for headers, banners, and other content that will appear on several pages. Django provides the extends tag in its template engine to solve this problem.

The extends tag allows you to create a parent template file that will contain website elements that appear in more than one HTML view. Then, as you create templates for various views, you will only need to create content for that specific view in the view's template. When the Django template parser encounters an extends tag, it parses the parent template first and then applies the child template.

The following text shows the syntax for enabling a view template to inherit from another template:

```
{% extends "site_base.html" %}
```

By the Way

The parent template, specified in quotation marks, is specified as a path relative to the paths defined in the TEMPLATE_DIRS setting in the settings.py file. If you defined c:\website\templates in the TEMPLATE_DIRS setting and you create a parent template called c:\website\templates\site\header.html, you would use the following extends statement:

```
{% extends "site/header.html" %}
```

Did you Know?

You can specify a variable name instead of a filename in the extends tag. This allows you to dynamically control what the content will be by specifying different template filenames from within the view code.

You use block tags to control where items from the child template will be placed in the parent template. The block tags need to appear in both the parent and child templates. In the parent template, the block tags designate where data, with a block with the same name, from the child template will be placed. In the child template, the block tag is used to partition a section of data and assign it a name that can be referenced from the parent.

Blocks begin with a block tag and end with an endblock tag. The following code snippet shows the syntax for creating a block and assigning it the name content:

```
{% block content %}
<block code here>
{% endblock %}
```

The best way to show you how to extend a template is through an example. Listing 7.6 defines a basic parent template.

LISTING 7.6   A Basic Parent Template File, `base.html`

```
<html>
<head>
<title>{% block content %}Title{% endblock %}</title>
</head>
<body>
{% block content %}
Base Site
{% endblock %}
</body>
</html>
```

Listing 7.7 shows how to apply the parent template shown in Listing 7.6 in a child template.

LISTING 7.7   A Basic Child Template File, `view.html`

```
{% extends "base.html" %}
{% block title %}My Template View{% endblock %}
{%block content %}
<h1> My Web Page</h1><hr>
<li>Testing templates.</li>
{% endblock %}
```

When the `view.html` template shown in Listing 7.7 is parsed, the Django template parser sees the `extends` tag and parses the `base.html` parent template. Then, as it encounters the `title` and `content` blocks in the `view.html` file, it applies the HTML code in those sections to the HTTP response. Listing 7.8 shows the resulting HTML code that is sent as the HTTP response.

LISTING 7.8   Resulting HTML Response When `view.html` Extends `base.html`

```
<html>
<head>
<title> My Template View </title>
</head>
<body>
<h1> My Web Page</h1><hr>
<li>Testing templates.</li>
</body>
</html>
```

By the Way

If a no block in the child matches a block in the parent, the data contained in the block and endblock statements is added to the HTML response. For example, if we had not included the title block in Listing 7.7, the Django parser would have included the value contained in the title block of Listing 7.6, and the <title> HTML tag in Listing 7.8 would have been <title>Title</title>.

Try It Yourself

Add a Base Template to Your Website

In this section, you will create a base template to use for the iFriends website and modify the template you created in the preceding section to extend the new parent template.

Follow these steps to create a base template called iFriends_base.html and to change the person_details.html template into a child template that extends iFriends.html:

1. In an editor, create and open a file called iFriends/templates/ iFriends_base.html.

2. Add the contents of Listing 7.9 to the iFriends_base.html file.

LISTING 7.9 Full Contents of iFriends/templates/ iFriends_base.html

```
<!DOCTYPE html>
<html xmlns="http://www.w3.org/1999/xhtml" lang="en-us" xml:lang="en-us" >
<head>
    <link rel="stylesheet" href="style.css" />
    <title>{% block title %}iFriends{% endblock %}</title>
</head>
<body>
<table width=100% bgcolor="111177">
<tr><td>
<font size="12" color="white">iFriends Webspace</font>
</td></tr>
<tr><td>
<font size="3" color="white">Home</font>
</td></tr>
</table>
{% block content %}{% endblock %}
</body>
</html>
```

3. Save the file.

4. Open the iFriends/templates/Person/person_details.html file in an editor.

5. Remove the following lines of code:

```
<!DOCTYPE html>
<html xmlns="http://www.w3.org/1999/xhtml" lang="en-us" xml:lang="en-us" >
<head>
<title>{{ p.name }}</title>
</head>
<body>
. . .
</body>
</html>
```

6. Add the following lines of code, as shown in Listing 7.10, to extend the
iFriends_base.html template and assign the title and content blocks:

```
{% extends "iFriends_base.html" %}
{% block title %}test{% endblock %}
{% block content %}
{% endblock %}
```

7. Save the file.

8. Access the following URL in a web browser to verify that the new view is working correctly, as shown in Figure 7.7:

```
http://127.0.0.1:8000/People/Info/2/
```

FIGURE 7.7
Web page
generated by
people_details.
html by extending
iFriends_
base.html.

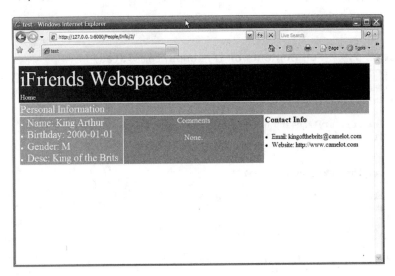

LISTING 7.10   Full Contents of iFriends/templates/
person_details.html

```
{% extends "iFriends_base.html" %}

{% block title %}test{% endblock %}
{% block content %}
<tr bgcolor="aabbcc"><td colspan="3">
```

LISTING 7.10 Continued

```
<font size="5" color="white">Personal Information</font>
</td></tr>
<tr valign="top"><td width=30% bgcolor="aaaaaa"><font color="white" size="5">
    <li>Name: {{p.name}}</li>
    <li>Birthday: {{ p.birthday }}</li>
    <li>Gender: {{ p.gender }}</li>
    <li>Desc: {{ p.desc }} </li>
</font></td>
<td width=40% bgcolor="aa99aa"><font color="white" size="4">
    <p align="center">Comments</p>
    <p align="center">None.
</font></td>
<td width=30%>
    <h3>Contact Info</h3>
    <li>Email: {{ p.email }}</li>
    <li>Website: {{ p.favoriteURL }}</li>
</td></tr>
{% endblock %}
```

Embedding Templates

In addition to extending templates with parent templates, Django allows you to load the entire contents of a template into an existing template using the `include` tag. Unlike the `extends` tag, the `include` tag simply inserts the full contents of the specified template file into the existing template.

The `include` tag can be useful for creating "canned" components for your website, such as a calendar, that need to be displayed on several web pages.

For example, the following line of code embeds a template named `comments.html` into a template:

```
{% include "comments.html" %}
```

> **Did you Know?**
>
> You can specify a variable name instead of a filename in the `include` tag. This allows you to dynamically control what the content will be by specifying different template filenames from within the view code.

> **By the Way**
>
> Variables that are available in the view template also are available in templates that are embedded using the `include` tag.

Embed a Template File in Another Template

In this section, you will create a `quote.html` template that can be embedded into other template files.

Follow these steps to create a template called `quote.html` and embed it into `person_details.html`:

1. In an editor, create and open a file called `iFriends/templates/quote.html`.

2. Add the contents of Listing 7.11 to the `quote.html` file.

LISTING 7.11   Full Contents of `iFriends/templates/quote.html`

```
<table width="100%">
<tr bgcolor="aa22aa" width="100%"><td align="center">
<font size="4">Quote of the Day</font>
</td></tr>
<tr><td align="center">
<font size="5">I think therefore I am.</font>
</td></tr>
<tr><td align="center">
<font size="2">- Rene Descartes</font>
</td></tr>
</table>
```

3. Save the file.

4. Open the `iFriends/templates/Person/person_details.html` file in an editor.

5. Remove the following lines of code:

```
<p align="center">Comments</p>
<p align="center">None.
```

6. Add the following line of code, as shown in Listing 7.12, to embed the `quote.html` file:

```
{% include "quote.html" %}
```

7. Save the file.

8. Access the following URL in a web browser to verify that the new view is working correctly, as shown in Figure 7.8:

```
http://127.0.0.1:8000/People/Info/2/
```

▼

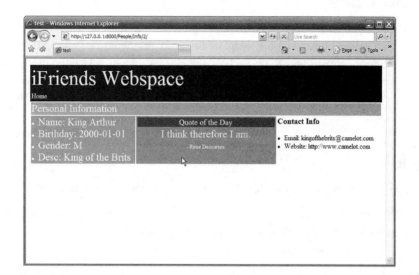

FIGURE 7.8
Web page
generated by
`people_
details.html`
by extending
`iFriends_base.
html` and
embedding
`quote.html`.

LISTING 7.12 Full Contents of `iFriends/templates/`
`person_details.html`

```
{% extends "iFriends_base.html" %}

{% block title %}test{% endblock %}
{% block content %}
<table width=100%>
<tr bgcolor="aabbcc"><td colspan="3">
<font size="5" color="white">Personal Information</font>
</td></tr>
<tr valign="top"><td width=30% bgcolor="aaaaaa"><font color="white" size="5">
    <li>Name: {{p.name}}</li>
    <li>Birthday: {{ p.birthday }}</li>
    <li>Gender: {{ p.gender }}</li>
    <li>Desc: {{ p.desc }} </li>
</font></td>
<td width=40% bgcolor="aa99aa"><font color="white" size="4">
    {% include "quote.html" %}
</font></td>
<td width=30%>
    <h3>Contact Info</h3>
    <li>Email: {{ p.email }}</li>
    <li>Website: {{ p.favoriteURL }}</li>
</td></tr>
{% endblock %}
```

Summary

In this hour, you learned how to configure Django to allow you to use HTML templates. You learned how to create template files and use them to enhance your views. You also learned how to create base templates that will reduce the amount of HTML code that is needed in your view templates. You also learned how to create templates for specific tasks and embed them into your view templates using the `include` tag.

Q&A

Q. Is there a way to tie the templates into the Django admin interface?

A. Yes. You can use the Django admin parent `base_site.html` in your view templates by using the following line of code to extend it:

```
{% extends 'admin/base_site.html' %}
```

Q. Is there a way to render a template to a string object so that I can parse and possibly manipulate it?

A. Yes. Django provides the `django.template.loader.render_to_string`
`(template_name, dictionary, context_instance)` function that will render a template file to a string object. The `render_to_string()` function accepts a template file name as the first argument, a dictionary containing variables as an optional second argument, and a `Context` object as an optional third argument. The following code will render the `someTemplate.html` template file to a string:

```
from django.template.loader import render_to_string
render_to_string('someTemplate.html', {'name': 'Brad', 'pID': 1})
```

Workshop

The workshop consists of a set of questions and answers designed to solidify your understanding of the material covered in this hour. Try answering the questions before looking at the answers.

Quiz

1. Where does Django begin looking for template files when they are specified in an `extends` or `include` command?

2. Which tag should be used to embed another template file into an existing one?

3. Which template file is parsed first—the parent or the child?

Quiz Answers

1. It looks in the directories specified by the TEMPLATE_DIRS setting in the settings.py file.

2. include.

3. The child template.

Exercises

1. Create an HTML template that displays a table of all Person objects in the database. The index() function of the iFriends/People/views.py file already generates the full HTML code. You will need to modify the file to generate the list as a string and add that string to the dictionary passed to render_to_response().

2. Modify the template you created in Exercise 1 to extend the iFriends/templates/iFriends_base.html template.

Using Built-in Template Tags to Enhance Views

What You'll Learn in This Hour:

▶ How to use `for` loops to generate HTML code from lists
▶ How to use if logic to add conditional HTML code to templates
▶ How to add dynamic links to templates
▶ How to reduce template code by using the `with` tag
▶ How to add cycling behavior to enhance table views

Django has several tags that allow you to implement some basic logic in your templates that helps you reduce the amount of HTML code that you need to write. This hour covers using Django's built-in template tags to create more complex and useful templates.

Implementing Loops

One of the most common tags that you will use will be the `for` tag to implement `for` loops inside your HTML documents. The `for` tag allows you to navigate through a list of strings or objects and generate HTML code for each item in the list.

For example, if you have a list of several URLs for which you want to write HTML links in a template, you could implement a `for` tag similar to the following code snippet, where `links` is a `list` object:

```
{% for lnk in links %}
    <li><a href="{{ lnk  }}"> {{ lnk }}</a></li>
{% endfor %}
```

Using this code in your template renders the list of links in the HTTP response. It doesn't matter how many links you need to put in the list. You do not need to add code to your HTML template to do so.

> You can add as many lines of code inside the for tag section as are needed and then add the {% endfor %} tag to close the section.

The for tag can also handle dictionary objects. Use the following syntax:

```
{% for key, value in dict %}
```

For example, if you have a dictionary containing people's names as the key and phone numbers as the value, you could use the following code snippet in a template to render the list of names and phone numbers:

```
{% for name, phone in phoneList %}
    <h2>Name:  {{ name }} </h2>
    <li>Phone:  {{ phone }} </li>
{% endfor %}
```

> You can access the items in a list in reverse order by using the reversed tag in a for tag statement. For example, the following code displays the entries in the books list in reverse order:
>
> ```
> {% for title in books reversed %}
> ```

Django also allows you to use for loops to process lists of lists as long as you can unpack the values in each sublist into a set of names. For example, if you have a list of GPS coordinates that are formatted as a [location, lat, long] list, you could use the following code snippet in a template to render the list of GPS locations:

```
{% for location, lat, long in gpsList %}
    <h2>Location:  {{ location }} </h2>
    <li>Coordinates:  {{ lat }}:{{ long }}</li>
{% endfor %}
```

Django provides the forloop variable in loop operations. It can provide you with information such as counters and parent loops. Table 8.1 lists the available fields in the forloop variable object.

TABLE 8.1   Fields Available in the `forloop` Variable

Variable	Description
`forloop.counter`	The loop's current iteration (1-based index)
`forloop.counter0`	The loop's current iteration (0-based index)
`forloop.revcounter`	The number of iterations from the end of the loop (1-based index)
`forloop.revcounter0`	The number of iterations from the end of the loop (0-based index)
`forloop.first`	Is true if this is the first iteration through the loop
`forloop.last`	Is true if this is the last iteration through the loop
`forloop.parentloop`	Accesses the `forloop` object in the loop before the current one (used when nesting loops)

Try It Yourself ▼

Use a `for` Loop to Render a List of Objects

In this example, you will create a template that renders a list of `Person` objects for the `index()` function of the People application view.

Follow these steps to create an HTML document to display `Person` details and turn it into a Django template:

1. Using a text editor, create a file called `iFriends/templates/People/person_index.html`.

2. Add the following line of code to `person_index.html` to extend the `iFriends_base.html` base template, as shown in Listing 8.1:

   ```
   {% extends "iFriends_base.html" %}
   ```

3. Add the following line of code to add a title block to be inserted into the `iFriends_base.html` template, as shown in Listing 8.1:

   ```
   {% block title %}People{% endblock %}
   ```

4. Add the following content block of code to generate a table that will contain the list of people, as shown in Listing 8.1:

   ```
   {% block content %}
   <table width=100%>
   <tr bgcolor="aabbcc"><td colspan="3">
   <font size="5" color="white">Personal List</font>
   </td></tr>
   <tr valign="top"><td width=30% bgcolor="aaaaaa"><font color="white"
   ➥size="5">
   ```

```
</font>
     </td></tr>
{% endblock %}
```

5. Add the following for loop to navigate through the list of people and generate a numbered list of people in the view, as shown in Listing 8.1:

   ```
   {% for p in pList %}
       <p>{{ forloop.counter }}. {{ p.name }}</p>
   {% endfor %}
   ```

6. Save the file.

7. Open the iFriends/People/views.py file in an editor.

8. Delete the current contents of the index() function.

9. Add the following line of code to the index() function to generate a list of
   Person objects, as shown in Listing 8.2:

   ```
   pList = Person.objects.all()
   ```

10. Add the following line of code to the index() function to render the view
    using the person_index.html template and adding the list of people gener-
    ated in step 9 to the dictionary, as shown in Listing 8.2:

    ```
    return render_to_response('people/person_index.html', {'pList': pList})
    ```

11. Save the views.py file.

12. Access the following URL in a web browser to verify that the view is working
    correctly, as shown in Figure 8.1:

    ```
    http://127.0.0.1:8000/People/
    ```

FIGURE 8.1
Web page gen-
erated by the
index() view of
the People
application.

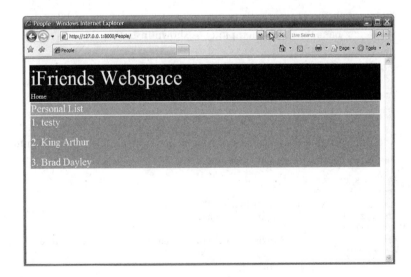

LISTING 8.1   Full Contents of `iFriends/templates/People/person_index.html`

```
{% extends "iFriends_base.html" %}

{% block title %}People{% endblock %}
{% block content %}
<table width=100%>
<tr bgcolor="aabbcc"><td colspan="3">
<font size="5" color="white">Personal List</font>
</td></tr>
<tr valign="top"><td width=30% bgcolor="aaaaaa"><font color="white" size="5">
{% for p in pList %}
    <p>{{ forloop.counter }}. {{ p.name }}</p>
{% endfor %}
</font></td></tr>
{% endblock %}
```

LISTING 8.2   Full Contents of `iFriends/People/views.py`

```
from django.http import HttpResponse
from iFriends.People.models import Person
from django.shortcuts import render_to_response, get_object_or_404

def index(request):
    pList = Person.objects.all()
    return render_to_response('people/person_index.html', {'pList': pList})

def details(request, pID='0', opts=()):
    p = get_object_or_404(Person, pk=pID)
    return render_to_response('people/person_details.html', {'p': p})
```

> Did you notice how much the `iFriends/People/views.py` file has shrunk? One of the best things about Django is that it really reduces the amount of code needed to generate web pages.

By the Way

Implementing `if` Logic

Django also provides rudimentary if logic to the template parser. You can use the if, ifchanged, ifequal, and ifnotequal tags to determine how and if content should be displayed. The following sections describe the different types of if tags and their uses.

Using if

The if tag evaluates a variable and determines if it is true. If the variable evaluates to true, the template engine renders the code inside the if block. You need to add an endif tag to end the block. You can also use the optional else tag with all the if tags to provide alternative template code.

For example, suppose your template is expecting a list of cars called carList. You could use the following code snippet to determine if the car list is empty and note that in the web page, instead of just having a blank section in the web page:

```
{% if carList %}
    {% for car in carList %}
        <li>{{ car.model }}</li>
    {% endfor %}
(% else %}
    No cars in list.
{% endif %}
```

You can use a not operator in the if tags to change the if logic. For example, the preceding code snippet could also be written as follows:

```
{% if not carList %}
   No cars in list.
 (% else %}
    {% for car in carList %}
        <li>{{ car.model }}</li>
    {% endfor %}
{% endif %}
```

You can also use or and and operators in the if tags to chain together logic. For example, if you want to display a list only if both teacherList and studentList have entries, you could use the following code snippet:

```
{% if studentList and teacherList %}
    <h2>Students</h2>
    {% for s in studentList %}
        <li>{{ student }}</li>
    {% endfor %}
    <h2>Students</h2>
    {% for s in studentList %}
        <li>{{ student }}</li>
    {% endfor %}
{% endif %}
```

Using ifchanged

The ifchanged tag is used inside for loops to determine if a variable value has changed since the last iteration. If the value has changed, the template engine renders the code inside the ifchanged block. You need to add an endifchanged tag to end the block.

For example, if your template is parsing blog entries that contain a date field, you could use the following code to note the change in dates:

```
{% for b in blogList %}
    {% ifchanged b.date.date %}
        <h2>Date: {{ b.date.date }} </h2>
    {% endifchanged %}
    <h1>{{ b.title }}</h1>
    {{ b.text }}
{% endfor %}
```

The `ifchanged` tag can also determine if its own rendered contents have changed. Instead of specifying variable(s) inside the `tag` statement, you just need to add the variable(s) inside the `ifchanged` block. If they change, the content changes from the last state and is rendered again by the template engine. For example:

```
{% ifchanged %}<h3>{{ b.date }}</h3> {% endifchanged %}
```

Using `ifequal`

The `ifequal` tag determines if two arguments are equal. The arguments can be either variables or hard-coded strings. If the arguments match, the template engine renders the code inside the `ifequal` block. You need to add an `endifequal` tag to end the block.

For example, if your template is parsing a list of users, and you want only users who have a last name of Arthur, you could use the following code snippet:

```
{% for user in userList %}
    <h1>Arthurs</h1>
    {% ifequal user.last "Arthur" %}
        <li>{{ user.first }}</li>
    {% endifequal %}
{% endfor %}
```

Using `ifnotequal`

The `ifnotequal` tag determines if two arguments are not equal. The arguments can be either variables or hard-coded strings. If the arguments do not match, the template engine renders the code inside the `ifnotequal` block. You need to add an `endifnotequal` tag to end the block.

For example, if your template is parsing a list of blogs, and you want to exclude blogs with the title of "test," you could use the following code snippet:

```
{% for blog in blogList %}
    {% ifnotequal blog.title "test" %}
        <h1>{{ blog.title }}</h1>
        {{ blog.text }}
    {% endifnotequal %}
{% endfor %}
```

▼   **Try It Yourself**

Use if Logic to Determine the View Content

In this section, you will use `ifequal` logic to control the content displayed by the `person_details.html` template. Follow these steps to modify the `person_details.html` template file so that it can determine if the person's gender is M or F. Add some character to the site by displaying the Australian terms "Bloke" and "Sheila" instead of M and F:

1. Open the `iFriends/templates/People/person_details.html` file in an editor.

2. Remove the following line of code from the file:

    ```
    <li>Gender: {{ p.gender }}</li>
    ```

3. Add the following `ifequal` tag code to the file to compare the value of gender to the string M. Then use the Australian terms Bloke and Sheila instead of M and F, as shown in Listing 8.3:

    ```
    <li>Gender:
        {% ifequal p.gender "M" %}
            Bloke
        {% else %}
            Sheila
        {% endifequal %}
    </li>
    ```

4. Save the file.

5. Access the `details()` view of the `People` object in a web browser to verify that the view now displays Bloke and Sheila correctly, as shown in Figure 8.2.

LISTING 8.3   Full Contents of `iFriends/templates/People/person_details.html`

```
{% extends "iFriends_base.html" %}

{% block title %}Details{% endblock %}
{% block content %}
<table width=100%>
<tr bgcolor="aabbcc"><td colspan="3">
<font size="5" color="white">Personal Information</font>
```

▼

LISTING 8.3 Continued

```
</td></tr>
<tr valign="top"><td width=30% bgcolor="aaaaaa"><font color="white" size="5">
    <li>Name: {{p.name}}</li>
    <li>Birthday: {{ p.birthday }}</li>
    <li>Gender:
        {% ifequal p.gender "M" %}
            Bloke
        {% else %}
            Sheila
        {% endifequal %}
    </li>
    <li>Desc: {{ p.desc }} </li>
</font></td>
<td width=40% bgcolor="aa99aa"><font color="white" size="4">
    {% include "quote.html" %}
</font></td>
<td width=30%>
    <h3>Contact Info</h3>
    <li>Email: {{ p.email }}</li>
    <li>Website: {{ p.favoriteURL }}</li>
</td></tr>
{% endblock %}
```

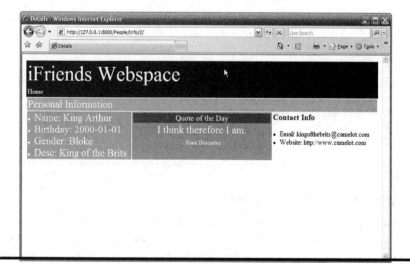

FIGURE 8.2
Web page generated by the details() view of the People application.

Adding Links with the url Tag

Django provides the url tag to help you add links to your web pages. If possible, it is best to avoid hard-coded links. If you modify the URLconf file and thus change the URL pattern, you might wind up needing to change every place in your code that you hard-coded the link.

To solve this problem, the `url` tag allows you to specify the view function, including arguments, directly. The `url` tag results in an absolute URL being placed in the rendered HTML document.

The first argument inside the `url` tag is a path to a view function, such as the path to the `details()` function in the `views.py` file of the People application in the iFriends project:

```
iFriends.People.views.details
```

Additional arguments are optional and should be separated by commas with no spaces. Arguments are considered positional unless you specify a *keyword=value*. For example:

```
{url mySite.arch.views.list arg1,arg2,year=2008 %}
```

By the Way

> If you are using named URL patterns, you can refer to the name of the pattern in the `url` tag instead of using the path to the view.

The arguments specified in the `url` tag must correspond to what is defined in the URLconf file. If they do not, no URL is returned.

Watch Out!

> The `url` tag searches for the first match in the URLconf file. If multiple patterns are pointing to the same view, either use named patterns, or make certain that the first one in the list is the one you want.

▼   **Try It Yourself**

Add Dynamic Links to a Template

In this section, you will modify the `person_index.html` file you created earlier in this hour to add dynamic links to the details page for each person in the list. Follow these steps to add dynamic links that refer to the view function directly to the index view of the People application:

1. Open the `iFriends/templates/People/person_index.html` file in an editor.

2. Remove the following line of code from the file:

   ```
   <li> {{ p.name }}</li>
   ```

▼

3. Add the following code to the file, as shown in Listing 8.4, to add links to the `details()` view function and pass the `Person.id` argument to the view:

```
<li>
<a href="{% url iFriends.People.views.details p.id %}">{{ p.name }}</a>
</li>
```

4. Save the file.

5. Open the `iFriends/urls.py` file in an editor.

6. Comment out the following line by putting a # in front of it so that the template parser won't pick it up when parsing the url tag from step 3.

```
#(r'^Info/$', 'details'),
```

7. Save the file.

8. Access the following URL in a web browser to bring up the index view, shown in Figure 8.3, and verify that the names are now links:

```
http://127.0.0.1:8000/People/
```

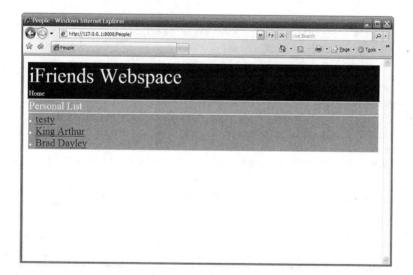

FIGURE 8.3
Web index web page generated with links to the `details()` view of the People application.

9. Click one of the person links to verify that the links are working correctly. That person's detail view should be loaded, as shown in Figure 8.4.

FIGURE 8.4
Web details web page view of the People application.

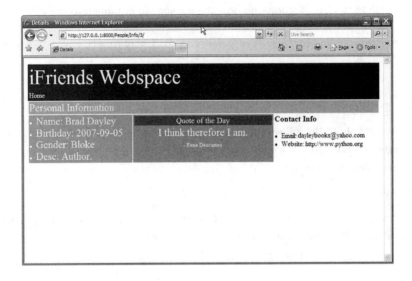

LISTING 8.4   Full Contents of `iFriends/templates/People/person_index.html`

```
{% extends "iFriends_base.html" %}

{% block title %}People{% endblock %}
{% block content %}
<table width=100%>
<tr bgcolor="aabbcc"><td colspan="3">
<font size="5" color="white">Personal List</font>
</td></tr>
<tr valign="top"><td width=30% bgcolor="aaaaaa"><font color="white" size="5">
{% for p in pList %}
    <li>
    <a href="{% url iFriends.People.views.details p.id %}">{{ p.name }}</a>
    </li>
{% endfor %}
</font></td></tr>
{% endblock %}
```

Reducing Code Using the with Tag

Another template tag that you will find useful is `with`. The `with` tag allows you to assign a complex variable name a simpler one. This is most helpful when you have to reference the object several times.

For example, consider the `business.accounting.contact_info` subobject. Referencing that object several times would take a lot of keystrokes. The following example shows how to use the `with` tag to reduce the code necessary to reference the object:

```
{% with business.accounting.contact_info as ci %}
Phone: {{ ci.phone }}
```

to Tables

to modify values as you cycle through a
rated list of arguments that will be cycled

table in your template and you wanted
t background color, you could use the
rows. The following code generates the

```
%}">
```

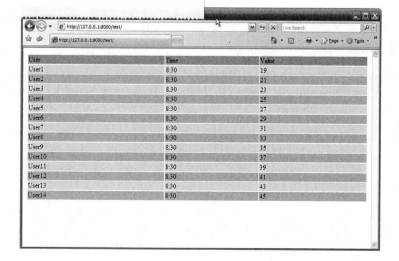

FIGURE 8.5
Table generated with alternating dark and light lines using the `cycle` tag.

Summary

In this hour, you learned how to use template tags to add logic in your templates. You learned how to generate several lines of HTML code from a list using the `for` tag. You also learned how to add HTML code conditionally using the `if`, `ifchanged`, `ifequal`, and `ifnotequal` tags.

Using loops, conditions, and other tags enables you to write simpler and more useable code and makes it easier to modify and update your website.

Q&A

Q. *Can I still use the {{ and {% character sets as text in my web pages?*

A. Yes. Django provides the `templatetag` tag to output character sets defined by the template to the rendered HTML. The following code shows how to use `templatetag` to output the {% character set:

```
{% templatetag openblock %}
```

Q. *Is there a way to add text to a template without displaying it in the rendered file?*

A. Yes. You can use the `comment` and `endcomment` tags. Anything between them will not get rendered.

Q. *Is there a way to quickly remove extra white spaces from the rendered text so that the HTTP response is smaller?*

A. Use the `spaceless` and `endspaceless` tags. The white spaces, including end-of-line characters, are removed from the HTML code between those tags.

Workshop

The workshop consists of a set of questions and answers designed to solidify your understanding of the material covered in this hour. Try answering the questions before looking at the answers.

Quiz

1. Which template tag would you use to recursively add HTML code for items in a list?

2. What method should you use to add links to other views in a template?

3. Which tag could you use to reduce the number of keystrokes necessary to write a template when you have objects with long names?

Quiz Answers

1. The `for` tag.

2. You should use the `url` tag method so that you can directly reference the view.

3. The `with` tag.

Exercises

1. Use the `cycle` tag to modify the `person_index.html` file so that every other line in the list is a different color.

2. Use the `url` tag to modify the `iFriends_base.html` file so that the word Home that appears in the website banner is actually a link to the `iFriends.People.views.index` view.

HOUR 9

Using Built-in Template Filters to Enhance Views

What You'll Learn in This Hour:

▶ How to apply filters in templates
▶ How to format text using filters
▶ How to create and manipulate lists using filters
▶ How to sort a list of dictionaries in a template
▶ How to format dates using filters

Django provides a robust library of built-in filters that you can use to manipulate data inside templates. In this hour, you will learn how to use filters to manipulate data that is rendered inside templates.

As you understand and use filters, you will see that they provide several necessary features that are needed when rendering data into HTML responses. The following sections will help you understand filters and how to use them to format text, manipulate lists, sort data, and display dates.

Understanding Filters

This section discusses how to apply filters in your templates. The filter examples discussed in this section are described in more detail in the following sections.

Each filter is a link to a function in Django's template library that performs a specific task. Filters can be applied in one of two ways—as a direct pipe to a variable, or using the `filter` tag.

Filters are applied to a variable using piping syntax. For example, to change the variable `place` to all lowercase, you could apply the `lower` filter using the following syntax:

```
{{ place|lower }}
```

Filters can also be applied to a block of template code or text using the `filter` tag. The template engine renders whatever is inside the filter block and then applies the filters to it. For example, the following `filter` tag applies the upper filter to a block of text and the `place` variable:

```
{% filter escape|upper %}
The meeting will be held at {{ place }}.
{% endfilter %}
```

The Django template engine renders the value of the `place` variable and then applies the `escape` and `upper` filters to the rendered contents.

Either method of applying filters works well. Often, applying the filter directly to a variable is the simplest method. However, using the `filter` tag is the best method if you need to apply the same filters to a larger amount of data or to a block of text.

Filters can be chained together using the | (pipe) character when applying them to a `filter` tag or variable. For example, the following `filter` tag code applies the escape, upper, and `linebreaks` filters to a block of text:

```
{% filter escape|upper|linebreaks %}
The meeting will be held at {{ place }}.
Please be on time.
{% endfilter %}
```

Some filters either allow or require arguments. The syntax for passing arguments to a filter is as follows:

```
filtername:"argument list"
```

For example, the following line of code applies the `removetags` filter to a text variable and passes to it the arguments `table`, `tr`, and `td`:

```
{{ tableText|removetags:"table tr td" }}
```

In the case of the `removetags` filter, the arguments are space-separated. Some filters require the arguments to be comma-separated. Make sure you know in what format the filter expects the variable list.

Formatting Text

Now that you understand how to apply filters, let's look at some filters that allow you to format text. Django provides several different filters that allow you to manipulate and enhance the text that is rendered to the web pages.

The following sections show some examples of some of the more common filters that you can use to format text.

Changing Text Case

Often you will parse text from an object or a web request, and you need to change the text's case. Django provides several filters for doing so. The following is a list of useful filters to change the case of text in a template:

- ▶ `capfirst` capitalizes only the first letter in the string and leaves the rest of the string alone.

- ▶ `title` capitalizes the first letter of each word in the string and lowercases all the remaining letters.

- ▶ `upper` changes the entire string to uppercase.

- ▶ `lower` changes the entire string to lowercase.

The following example shows what happens with the `capfirst`, `title`, `upper`, and `lower` filters:

```
{{ title|capfirst}}<p>
{{ title|title}}<p>
{{ title|upper}}<p>
{{ title|lower}}<p>
```

When these filters are applied to a variable `title` with a value of `teST titLE`, the following HTML code is rendered:

```
TeST titLE<p>
Test Title<p>
TEST TITLE<p>
test title
```

> Notice that the `capfirst` filter results in `TeST titLE`. You could pipe the `title` variable through the `lower` filter first to render `title` as `Test title`:
>
> ```
> {{ title|lower|capfirst}}<p>
> ```

By the Way

escape

The escape filter allows you to escape HTML code in a string so that the code appears in the view as text. The web browser does not parse the HTML code in the text. This can be useful if you want to display HTML code as part of the view.

The HTML characters in the string are replaced with the HTML escape codes. The < character is replaced with &lt, the > character is replaced with &gt, and so on. The result is that the HTML tags in the filtered block of text show up as text in the web page.

For example, the following template code results in the HTML code being displayed in the browser, as shown in Figure 9.1:

```
<h2>The following code:</h2><p>
{% filter escape %}
<li>List Item1</li>
<li>List Item2</li>
<li>List Item3</li>
<li>List Item4</li>
<li>List Item5</li>
{% endfilter %}
<h2>Generates this list:</h2>
<li>List Item1</li>
<li>List Item2</li>
<li>List Item3</li>
<li>List Item4</li>
<li>List Item5</li>
```

FIGURE 9.1
Web page that displays HTML code as plain text.

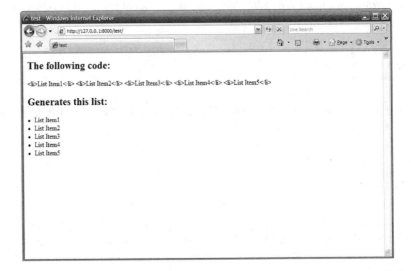

length

The length filter returns the length of the object being filtered. If the object is a string, it returns the number of characters in the string. If the object is a list, it returns the number of elements in the list.

The length filter is especially useful for formatting HTML elements around the length of a string or the number of items in a list. An example of how length can be used to format HTML elements is using the length of a list to define the number of columns to span in a table. If you pass into the template a list of headers and a title, you can use the following code snippet to build the table and span the title row across all the columns that the headers form:

```
<table>
  <tr>
     <td colspan="{{ headers|length }}">{{ title }}</td>
  </tr>
  <tr>
    {% for h in headers %}
       <td>{{ h }}</td>
    {% endfor %}
  </tr>
</table>
```

linebreaks

The linebreaks filter replaces the line breaks in plain text with the HTML line break <br />. Because the HTML parser ignores line breaks and allows the text to run together, the linebreaks filter is indispensable when you render large amounts of text.

The linebreaks filter does not accept any arguments. For example, to apply the linebreaks filter to a variable called data, use the following syntax:

```
{{ data|linebreaks }}
```

If the linebreaks filter encounters two consecutive line breaks, it replaces them with an HTML paragraph <p>.

stringformat

The stringformat filter formats the variable according to the Python string formatting syntax specified as an argument. The stringformat filter accepts only one argument—a valid Python string formatting operation with the leading % character dropped.

The best way to illustrate the string format function is with the following examples, where the value of num is 380:

```
int = {{ num|stringformat:"i" }}
hex = {{ num|stringformat:"x" }}
padded = {{ num|stringformat:"08X" }}
prec2float = {{ num|stringformat:"2.f" }}
```

This renders the following:

```
int = 380
hex = 17c
padded = 0000017C
prec2float = 380.00
```

> You can find more information about the Python string formatting options at:
> http://docs.python.org/lib/typesseq-strings.html.

striptags

The striptags filter removes all (X)HTML tags from a string of text. The striptags filter can be used for several purposes. One of the best uses is to clear out HTML codes before displaying text that was retrieved from an unsecured source, such as a user form. You can protect against users adding HTML code that could pose problems.

For example, if you accept blog entries and then display them, you can use the following line of code to render the blog text without any HTML elements the user may have added:

```
{{ blog.text|striptags }}
```

> Django also includes the removetags filter, which allows you to remove specific HTML codes from text. The removetags filter accepts a list of space-separated codes. For example, the following line of code removes all the <li>, <p>, and <br> tags from blog.text:
>
> ```
> {{ blog.text|removetags:"li p br"}}
> ```

wordwrap

The wordwrap filter allows you to specify a length at which lines of text should wrap. When the wordwrap filter renders text, it determines if the next word will exceed the maximum line length. If it will, the filter enters a line break after the current word.

For example, to render text with a maximum line length of 40, you would use the following line of code:

```
{{ text|wordwrap:"40" }}
```

> The wordwrap filter adds only plain-text line breaks to the text. If you want to wrap the text inside an HTML element such as a table cell, use the `linebreaks` filter also:
>
> ```
> {{ text|wordwrap:"40"|linebreaks}}
> ```

pluralize

The `pluralize` filter is used to add a plural suffix if the value of a variable is not 1. This can be useful in adding a human element to the website by eliminating messages such as "You have 1 unread messages." Using the `pluralize` filter enables you to write code in your template to print the message correctly. For example:

```
You have {{ msgNum }} unread message{{ msgNum|pluralize }}
```

If the value of msgNum is 1, the template renders "You have 1 unread message." If the value of msgNum is 3, the template renders "You have 3 unread messages."

The default suffix is s, but the `pluralize` filter also accepts a comma-separated list. If only one argument is passed into the `pluralize` filter, it is treated as the alternate string to apply for plural values. The following example uses the plural suffix es instead of s:

```
I rode {{ busCnt }} bus{{ busCnt|pluralize:"es" }}
```

The `pluralize` filter can also handle cases when a singular suffix must be applied. If two arguments are passed into the `pluralize` filter, the first argument is treated as the singular suffix, and the second is treated as the plural suffix. For example, if you wanted to render the string "Updated # entry(ies)" in a more user-friendly format, you could use the following `pluralize` filter:

```
Updated {{ eNum }} entr{{ eNum|pluralize:"y,ies" }}
```

> The length filter can help a lot with the pluralize filter. For example, if all you
> have is a list of entries, you could apply the length filter to the list first to get a
> count to use for the pluralize filter:
>
> entr{{ entries|length|pluralize:"y,ies" }}

yesno

The yesno filter can be applied to a variable. It accepts either a "yes,no" or
"yes,no,maybe" string of arguments. The yesno filter tests the variable and renders
the yes string if the variable is true, the no string if the variable is false, and
the maybe string if the variable value is none. If only a "yes,no" string is passed, the
filter renders the no string if the variable value is none.

For example, the following line of code renders the string It is true if the variable
is true and the string It is false if the variable is not true:

```
{{ var|yesno:"It is true,It is false" }}
```

Obviously, the variable can be a Boolean True or False value, and it can be a None
value. If the variable is in numeric form, a value of 0 renders the no string, and any
other value renders the yes string. If the variable is a list or dictionary, if the
variable is empty, the no string is rendered. If the variable has at least one entry, the
yes string is rendered.

The yesno tag may seem simple, but it can be used in many creative ways to save a
lot of code. The following code snippet shows an example of using the yesno tag in
a for loop to build a table:

```
{% for i in myList %}
{{ forloop.first|yesno:"<table>,"}}
<tr><td>{{ i }}</td></tr>
{{ forloop.last|yesno:"</table>,"}}
{% endfor %}
```

If the <table> tags in the preceding example were placed outside the for loop, they
would appear in the rendered text even if there were no items in the text to render.
The yesno filter lets you place the <table> tags only if you are on the first or last
item in the list.

> The preceding example shows a couple of things. One is that the yesno filter
> accepts an empty string as one of its arguments. The other is that you can use
> HTML code in the string.

Try It Yourself ▼

Add Text Formatting Filters to Templates

In this section, you will extend the person_details.py template to include the friends and blogs fields of the Person object. You will also use text formatting filters to enhance the text that is rendered by the template:

Follow these steps to modify the person_details.py template:

1. Open the iFriends/templates/person_details.py file in an editor.

2. Add the following HTML table row code, after the last </tr> tag in the table, to add new table cells for the friends and blogs fields:

```
<tr>
<td width="30%" bgcolor="556677" valign="top">
    <font color="white" size="4">
    <h3>
        iFriends
    </h3>
    </font>
</td>
<td width="70%" bgcolor="555555" colspan="2" valign="top">
    <font color="white" size="4">
    <h3>
        Blogs
    </h3>
    </font>
</td>
</tr>
```

3. The Person object is stored in variable p, so you can access the list of friends and blogs using p.friends.all and p.blogs.all, respectively. Create a with tag block for each, inside the <font> tag of each table cell, using the following code:

```
{% with p.friends.all as fl %}
{% endwith %}
{% with p.blogs.all as bl %}
{% endwith %}
```

4. Modify the Friends header created in step 2 using the following code so that the header renders No iFriends, iFriend, or iFriends, depending on whether there are zero, one, or more friends, respectively:

```
<h3>
    {{ fl|length|yesno:"iFriend,No Friend"}}{{fl|length|pluralize}}
</h3>
```

5. Modify the Blogs header created in step 2 using the following code so that the header renders No Blogs, Blog Entry, or Blog Entries, depending on whether there are zero, one, or more blogs, respectively:

▼

```
<h3>
    {{ bl|length|yesno:"Blog,No Blog"}}
    Entr{{ bl|length|pluralize:"y,ies"}}
</h3>
```

6. Add the following code to the template to generate a list of friends:

```
{% for f in fl %}
 <li>{{ f.name }}</li>
{% endfor %}
```

7. Add the following code to the template to generate a list of blogs:

```
{% for b in bl %}
<li>{{ b.title }}</li>
{% endfor %}
```

8. Save the file.

9. Access some different person details pages on the website to verify that the filters are working correctly. Figures 9.2 and 9.3 show web pages with different
   headers for the friends and blogs lists.

By the Way

If you haven't already created some more users, you might need to do so. You
might want to use the admin interface to create the new objects. To add blog
entries, you may need to enable the admin interface for the blog class, as discussed in Hour 3, "Adding Models and Objects to Your Website."

FIGURE 9.2
Person details
view that has a
couple friend
entries but only
one blog entry.

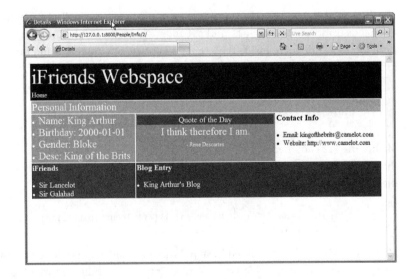

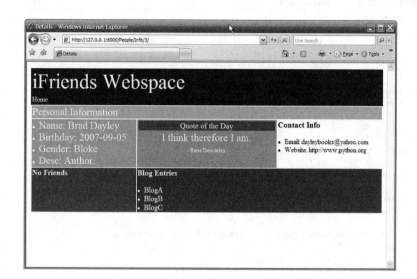

FIGURE 9.3
Person details
view that has
no friend entries
but several blog
entries.

Listing 9.1 shows the complete `person_details.py` file.

LISTING 9.1   Full Contents of `iFriends/template/person_details.py`

```
{% extends "iFriends_base.html" %}

{% block title %}Details{% endblock %}
{% block content %}
<table width=100%>
<tr bgcolor="aabbcc"><td colspan="3">
<font size="5" color="white">Personal Information</font>
</td></tr>
<tr valign="top"><td width=30% bgcolor="aaaaaa"><font color="white" size="5">
    <li>Name: {{p.name}}</li>
    <li>Birthday: {{ p.birthday }}</li>
    <li>Gender:
        {% ifequal p.gender "M" %}
            Bloke
        {% else %}
            Sheila
        {% endifequal %}
    </li>
    <li>Desc: {{ p.desc }} </li>
</font></td>
<td width=40% bgcolor="aa99aa"><font color="white" size="4">
    {% include "quote.html" %}
</font></td>
```

LISTING 9.1   Continued

```
<td width=30%>
    <h3>Contact Info</h3>
    <li>Email: {{ p.email }}</li>
    <li>Website: {{ p.favoriteURL }}</li>
</td></tr>
<tr>
<td width="30%" bgcolor="556677" valign="top">
    <font color="white" size="4">
    {% with p.friends.all as fl %}
    <h3>
        {{ fl|length|yesno:"iFriend,No Friend"}}{{fl|length|pluralize}}
    </h3>
    {% for f in fl %}
    <li>{{ f.name }}</li>
    {% endfor %}
    {% endwith %}
    </font>
</td>
<td width="70%" bgcolor="555555" colspan="2" valign="top">
    <font color="white" size="4">
    {% with p.blogs.all as bl %}
    <h3>
        {{ bl|length|yesno:"Blog,No Blog"}}
        Entr{{ bl|length|pluralize:"y,ies"}}
    </h3>
    {% for b in bl %}
    <li>{{ b.title }}</li>
    {% endfor %}
    {% endwith %}
    </font>
</td>
</tr>
</table>
{% endblock %}
```

Manipulating Lists

This section discusses using filters to create and manipulate lists inside the template files. You probably will work quite a bit with lists inside the templates, and you won't have the control that you normally would inside Python code. However, the template engine does provide some much-needed filters to help you manage lists.

The following sections describe the slice, make_list, join, and random filters and how to apply them to lists.

slice

The slice filter accepts an argument containing Python list slicing syntax. Depending on the argument's value, it renders a subset of the original list.

This is useful if you need to limit the number of entries from the list that you want to render to the HTML output. For example, if a template is used to render items returned from a search, you could use the `slice` filter in the following line of code to filter only the top ten:

```
{{ searchResults|slice":10" }}
```

Just as in Python, the number on the left of the : refers to the starting index, and the number on the right refers to the ending index. If no value is specified for the starting index, the `slice` filter starts at the first item. If no value is specified for the ending index, the `slice` filter stops after the last item.

Also, just like Python, the index is 0-based, and negative numbers access items from the end of the list. If you wanted the template in the preceding example to retrieve the last 10 items in the search routine, you would use the following syntax:

```
{{ searchResults|slice"-10:" }}
```

The `slice` filter can be applied to a string variable as well. For example, if you have a string, `str`, with a value of `Hello World`, you could use the `slice` filter in the following code to display only `Hello`:

```
{{ str|slice:":5" }}
```

Did you Know?

---

make_list

The `make_list` filter renders the variable as a list. The `make_list` filter accepts no arguments. If the variable is numeric, the `make_list` filter renders a list of digits. If the variable is a string, it renders a list of characters.

The following example shows the result of applying the `make_list` filter to a string, s, with a value of `Python`:

```
{{ s|make_list }}
```

It renders the following:

```
['P','y','t','h','o','n']
```

The following example shows the result of applying the `make_list` filter to a number, n, with a value of `2008`:

```
{{ n|make_list }}
```

It renders the following:

```
['2','0','0','8']
```

The `make_list` filter can be used in many different ways, depending on how creative you get. For example, you can split a large number into a list of characters and then process each digit separately.

join

The `join` filter works similarly to the Python `str.join(list)` function. The `join` filter accepts a string object as the only argument. The entries in the list are joined, with the value of the string argument placed between each entry and rendered as a string.

The `join` filter is useful if you need to display the elements of a list in comma- or space-separated form. For example, if you simply want to display names in a person list, you could use the following code in a template:

```
{% filter linebreaks %}
There are {{ people.length }} people in the list.
Their names are : {{ people|join:", " }}.
{% endfilter %}
```

The rendered output from this filter would look something like this:

```
There are 5 people in the list.
Their names are: Arthur, Lancelot, Galahad, Robin, Tim.
```

Did you Know?

> The `join` filter can be applied to a string variable as well. For example, if you have a string, s, with a value of Title, you could use the `join` filter as follows to display T-i-t-l-e:
>
> `{{ s|join:"-" }}`

random

The `random` filter selects a random item from a list. This can be useful for keeping web content from getting too stale. For example, if you use a quote of the day on your website, you could pass a list of quotes, and the `random` filter would allow you to generate a random quote each time the web page is accessed.

Here's the syntax for using the random filter:

```
{{ QuoteOfTheDay|random }}
```

Try It Yourself ▼

Apply a Filter to a List Object

In this section, you will modify the quote.html template to select a random quote from the list. Currently the quote is hard-coded in, so you need to add code to the details view function to send the quote as part of the context dictionary.

In this section, you will stop the development server and create a new application called Quotes. After the application is created, you will add some quotes to the database using the admin interface. If you've forgotten how to do some of these tasks, refer to Hours 2 and 3.

By the Way

Following these steps to randomize the quote displayed on the person details view:

1. Stop the development server.

2. From the iFriends root directory, use the following command to create an application called Quotes:

   ```
   python manage.py startapp Quotes
   ```

3. Open the iFriends/Quotes/models.py file in an editor.

4. Add the following line of code to the file to import the models class:

   ```
   from django.db import models
   ```

5. Add the following code to the file, as shown in Listing 9.2, to define a Quotes model and enable it in the admin interface:

   ```
   class Quote(models.Model):
       text = models.TextField('text', max_length=200)
       by = models.CharField ('by', max_length=50)

       def __str__(self):
           return '%s' % (self.text)

       class Admin:
           pass
   ```

6. Save the iFriends/Quotes/models.py file.

7. Open the iFriends/settings.py file in an editor.

8. Add the following line to the INSTALLED_APPS setting of the settings.py file to activate the Quotes model:

   ```
   'iFriends.Quotes',
   ```

9. Save the iFriends/settings.py file.

▼

Watch
Out!

Whenever you run the syncdb utility, you change the structure of the database. The syncdb utility should be able to install new applications into the database without problems. I've noticed that Django sometimes has a hard time updating the database. If you get errors, check the structure of the database to make sure the application was added. You might need to add 'iFriends.Quotes' as the first line in the settings.py file to get it added to the database. Hopefully, database synching will be improved in the future.

10. Use the following command from the iFriends root directory to synchronize the new Quotes model to the database:

```
python manage.py syncdb
```

11. Use the following command from the iFriends root directory to start the development server:

```
python manage.py runserver
```

12. Access the admin interface at the following address, and add some Quote objects to the database.

```
http://127.0.0.1:8000/admin
```

13. Open the iFriends/People/views.py file in an editor.

14. Add the following line of code, as shown in Listing 9.3, to import the Quotes model:

```
from iFriends.Quotes.models import Quote
```

15. Make the following change to the details() function, as shown in Listing 9.3, to get a list of Quote objects and pass it into the render_to_response() function:

```
def details(request, pID='0', opts=()):
    rDict = {}
    p = get_object_or_404(Person, pk=pID)
    rDict['p'] = p
    quotes = Quote.objects.all()
    rDict['quotes'] = quotes
    return render_to_response('people/person_details.html', rDict)
```

16. Save the iFriends/People/views.py file.

17. Open the iFriends/templates/quote.html file in an editor.

18. Add the following with tag block on the outside of the `<font>` tags, as shown in Listing 9.4, to assign a random item from the quotes list to the variable quote using the random filter:

```
{% with quotes|random as quote %}
...
{% endwith %}
```

> No changes are needed to iFriends/templates/People/person_details.html because the quotes variable is passed to the quote.html template.

By the Way

19. Replace the quote and the byline text with variable references to the quote.text and quote.by fields of the Quote object, as shown in Listing 9.4:

```
{{ quote.text }}
. . .
{{quote.by }}
```

20. Save the iFriends/templates/quote.html file.

21. Access one of the Person details pages from the following address in a web browser, and click the Refresh button. Each time you refresh the browser, the quote should change, as shown in Figures 9.4 and 9.5.

```
http://127.0.0.1:8000/People/Info/1/
```

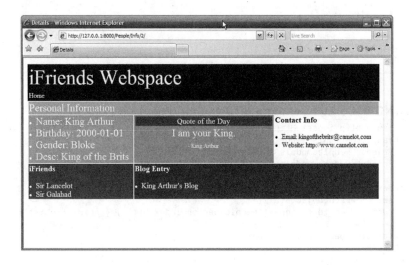

FIGURE 9.4
The first quote of the day.

FIGURE 9.5
The next quote
of the day.

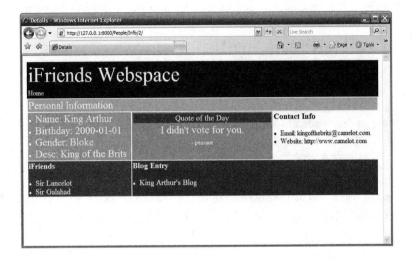

LISTING 9.2   Full Contents of iFriends/Quotes/models.py

```python
from django.db import models

class Quote(models.Model):
    text = models.TextField('text', max_length=200)
    by = models.CharField('by', max_length=50)

    def __str__(self):
        return '%s' % (self.text)

    class Admin:
        pass
```

LISTING 9.3   Full Contents of iFriends/People/views.py

```python
from django.http import HttpResponse
from django.shortcuts import render_to_response, get_object_or_404
from iFriends.People.models import Person
from iFriends.Quotes.models import Quote

def index(request):
    pList = Person.objects.all()
    return render_to_response('people/person_index.html', {'pList': pList})

def details(request, pID='0', opts=()):
    rDict = {}
    p = get_object_or_404(Person, pk=pID)
    rDict['p'] = p
    quotes = Quote.objects.all()
    rDict['quotes'] = quotes
    return render_to_response('people/person_details.html', rDict)
```

LISTING 9.4   Full Contents of `iFriends/templates/quote.html`

```
<table width="100%">
<tr bgcolor="aa22aa" width="100%"><td align="center">
<font size="4">Quote of the Day</font>
</td></tr>
<tr><td align="center">
{% with quotes|random as quote %}
<font size="5">{{ quote.text }}</font>
</td></tr>
<tr><td align="center">
<font size="2">- {{quote.by }}</font>
{% endwith %}
</td></tr>
</table>
```

Sorting Dictionaries

The `dictsort` filter is a useful tool when you want to display the data from a template in a different order. The `dictsort` filter can be applied to a list of dictionaries. It accepts a key name as the only argument. The filter renders a sorted list based on the key given in the argument.

> **By the Way**
>
> If you need to sort the list of dictionaries in reverse order, you can use the `dictsortreversed` filter in the same way that you use `dictsort`. The only difference is that the dictionaries are sorted in reverse order.

To show an example of using a `dictsort` filter table, the following template code renders a table of flight data that comes from a list of flights stored in dictionaries. The sample code sorts the list using the `dictsort:'departure'` filter to sort the list by the departure key before rendering the table.

```
<h1>Departure Table</h1>
<table border="1" cellpadding="2">
<tr bgcolor="dddddd">
    <td>Departure</td>
    <td>Arrival</td>
    <td>Flight Number</td>
</tr>
{% for f in flights|dictsort:"departure" %}
<tr>
    <td>{{ f.depeparture }}</td>
    <td>{{ f.arrival }}</td>
    <td>{{ f.flightnum }}</td>
</tr>
{% endfor %}
</table>
```

As another example, use the same code, but change the <h1> text to "Arrival Table," and change the `dictsort` argument for tag to the following code:

```
{% for f in flights|dictsort:"arrival" %}
```

By doing this, you can render another table with the flights sorted by the `arrival` key. The result is a web page similar to the one shown in Figure 9.6.

FIGURE 9.6
Two tables generated with the same date in a different sort order using the `dictsort` filter.

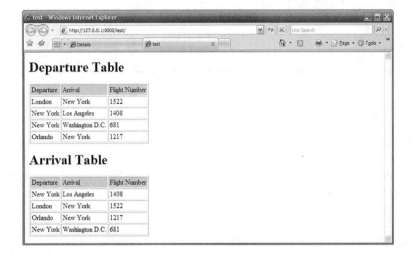

Formatting Dates

This section discusses using filters to display and format date and time variables inside the template files. You probably will work with dates to either display the current date or display dates that are fields in a model.

The following sections describe the date, `time`, `now`, `timesince`, and `timeuntil` filters and how to apply them in a template.

date

The `date` filter can be applied to Python `date` variables, including `date` fields in a model object. The `date` filter accepts a string of format characters as an argument and formats the date based on those characters. For a full description of the `datetime` format characters, refer to Appendix C, "Formatting Dates and Times."

The following examples should help you understand how the `date` filter works. The `entryDate` variable is a `date` instance with a value of February 7, 2005.

The following code applies the j character to render the day of the week without the leading 0, the S character to render the English day/month suffix, the F character to render the month as textual, and the Y character to render the four-digit year:

```
{{ entryDate|date:"jS F Y" }}
renders
7th February 2005
```

The following code applies the D character to render the three-character day-of-the-week text, the F character to render the month as textual, the j character to render the day of the week without the leading 0, the S character to render the English day/month suffix, and the Y character to render the four-digit year:

```
{{ entryDate|date:"D, F jS, Y" }}
renders
Mon, February 7th, 2005
```

The following code applies the m character to add the two-digit month value, the d character to add the two-digit day value, and the Y character to add the four-digit year:

```
{{ entryDate|date:"m/d/Y" }}
renders
02/07/2005
```

Did you notice that the comma and slash characters that were added to the format string for the date filter get rendered with the values specified by the format characters?

Did you Know?

time

The time filter can be applied to Python date and datetime variables, including datetime fields in a model object, the same way that the date filter is. The time filter also accepts a string of format characters as an argument and formats the time based on those characters. For a full description of the datetime format characters, refer to Appendix C.

You can use only the characters that format time specifically in the time filter. The date characters will not work.

By the Way

The following examples should help you understand how the time filter works. The someTime variable is a time instance with a value of 10:51 p.m. MDT.

The following code applies the h character to render the two-digit hour in 12-hour format, the i character to render the two-digit minutes value, the a character to render the a.m./p.m. text string, and the T character to render the timezone string:

```
{{ someTime|date:"h:ia T" }}
renders
10:51p.m. Mountain Daylight Time
```

The following code applies the H character to render the two-digit hour in 24-hour format, the i character to render the two-digit minutes value, the s character to render the two-digit seconds value, the a character to render the AM/PM text string, and the O character to render the offset to Greenwich time:

```
{{ someTime|date:"H:i:sAO" }}
renders
22:51:46PM+1800
```

> Did you notice that the colon characters that were added to the format string for the time filter get rendered with the values specified by the format characters?

now

Because we are discussing the date and time filters in this section, it would be a good idea to discuss the now tag as well. The now tag works similarly to the date and time filters in that it accepts a string of format characters to format the current date and time. However, the now tag uses tag syntax instead of filter syntax and is not applied to a variable object. The following line of code shows how to render the current date and time in a template using the now filter:

```
{% now "M d, Y g:ma" %}
```

This line of code renders the date and time in the following format:

```
Jan 17, 2008 3:01p.m.
```

For a full description of the datetime format characters, refer to Appendix C.

timesince **and** timeuntil

The timesince filter can be applied to either a time or datetime variable. It accepts an optional time or datetime object as the only argument. The timesince filter determines the time since the time or datetime variable to the current time and renders a textual string noting the difference.

The timeuntil filter can also be applied to either a time or datetime variable. It also accepts an optional time or datetime object as the only argument. However, the timeuntil filter subtracts the current time from the time or datetime variable and renders a textual string noting the delta.

If a time or datetime argument is added, the timesince and timeuntil filters determine the time elapsed between the filter argument and the variable, and render a textual string noting the difference.

> Currently, the time or datetime argument should be earlier than that of the original variable in both the timeuntil and timesince filters. This was different than I expected. I'm not certain if this will change in the future.

The timesince and timeuntil filters measure the difference in units of years, months, days, minutes, and seconds. However, only the two largest units are displayed, such as years and months, months and days, days and hours, hours and minutes, and minutes and seconds.

The following code snippet shows an example of using the timeuntil and timesince filters to display textual information about the last archive date, next archive date, and current date and time:

```
<h1>Archive Data</h1>
<table border=1 padding=2>
<tr>
    <td>Current Time</td>
    <td>Last Archive</td>
    <td>Next Archive</td>
</tr>
<tr>
    <td>{% now "M d, Y h:m:sa" %}</td>
    <td>{{ lastArch|date:"M d, Y h:m:sa" }}</td>
    <td>{{ nextArch|date:"M d, Y h:m:sa" }}</td>
</tr>
</table>
<p>
It has been {{ lastArch|timesince }}
since the last archive.<p>
The next archive will take place in
{{ nextArch|timeuntil }}.<p>

The time between the archives will be
{{ nextArch|timeuntil:lastArch }}.
```

Figure 9.7 shows the output of the code in the web browser.

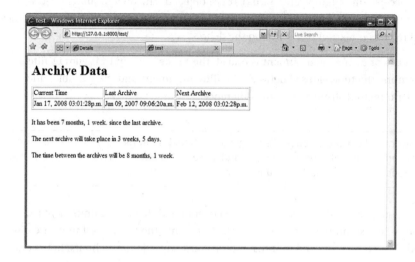

▼   **Try It Yourself**

Format Date and Time Variables in a Template

In this section, you will add a datetime field to the Blog model in the Person application. You will use the date formatting filters to display the dates correctly in the Person details view.

Follow these steps to add the datetime field to the Blog model and update the person_details.py template:

1. Stop the development server.

2. Open the iFriends/People/models.py file in an editor.

3. Add the following line of code to the Blog model to add a datetime field called Last Modified:

   ```
   date = models.DateTimeField('Last Modified')
   ```

▼   4. Save the iFriends/People/models.py file.

> You need to synchronize the changes to the `Blog` model to the database. Django currently cannot do this. It is recommended that you sync the application to the database only once (when it is created). However, in the real world, we know that isn't possible. I've been able to update the database by removing the table(s) for the model that is changed and then synchronizing the database. To get the models in the database to update, you need to drop the people_blog table in the database, which means that all the data in that table will be lost. The following steps take you through the process of updating the database properly. Hopefully, Django will fix this in the future. If Django changes things and these steps do not work, you may need to drop the entire database (lose all your data) and then synchronize.

5. Open a MySQL command-line client.

6. From the MySQL command prompt, enter the following commands to drop the people_blog table:

```
use ifriendsdb;
drop table people_blog;
```

7. Use the following command from the iFriends root directory to synchronize the updated `Blog` model to the database:

```
python manage.py syncdb
```

8. Use the following command from the iFriends root directory to start the development server:

```
python manage.py runserver
```

9. Access the admin interface using the following URL. Verify that the `Blog` objects have the new Last Modified field, and create some new blog entries.

```
http://127.0.0.1:8000/admin
```

> Django doesn't display the Last Modified `datetime` field because we used the `auto_now` option, which overrides any value you might add in the admin interface.

10. Open the `iFriends/templates/Person/person_details.py` file in a web browser.

11. Modify the following line to format the birthday date field correctly, as shown in Listing 9.5:

```
<li>Birthday: {{ p.birthday|date:"m/d/Y" }}</li>
```

12. Add the following lines of code to the blog list to display the blog's Last Modified date, as shown in Listing 9.5:

```
<li>
    {{ b.title }} -
    <font size="2"> {{ b.date|date:"M d, Y g:ma" }}</font>
</li>
```

13. Save the iFriends/templates/Person/person_details.py file.

14. Access one of the Person details pages from the following address in a web browser, as shown in Figure 9.8, and view the new dates you added.

```
http://127.0.0.1:8000/People/Info/1/
```

FIGURE 9.8
Person details view that has formatted dates for the birthday and blog list items.

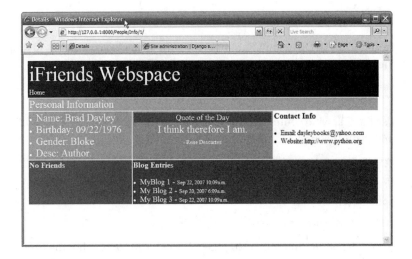

Listing 9.5 shows the complete person_details.py file.

LISTING 9.5 Full Contents of iFriends/templates/Person/ person_details.py

```
{% extends "iFriends_base.html" %}

{% block title %}Details{% endblock %}
{% block content %}
<table width=100%>
<tr bgcolor="aabbcc"><td colspan="3">
<font size="5" color="white">Personal Information</font>
</td></tr>
<tr valign="top"><td width=30% bgcolor="aaaaaa"><font color="white" size="5">
    <li>Name: {{p.name}}</li>
    <li>Birthday: {{ p.birthday|date:"m/d/Y" }}</li>
    <li>Gender:
        {% ifequal p.gender "M" %}
```

LISTING 9.5 Continued

```
            Bloke
        {% else %}
            Sheila
        {% endifequal %}
    </li>
    <li>Desc: {{ p.desc }} </li>
</font></td>
<td width=40% bgcolor="aa99aa"><font color="white" size="4">
    {% include "quote.html" %}
</font></td>
<td width=30%>
    <h3>Contact Info</h3>
    <li>Email: {{ p.email }}</li>
    <li>Website: {{ p.favoriteURL }}</li>
</td></tr>
<tr>
<td width="30%" bgcolor="556677" valign="top">
    <font color="white" size="4">
    {% with p.friends.all as fl %}
    <h3>
        {{ fl|length|yesno:"iFriend,No Friend"}}{{fl|length|pluralize}}
    </h3>
    {% for f in fl %}
    <li>{{ f.name }}</li>
    {% endfor %}
    {% endwith %}
    </font>
</td>
<td width="70%" bgcolor="555555" colspan="2" valign="top">
    <font color="white" size="4">
    {% with p.blogs.all as bl %}
    <h3>
        {{ bl|length|yesno:"Blog,No Blog"}}
        Entr{{ bl|length|pluralize:"y,ies"}}
    </h3>
    {% for b in bl %}
    <li>{{ b.title }} -
        <font size="2"> {{ b.date|date:"M d, Y g:ma" }}</font>
    </li>
    {% endfor %}
    {% endwith %}
    </font>
</td>
</tr>
</table>
{% endblock %}
```

Summary

In this hour, you learned how to apply filters to variables in templates to alter the rendered output. You learned how to format text, dates, and times. You also learned how to manipulate lists, create lists on-the-fly, and randomly select items in a list from within the template using list filters. This hour also covered using the `dictsort` filter to filter sort lists of dictionaries before rendering them to the HTTP response.

Q&A

Q. Is there a way to add one numeric variable to another in a template?

A. Yes. The add filter can be applied to a variable to add another variable to it using the following syntax:

```
{{ varA|add:varB }}
```

Q. Is there a way to retrieve a specific digit from a numeric variable?

A. Yes. The get_digit filter retrieves a specific digit based on a numeric argument, where an argument with a value of 1 is the rightmost digit:

```
{{ varA|get_digit:"1" }}
```

Q. Is there a quick way to add HTML markup to an URL that is in plain text so that it will be rendered as a clickable link?

A. Yes. The urlize filter adds HTML markup to a plain-text URL:

```
{{ myURL|urlize }}
```

Q. Are any other filter libraries available for templates?

A. Yes. You can add the django.contrib.humanize, django.contrib.markup, and django.contrib.webdesign libraries to the INSTALLED_APPS setting and load them into the templates using the following load tag syntax:

```
{% load humanize %}
```

Workshop

The workshop consists of a set of questions and answers designed to solidify your understanding of the material covered in this hour. Try answering the questions before looking at the answers.

Quiz

1. Which filter would you use to render all the end-of-line characters in text to HTML line-break codes?

2. Which filter would you use to sort a list of dictionaries?

3. What argument does the date filter accept?

Quiz Answers

1. The linebreaks tag

2. The dictsort tag

3. A string of time format characters

Exercises

1. Use the now tag to add the current time somewhere in the header template iFriends/templates/iFriends_base.html.

2. Use datetime formatting to format the time created in Exercise 1 to the following format:

```
Tuesday, Jan 1st, 2008
```

HOUR 10

Adding Forms to Views

What You'll Learn in This Hour:

▶ How to create Form instances

▶ How to render Form objects as HTML code

▶ How to render forms for models and objects

▶ How to create custom forms by customizing Widgets and using custom templates

Forms are a basic element of any website. HTML forms are used to collect input from users. This input can be used to change data in the database, configure settings, send emails, and perform various other tasks.

Django provides a useful library to help you create and handle forms. The Django forms library is intended to handle HTML form display, data processing, and redisplay. In this hour, you will learn how to create forms and display them in your HTML views. We won't actually gather any input from the forms in this hour; that topic is covered in the next hour.

Before starting this hour, you need to understand a few terms:

▶ **Model:** We covered models earlier. You should remember that a model is an object-definition with several fields defined that define attributes of the object.

▶ **Form:** In this hour, form refers to a Django Form class that is used to render HTML forms.

▶ **Field:** Both models and forms have Field objects. The Field objects for models and forms are similar and are somewhat related, but they are not the same. Appendix B, "Django Form Field Objects," contains a table that maps Model Fields to Form Fields.

▶ **Widget:** A Widget is an object that renders to an HTML form element. Each
Form Field has an associated Widget object that is used when rendering the
Form as HTML. For example, a CharField Widget renders to an HTML text
input element. Appendix B lists the Widget objects.

Currently, the two form libraries are forms and newforms. The forms library is old,
so it isn't covered in this book. The Django project suggests that you import the
newforms library as forms to maintain backward compatibility. Perhaps the Django
developers intend to remove the old forms library and replace it with newforms. In
this book, however, I always import the newforms library using the following
import statement:

```
from django import newforms as forms
```

When I refer to the forms library, I am really referring to the newforms library.

Creating Form Instances

You can define forms in Django by creating a class that inherits the Form class and
then defining Field objects as members of the form. For example, to create an
address book form that includes name, address, and email fields, you would use the
following class definition:

```
from django import newforms as forms
class AddressForm(forms.Form):
    name = forms.CharField()
    address = forms.CharField()
    email = forms.EmailField()
```

After the form has been created, you can create instances of the form by calling this
constructor:

```
adr = AddressForm()
```

The following sections describe the different fields you can use when defining forms,
how to create bound and unbound instances of the forms, and how to override
built-in form methods.

Form Fields

You can add several different types of fields to forms. The advantage of different
types of fields is that the form can more closely match the data types that will be
put into it and validated.

Several Field objects are available in the forms package. The following is a list of the Field objects and their uses. For more information about each Field object, see Appendix B.

► The BooleanField object is used to add true/false values. It renders a check box.

► The CharField object is used for most textual input. It renders a text box.

► The ChoiceField object is used to select an item from a list. It renders a select box.

► The DateField object is used to specify a date. It renders a text box.

► The DateTimeField object is used to specify a date/time. It renders a text box.

► The DecimalField object is used to specify numeric data in the form of a decimal value. It renders a text box.

► The EmailField object is used to specify an email address. It renders a text box.

► The FileField object is used to specify a file. It renders a file upload.

► The ImageField object is used to specify an image file. It renders a file upload.

► The IntegerField object is used to specify numeric data in the form of an integer value. It renders a text box.

► The IPAddressField object is used to specify an IPv4 address. It renders a text box.

► The MultipleChoiceField object is used to select multiple items from a list. It renders a multiple-select box.

► The NullBooleanField object is used to select a true/false/none value. It renders a null Boolean select.

► The RegexField object is used to specify that you want a specific regular expression as the input. It renders a text box.

► The TimeField object is used to specify a time. It renders a text box.

► The URLField object is used to specify a valid URL. It renders a text box.

Each `Field` object has the following core field arguments available when you define the form:

▶ The `required` argument can be set to `True` or `False`; it defaults to `True`. If `required` is set to `False`, no value is required when creating or validating the form.

▶ The `label` argument allows you to specify a textual label that is displayed when the form is rendered. If `label` is not specified, the name of the field is used.

▶ The `initial` argument allows you to specify an initial value for the field. `initial` is used only with unbound forms.

▶ The `widget` argument allows you to specify a `Widget` object to use when rendering the field. The `Widget` object determines what HTML element is used in the form when it is rendered. For more details about the types of `Widget` objects you can assign to fields, see Appendix B.

▶ The `help_text` argument allows you to specify a string that is displayed next to the field when the field is rendered.

The following example shows a simple `Field` definition that uses the core field arguments:

```
desc = forms.CharField(required=False, label='Description',
        widget=forms.Textarea(), help_text='Your description here.')
```

Bound and Unbound Forms

You can create two different types of form instances, depending on what you need from the form. You can create forms that are either bound or unbound to data. A bound form is a form that contains data bound to each element in the form. An unbound form is a blank form that contains no data values for the elements in the form.

A form that is unbound to data cannot do validation, but it can still render the form so that it can be displayed as HTML. To create an unbounded instance of a form, you simply need to call the `Form` constructor. The following example creates an unbound form:

```
adr = AddressForm()
```

A form that is bound to data can validate that data as well as render it to be displayed as HTML. To create a bound instance of a form, you need a dictionary. The dictionary's keys need to match the names of the fields you specified when you defined the form. The values need to be valid for the `Field` object that the key specifies. The following example shows how to create a form that is bound to a dataset:

```
from django import newforms as forms
class AddressForm(forms.Form):
    name = forms.CharField()
    address = forms.CharField()
    email = forms.EmailField()
. . .
dset = {'name': 'Surfs Up',
        'address': 'Somewhere Wet',
        'email': 'blue@ocean.waves'}
adr = AddressForm(dset)
```

When the `AddressForm` instance is created, it is bound to the data in `dset`.

Bound forms should be considered immutable. You cannot change the data after the form has been created. To change the data, you need to create another instance of the form.

Watch Out!

To determine whether a form instance is bound, you can access the `is_bound` attribute of the `Form` object. For the preceding example, the following line of code would evaluate to `True`:

```
adr.is_bound
```

By the Way

Rendering Forms as HTML

An instance of a `Form` object can be rendered as HTML in a couple of ways. The first way is to render the form inside Python code—for example, inside a view function when building the text for the `HttpResponse`. The second way is to pass the form object as a variable to an HTML template file and then render the form inside the template itself.

Django provide three different versions of form rendering. The following sections discuss rendering forms as tables, lists, and paragraphs. The table version seems to be the most popular. Which one you use depends on how you want the form to be displayed.

Rendering Forms as a Table

Django provides the `as_table()` function to render forms as an HTML table. This method is also the default method if you simply use the `print` function to print the form.

When forms are rendered as an HTML table, each `Field` in the form is rendered as a two-column row. The first column displays the label in a `<th>` tag. The second column uses the HTML equivalent of the `Widget` object assigned to the `Field` to display the value in a `<td>` tag. For example, a `CharField` that is labeled `Name` and has a value of `Tim` renders to the following HTML:

```
<tr><th><label for"id_name"Name:</label><th>
<td><input type="text" name="name" value="Tim" /></td></tr>
```

> There are no `<table>` or `<form>` tags around the rendered table. This gives you much more flexibility in building the view.

The following line of code shows how to render a `Form` object as an HTML table in Python code:

```
html += myForm.as_table()
```

The following line of code shows how to render a `Form` object as an HTML table in an HTML template:

```
{{ myForm.as_table }}
```

Rendering Forms as a List

Django provides the `as_ul()` function to render forms as an HTML list. When forms are rendered as an HTML list, each `Field` in the form is rendered as a list item with a `<label>` and `<input>` tag. The `<label>` tag displays the label of the `Field`. The `<input>` tag displays the HTML equivalent of the `Widget` object assigned to the `Field`. For example, a `CharField` that is labeled `Name` and has a value of `Tim` renders to the following HTML:

```
<li><label for"id_name"Name:</label>
<input type="text" name="name" value="Tim" /></li>
```

By the Way

> There are no `<form>` tags around the rendered list. This gives you much more flexibility in building the view.

The following line of code shows how to render a Form object as an HTML list in Python code:

```
html += myForm.as_ul()
```

The following line of code shows how to render a Form object as an HTML list in an HTML template:

```
{{ myForm.as_ul }}
```

Rendering Forms as Paragraphs

Django provides the as_p() function to render forms as HTML paragraphs. When forms are rendered as HTML paragraphs, each Field in the form is rendered inside <p> tags with <label> and <input> tags. The <label> tag displays the label of the Field. The <input> tag displays the HTML equivalent of the Widget object assigned to the Field. For example, a CharField that is labeled Name and has a value of Tim renders to the following HTML:

```
<p><label for"id_name"Name:</label>
<input type="text" name="name" value="Tim" /></p>
```

> There are no <form> tags around the rendered paragraph. This gives you much more flexibility in building the view.

By the Way

The following line of code shows how to render a Form object as an HTML paragraph in Python code:

```
html += myForm.as_p()
```

The following line of code shows how to render a Form object as an HTML paragraph in an HTML template:

```
{{ myForm.as_p }}
```

Try It Yourself   ▼

Render a Form as HTML

In this section, you will add a contact_view() view to the iFriends website and create a basic form that will allow users to send emails to the site admin. You will create a new application called Home to store the contact_view() view in.

▼

When you add the Home application, you do not need to stop and then restart the server or add a line to the INSTALLED_APPS setting in the settings.py file. You will not be adding any model information that will need to be synchronized to the database.

Follow these steps to create the Home application, add a contact_view(), and create a contact form:

1. From the iFriends root directory, use the following command to create an application called Home:

```
python manage.py startapp Home
```

2. Open the iFriends/Home/views.py file in an editor.

3. Add the following code to the file, as shown in Listing 10.1, to import the render_to_response and forms objects:

```
from django.shortcuts import render_to_response
from django import newforms as forms
```

4. Add the following code to the file, as shown in Listing 10.1, to define the EmailForm form:

```
class EmailForm(forms.Form):
        title = forms.CharField(max_length=50)
        sender = forms.EmailField()
        date = forms.DateTimeField()
        text = forms.CharField(max_length=200)
```

5. Add the following contact_view() function, as shown in Listing 10.1, to create an instance of the EmailForm and call the contact_form.html template:

```
def contact_view(request):
    eForm = EmailForm()
    return render_to_response('home/contact_form.html', { 'eForm':eForm })
```

6. Save the iFriends/Home/views.py file.

7. Create a directory called iFriends/templates/Home.

8. Create and open an iFriends/templates/Home/contact_form.html file in an editor.

9. Add the template code shown in Listing 10.2 to extend the base template and render the eForm variable as a table.

10. Save the iFriends/templates/Home/contract_form.html file.

11. Open the iFriends/urls.py file in an editor.

12. Add the following line to the URL patterns to provide the URL link to the `contact_view()` view function:

```
(r'^Home/contact/$', 'iFriends.Home.views.contact_view'),
```

13. Save the `iFriends/urls.py` file.

14. Access the following URL in a web browser to bring up the contact view, shown in Figure 10.1, and verify that the form renders correctly:

```
http://127.0.0.1:8000/Home/contact/
```

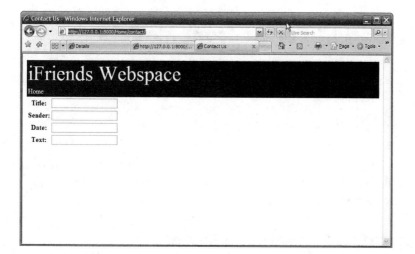

FIGURE 10.1
Contact form rendered as an HTML table in the `contact_form.html` template.

LISTING 10.1   Full Contents of `iFriends/Home/views.py`

```python
from django.shortcuts import render_to_response, get_object_or_404
from datetime import datetime
from django import newforms as forms

class EmailForm(forms.Form):
        title = forms.CharField(max_length=50)
        sender = forms.EmailField()
        date = forms.DateTimeField()
        text = forms.CharField(max_length=200)

def contact_view(request):
    eForm = EmailForm()
    return render_to_response('home/contact_form.html', { 'eForm':eForm })
```

▼

LISTING 10.2   Full Contents of iFriends/templates/Home/
contact_form.html

```
{% extends "iFriends_base.html" %}

{% block title %}Contact Us{% endblock %}
{% block content %}
<table>
{{ eForm }}
</table>
{% endblock %}
```

▲

Rendering Forms from Models

In the previous sections, you learned how to define new Form objects and render them as HTML. Django also allows you to create Form objects from a model or an instance of a model.

Creating forms from models is easy and limits coding errors. However, you do not have as much control over forms created from models as forms you create yourself.

The following sections describe the process of creating a form from a model class using the form_for_model() helper function and creating a form from a model instance using the form_for_instance() helper function.

Creating a Form from a Model

The form_for_model() function accepts a model class and creates a Form class with a Field object that corresponds to each Field object in the model. You can then use the Form class to create Form instances that can be rendered as HTML. For a mapping of Form Fields to Model Fields, see Appendix B.

For example, let's look at creating a Form object from this Blog model:

```
class Blog(models.Model):
    title = models.CharField('Title', max_length=200)
    text = models.TextField('Text', max_length=2048)
    date = models.DateTimeField('Last Modified')
```

The following code snippet creates a Form class from the Blog model, creates a Form instance from the Form class, and renders it as HTML paragraphs, as shown in Figure 10.2:

```
from django.http import HttpResponse
from iFriends.People.models import Blog
from django import newforms as forms
. . .
```

```
BlogForm = forms.form_for_model(Blog)
bf = BlogForm()
return HttpResponse(bf.as_p())
```

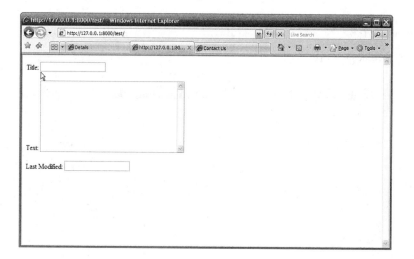

FIGURE 10.2
Blog form
generated from
form_for_
model() and
rendered
as HTML
paragraphs.

> If you set the editable=False option when creating a Field in a model, that
> Field is not added to the Form class created by form_for_model() or
> form_for_instance().

Creating a Form from an Object

You can use the form_for_instance() helper function to create a Form class from
an object that is a model instance. The form_for_instance() function works basically the same way as the form_for_model() function. For each Field object in the
model, a corresponding Field is created in the Form class.

The big difference is that the data values from the model instance are assigned as
initial values of the form. When the Form is rendered as HTML, those values are
placed as initial values in the form.

Another advantage of using the form_for_instance() function is that you don't
necessarily need to know what model is being rendered. This can be helpful if you
want to write generic views that will render forms from different types of objects.

For an example, let's use the Blog class defined in the preceding section. The following code snippet uses form_for_instance() to create a Form class from the Blog
object instance, creates a Form instance from the Form class, and renders it as HTML
paragraphs, as shown in Figure 10.3:

```
from django.http import HttpResponse
from django.shortcuts import get_object_or_404
from iFriends.People.models import Blog
from django import newforms as forms
. . .
blog = get_object_or_404(Blog, pk=1)
BlogForm = forms.form_for_instance(blog)
bf = BlogForm()
return HttpResponse(bf.as_p())
```

FIGURE 10.3
Blog form with
initial values
filled in,
generated from
form_for_
instance(),
and rendered
as HTML
paragraphs.

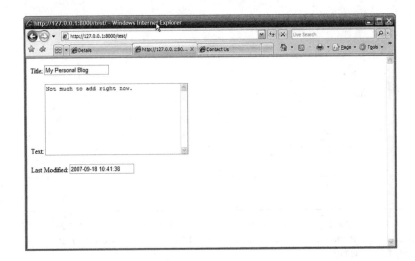

Notice that the form's values are already filled in with the values in the Blog
instance.

Creating Partial Forms from Models

The form_for_model() and form_for_instance() functions accept a fields argument that allows you to specify which Field objects are added to the Form class.
The fields argument is set to a list of Field names that exist in the model. Only
the fields that are listed in the fields argument are added to the Form class.

The fields argument gives you more flexibility when creating forms for models. For
example, consider the Blog class from the previous sections. The Last Modified
field isn't something that the user needs to modify. The following code snippet uses
the fields argument in form_for_instance() to create a Form class that is a subset of the Blog object instance. The Form class includes only the title and text
fields that are listed in the fields argument, as shown in Figure 10.4:

```
from django.http import HttpResponse
from django.shortcuts import get_object_or_404
from iFriends.People.models import Blog
```

```
from django import newforms as forms
. . .
blog = get_object_or_404(Blog, pk=1)
BlogForm = forms.form_for_instance(blog, fields=('title', 'text')
bf = BlogForm()
return HttpResponse(bf.as_p())
```

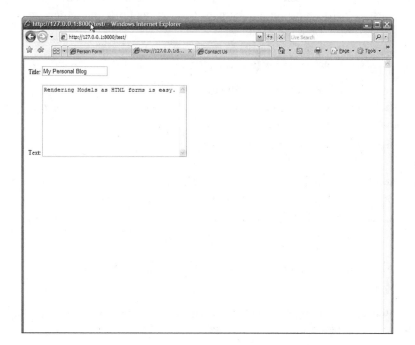

FIGURE 10.4
Blog form that
includes only
the title and
text fields ren-
dered as HTML
paragraphs.

Notice that the Last Modified field is not present in the form because it is not
listed in the fields argument.

> Fields that are omitted from the fields argument must not be required for valida-
> tion. They need to be allowed to have a None value by setting Blank=True, contain
> a default value, or be filled in automatically.

Try It Yourself

Create and Render a Form for a Model

In this section, you will create a person_form() view that displays a Person object
as a form. Follow these steps to add the person_form() that creates a form from a

Person object, create an HTML template to display the form, and update the URLconf file to enable the view:

1. Open the iFriends/People/views.py file in an editor.

2. Add the following code to the file, as shown in Listing 10.3, to define a person_form() function that accepts the argument pID and retrieves a Person object from the database:

```
def person_form(request, pID='0'):
    p = get_object_or_404(Person, pk=pID)
```

3. Add the following code to the function created in step 2 to create a PersonForm class from the Person object instance, and then create an instance of the PersonForm:

```
PersonForm = forms.form_for_instance(p)
pForm = PersonForm()
```

4. Add the following line of code to the person_form() function, as shown in Listing 10.3, to render the form to a template called person_form.html:

```
return render_to_response('People/person_form.html', {'pForm':pForm})
```

5. Save the iFriends/People/views.py file.

6. Create and open a file named iFriends/templates/People/person_form.html in an editor.

7. Add the template code shown in Listing 10.4 to extend the base template and render the pForm variable as a table.

8. Save the iFriends/templates/Person/person_form.html file.

9. Open the iFriends/People/urls.py file in an editor.

10. Add the following line to the URL patterns to provide the URL link to the person_form() view function:

```
(r'^Form/(?P<pID>\d+)/$', 'person_form'),
```

11. Save the iFriends/People/urls.py file.

12. Access the following URL in a web browser to bring up the person form view, as shown in Figure 10.5, and verify that the form renders correctly:

```
http://127.0.0.1:8000/People/Form/1/
```

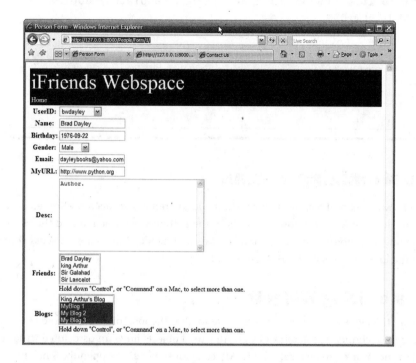

FIGURE 10.5
Person form
rendered as
an HTML table
in the
person_form.
html template.

LISTING 10.3 Full Contents of iFriends/People/views.py

```python
from django.http import HttpResponse
from django.shortcuts import render_to_response, get_object_or_404
from iFriends.People.models import Person, Blog
from iFriends.Quotes.models import Quote
from datetime import datetime
from django import newforms as forms

def index(request):
    pList = Person.objects.all()
    return render_to_response('people/person_index.html', {'pList': pList})

def details(request, pID='0', opts=()):
    rDict = {}
    p = get_object_or_404(Person, pk=pID)
    rDict['p'] = p
    quotes = Quote.objects.all()
    rDict['quotes'] = quotes
    return render_to_response('people/person_details.html', rDict)

def person_form(request, pID='0'):
    p = get_object_or_404(Person, pk=pID)
    PersonForm = forms.form_for_instance(p)
    pForm = PersonForm()
    return render_to_response('People/person_form.html', {'pForm':pForm})
```

LISTING 10.4   Full Contents of `iFriends/templates/People/`
`person_form.html`

```
{% extends "iFriends_base.html" %}

{% block title %}Person Form{% endblock %}
{% block content %}
<table>
{{ pForm }}
</table>
{% endblock %}
```

Customizing Forms

The HTML look and feel of the forms that Django renders seems a bit limited and plain. However, you can add code to both the Python view function and the HTML template to customize the form's look and feel. The following sections discuss changing the look and feel of the HTML forms.

Customizing Widgets

One of the biggest changes you can make to alter the look and feel of a `Form Field` object is to change the `Widget` object. All `Field` objects have an associated `Widget` object that is used to generate the HTML code for the `Field`. Appendix B has more information on `Form Fields` and Widgets.

Django allows you to specify attributes for the Widget as well as specify a totally different Widget to use for the form. Changing the Widget results in changing the HTML code that is generated when the form is rendered as HTML.

For example, consider the following `Form` code, which renders a form similar to the one shown in Figure 10.6:

```
class MForm(forms.Form):
    name = forms.CharField(max_length=50)
    location = forms.CharField(max_length=80)
    size = forms.CharField(max_lenght=20))
    desc = forms.CharField(max_length=200)
```

All the HTML elements are text inputs and are the same size even though the `Fields` are for different types of data. The following definition for the form sets the `size` attribute of the `length` field and changes the `size` field to a `RadioSelect` and the desc field to a `Textarea`, as shown in Figure 10.7:

```
sList = [('S', 'Hill'),('M','Peak'), ('L', 'Climber')]
class MForm(forms.Form):
    name = forms.CharField(max_length=50)
    location = forms.CharField(widget=
```

```
                forms.TextInput(attrs={'size':'40'}))
size = forms.CharField(widget=
                forms.RadioSelect(choices=sList))
desc = forms.CharField(widget=forms.Textarea(
                attrs={'rows':'4','cols':'40'}))
```

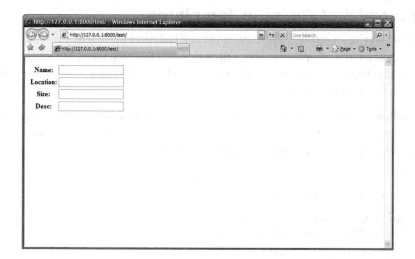

FIGURE 10.6
Simple form rendered as an HTML table.

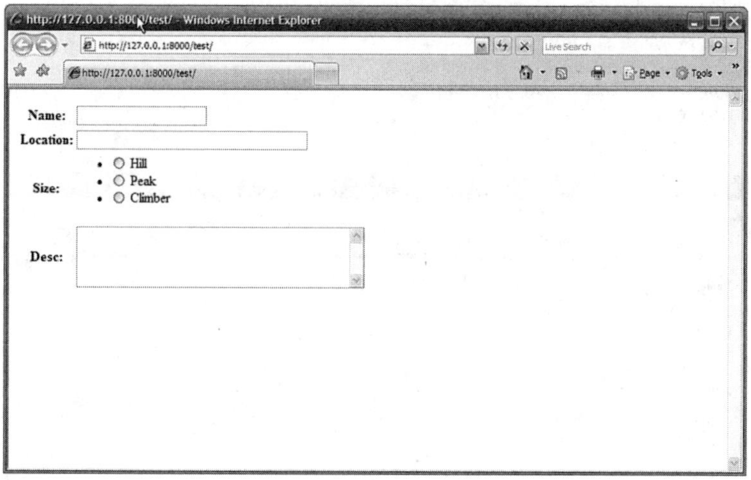

FIGURE 10.7
Form class with customized Widgets rendered as an HTML table.

The form in Figure 10.7 would be much more useful, and it doesn't take that much extra code.

> The only thing you really need to watch out for when customizing forms is to make
> sure that they still conform to the data that you work with.

Customizing Forms in Templates

Another way to customize your forms is using HTML templates. When you pass
forms into a template, you can access the fields directly using the . (dot) syntax. This
allows you to access not only the value of the field, but also the field attributes, such
as `label_tag` and `help_text`.

The following code snippet from an HTML template shows how you can access an
instance of the `MForm` from the preceding section and use your own HTML code to
control how it is displayed, as shown in Figure 10.8:

```
<table>
<tr>
    <th>{{ MForm.name.label_tag }}</th>
    <td>{{ MForm.name }}</td>
    <th>{{ MForm.location.label_tag }}:</th>
    <td>{{ MForm.location }}</td>
</tr>
<tr>
    <th>{{ MForm.desc.label_tag }}:</th>
    <td colspan="3">{{ MForm.desc }}</td>
</tr>
</table>
<h3>{{ MForm.size.label_tag }}</h3>
{{ MForm.size }}
```

FIGURE 10.8
Form class with
customized
Widgets ren-
dered using -
custom
template code.

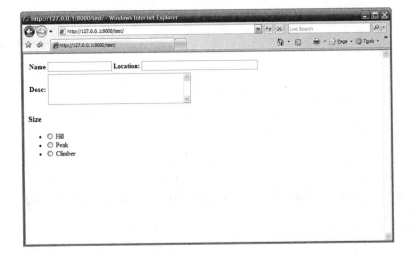

By the Way

You can also access the Form as a list in the template and use it in a for loop. This makes it easy to apply the same HTML code to several fields. For example:

```
{% for field in MForm %}
<h2>{{ field.label_tag }}</h2>
{{ field }}
{% endfor %}
```

Try It Yourself ▼

Create and Generate a Customized Form

In this section, you will modify the contact form created earlier in this hour to display a better-looking form. Follow these steps to modify the Form definition and HTML template files:

1. Open the iFriends/Home/views.py file in an editor.

2. Modify the title and sender fields of the EmailForm to the following code, as shown in Listing 10.5, so that the Widget size corresponds to the maximum length:

```
title = forms.CharField(max_length=50,
        widget=forms.TextInput(attrs={'size':'50'}))
sender = forms.EmailField(max_length=30,
        widget=forms.TextInput(attrs={'size':'30'}))
```

3. Change the text field to the following code to use the Textarea Widget instead of TextInput, as shown in Listing 10.5:

```
text = forms.CharField(widget=forms.Textarea(
                    attrs={'rows':'6','cols':'75'}))
```

4. Save the iFriends/Home/views.py file.

5. Open the iFriends/templates/Home/contact_form.html file in an editor.

6. Use the following code to change how the form is rendered as a table. Combine the title and sender elements in the same row and place the text element on the next row, as shown in Listing 10.6:

```
<tr>
    <th>{{ eForm.title.label_tag }}</th>
    <td>{{ eForm.title }}</td>
    <th>{{ eForm.sender.label_tag }}:</th>
    <td>{{ eForm.sender }}</td>
</tr>
<tr>
    <th>{{ eForm.text.label_tag }}:</th>
    <td colspan="3">{{ eForm.text }}</td>
</tr>
```

Notice that the date field doesn't get added in the template. We don't want the user to be able to set the date, so that can be handled later by the view function.

7. Save the iFriends/templates/Home/contact_form.html file.

8. Access the following URL in a web browser to bring up the contact form view, shown in Figure 10.9, and verify that the form renders correctly:

    http://127.0.0.1:8000/Home/contact/

FIGURE 10.9
Modified contact form displayed as an HTML table in the contact_form.html template.

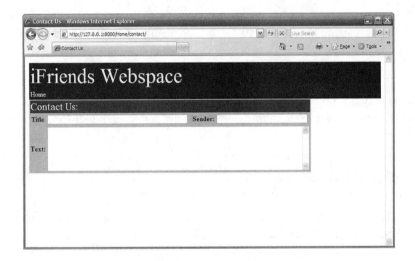

LISTING 10.5   Full Contents of iFriends/Home/views.py

```python
from django.shortcuts import render_to_response, get_object_or_404
from datetime import datetime
from django import newforms as forms

class EmailForm(forms.Form):
        title = forms.CharField(max_length=50,
                            widget=forms.TextInput(attrs={'size':'50'}))
        sender = forms.EmailField(max_length=30,
                            widget=forms.TextInput(attrs={'size':'30'}))
        date = forms.DateTimeField()
        text = forms.CharField(widget=forms.Textarea(
                            attrs={'rows':'6','cols':'75'}))

def contact_view(request):
    eForm = EmailForm()
    return render_to_response('home/contact_form.html', { 'eForm':eForm })
```

LISTING 10.6 Full Contents of `iFriends/templates/Home/contact_form.html`

```
{% extends "iFriends_base.html" %}

{% block title %}Contact Us{% endblock %}
{% block content %}
<table bgcolor="aaccdd">
<tr bgcolor="1111cc">
    <td colspan="4"><font color="white" size="5">
        Contact Us:
    </font></td>
</tr>
<tr>
    <th>{{ eForm.title.label_tag }}</th>
    <td>{{ eForm.title }}</td>
    <th>{{ eForm.sender.label_tag }}:</th>
    <td>{{ eForm.sender }}</td>
</tr>
<tr>
    <th>{{ eForm.text.label_tag }}:</th>
    <td colspan="3">{{ eForm.text }}</td>
</tr>
</table>
{% endblock %}
```

Summary

This hour discussed how to create Form objects in Django by defining each field. It also discussed how to quickly create Form objects from models using the `form_for_model()` and `form_for_instance()` functions. This hour discussed rendering forms to HTML as well.

In the final section of this hour, you learned how to customize the look and feel of the rendered form by customizing the Widget and using custom template code.

Q&A

Q. *Is there a way to find out what model is associated with a* **Form** *instance?*

A. Yes. The model can be accessed using the _model of the Form instance. Here's an example:

```
objClass = ContactForm._model
```

Q. *Can I create my own Widget?*

A. Yes. The following code defines a custom `TextInput` Widget that can be used in Forms:

```
class myWidget(forms.TextInput):
    def __init__(self, *args, **kwargs):
        kwargs.setdefault('attrs', {}).update({'size': '60'})
        super(myWidget, self).__init __(*args, **kwargs)
```

Workshop

The workshop consists of a set of questions and answers designed to solidify your understanding of the material covered in this hour. Try answering the questions before looking at the answers.

Quiz

1. What format is a form rendered in if you do not use the as_p, as_ul, or as_table functions?

2. How do you set the initial values for a form?

3. How to you create a form directly from a model?

4. How can you access the value of form elements from within a template?

Quiz Answers

1. The form is rendered as a table.

2. There are three ways. You can create the form from an instance of an object. You can set the `initial` attribute of the `Fields` in the form when you define it. You can pass a dictionary to the `Form` constructor when you create an instance of the form.

3. Call the `django.newforms.form_for_model()` function and pass it the model class.

4. You can use the dot syntax in a template to access form elements; for example, `form1.name`.

Exercises

1. Create a view function in the `iFriends/People/views.py` file that creates a `Form` instance for a `Blog` object.

2. Create an HTML template in the iFriends/templates/People directory that displays the `Blog` form you created in Exercise 1. Add a `render_to_response()` call to the view function to render the view to the new template.

3. Add an entry to the `URLconf` file to enable the `Blog` view to be accessed from a web browser.

HOUR 11

Using Views to Add and Update Data in the Database

What You'll Learn in This Hour:

▶ How to detect and handle GET and POST requests
▶ How to validate data from POST requests against the model
▶ How to update data in the database using forms
▶ How to add new objects to the database using forms

In Hour 10, "Adding Forms to Views," you learned how to create Form objects and render them as HTML. In this hour, we will extend that concept and show you how to use rendered forms to update the database.

The following sections take you through the process of displaying the Form during a GET request, retrieving the updated data from the form in a POST request, validating the data, and updating the database.

Handling GET and POST Requests

The first step in using Django Forms to update the database is to handle the GET and POST requests properly. Because the GET request is the initial request to just view the page, the request has no form data. When the user clicks the submit button on the form, Django receives a POST request that contains the form data and that can be processed.

The type of request can be determined by accessing the HttpRequest object that is sent to the view function. For a GET request, the value of the request is 'GET'. For a POST request, the value is 'POST'.

For example, the following code snippet checks to see if the `HttpRequest` is a GET or POST request:

```
def my_view(request):
    if request.method == 'GET':
        #handle GET
    if request.method == 'POST':
        #handle POST
```

▼
Try It Yourself

Handle GET and POST Requests in a View

In this section, you will add an update button to the person_from.html template and update the person_form() view to detect whether the request is a GET or POST. Follow these steps to add GET and POST request handling to the person_form() view:

1. Open the `iFriends/templates/People/person_form.html` file in an editor.

2. Add the following line of code, shown in Listing 11.1, to display a message at the top of the form page. The message variable is used to relay information about form processing to the web browser:

   ```
   <h3>{{ message }}</h3>
   ```

3. Add the following `<form>` and `<input>` tags around the table that renders the pForm form, shown in Listing 11.1, to add a POST method and a submit button to the form:

   ```
   <form method="post" action=".">
   . . .
   <input type="submit" name="submit" value="update" />
   </form>
   ```

4. Save the `iFriends/templates/People/person_form.html` file.

5. Open the `iFriends/People/views.py` file in an editor.

6. Remove the current contents of the person_form() view function.

7. Add the following lines of code to the person_form() view, shown in Listing 11.2, to set initial values for the Form, message, and Person objects:

   ```
   PersonForm = forms.form_for_model(Person)
   f = PersonForm()
   message = 'Unknown Request'
   p = get_object_or_404(Person, pk=pID)
   ```

▼

8. Add the following lines of code to the `person_form()` view, shown in Listing 11.2, to determine if the request is a GET request. If it is, create a Form instance, and set the message to an editing message:

```
if request.method == 'GET':
    PersonForm = forms.form_for_instance(p)
    f = PersonForm()
    message = 'Editing person %s ' % p.name
```

9. Add the following lines of code to the `person_form()` view, shown in Listing 11.2, to determine if the request is a POST request. If it is, set the message to an update request message (the code to actually update the data will be added later in this hour):

```
if request.method == 'POST':
    if request.POST['submit'] == 'update':
        message = 'Update Request for %s.' % p.name
```

10. Add the following lines of code to the `person_form()` view, shown in Listing 11.2, to render the response to the `person_form.html` template, and pass in the Form and message objects:

```
return render_to_response(
    'People/person_form.html',
    {'pForm':f,
     'message': message})
```

11. Save the `iFriends/People/views.py` file.

12. Access the following URL in a web browser to bring up the Person form view, shown in Figure 11.1, and verify that the form renders correctly with the update button and message:

```
http://127.0.0.1:8000/Person/Form/1/
```

13. Click the update button. The form should be displayed with the update request message and blank data, shown in Figure 11.2.

Notice that the form's data is blank after the POST request is submitted. This is because in the POST handler, we did not get the instance of the Person object and apply it to the form.

By the Way

FIGURE 11.1
Person form
view rendered
with an update
button in the
person_form.
html template.

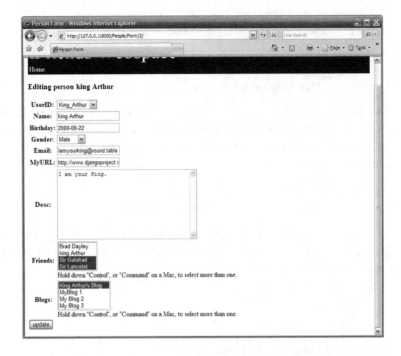

FIGURE 11.2
Person form
view generated
by clicking the
update button.

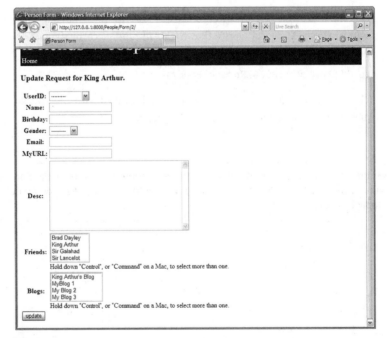

LISTING 11.1 Full Contents of iFriends/templates/People/person_form.html

```
{% extends "iFriends_base.html" %}
{% block title %}Person Form{% endblock %}
{% block content %}
<h3>{{ message }}</h3>

<form method="post" action=".">
<table>
{{ pForm }}
</table>
<input type="submit" name="submit" value="update" />
</form>
{% endblock %}
```

LISTING 11.2 Full Contents of the person_form() view in iFriends/People/views.py

```
def person_form(request, pID='0'):
    #default
    PersonForm = forms.form_for_model(Person)
    f = PersonForm()
    message = 'Unknown Request'
    p = get_object_or_404(Person, pk=pID)

    if request.method == 'GET':
        PersonForm = forms.form_for_instance(p)
        f = PersonForm()
        message = 'Editing person %s ' % p.name

    if request.method == 'POST':
        if request.POST['submit'] == 'update':
            message = 'Update Request for %s.' % p.name

    return render_to_response(
        'People/person_form.html',
        {'pForm':f,
         'message': message})
```

Validating Data from a POST Against the Model

The preceding section covered how to determine whether the request is a GET or POST. This section covers retrieving the values that the user entered into the HTML form and validating them before saving the data to the database.

The following sections describe the process of retrieving data from the post, validating the data, handling errors, and cleaning data.

Retrieving Data from a POST

The form data can be retrieved from a POST request by accessing the POST attribute of the HttpRequest object. The POST attribute of the HttpRequest object acts like a Python dictionary, with the labels of the form fields acting as keys.

For example, suppose we're handling a POST request from an HTML form that was rendered from the following Form class:

```
class DataForm(forms.Form):
    title = forms.CharField(max_length=20)
    text = forms.CharField()
    num = forms.IntegerField()
```

The following code snippet from a view function would be able to access the name, text, and num fields from the POST request:

```
name = request.POST['name']
text = request.POST['text']
num = request.POST['num']
```

Using this code, the view function now has the name, text, and num values that the user entered into the form. However, that data needs to be validated. You can't trust that the user will always input proper values in the form.

Validating the Data from a POST

Django provides the is_valid() function to verify that the values of fields in the Form object are the proper type and conform to the limits defined in the Field definitions.

The first step in validating the data that was retrieved from the POST request is to create a Form instance from the data. The following code collects the form data into a dictionary and uses that dictionary to create an instance of a BlogForm:

```
data = {'title': request.POST['title'],
        'text': request.POST['text'],
vForm = BlogForm(data)
```

This code creates an instance of the BlogForm class. The following code snippet uses that instance to verify whether the values in the form are valid:

```
if vForm.is_valid():
    #Use the form data
else:
    #Handle the invalid data
```

There is a quicker way to add all the values of a POST to create an instance of the Form object. Because the POST attribute of the HttpRequest acts like a dictionary, the POST attribute itself can act as the dictionary to create an instance of the Form. For example, the following line of code creates an instance of the BlogForm from the preceding example:

```
vForm = BlogForm(request.POST)
```

By the Way

Handling Errors in the POST Data

Handling errors in the POST data is determined by the form's flexibility. Usually the best thing to do is report back to the user that the form has problems and ask him or her to fix the problem and resubmit.

Django provides some tools to help fix forms, as well as to let users know that the form has a problem. We covered the is_valid() function in the preceding section. The problem with is_valid() is that all it does is return a True or False answer. It doesn't actually tell you which fields have a problem.

To find out what which fields have a problem, you can access the errors attribute of the Form object. When you do so, the Form is validated, and any fields that have problems are returned as a dictionary of Field names as keys and help text strings as the values. If the Form has no errors, an empty dictionary is returned.

For example, if a Form instance called vForm has an IntegerField named num that receives the string 'one' as the value from the POST, consider the following line of code:

```
badFields = vForm.errors
```

The value of badFields would be equal to the following:

```
{'num', [u'Enter ca whole number']}
```

The dictionary returned by the errors attribute can be used in several different ways. One way is to pass the dictionary to an error-handling template that displays the invalid forms with the help text. Another way the dictionary can be used is to parse the dictionary and use a helper function in the view to add default values to the invalid fields.

Accessing Clean Data in the Form

Accessing clean data in the form is not really part of validation, but it definitely is worth mentioning, and there isn't a better place to do so. One of the neat things about Django Forms is that they allow you to enter data in several different formats. The Form then normalizes the data to a consistent format. Appendix B, "Django Form Field Objects," lists the normalized value that the different Form Fields use.

The best examples of this are the date and time fields. You can add dates to a DateField in the form of '1999-12-31' or '12/31/1999', but they both normalize to a Python datetime.date object.

The concept of clean data is the normalized values of data from a Form. Clean data can be accessed using a couple of methods. The cleaned_data() function of a Form instance returns a dictionary containing the Field names as keys and the normalized values as the values.

For example, consider the following code:

```
class DataForm(forms.Form):
    title = forms.CharField(max_length=20)
    date = forms.DateField()
data = {'title': 'title', 'date':'2008-1-1'}
f = DataForm(data)
cleanData =  f.cleaned_data
```

The value of cleanData would be the following dictionary:

```
{'date': datetime.date(2008, 1, 1), 'title': u'title'}
```

Watch Out!

> If the form has errors, cleaned_data() raises an attribute error.

Clean data can also be accessed at the Field level by calling the clean() function of an instance of the Field class and passing in a valid value. The following code from the Django shell shows an example of using several different formats on a DateField object:

```
>>> fld = forms.DateField()
>>> fld.clean('2008-2-2')
datetime.date(2008, 2, 2)
>>> fld.clean('2/3/2008')
datetime.date(2008, 2, 3)
>>> fld.clean('Feb 4, 2008')
datetime.date(2008, 2, 4)
```

Try It Yourself ▼

Retrieve and Validate the Data from a POST Request

In the preceding "Try It Yourself" section, you modified the person_form() view function to determine if the request was a GET or POST. In this section, you will modify the POST handler to retrieve and validate the data from the POST request.

Follow these steps to modify the person_form() view to create a Form instance for a Person object and validate the data from the POST against that form:

1. Open the iFriends/Person/views.py file in an editor.

2. Add the following line of code to the POST handler in the person_form() view, shown in Listing 11.3, to create a Form class for the Person model:

   ```
   PersonForm = forms.form_for_instance(per)
   ```

3. Add the following line of code, shown in Listing 11.3, to create an instance of the PersonForm class using the data from the POST request:

   ```
   f = PersonForm(request.POST.copy())
   ```

> We use the copy() function to create a copy of the POST data as a new dictionary object. This is useful if you need to modify the data without affecting the HttpRequest.
>
> **By the Way**

4. Add the following lines of code, shown in Listing 11.3, to validate the Form data returned from the POST and to modify the message variable accordingly:

   ```
   if f.is_valid():
       message += ' Valid.'
   else:
       message += ' Invalid.'
   ```

5. Save the iFriends/Person/views.py file.

6. Access the following URL in a web browser to bring up the Person form view, shown in Figure 11.3:

   ```
   http://127.0.0.1:8000/Person/Form/1/
   ```

7. Modify the form with valid data, and click the update button. Verify that the validated message appears at the top of the form, as shown in Figure 11.3.

8. Modify the form with invalid data (set the UserID choice field to blank), and click the update button. Verify that the invalid message appears at the top of the form, as shown in Figure 11.4. ▼

FIGURE 11.3
Person form view generated by adding valid data and clicking the submit button.

FIGURE 11.4
Person form view generated by adding invalid data and clicking the submit button.

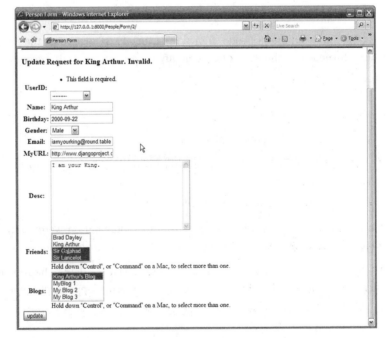

Did you notice the help text above the UserID field in the form? This is an added bonus of Django forms. Because the field was invalid when the instance was created, Django automatically puts in the help text.

LISTING 11.3 Full Contents of the `person_form()` view in iFriends/People/views.py

```
def person_form(request, pID='0'):
    #default
    PersonForm = forms.form_for_model(Person)
    f = PersonForm()
    message = 'Unknown Request'

    p = get_object_or_404(Person, pk=pID)

    if request.method == 'GET':
        PersonForm = forms.form_for_instance(p)
        f = PersonForm()
        message = 'Editing person %s ' % p.name

    if request.method == 'POST':
        if request.POST['submit'] == 'update':
            message = 'Update Request for %s.' % p.name
            PersonForm = forms.form_for_instance(p)
            f = PersonForm(request.POST.copy())
            if f.is_valid():
                message += ' Valid.'
            else:
                message += ' Invalid.'

    return render_to_response(
        'People/person_form.html',
        {'pForm':f,
         'message': message})
```

Updating Data in the Database

When you have finished validating data in the Form, the data can be saved in the database. To save the data in the Form to the database, use the save() function of the Form instance. The save() function of the Form object works the same way as the save() function of Model objects that was discussed in Hour 5, "Using Data from the Database in Views."

The save() function preprocesses the data in the Form, prepares the data to be inserted into the database, and inserts the data into the database. The Form save() function uses the same database table, so as long as the primary key matches, the object in the database is updated.

▼   **Try It Yourself**

Save Form Data to the Database

In this section, you will add save functionality to the person_form() view function so that when the update button is clicked, the data actually gets saved to the database. Follow these steps to call the save() function on the PersonForm object created in person_form():

1. Open the iFriends/Person/views.py file in an editor.

2. Add the following try block to the POST handler in the person_form() view, shown in Listing 11.4, to save the Form data to the database or to adjust the message with a database error:

   ```
   try:
           f.save()
           message += ' Updated.'
   except:
           message = ' Database Error.'
   ```

3. Save the iFriends/Person/views.py file.

4. Open the iFriends/templates/People/person_details.html file in an editor.

5. Add the following line of code to the first row of the HTML table, shown in Listing 11.4, in the person_details.html template file to add a dynamic link to the person_form() view:

   ```
   <a href="{% url iFriends.People.views.person_form pID=p.id %}">[Edit]</a>
   ```

6. Save the iFriends/templates/People/person_details.html file.

7. Access the following URL in a web browser to bring up the Person details() view, shown in Figure 11.5:

   ```
   http://127.0.0.1:8000/Person/Info/1/
   ```

8. Click the new Edit link to bring up the person_form() view, shown in Figure 11.5.

9. Modify the form with valid data, and click the update button.

10. Access the following URL again in a web browser to bring up the Person details() view, shown in Figure 11.5, and verify that the data has been updated:

    ```
    http://127.0.0.1:8000/Person/Info/1/
    ```

▼

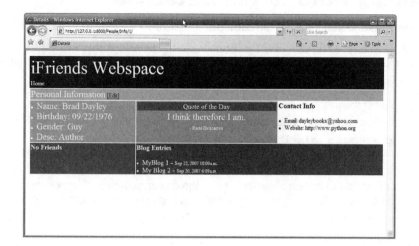

FIGURE 11.5
Person
details() view
with updated
values from the
Person form
view.

LISTING 11.4   Full Contents of the `person_form()` View in iFriends/
People/views.py

```python
def person_form(request, pID='0'):
    #default
    PersonForm = forms.form_for_model(Person)
    f = PersonForm()
    message = 'Unknown Request'

    p = get_object_or_404(Person, pk=pID)

    if request.method == 'GET':
        PersonForm = forms.form_for_instance(p)
        f = PersonForm()
        message = 'Editing person %s ' % p.name

    if request.method == 'POST':
        if request.POST['submit'] == 'update':
            message = 'Update Request for %s.' % p.name
            PersonForm = forms.form_for_instance(p)
            f = PersonForm(request.POST.copy())
            if f.is_valid():
                try:
                    f.save()
                    message += ' Updated.'
                except:
                    message = ' Database Error.'
            else:
                message += ' Invalid.'

    return render_to_response(
        'People/person_form.html',
        {'pForm':f,
         'message': message})
```

Adding Data to the Database

The process of adding data to the database is basically the same as updating existing data. You start with an empty form, add data to it, and then use save() to update the database. The difference is that the primary key of the Form object either doesn't already exist in the database or is not present in the object.

Django adds the primary key ID to objects if one is not specified in the model. However, you can assign your own primary key in the model and then set the value in the view function to tell Django to add the data as a new object.

Watch Out!

> If you do decide to assign a primary key to the object, you need to make certain that the key is unique. Otherwise, existing data might be overwritten.

▼ **Try It Yourself**

Add New Objects to the Database Using Form Data

In this section, you will add a new view to the People views that will render a form to create Blog objects and assign them to a Person object. You will add a POST handler just as you did in the person_form() view that will collect data from the POST request. However, this time you will start with a blank Blog Form so that a new Blog object is added to the database. You will also be required to add code to add the Blog object to a specific Person object.

Follow these steps to add the add_blog() view to the iFriends project:

1. Open the iFriends/Person/views.py file in an editor.

2. Create a new view function called add_blog(), as shown in Listing 11.5.

3. Add the following lines of code, shown in Listing 11.5, to initialize a BlogForm instance and message and to get the Person object that the new Blog will be added to:

```
BlogForm = forms.form_for_model(Blog, fields=('title', 'text'))
bf = BlogForm()
message = 'Unknown Request'
p = get_object_or_404(Person, pk=pID)
```

4. Add the following lines of code, shown in Listing 11.5, to add a simple GET handler:

```
if request.method == 'GET':
    message = 'Add Blog for %s ' % p.name
```

▼

5. Add the following lines of code, shown in Listing 11.5, to begin adding the POST handler to the view:

```
if request.method == 'POST':
    if request.POST['submit'] == 'Add':
```

6. Add the following line of code to the POST handler, shown in Listing 11.5, to create an instance of the BlogForm with only the title and text Fields from the POST data that will be rendered in the template:

```
bf = BlogForm(request.POST.copy())
```

7. Add the following lines of code to the POST handler, shown in Listing 11.5, to create a Form class for the full Blog. Add the title and text Fields from the POST data and a date Field set to the current time to a dictionary. Use that dictionary to create an instance of the SaveForm for the Blog object:

```
SaveForm = forms.form_for_model(Blog)
postDict = request.POST.copy()
postDict['date'] = datetime.now()
save_bf = SaveForm(postDict)
```

8. Add the following line of code to the POST handler to validate the instance of the Blog SaveForm and either save the object or set the error message:

```
if save_bf.is_valid():
    try:
        bObj = save_bf.save()
. . .
        message = 'Blog added to %s.' % p.name
    except:
        message = 'Database Error.'
else:
    message = 'Invalid data in Form.'
```

9. Add the following lines of code to the try block in the POST handler, shown in Listing 11.5, to add the new Blog object to the Person object, and save the Person object:

```
p.blogs.add(bObj)
p.save()
```

10. Add the following lines of code to the end of the add_blog() function, shown in Listing 11.5, to render the data to an add_blog_form.html template file.

```
return render_to_response(
    'People/add_blog_form.html',
    {'bForm':bf, 'message': message})
```

11. Save the iFriends/Person/views.py file.

12. Create and open a file called iFriends/templates/Person/add_blog_form. html in an editor.

13. Add the code shown in Listing 11.6 to the file to render a `Blog Form` object, bForm, as a table, and add an Add button to submit the form.

14. Save the `iFriends/templates/Person/add_blog_form.html` file.

15. Open the `iFriends/templates/Person/person_details.html` file in an editor.

16. Add the following lines of code to the `<h3>` header "Blog Entries," shown in Listing 11.7, to add a link to the `add_blog()` view function:

```
<a href="
 {% url iFriends.People.views.add_blog pID=p.id %}
 ">[+]</a>
```

17. Open the `iFriends/People/urls.py` file in an editor.

18. Add the following line to the URL patterns to enable the `add_blog()` view function:

```
(r'^AddBlogForm/(?P<pID>\d+)/$', 'add_blog'),
```

19. Save the `iFriends/People/urls.py` file.

20. Access the following URL in a web browser to bring up the `Person details()` view, shown in Figure 11.6, and verify that the new link has been added to the Blog object:

```
http://127.0.0.1:8000/Person/Info/1/
```

FIGURE 11.6
Person details() view with a link to the add_blog() view.

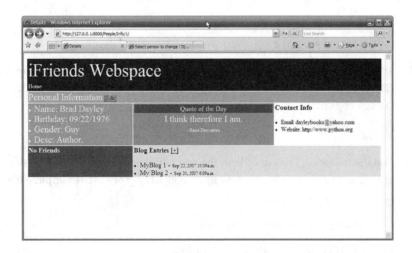

21. Click the + link to bring up the `blog_add()` view, shown in Figure 11.7.

22. Add data to the form, and click the Add button. The message should indicate that the new blog entry was added.

FIGURE 11.7
add_blog()
view rendering a
Blog Form.

23. Access the following URL again in a web browser to bring up the Person details() view, shown in Figure 11.8. This time the new entry you created in step 22 should show up in the blog list.

```
http://127.0.0.1:8000/Person/Info/1/
```

You may need to refresh the browser to retrieve a fresh copy of the details() view to see the new blog entry.

Watch Out!

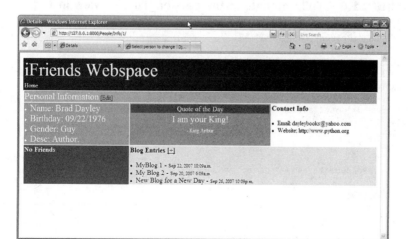

FIGURE 11.8
Person
details() view
with an updated
blog entry from
the add_blog()
view.

LISTING 11.5   Full Contents of the add_blog() view in
`iFriends/People/views.py`

```python
def add_blog_form(request, pID='0'):
    BlogForm = forms.form_for_model(Blog, fields=('title', 'text'))
    bf = BlogForm()
    message = 'Unknown Request'
    p = get_object_or_404(Person, pk=pID)

    if request.method == 'GET':
        message = 'Add Blog for %s ' % p.name

    if request.method == 'POST':
        if request.POST['submit'] == 'Add':
            bf = BlogForm(request.POST.copy())
            SaveForm = forms.form_for_model(Blog)
            postDict = request.POST.copy()
            postDict['date'] = datetime.now()
            save_bf = SaveForm(postDict)
            if save_bf.is_valid():
                try:
                    bObj = save_bf.save()
                    p.blogs.add(bObj)
                    p.save()
                    message = 'Blog added to %s.' % p.name
                except:
                    message = 'Database Error.'
            else:
                message = 'Invalid data in Form.'

    return render_to_response(
        'People/add_blog_form.html',
        {'bForm':bf, 'message': message})
```

LISTING 11.6   Full Contents of the person_form() view in
`iFriends/People/views.py`

```
{% extends "iFriends_base.html" %}

{% block title %}Blog Form{% endblock %}
{% block content %}
<h3>{{ message }}</h3>

<form method="post" action=".">
<table>
{{ bForm }}
</table>

<input type="submit" name="submit" value="Add" />
</form>
{% endblock %}
```

LISTING 11.7   Full Contents of iFriends/templates/People/ person_details.html

```
% extends "iFriends_base.html" %}

{% block title %}Details{% endblock %}
{% block content %}
<table width=100%>
<tr bgcolor="aabbcc"><td colspan="3">
<font size="5" color="white">Personal Information</font>
<a href="{% url iFriends.People.views.person_form pID=p.id %}">[Edit]</a>
</font>
</td></tr>
<tr valign="top"><td width=30% bgcolor="aaaaaa"><font color="white" size="5">
    <li>Name: {{p.name}}</li>
    <li>Birthday: {{ p.birthday|date:"m/d/Y" }}</li>
    <li>Gender:
        {% ifequal p.gender "M" %}
            Guy
        {% else %}
            Gal
        {% endifequal %}
    </li>
    <li>Desc: {{ p.desc }} </li>
</font></td>
<td width=40% bgcolor="aa99aa"><font color="white" size="4">
    {% include "quote.html" %}
</font></td>
<td width=30%>
    <h3>Contact Info</h3>
    <li>Email: {{ p.email }}</li>
    <li>Website: {{ p.favoriteURL }}</li>
</td></tr>
<tr>
<td width="30%" bgcolor="556677" valign="top">
    <font color="white" size="4">
    {% with p.friends.all as fl %}
    <h3>
        {{ fl|length|yesno:"iFriend,No Friend"}}{{fl|length|pluralize}}
    </h3>
    {% for f in fl %}
    <li>{{ f.name }}</li>
    {% endfor %}
    {% endwith %}
    </font>
</td>
<td width="70%" bgcolor="eeeeee" colspan="2" valign="top">
    <font size="4">
    {% with p.blogs.all as bl %}
    <h3>
        {{ bl|length|yesno:"Blog,No Blog"}}
        Entr{{ bl|length|pluralize:"y,ies"}}
        <a href="
        {% url iFriends.People.views.add_blog pID=p.id %}
        ">[+]</a>
    </h3>
    {% for b in bl %}
    <li>{{ b.title }} -
```

LISTING 11.7   continued

```
     <font size="2"> {{ b.date|date:"M d, Y g:ma" }}</font>
    </li>
    {% endfor %}
    {% endwith %}
    </font>
</td>
</tr>
</table>
{% endblock %}
```

Summary

In this hour, you learned how to handle GET and POST requests inside view functions. You also learned how to retrieve data from a POST request. In addition, you learned how to use Form objects to validate and save the data from a POST in the database.

Q&A

Q. *Is there a way to determine if a* **Form** *object has errors from the template file?*

A. Yes. If you access the has_errors attribute of a Form object in a template, it returns true if the form does not pass validation:

```
{% if pForm.has_errors %}
<p>Form Error. Please try again.</p>
{% endif %}
```

Q. *Is there a way to modify the* **save** *function of a* **Form** *object to perform extra tasks before the save takes place?*

A. Yes. The following code snippet from a Form class definition overrides the save() function:

```
class FormClass(forms.Form):
    . . . .
    def save(self):
        #Do Something
        super(FormClass, self).save()
```

Workshop

The workshop consists of a set of questions and answers designed to solidify your understanding of the material covered in this hour. Try answering the questions before looking at the answers.

Quiz

1. What are two ways you can determine if the data in a Form object is valid?

2. How can the data from an HTML form be retrieved from a POST request?

3. How do you save the data in a Form object to the database?

Quiz Answers

1. Call the is_valid() function of the object. Access the errors attribute of the object.

2. From the POST attribute of the HttpRequest object that is passed into the view function.

3. Use the save() function of the Form object.

Exercises

1. Add a new view to the Quotes application to add Quote objects to the database.

2. Add another view to the Quotes application to modify Quote objects in the database.

HOUR 12

Utilizing Generic Views

What You'll Learn in This Hour:

▶ How to use simple generic views
▶ How to display a list of objects using generic views
▶ How to display object details using generic views
▶ How to display date-based object indexes using generic views
▶ How to use generic views to create objects
▶ How to use generic views to update objects
▶ How to use generic views to delete objects

Django provides a set of easy-to-use packages called generic views that allow you to generate basic generic views quickly. Generic views do a good job of abstracting common tasks such as building web views to display lists of objects, as well as create, update, and delete objects.

Basically, generic views do the work that is normally done in an application's `views.py` file. Using generic views, you can create useful views without having to use any Python code.

The following sections describe generic views and how to use them to display objects, lists of objects, and forms to create, change, and delete objects.

Understanding Generic Views

Generic views are easy to implement. To implement a generic view, you create a template for the generic view to render and then add an URL pattern to the `URLconf` file that enables the view.

The four basic parts of implementing generic views are the arguments dictionary, URL pattern, context variables, and HTML template. The following sections discuss each part.

Arguments Dictionary

The arguments dictionary is a Python dictionary of arguments that are passed to the generic view function when the URL is accessed. Each generic view has a list of required and optional arguments. The arguments allow you to define the view's behavior and attributes.

Some arguments define the behavior of the view function, and others are used as data in the template file. For example, the following dictionary defines arguments that can be passed to an `object_list` generic view:

```
quote_list_info = {
    'queryset' : Quote.objects.all(),
    'allow_empty' : True,
}
```

The argument `queryset` is a `QuerySet` object of all objects in the `Quote` model. The `queryset` argument gives the generic list a set of data that can be accessed from the generic view template. The `allow_empty` argument tells the generic list function to accept an empty list.

The arguments that are available to the generic view functions handle most of the views' needs. However, sometimes you want to pass your own custom variables to the view. Django provides the `extra_context` argument to solve this problem. The `extra_context` argument is a dictionary that defines auxiliary data that you want to pass to the template. You can pass objects or callables as part of the `extra_context` dictionary.

> Be careful if you pass `QuerySet` objects as part of the `extra_context` dictionary. `QuerySets` are cached when they are first evaluated, so the data might be stale by the time it is passed to the view. If you need fresh data in the `QuerySet`, you can pass the `QuerySet` by passing a function and having the function create the `QuerySet`.

Table 12.1 lists all the arguments that can be used in the different generic views.

TABLE 12.1   Generic View Arguments That Can Be Added to the Info Dictionary for Generic Views

Argument	Description
allow_empty	Boolean. Defaults to False. If set to True, the page is displayed even if no objects are in the list. Otherwise, a 404 error is displayed.
allow_future	Boolean. Defaults to False. If set to True, date-based views display dates even if they are in the future.
context_processors	A list of template-context processors to apply to the views template.
date_field	Specifies the name of the DateField or DateTimeField of the model that date-based views use to query dates to build a list of objects.
day	Specifies the day, formatted by the day_format argument, that date-based views use to query dates to build a list of objects.
day_format	Defaults to %d. Specifies the format to use when specifying the day argument.
extra_context	A dictionary object that contains whatever extra objects, functions, and auxiliary information you want to pass to the view.
login_required	Boolean. Defaults to False. If set to True, displays the view only if the user is logged in.
make_object_list	Boolean. Defaults to False. If set to True, the archive_year view retrieves a list of objects and passes it to the template as the object_list context variable.
mimetype	Defaults to DEFAULT_CONTENT_TYPE. Specifies the MIME type to use for the resulting document.
model	Specifies which model to use when building forms to create, update, and delete generic views.
month	Specifies the month, formatted by the month_format argument, that date-based views use to query dates to build a list of objects.
month_format	Defaults to %d. Specifies the format to use when specifying the month argument.
num_latest	Defaults to 15. Specifies the number objects to send to the template as the latest context variable.

TABLE 12.1   Continued

Argument	Description
object_id	Specifies the primary key value to use when accessing objects directly.
page	Specifies a 1-based integer designating the current page number.
paginate_by	An integer. Specifies the number of objects to be displayed per page. If you use the paginate_by argument, a page argument is required as well.
post_delete_redirect	Specifies an URL to redirect the browser to after the delete operation.
post_save_redirect	Specifies an URL to redirect the browser to after the save operation.
queryset	Specifies a QuerySet object to use as a list of objects.
slug_field	A slug and slug_field can be used instead of the object_id argument in some views.
template	The full name and path, relative to the template directory, to use in the direct_to_template view.
template_loader	The template loader to use when loading the template.
template_name	The full name and path, relative to the template directory, of a template file to use to render the page.
template_object_name	Designates the name of the context variable that is assigned to the object.
url	Specifies the URL to redirect the browser to in the redirect_to view.
week	Specifies the two-digit week that date-based views use to query dates to build a list of objects.
year	Specifies the four-digit year that date-based views use to query dates to build a list of objects.

Which arguments are required and which are optional for each generic view function depends on which view function you are using. This topic is discussed later in this hour.

URL Pattern

Generic template URL patterns follow the same syntax as normal URL patterns. The only differences are that the second argument points to a generic view package instead of a view function in the application, and the dictionary of arguments is required as the third argument.

For example, to create an URL pattern to access the `object_list` generic view, you would define an argument dictionary and add an URL pattern similar to the following to the `URLconf` file:

```
obj_dict = {
    'queryset' : Quotes.objects.all()
    'allow_empty' : True
}
urlpatterns = patterns('django.views.generic.list_detail',
    (r'^obj_list/$', object_list, obj_dict),
}
```

Context Variables

Context variables are variables that can be accessed from within the template file. Context variables in generic views are the same as creating a dictionary and passing it to the `render_to_response()` function.

Table 12.2 lists the context variables that get passed to the template.

TABLE 12.2 Context Variables Generated by Generic Views That Are Available in the Templates

Variable	Description
date_list	A list of `datetime` objects representing all the dates that have objects available for the date-based view. For `archive_index`, the objects are year-based for all objects. For `archive_year`, the objects are month-based for one year.
day	A `datetime` object representing the day of the date-based view.
first_on_page	The 1-based index for the first result on the current page in pagination.
form	A `Form` object created for a model in the object creation, update, and deletion views.

TABLE 12.2   Continued

Variable	Description
has_next	Boolean. Is True if there is a next page in pagination.
has_previous	Boolean. Is True if there is a previous page in pagination.
hits	The total number of pages in pagination.
is_paginated	Boolean. Is True if the paginate_by argument was added to the view.
last_on_page	The 1-based index for the last result on the current page in pagination.
latest	A list of the latest arguments in the system. The number of latest objects corresponds to the num_latest argument.
month	A datetime object representing the month of the date-based view.
next	The 1-based page number for the next page in pagination.
next_day	A datetime object representing the next day of the date-based view.
next_month	A datetime object representing the next month of the date-based view.
object	An object passed to the template by the view function. The context variable object is the default value of the template_object_name argument.
object_list	A list of objects passed to the template by the view function.
page	The current page number in pagination.
pages	The total number of pages in pagination.
params	A dictionary of parameters captured by the URLconf and passed to the direct_to_template view.
previous	The 1-based page number for the previous page in pagination.
previous_day	A datetime object representing the previous day of the date-based view.
previous_month	A datetime object representing the previous month of the date-based view.
results_per_page	The number that was specified by the paginate_by argument.
week	A datetime object representing the week of the date-based view.
year	A datetime object representing the year of the date-based view.

> Which context variables that are available in the template for each generic view depends on which view function rendered it. This topic is discussed later in this hour.

By the Way

Generic HTML Template

Generic templates are the same as other Django HTML template files. You need to create a template file to render each generic view. The context variables listed in the preceding section can be accessed from the generic view.

For example, you would use the following code to access the year context variable of a `django.views.generic.date_based.archive_year` view from the template:

```
{{ year }}
```

Using Simple Generic Views

The first two generic views we will look at are the simple generic views `django.views.generic.simple.direct_to_template` and `django.views.generic.simple.redirect_to`.

direct_to_template

The `direct_to_template` view allows you to render a template file directly from the URLconf without using a view function.

The following list describes the required arguments, optional arguments, and context variables available when using the `direct_to_template` view (see Tables 12.1 and 12.2 for information about the arguments and context variables):

- ▶ The required argument is `template`.
- ▶ The optional arguments are `extra_context` and `mimetype`.
- ▶ The context variable is `params`.

The following is a sample URL pattern for the `direct_to_template` view:

```
(r'^(?P<num>\d+/$', 'direct_to_template', { 'template' : 'index.html'}),
```

Any arguments passed in from the URL are available in the template from the params context variable. For example, you could use the following line of code to access the num argument from the preceding URL pattern:

```
{{ params.num }}
```

redirect_to

The `redirect_to` view allows you to redirect the HTTP request to another URL. This can be useful if you want to support old URLs or redirect several URLs to a specific view.

For example, the following URL pattern redirects /files/2008 to /arch/2008:

```
(r'^files/(?P<year>\d{4}/$', 'redirect_to', { 'url' : '/arch/%(year)'}),
```

The following list describes the required arguments, optional arguments, and context variables available when using the `redirect_to` view (see Tables 12.1 and 12.2 for information about the arguments and context variables):

- ▶ The required argument is `url`.
- ▶ There are no optional arguments.
- ▶ The context variable is `params`.

Displaying an Object List in a Generic View

The `django.views.generic.list_detail.object_list` view creates a generic view for rendering a list of objects. The `object_list` view requires a QuerySet argument, `queryset`, that contains the objects you want to list.

For example, if you wanted to list all the objects in the `Blog` model with a title that contains the word "test," you would make the following assignment to the `queryset` argument:

```
list_info = { 'queryset' : Blog.objects.filter(title__contains='test')}
```

The following list describes the required arguments, optional arguments, and context variables available when using the `object_list` view (see Tables 12.1 and 12.2 for information about the arguments and context variables):

- ▶ The required argument is `queryset`.
- ▶ The optional arguments are `paginate_by`, `page`, `template_name`, `template_loader`, `extra_context`, `allow_empty`, `context_processors`, `template_object_name`, and `mimetype`.
- ▶ The context variables are `object_list`, `is_paginated`, `results_per_page`, `has_next`, `has_previous`, `page`, `next`, `previous`, `last_on_page`, `first_on_page`, `pages`, and `hits`.

▶ The default `template_name` is *app_label*/*model_name*_list.html (such as People/Person_list.html).

The following code snippet shows an example of defining a generic `object_list` view in the URLconf file:

```
list_info = {
    'queryset' : Blog.objects.filter(title__contains='test'),
    'allow_empty' : True,
}
urlpatterns = patterns('django.views.generic.list_detail',
    (r'^blog_list/$', object_list, list_info),
}
```

The following template code snippet shows an example of accessing the context variable `object_list` in a template:

```
{% for blog in object_list %}
    <li>{{ blog.title }}</li>
{% endfor %}
```

Try It Yourself ▼

Use a Generic View to Display a List of Objects

In this section, you will use the `object_list` generic view to display a list of Quote objects. Follow these steps to create a template and update the URLconf file to enable the view:

1. Create and open a file called iFriends/templates/Quotes/quote_list.html in an editor.

2. Add the following for loop code that accesses the `object_list` context variable to generate a list of Quote objects:

```
{% for q in object_list %}
    <li>
        {{ q.text }}
        <font size="3">-{{ q.by }}
        <a href="/generic/quote_update/{{q.id}}/">[Update]</a>
        <a href="/generic/quote_delete/{{q.id}}/">[Delete]</a>
        </font>
    </li>
{% endfor %}
```

3. Add the rest of the code, shown in Listing 12.1, to extend the site base template and add the rest of the supporting HTML code for the view.

4. Save the iFriends/templates/Quotes/quote_list.html file.

▼

5. Open the `iFriends/urls.py` file in an editor.

6. Add the following lines of code to import the `list_detail` view and the `Quote` model:

```
from django.views.generic import list_detail
from iFriends.Quotes.models import Quote
```

7. Add the following lines of code, shown in Listing 12.2, to create a dictionary to use for the `object_list` view:

```
quote_list_info = {
    'queryset' : Quote.objects.all(),
    'allow_empty' : True,
}
```

8. Add the following URL patterns to enable the generic `object_list` view:

```
urlpatterns += patterns('',
    (r'^generic/quote_list/$',
        list_detail.object_list, quote_list_info),
)
```

9. Save the `iFriends/urls.py` file.

10. Access the following URL in a browser, as shown in Figure 12.1, to verify that the `object_list` view works:

```
http://127.0.0.1:8000/generic/quote_list/
```

FIGURE 12.1
Generic object
list view for the
Quote objects.

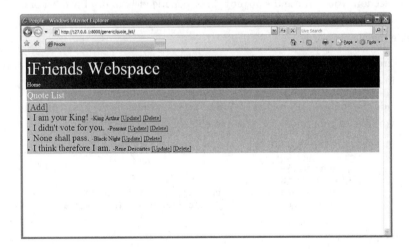

LISTING 12.1 Full Contents of `iFriends/templates/Quotes/`
`quote_list.html`

```
{% extends "iFriends_base.html" %}

{% block title %}Quote List{% endblock %}
{% block content %}
<table width=100%>
<tr bgcolor="aabbcc"><td colspan="3">
<font size="5" color="white">Quote List</font>
</td></tr>
<tr valign="top"><td width=30% bgcolor=" aadddd ">
<font size="5">
<a href="/generic/quote_add">[Add]</a>
{% for q in object_list %}
    <li>
        {{ q.text }}
        <font size="3">-{{ q.by }}
        <a href="/generic/quote_update/{{q.id}}/">[Update]</a>
        <a href="/generic/quote_delete/{{q.id}}/">[Delete]</a>
        </font>
    </li>
{% endfor %}
</font></td></tr>
{% endblock %}
```

The [Add], [Update], and [Delete] links are for generic views that will be created later in this hour.

By the Way

LISTING 12.2 Generic Section Fragment for `Quote` Objects in the
`iFriends/urls.py` File

```
. . .
#Quote generic section
from django.views.generic import list_detail
from iFriends.Quotes.models import Quote

quote_list_info = {
    'queryset' : Quote.objects.all(),
    'allow_empty' : True,
}

urlpatterns += patterns('',
    (r'^generic/quote_list/$',
      list_detail.object_list, quote_list_info),
)
```

Displaying Object Details in a Generic View

The `django.views.generic.list_detail.object_detail` view creates a generic view for rendering a specific object. The `object_detail` view requires a queryset argument that contains objects to search, and an `object_id` argument that contains the primary key for the object you want to display.

The following list describes the required arguments, optional arguments, and context variables available when using the `object_details` view (see Tables 12.1 and 12.2 for information about the arguments and context variables):

▶ The required argument is `queryset`.

▶ The optional arguments are `paginate_by`, `page`, `template_name`, `template_loader`, `extra_context`, `allow_empty`, `context_processors`, `template_object_name`, and `mimetype`.

▶ The context variables are `object_list`, `is_paginated`, `results_per_page`, `has_next`, `has_previous`, `page`, `next`, `previous`, `last_on_page`, `first_on_page`, `pages`, and `hits`.

▶ The default `template_name` is *app_label*/*model_name*_details.html (such as People/Person_details.html).

The following `URLconf` code snippet shows an example of defining a generic `object_details` view that retrieves the `object_id` variable from the URL and assigns the object name to `blog` in the context variables:

```
detail_info = {
    'queryset' : Blog.objects.all(),
    'template_object_name' : 'blog',
}
urlpatterns = patterns('django.views.generic.list_detail',
    (r'^blog_detail/(?P<object_id>\d+)/$',
        object_details, detail_info),
}
```

The following template code snippet shows an example of accessing the `blog` context variable just assigned in the template:

```
<h1>{{ blog.title }}</li>
{{ blog.text }}
```

Try It Yourself ▼

Use a Generic View to Display Object Details

In this section, you will use the object_details generic view to display the fields of a Blog object. Follow these steps to create a template and update the URLconf file to enable the view:

1. Create and open a file called iFriends/templates/Blogs/blog_details. html in an editor.

2. Add the following code that accesses the blog context variable, which will be defined later in the URLconf file, to display the details of the Quote object:

```
<font size="5" color="white">{{ blog.title }}</font>
<font size="2">{{ blog.date }}</font>
```

3. Add the rest of the code, shown in Listing 12.3, to extend the site base template and add the rest of the supporting HTML code for the view.

4. Save the iFriends/templates/Blogs/blog_details.html file.

5. Open the iFriends/urls.py file in an editor.

6. Add the following lines of code to import the list_detail view and the Blog model:

```
from django.views.generic import list_detail
from iFriends.People.models import Blog
```

7. Add the following lines of code, shown in Listing 12.4, to create a dictionary to use for the object_details view that sets the object name to blog and defines a custom template file:

```
blog_detail_info = {
    'queryset' : Blog.objects.all(),
    'template_object_name' : 'blog',
    'template_name' : 'Blogs/blog_detail.html',
}
```

8. Add the following URL patterns to enable the generic object_detail view:

```
urlpatterns += patterns('',
    (r'^generic/blog_details/(?P<object_id>\d+)/$',
        list_detail.object_detail, blog_detail_info),
)
```

9. Save the iFriends/urls.py file.

10. Access the following URL in a browser, as shown in Figure 12.2, to verify that the object_detail view works:

```
http://127.0.0.1:8000/generic/blog_details/1/
```
▼

FIGURE 12.2
Generic object
details view for
a Blog object.

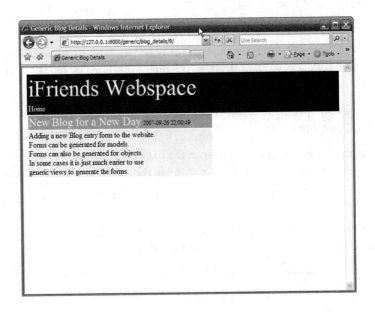

LISTING 12.3   Full Contents of `iFriends/templates/Blogs/`
`blog_detail.html`

```
{% extends "iFriends_base.html" %}

{% block title %}Generic Blog Details{% endblock %}
{% block content %}
<table width="400">
<tr bgcolor="aabbcc"><td colspan="3">
<font size="5" color="white">{{ blog.title }}</font>
<font size="2">{{ blog.date }}</font>
</td></tr>
<tr valign="top"><td bgcolor="ddffff">
{{ blog.text }}
</td></tr>
{% endblock %}
```

LISTING 12.4   Generic Section for `Blog` Objects in the
`iFriends/urls.py` File

```
#Blog generic section
from django.views.generic import list_detail
from iFriends.People.models import Blog

blog_detail_info = {
    'queryset' : Blog.objects.all(),
    'template_object_name' : 'blog',
```

```
        'template_name' : 'Blogs/blog_detail.html',
}

urlpatterns += patterns('',
    (r'^generic/blog_details/(?P<object_id>\d+)/$',
        list_detail.object_detail, blog_detail_info),
)
```

Displaying Date-Based Objects in a Generic View

Django provides several date-based generic views in the django.views.generic. date_based package to help you build views based on date Fields in the model. All these date-based views require a queryset argument that contains objects to search, and a date_field argument that contains the Field name to query when building the date-based view.

Each date-based view uses the date_field argument to query the queryset based on day, month, week, or year arguments to generate a list of either dates or objects.

The following sections describe each of the date-based views and list the required arguments, optional arguments, and context variables (see Tables 12.1 and 12.2 for information about the arguments and context variables).

If the date in the object's date_field is in the future, it is not displayed by the date-based views unless the allow_future argument is set to True.

Did you Know?

archive_index

The archive_index view is used to generate a year-based index view. Basically, the archive_index view creates a date object for each different year represented in the queryset and sends that list the template as the date_list variable. You can then use the date_list variable to list the years represented in the index.

► The required arguments are queryset and date_field.

► The optional arguments are num_latest, template_name, template_loader, extra_context, allow_empty, context_processors, mimetype, allow_future, and template_object_name.

► The context variables are date_list, latest, and extra_context.

► The default template_name is *app_label/model_name*_archive.html.

archive_year

The archive_year view is used to generate a month-based index view. In addition to the queryset and date_field arguments, the archive_year view requires a year argument. The queryset is reduced to objects which have a date_field that matches the year argument.

The archive_year view creates a date object for each month represented in the queryset and sends that list the template as the date_list variable. You can then use the date_list variable to list the years represented in the index.

- ▶ The required arguments are year, queryset, and date_field.
- ▶ The optional arguments are make_object_list, template_name, template_loader, extra_context, allow_empty, context_processors, mimetype, allow_future, and template_object_name.
- ▶ The context variables are year, date_list, latest, object_list, and extra_context.
- ▶ The default template_name is *app_label/model_name*_year.html.

archive_month

The archive_month view is used to generate a month-based object view. In addition to the queryset and date_field arguments, the archive_month view requires year and month arguments. The queryset is reduced to objects whose date_field matches the year and month arguments.

The archive_month view sends that queryset to the template as the object_list variable. You can then use the object_list variable to list the objects in the template.

- ▶ The required arguments are month, year, queryset, and date_field.
- ▶ The optional arguments are month_format, template_name, template_loader, extra_context, allow_empty, context_processors, mimetype, allow_future, and template_object_name.
- ▶ The context variables are month, next_month, previous_month, object_list, and extra_context.
- ▶ The default template_name is *app_label/model_name*_month.html.

archive_week

The archive_week view is used to generate a week-based object view. In addition to the queryset and date_field arguments, the archive_week view requires year and week arguments. The queryset is reduced to objects whose date_field matches the year and week arguments.

The archive_week view sends that queryset to the template as the object_list variable. You can then use the object_list variable to list the objects in the template.

- ▶ The required arguments are week, year, queryset, and date_field.

- ▶ The optional arguments are template_name, template_loader, extra_context, allow_empty, context_processors, mimetype, allow_future, and template_object_name.

- ▶ The context variables are week, object_list, and extra_context.

- ▶ The default template_name is *app_label/model_name*_week.html.

archive_day

The archive_day view is used to generate a day-based object view. In addition to the queryset and date_field arguments, the archive_month view requires year, month and day arguments. The queryset is reduced to objects whose date_field matches the year, month, and day arguments.

The archive_day view sends that queryset to the template as the object_list variable. You can then use the object_list variable to list the objects in the template.

- ▶ The required arguments are day, month, year, queryset, and date_field.

- ▶ The optional arguments are day_format, month_format, template_name, template_loader, extra_context, allow_empty, context_processors, mimetype, allow_future, and template_object_name.

- ▶ The context variables are day, next_day, previous_day, object_list, and extra_context.

- ▶ The default template_name is *app_label/model_name*_day.html.

archive_today

The `archive_today` view is the same as the `archive_day` view, except that it does not require the year, month, and day arguments. Instead, it uses the current system values of year, month, and day.

archive_detail

The `archive_detail` view works similar to the `archive_day` view, with two exceptions. The first is that it requires an additional `object_id` or `slug` argument. The second is that the only context variables available are `extra_context` and `object`. The `object` variable allows you to access the object to display the details.

URL Patterns for Date-Based Views

The following code illustrates the basic URL patterns for the `archive_day`, `archive_week`, `archive_month`, `archive_year`, and `archive_index` views, respectively:

```
urlpatterns = patterns('django.views.generic.date_based',
    (r'^(?P<year>\d{4})/(?P<month>[a-z]{3})/(?P<day>\w{1,2})/(?P<slug>[-\w]+)/$',
        'object_detail', info_dict),
    (r'^(?P<year>\d{4})/(?P<month>[a-z]{3})/(?P<day>\w{1,2})/$',
        'archive_day',   info_dict),
    (r'^(?P<year>\d{4})/(?P<week>\d{2})/$',
        'archive_week', info_dict),
    (r'^(?P<year>\d{4})/(?P<month>[a-z]{3})/$',
        'archive_month', info_dict),
    (r'^(?P<year>\d{4})/$', 'archive_year',  info_dict),
    (r'^$','archive_index', info_dict),
)
```

▼   **Try It Yourself**

Use a Generic View to Display a Date-Based Index of Objects

In this section, you will use the `archive_index`, `archive_year`, and `archive_month` generic views to display a date-based index of `Blog` objects. Follow these steps to create a template for year index, month index, and blog index views and update the URLconf file to enable the views:

1. Create and open a file called `iFriends/templates/Blogs/blog_arch.html` in an editor.

▼

2. Add the following for loop code to the file to generate a list of years containing Blog objects and add links to the blog_year index view for each year:

```
{% for date in date_list %}
    <li>
    <a href="/generic/blog_arch/{{ date|date:"Y" }}/">
        {{ date|date:"Y" }}</a>
    </li>
{% endfor %}
```

3. Add the rest of the code, shown in Listing 12.5, to extend the site base template and add the rest of the supporting HTML code for the view.

4. Save the iFriends/templates/Blogs/blog_arch.html file.

5. Create and open a file called iFriends/templates/Blogs/blog_year.html in an editor.

6. Add the following for loop code to the file to generate a list of months containing Blog objects and add links to the blog_month index view for each month:

```
{% for date in date_list %}
    <li>
    <a href="/generic/blog_arch/{{date|date:"Y"}}/{{date|date:"b"}}/">
        {{ date|date:"F" }}</a>
    </li>
{% endfor %}
```

7. Add the rest of the code, shown in Listing 12.6, to extend the site base template and add the rest of the supporting HTML code for the view. The year context variable is accessed to display the year in the heading.

8. Save the iFriends/templates/Blogs/blog_year.html file.

9. Create and open a file called iFriends/templates/Blogs/blog_month.html in an editor.

10. Add the following for loop code to the file to generate a list of Blog objects and add links to the generic blog_details view for each Blog:

```
{% for blog in object_list %}
    <li>
    <a href="/generic/blog_details/{{blog.id}}/">{{ blog }}</a>
    </li>
{% endfor %}
```

11. Add the rest of the code, shown in Listing 12.7, to extend the site base template and add the rest of the supporting HTML code for the view. The month context variable is accessed to display the textual month in the heading.

12. Save the iFriends/templates/Blogs/blog_month.html file.

13. Open the iFriends/urls.py file in an editor.

14. Modify the following lines of code to import the date_based view package:

```
from django.views.generic import list_detail, date_based
```

15. Add the following lines of code, shown in Listing 12.8, to create a dictionary to use for the blog_arch view that sets the queryset date_field to blog and defines a custom template file:

```
blog_arch_info = {
    'queryset' : Blog.objects.all(),
    'date_field' : 'date',
    'template_name' : 'Blogs/blog_arch.html',
}
```

16. Add the following lines of code, shown in Listing 12.8, to create a dictionary to use for the blog_year view that sets the queryset date_field to blog and defines a custom template file:

```
blog_month_info = {
    'queryset' : Blog.objects.all(),
    'date_field' : 'date',
    'template_name' : 'Blogs/blog_month.html',
}
```

17. Add the following lines of code, shown in Listing 12.8, to create a dictionary to use for the blog_month view that sets the queryset date_field to blog and defines a custom template file:

```
blog_year_info = {
    'queryset' : Blog.objects.all(),
    'date_field' : 'date',
    'template_name' : 'Blogs/blog_year.html',
}
```

18. Add the following URL patterns, shown in Listing 12.8, to enable the generic blog_arch, blog_year, and blog_month views:

```
urlpatterns += patterns('',
    (r'^generic/blog_arch/(?P<year>\d{4})/(?P<month>[a-z]{3})/$',
      date_based.archive_month, blog_month_info),
    (r'^generic/blog_arch/(?P<year>\d{4})/$',
      date_based.archive_year, blog_year_info),
    (r'^generic/blog_arch/$',
      date_based.archive_index, blog_arch_info),
)
```

19. Save the iFriends/urls.py file.

20. Access the following URL in a browser, as shown in Figure 12.3, to verify that the blog_arch view works:

```
http://127.0.0.1:8000/generic/blog_arch/
```

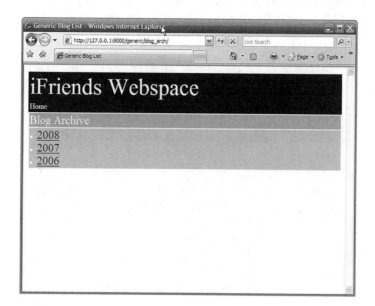

FIGURE 12.3
Generic date-based index view for `Blog` objects showing years that have `Blog` objects archived.

21. Click one of the year links to access the `blog_year` view, shown in Figure 12.4, to verify that the `blog_year` view works.

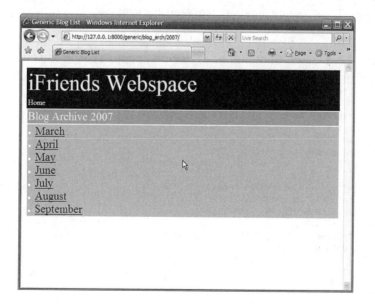

FIGURE 12.4
Generic date-based year view for `Blog` objects showing months that have `Blog` objects archived.

22. Click one of the month links to access the `blog_month` view, shown in Figure 12.5, to verify that the `blog_month` view works.

FIGURE 12.5
Generic date-based month view for `Blog` objects showing `Blog` objects archived for that month.

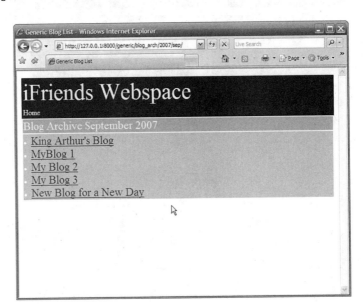

23. Click one of the blog links to access the `blog_details` view, shown in Figure 12.2, to verify that the `blog_year` link works.

LISTING 12.5   Full Contents of `iFriends/templates/Blog/ blog_arch.html`

```
{% extends "iFriends_base.html" %}

{% block title %}Generic Blog List{% endblock %}
{% block content %}
<table width=100%>
<tr bgcolor="aabbcc"><td colspan="3">
<font size="5" color="white">Blog Archive</font>
</td></tr>
<tr valign="top"><td width=30% bgcolor="aaddee">
<font color="white" size="5">
{% for date in date_list %}
    <li>
    <a href="/generic/blog_arch/{{ date|date:"Y" }}/">
        {{ date|date:"Y" }}</a>
    </li>
{% endfor %}
</font></td></tr>
{% endblock %}
```

LISTING 12.6 Full Contents of `iFriends/templates/Blogs/`
`blog_year.html`

```
{% extends "iFriends_base.html" %}

{% block title %}Generic Blog List{% endblock %}
{% block content %}
<table width=100%>
<tr bgcolor="aabbcc"><td colspan="3">
<font size="5" color="white">Blog Archive {{ year }}</font>
</td></tr>
<tr valign="top"><td width=30% bgcolor="aaddee">
<font color="white" size="5">
{% for date in date_list %}
    <li>
    <a href="/generic/blog_arch/{{date|date:"Y"}}/{{date|date:"b"}}/">
        {{ date|date:"F" }}</a>
    </li>
{% endfor %}
</font></td></tr>
{% endblock %}
```

LISTING 12.7 Full Contents of `iFriends/templates/ Blogs/blog_`
`month.html`

```
{% extends "iFriends_base.html" %}

{% block title %}Generic Blog List{% endblock %}
{% block content %}
<table width=100%>
<tr bgcolor="aabbcc"><td colspan="3">
<font size="5" color="white">
Blog Archive {{ month|date:"F Y" }}
</font></td></tr>
<tr valign="top"><td width=30% bgcolor="aaddee">
<font color="white" size="5">
{% for blog in object_list %}
    <li>
    <a href="/generic/blog_details/{{blog.id}}/">{{ blog }}</a>
    </li>
{% endfor %}
</font></td></tr>
{% endblock %}
```

LISTING 12.8 Generic Section for Blog Objects in the `iFriends/`
`urls.py` File

```
#Blog generic section
from django.views.generic import list_detail, date_based
from iFriends.People.models import Blog

blog_detail_info = {
    'queryset' : Blog.objects.all(),
    'template_object_name' : 'blog',
```

LISTING 12.8   Continued

```
        'template_name' : 'Blogs/blog_detail.html',
}
blog_arch_info = {
        'queryset' : Blog.objects.all(),
        'date_field' : 'date',
        'template_name' : 'Blogs/blog_arch.html',
        'allow_future': True
}
blog_month_info = {
        'queryset' : Blog.objects.all(),
        'date_field' : 'date',
        'template_name' : 'Blogs/blog_month.html',
}
blog_year_info = {
        'queryset' : Blog.objects.all(),
        'date_field' : 'date',
        'template_name' : 'Blogs/blog_year.html',
}

urlpatterns += patterns('',
        (r'^generic/blog_details/(?P<object_id>\d+)/$',
            list_detail.object_detail, blog_detail_info),
)

urlpatterns += patterns('',
        (r'^generic/blog_arch/(?P<year>\d{4})/(?P<month>[a-z]{3})/$',
            date_based.archive_month, blog_month_info),
        (r'^generic/blog_arch/(?P<year>\d{4})/$',
            date_based.archive_year, blog_year_info),
        (r'^generic/blog_arch/$',
            date_based.archive_index, blog_arch_info),
)
```

Using Generic Object-Creation Views

The django.views.generic.create_update.create_object view renders a
generic view that displays a form for creating objects. The create_object view
requires a model argument containing the model of the class you want to create. A
Form object is generated for the model and is passed to the template in the context
variable form.

By the Way

> If the object has validation errors, create_object displays them.

The form is displayed if accessed with a GET request, and the object is saved on a
POST request.

The `create_object` function actually modifies data in the database. You should use the `login_required` object to make certain that users are logged in before accessing the view.

Watch Out!

▶ The required argument is `model`.

▶ The optional arguments are `post_save_redirect`, `login_required`, `template_name`, `template_loader`, `extra_context`, and `context_processors`.

▶ The context variables are `form` and `extra_context`.

▶ The default `template_name` is *app_label*/*model_name*_form.html (such as People/Person_form.html).

The following code snippet shows an example of defining a generic `create_object` view in the URLconf file:

```
blog_info = {
    'model' : Blog,
    'post_save_redirect' : '/blog/list',
}
urlpatterns += patterns('',
    (r'^generic/blog_add/$',
      create_update.create_object, blog_info),
```

The following template code snippet shows an example of accessing the context variable `form` in a template:

```
<form action="" method="post">
    <p><label for"id_text">Title:</label>{{ form.title}}</p>
    <p><label for"id_by">By:</label>{{ form.text }}</p>
<input type="submit" />
```

Try It Yourself ▼

Use a Generic View to Implement an Object Creation Form

In this section, you will use the `create_object` generic view to display a `Quote` object creation form and create `Quote` objects. Follow these steps to create a template and update the URLconf file to enable the view:

1. Create and open a file called `iFriends/templates/Quotes/quote_add.html` in an editor. ▼

2. Add the following for form code to the file to generate a creation form for the Quote object using the form context variable to access the text and by form elements:

```
<form action="" method="post">
    <p><label for"id_text">Text:</label>{{ form.text }}</p>
    <p><label for"id_by">By:</label>{{ form.by }}</p>
<input type="submit"  value="Add"/>
</form>
```

3. Add the rest of the code, shown in Listing 12.9, to extend the site base template and add the rest of the supporting HTML code for the view.

4. Save the iFriends/templates/Quotes/quote_add.html file.

5. Open the iFriends/urls.py file in an editor.

6. Modify the following line of code in Listing 12.10 to import the create_update view:

```
from django.views.generic import list_detail, create_update
```

7. Add the following lines of code, shown in Listing 12.10, to create a dictionary to use for the quote_add view that defines a custom template file and a post_save_redirect URL:

```
quote_add_info = {
    'model' : Quote,
    'template_name' : 'Quotes/quote_add.html',
    'post_save_redirect' : '/generic/quote_list',
}
```

8. Add the following URL pattern to enable the generic quote_add view:

```
(r'^generic/quote_add/$',
  create_update.create_object, quote_add_info),
```

9. Save the iFriends/urls.py file.

10. Access the following URL in a browser, as shown in Figure 12.1.

```
http://127.0.0.1:8000/generic/quote_list/
```

11. Click the Add link to access the quote_add view, shown in Figure 12.6.

12. Add data to the quote_add form, and click the Add button to create the new Quote object.

13. Verify that the quote_add view redirects you to the quote_list view and that the new quote has been added to the list, as shown in Figure 12.7.

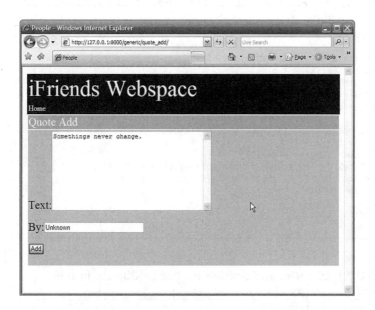

FIGURE 12.6
Generic Quote object creation form.

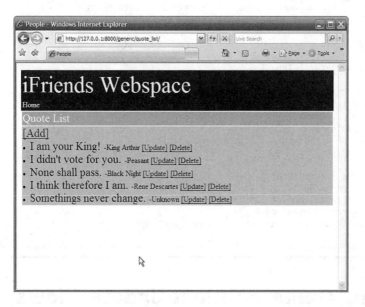

FIGURE 12.7
Generic Quote object list form showing the new quote entry added by the quote_add view.

LISTING 12.9   Full Contents of `iFriends/templates/Quotes/`
`quote_add.html`

```
{% extends "iFriends_base.html" %}

{% block title %}People{% endblock %}
{% block content %}
<table width=100%>
<tr bgcolor="aabbcc"><td colspan="3">
<font size="5" color="white">Quote Add</font>
</td></tr>
<tr valign="top"><td width=30% bgcolor="aadddd">
<font size="5">
<form action="" method="post">
    <p><label for"id_text">Text:</label>{{ form.text }}</p>
    <p><label for"id_by">By:</label>{{ form.by }}</p>
<input type="submit"  value="Add"/>
</form>
</font></td></tr>
{% endblock %}
```

LISTING 12.10   Generic Section for `Quote` Objects in the
`iFriends/urls.py` File

```
#Quote generic section
from django.views.generic import list_detail, create_update
from iFriends.Quotes.models import Quote

quote_list_info = {
    'queryset' : Quote.objects.all(),
    'allow_empty' : True,
}

quote_add_info = {
    'model' : Quote,
    'template_name' : 'Quotes/quote_add.html',
    'post_save_redirect' : '/generic/quote_list',
}

urlpatterns += patterns('',
    (r'^generic/quote_list/$',
      list_detail.object_list, quote_list_info),
    (r'^generic/quote_add/$',
      create_update.create_object, quote_add_info),
)
```

Using Generic Object-Update Views

The `django.views.generic.create_update.update_object` view renders a
generic view that displays a form for updating objects. The `update_object` view
requires a model argument and an `object_id` or `slug` argument. The view retrieves

the object and uses it to create a `Form` object that is passed to the template in the context variable `form`.

> If the object has validation errors, `update_object` displays them.

The form is displayed if accessed with a `GET` request and the object is updated on a `POST` request.

> The `update_object` function actually modifies data in the database. You should use the `login_required` object to make certain that users are logged in before accessing the view.

▶ The required arguments are `model` and `object_id` or `slug`.

▶ The optional arguments are `post_save_redirect`, `login_required`, `template_name`, `template_loader`, `extra_context`, and `context_processors`.

▶ The context variables are `form`, `object`, and `extra_context`.

▶ The default `template_name` is *app_label*/*model_name*_form.html (such as People/Person_form.html).

The following code snippet shows an example of defining a generic `update_object` view in the `URLconf` file:

```
blog_info = {
    'model' : Blog,
    'post_save_redirect' : '/blog/list',
}
urlpatterns += patterns('',
    (r'^generic/blog_update/(?P<object_id>\d+)/$',
}
```

The following template code snippet shows an example of accessing the context variable `form` in a template to display the object being updated:

```
<form action="" method="post">
    <p><label for"id_title">Title:</label>{{ form.title}}</p>
    <p><label for"id_text">By:</label>{{ form.text }}</p>
<input type="submit" />
```

Try It Yourself

Use a Generic View to Implement an Object Update Form

In this section, you will use the update_object generic view to display a Quote object update form that updates Quote objects. Follow these steps to create a template and update the URLconf file to enable the view:

1. Create and open a file called iFriends/templates/Quotes/quote_update. html in an editor.

2. Add the following for form code to the file to generate an update form for the Quote object using the form context variable to access the text and by form elements:

```
<form action="" method="post">
    <p><label for"id_text">Text:</label>{{ form.text }}</p>
    <p><label for"id_by">By:</label>{{ form.by }}</p>
<input type="submit"  value="Update"/>
</form>
```

3. Add the rest of the code, shown in Listing 12.11, to extend the site base template and add the rest of the supporting HTML code for the view.

4. Save the iFriends/templates/Quotes/quote_update.html file.

5. Open the iFriends/urls.py file in an editor.

6. Add the following lines of code, shown in Listing 12.12, to create a dictionary to use for the quote_update view that defines a custom template file and a post_save_redirect URL:

```
quote_update_info = {
    'model' : Quote,
    'template_name' : 'Quotes/quote_update.html',
    'post_save_redirect' : '/generic/quote_list',
}
```

7. Add the following URL pattern to enable the generic quote_update view:

```
(r'^generic/quote_update/$',
    create_update.update_object, quote_update_info),
```

8. Save the iFriends/urls.py file.

9. Access the following URL in a browser, shown in Figure 12.1.

```
http://127.0.0.1:8000/generic/quote_list/
```

10. Click the Update link for one of the quotes to access the quote_update view, shown in Figure 12.8.

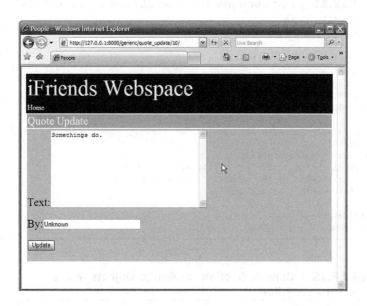

FIGURE 12.8
Generic Quote
object update
form.

11. Add data to the quote_update form, and click the Update button to update
the Quote object.

12. Verify that the quote_update view redirects you to the quote_list view and
that the quote has been updated in the list, as shown in Figure 12.9.

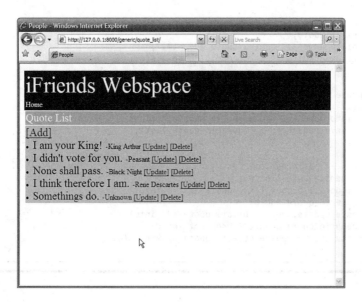

FIGURE 12.9
Generic Quote
object list form
showing the
quote entry
updated by the
quote_update
view.

LISTING 12.11   Full Contents of `iFriends/templates/Quotes/quote_update.html`

```
{% extends "iFriends_base.html" %}

{% block title %}People{% endblock %}
{% block content %}
<table width=100%>
<tr bgcolor="aabbcc"><td colspan="3">
<font size="5" color="white">Quote Update</font>
</td></tr>
<tr valign="top"><td width=30% bgcolor="aadddd">
<font size="5">
<form action="" method="post">
    <p><label for"id_text">Text:</label>{{ form.text }}</p>
    <p><label for"id_by">By:</label>{{ form.by }}</p>
<input type="submit"  value="Update"/>
</form>
</font></td></tr>
{% endblock %}
```

LISTING 12.12   Generic Section for `Quote` Objects in the `iFriends/urls.py` File

```
#Quote generic section
from django.views.generic import list_detail, create_update
from iFriends.Quotes.models import Quote

quote_list_info = {
    'queryset' : Quote.objects.all(),
    'allow_empty': True,
}

quote_add_info = {
    'model' : Quote,
    'template_name' : 'Quotes/quote_add.html',
    'post_save_redirect' : '/generic/quote_list',
}

quote_update_info = {
    'model' : Quote,
    'template_name' : 'Quotes/quote_update.html',
    'post_save_redirect' : '/generic/quote_list',
}

urlpatterns += patterns('',
    (r'^generic/quote_list/$',
      list_detail.object_list, quote_list_info),
    (r'^generic/quote_add/$',
      create_update.create_object, quote_add_info),
    (r'^generic/quote_update/(?P<object_id>\d+)/$',
      create_update.update_object, quote_update_info),
)
```

Using Generic Object-Deletion Views

The `django.views.generic.create_update.delete_object` view renders a generic view that displays a form for deleting objects. The `delete_object` view requires a `model`, an `object_id`, and a `post_delete_redirect` object. The view retrieves the object and uses it to create a `Form` object that is passed to the template in the context variable `form`.

The form is displayed if it is accessed with a GET request, and the object is deleted on a POST request.

▶ The required arguments are `model`, `object_id`, and `post_delete_redirect`.

▶ The optional arguments are `login_required`, `template_name`, `template_loader`, `extra_context`, and `context_processors`.

▶ The context variables are `object` and `extra_context`.

▶ The default `template_name` is *app_label*/*model_name*_form.html (such as People/Person_form.html).

The following code snippet shows an example of defining a generic `update_object` view in the URLconf file:

```
blog_info = {
    'model' : Blog,
    'post_delete_redirect' : '/blog/list',
}
urlpatterns += patterns('',
    (r'^generic/blog_delete/(?P<object_id>\d+)/$',
}
```

The following template code snippet shows an example of accessing the context variable `object` in a deletion template to display the `Blog` object being deleted:

```
<form action="" method="post">
    <p>{{ object.title }}</p>
    <p> -{{ object.text }}</p>
<input type="submit" />
</form>
```

Try It Yourself ▼

Use a Generic View to Implement an Object Deletion Form

In this section you will use the `delete_object` generic view to display a `Quote` object deletion form that deletes `Quote` objects. Follow these steps to create a template and update the URLconf file to enable the view:

▼

1. Create and open a file called iFriends/templates/Quotes/quote_delete. html in an editor.

2. Add the following form code to the file to generate a deletion form for the Quote object. This code uses the object context variable to access the text and by form elements:

```
<form action="" method="post">
    <p>{{ object.text }}</p>
    <p> -{{ object.by }}</p>
<input type="submit" value="Delete"/>
</form>
```

3. Add the rest of the code, shown in Listing 12.13, to extend the site base template and add the rest of the supporting HTML code for the view.

4. Save the iFriends/templates/Quotes/quote_delete.html file.

5. Open the iFriends/urls.py file in an editor.

6. Add the following lines of code, shown in Listing 12.14, to create a dictionary to use for the quote_delete view that defines a custom template file and a post_delete_redirect URL:

```
quote_delete_info = {
    'model' : Quote,
    'template_name' : 'Quotes/quote_delete.html',
    'post_delete_redirect' : '/generic/quote_list',
}
```

7. Add the following URL pattern to enable the generic quote_delete view:

```
(r'^generic/quote_delete/(?P<object_id>\d+)/$',
    create_update.delete_object, quote_delete_info),
```

8. Save the iFriends/urls.py file.

9. Access the following URL in a browser, shown in Figure 12.1.

```
http://127.0.0.1:8000/generic/quote_list/
```

10. Click the Delete link for one of the quotes to access the quote_delete view, shown in Figure 12.10.

11. Add data to the quote_delete form, and click the Delete button to delete the Quote object.

12. Verify that the quote_delete view redirects you to the quote_list view and that the quote has been removed from the list, shown in Figure 12.11.

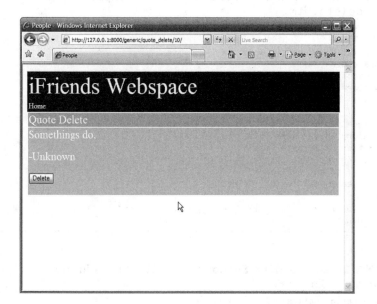

FIGURE 12.10
Generic Quote object delete form.

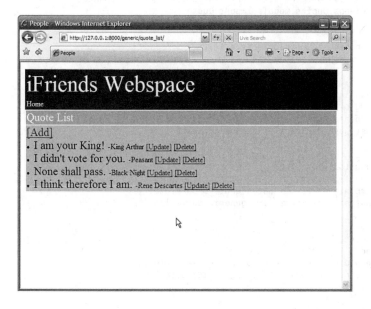

FIGURE 12.11
Generic Quote object list form showing that the quote entry has been deleted by the quote_delete view.

LISTING 12.13   Full Contents of `iFriends/templates/Quotes/`
`quote_delete.html`

```
{% extends "iFriends_base.html" %}

{% block title %}People{% endblock %}
{% block content %}
<table width=100%>
<tr bgcolor="aabbcc"><td colspan="3">
<font size="5" color="white">Quote Delete</font>
</td></tr>
<tr valign="top"><td width=30% bgcolor="aadddd">
<font color="white" size="5">
<form action="" method="post">
    <p>{{ object.text }}</p>
    <p> -{{ object.by }}</p>
<input type="submit" value="Delete"/>
</form>
</font></td></tr>
{% endblock %}
```

LISTING 12.14   Generic Section for `Quote` Objects in the
`iFriends/urls.py` File

```
#Quote generic section
from django.views.generic import list_detail, create_update
from iFriends.Quotes.models import Quote

quote_list_info = {
    'queryset' : Quote.objects.all(),
    'allow_empty' : True,
}

quote_add_info = {
    'model' : Quote,
    'template_name' : 'Quotes/quote_add.html',
    'post_save_redirect' : '/generic/quote_list',
}

quote_update_info = {
    'model' : Quote,
    'template_name' : 'Quotes/quote_update.html',
    'post_save_redirect' : '/generic/quote_list',
}

quote_delete_info = {
    'model' : Quote,
    'template_name' : 'Quotes/quote_delete.html',
    'post_delete_redirect' : '/generic/quote_list',
}

urlpatterns += patterns('',
    (r'^generic/quote_list/$',
      list_detail.object_list, quote_list_info),
    (r'^generic/quote_add/$',
      create_update.create_object, quote_add_info),
```

```
(r'^generic/quote_update/(?P<object_id>\d+)/$',
    create_update.update_object, quote_update_info),
(r'^generic/quote_delete/(?P<object_id>\d+)/$',
    create_update.delete_object, quote_delete_info),
)
```

▲

Summary

In this hour, you learned how to implement the `list_details` generic views to generate views without having to implement Python view functions. You learned how to use the simple generic views to redirect URL requests and directly access template files. We also covered using the `date_based` package to implement an object archive index. Using the `create_update` package, you can use generic views to create, update, and delete objects.

Q&A

Q. Is there a way to implement page numbers for generic list views?

A. Yes. Django provides the `paginate_by` argument to generic list views to implement a pagination system. The pagination information can be accessed in the templates through `page`, `pages`, `last_on_page`, `first_on_page`, `previous`, `next`, `has_next`, `has_previous`, `hits`, and `results_per_page`.

Q. Is there a way to access functions from generic views?

A. Yes. If you pass a function as a member of the `extra_context` dictionary argument, it is evaluated just before it is passed to the template.

Workshop

The workshop consists of a set of questions and answers designed to solidify your understanding of the material covered in this hour. Try answering the questions before looking at the answers.

Quiz

1. Which argument would you pass into a generic object-creation form to redirect to a different URL?

2. Is there a way to verify if the user is logged in before allowing him or her to create, update, or delete objects using generic forms?

3. What additional argument is required for generic URL patterns?

4. What view would you use to render an URL template without having to call a view function?

Quiz Answers

1. The `post_save_redirect` argument.

2. Yes. Set the `login_required` argument to `True` in the `create_object`, `update_object`, and `delete_object` views.

3. An additional dictionary of arguements is required in the generic view URL patterns.

4. The `direct_to_template` view.

Exercises

1. Add a generic view to list the `Blog` objects in the iFriends database.

2. Add generic views to create, update, and delete `Blog` objects in the iFriends database and tie them into the view you created in Exercise 1.

Advanced View Configurations

What You'll Learn in This Hour:

▶ How to load templates from applications
▶ How to create custom libraries to customize the template system
▶ How to create custom filters
▶ How to create custom tags
▶ How to create `simple_tags`
▶ How to create `inclusion_tags`

This hour covers extending the template engine to create advanced view configurations. Django provides many capabilities with its built-in tags. However, as you begin creating new custom tags and filters in your projects, a whole new world opens up.

This hour also discusses how to create custom tags and filters that you can use in your templates to reduce the amount of code necessary to generate web pages. The examples in this hour are simple to enable you to quickly understand customizing the template engine. Keep in mind that you can really do much more in your custom tags to solve problems.

The following sections discuss how to load template files from applications. They also show you how to create custom tag and filter libraries to extend Django's template system.

Loading Templates from Applications

In Hour 7, "Implementing Django Templates to Create Custom Views," we discussed how to configure a template directory by setting TEMPLATE_DIRS in the project's settings.py file. The TEMPLATE_DIRS setting is used by the django.template.loaders.filesystem loader, which is the default loader.

Django has another template loader that is useful when organizing your templates for specific applications. The `django.template.app_directories` loader searches for templates in a templates subdirectory of installed applications.

For example, if you enable the `app_directories` loader for a site called mySite that has an application called myApp, you could store templates in the mySite/myApp/templates directory.

> As a security measure, the `app_directories` loader searches only template directories in applications that are listed in the INSTALLED_APPS setting of the `settings.py` file.

To enable the `app_directories` loader, add the following line to the TEMPLATE_LOADERS setting of the `settings.py` file:

```
'django.template.loaders.app_directories.load_template_source',
```

By the Way

> If you plan to distribute your applications using Python eggs, you can use the `django.template.loaders.eggs.load_template_source` template loader. The eggs template loader works the same as the `app_directories` loader, except that it loads templates from Python eggs rather than directly from the file system.

Extending the Template System

Django's built-in tags and filters provide enough features for most web pages. However, sometimes you will want to implement your own filters and tags.

Django makes it easy to add your own custom filters and tags to extend the template system by creating your own templatetags application.

To create a templatetags application, you create a templatetags directory as a subdirectory inside an installed application at the same level as the application's `models.py` file. Then you create an `__init__.py` file in that directory to tell Python that this is a package containing Python code.

After you have created the templatetags application, you can create custom template tag and filter libraries. To create a template tag or filter library, create a blank Python document in the templatetags directory. Then add the following lines of code at the top of the document to create a Library object so that Django knows that it is a valid tag or filter library:

```
from django import template
register = template.Library()
```

> **Did you Know?**
>
> Custom template tag and filter libraries need to be placed inside installed applications. They can still be accessed by templates for other applications. If you do not want the custom templates to be placed in one of your currently installed applications, you could install a new application and leave the models.py and views.py files blank and create the templatetags application in the blank application.

You can load the custom template tag and filter libraries into templates by using the load tag and specifying the library filename without the .py extension:

```
{% load custom_tags %}
```

> **Watch Out!**
>
> After you create a new templatetags package, you must stop and then restart the Django server so that the new package will be available.

Try It Yourself

Create a Templatetags Application to Implement Custom Tags and Filters

In this section, you will create a templatetags application in which you can create custom template tag and filter libraries.

Follow these steps to install a blank Custom application and create a templatetags package in that application:

1. Stop the Django development server.

2. Use the following command from the root of the iFriends project to create a new application called Custom:

   ```
   python manage.py startapp Custom
   ```

3. Create a directory in the new Custom application called iFriends/Custom/templatetags/.

▼

4. Copy the blank __init.py__ file from the iFriends/Custom/ directory to the iFriends/custom/templatetags/ directory to tell Python that this is an application with Python code in it.

5. Open the iFriends/settings.py file in an editor.

6. Add the following line of code to the INSTALLED_APPS setting file to install the Custom application:

   ```
   'iFriends.Custom',
   ```

7. Save the iFriends/settings.py file.

▲

8. Start the development server.

Creating Custom Filters

Creating custom filters is easy. Filters are really just Python functions that accept either one or two arguments. The first argument is the value to which the filter will be applied. The second argument is the filter argument, if any, that is attached to the filter in the template.

For example, consider the following template code:

```
{{ "1.2.3.4"|drop:"." }}
```

The arguments value and arg in the following filter function would be set to 1.2.3.4 and . respectively:

```
def drop(value, arg):
  return value.replace(arg, '')
```

After you have created the filter function, you need to register it with the Library object in the module. To register a filter with a Library object, you call the filter() function of the Library object and pass in the filter name as the first parameter and the filter function as the second:

```
from django import template
register = template.Library()

def drop(value, arg):
  return value.replace(arg, '')
register.filter('drop', drop)
```

If you are using Python 2.4 or later, you can register the filter using a decorator function. If you do not pass a name argument to the decorator function, the filter function name is used as the filter name. For example, in the following two decorator statements, the name of the filter is DropChar in the first decorator and drop in the second:

```
@register.filter(name="DropChar")
def drop(value, arg):
. . .
@register.filter()
def drop(value, arg):
```

If your filter is expecting a string, you can use the @stringfilter decorator for the filter function. The @stringfilter decorator converts objects to their string values before passing them to the filter function. The following code snippet shows an example of using the @stringfilter decorator:

```
@register.filter(name=" FilterText")
@stringfilter
def FilterText(value, arg):
```

Try It Yourself ▼

Create a Custom Template Filter

In this section, you will create a custom template filter to display datetime objects in a specific format without having to use the date filter and filter string. This type of filter can save you keystrokes and time if you have a set way you want datetime objects to be displayed.

Follow these steps to create a custom filter module and add the time filter to it:

1. Create and open a file called iFriends/Custom/templatetags/custom_filters.py.

2. Add the following lines of code, shown in Listing 13.1, to import the django.template package and create a Library object so that Django recognizes the module as a valid filter library:

```
from django import template
register = template.Library()
```

3. Add the following lines of code, shown in Listing 13.1, to import the datetime and create a filter function longTime that accepts a datetime object and returns it as a specific string format:

```
import datetime
. . .
def longTime(aTime):
    return aTime.strftime("%m/%d/%Y %I:%M%p")
```

▼

4. Add the following line of code to register the filter with the `Library` object for the module:

```
@register.filter(name="longTime")
```

If you are using Python 2.3 or earlier, you must use the following line of code after the function to register it with the library:

```
register.filter('drop', drop)
```

5. Save the `iFriends/Custom/templatetags/custom_filters.py` file.

6. Open the `iFriends/templates/Blogs/blog_details.html` file in an editor.

7. Add the following line of code, shown in Listing 13.2, to load the `custom_filters.py` library module you created in step 1:

```
{% load custom_filters %}
```

8. Modify the following line of code to use the `longTime` filter to display the `blog.date` field:

```
<font size="2">{{ blog.date|longTime }}</font>
```

9. Save the `iFriends/templates/Blogs/blog_details.html` file.

10. Open the following URL in a web browser to bring up the `blog_details` generic view, shown in Figure 13.1, to verify that the date is formatted correctly:

```
http://127.0.0.1:8000/generic/blog_details/1/
```

FIGURE 13.1
The `blog_details` generic view showing the date and time formatted using the `longTime` custom filter.

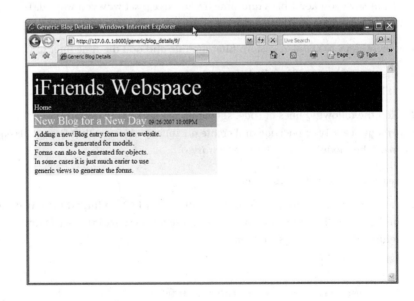

LISTING 13.1 Full Contents of `iFriends/Custom/templatetags/custom_filters.py`

```python
from django import template
register = template.Library()
import datetime

@register.filter(name="longTime")
def longTime(aTime):
    return aTime.strftime("%m/%d/%Y %I:%M%p")
```

LISTING 13.2 Full Contents of `iFriends/templates/Blogs/blog_details.html`

```html
{% extends "iFriends_base.html" %}

{% block title %}Generic Blog Details{% endblock %}
{% block content %}
{% load custom_filters %}
<table width="400">
<tr bgcolor="aabbcc"><td colspan="3">
<font size="5" color="white">{{ blog.title }}</font>
<font size="2">{{ blog.date|longTime }}</font>
</td></tr>
<tr valign="top"><td bgcolor="ddffff">
{{ blog.text|linebreaks }}
</td></tr>
{% endblock %}
```

Creating Custom Tags

Custom filters are useful and simple to create. However, for more complex actions on data, you will want to use custom tags. Custom tags can do just about anything because of how they are implemented.

Custom tags split the work between distinct parts—a compilation function and a renderer object. Creating a custom tag involves first creating a renderer object, and then creating a compilation function that returns an instance of the renderer object, and, finally, registering the tag with the custom tag library.

The renderer object is a subclass of the template Node object that includes a render() function that outputs the contents of the Node.

To create the renderer object, create a new class that extends the `template.Node` object and includes a render function that renders the output. For example, the following code snippet creates a renderer class that accepts a string object when it is created and renders the string to lowercase:

```python
class doLOWNode(template.Node):
    def __init__(self, aStr):
```

```
        self.aStr = aStr
    def render(self, context):
        return self.aStr.lower()
```

The compilation function determines how the tag is rendered into a template Node. When the custom tag is encountered in a template, the parser calls the compilation function with the parser object and the tag contents. For example, in the following tag:

```
{% doLOW "Some Text" %}
```

the following value is passed to the compilation function:

```
doLOW "Some Text"
```

The compilation function is responsible for returning a template Node object based on the tag's contents.

For example, the following code defines a compilation function that processes a tag that accepts a string argument and uses that string to return an instance of the doLOWNode object defined a moment ago:

```
def doLOW(parser, token):
    try:
        tag_name, aStr = token.split_contents()
    except ValueError:
        raise template.TemplateSyntaxError, "Requires 1 argument"
    if not (aStr[0] == aStr[-1] and aStr[0] in ('"', "'")):
        raise template.TemplateSyntaxError, "Argument should use quotes"
    return doLOWNode(aStr[1:-1]) #Removes the beginning and ending quotes
```

Watch Out!

The preceding code uses the split_contents() function of the token object to split the tag and argument from the tag contents variable token. You should use the split_contents() method instead of the Python string function split(). split() doesn't understand that values in quotes shouldn't be split, so any spaces in the string would be split into separate tokens.

By the Way

The compilation function is responsible for raising TemplateSyntaxError exceptions if the contents do not match what is expected. Notice that the preceding code checks the number of arguments and encloses the argument in quotes.

After you have defined the renderer object and the compilation class, you need to register the custom tag with the Library object using the following syntax:

```
register.tag('doLOW', doLOW)
```

Did you Know?

Just as with custom filters, if you are using Python 2.4 or later, you can register the tag using a decorator function, as shown in the following example:

```
@register.tag(name="doLOW")
```

The following sections describe some custom tags that help you make more dynamic custom tag libraries.

Creating Simple Custom Tags

Frequently you may find yourself creating tags that accept a string and simply output a different form of the string. Django provides a special type of filter that is much easier to create and manage to handle these needs.

The `simple_tag` filter allows you to quickly define a tag function that accepts one or more arguments, processes them, and returns a string. To show you how simple this process is, the following code creates a `simple_tag` that accepts a string and converts it to uppercase:

```
def doUP(aStr):
    return aStr.upper()
register.simple_tag(doUP)
```

Basically the doUP example works the same as the doLOW tag, except that doUP is done in only three lines of code.

You could access it from the template using the following code:

```
{% doUP "Some Text" %}
```

By the Way

If you pass variables to the `simple_tag`, the value of the objects gets passed, not the variables themselves.

Creating Custom Block Tags

At times you may want to create a filter that processes a block of text, variables, and other data. This is where the `parser` argument to the compilation function comes in. Using the `parse()` function of the `parser` object, you can parse from the beginning block tag to an end block tag.

The `parse()` function returns a list of template Node objects that exist between the two blocks. You can pass that Node list to the renderer, and then the renderer can apply the tag function to all nodes in the block.

For example, you could create the following compilation function that parses the template until it finds the endUToSpace tag to create a Node list:

```
def doUToSpace(parser, token):
    nodelist = parse(('endUToSpace',))
    parser.delete_first_token()
    return doUToSpaceNode(nodelist)
```

The following code defines the renderer object for the compilation function just shown. It accepts the Node list on creation. Then it renders the Node list using the render() function to get all the text that is output by the Nodes. Finally, it applies the replace() function to the entire output:

```
class doUToSpaceNode(template.Node):
    def __init__(self, nodelist):
        self.nodelist = nodelist
    def render(self, context):
        outText = self.nodelist.render(context)
        return outText.replace('_', ' ')
```

The following line of code registers the UToSpace tag in the library:

```
@register.tag(name="UToSpace")
```

The following line of code accesses the UToSpace tag using both text and variables:

```
{% UToSpace %}
This_block_of_text_is_filled_with_underscores.
So_is_this_variable_{{ NoSpaceData }}.
{% endUToSpace %}
```

Retrieving and Setting Variables in the Context

One of the most valuable things about using custom tags is that you have access to the template context. That means that you can both read variables from the context and create new variables in the context that can be accessed in the template.

Remember that the tag contents argument that gets passed to the compilation function includes only the text inside the tag statement. So if you pass a variable as an argument to the tag, it shows up as just the variable name.

To solve this problem, Django provides the Variable class. The Variable class accepts the variable name in its constructor. The Variable class contains a `resolve()` function that resolves the variable name inside the template context and returns the actual variable object.

For example, the following compilation function parses the `makeFTime` tag contents, gets the variable name of a `datetime` object, and uses that variable object to create a `makeFTimeNode` object:

```
def makeFTime(parser, token):
    try:
        tag_name, aTime = token.split_contents()
    except ValueError:
        raise template.TemplateSyntaxError
    return makeFTimeNode(aTime)
```

The following renderer class uses the variable name to create a `Variable` object when creating an instance of the class. Then, in the render function, it uses the `resolve()` function of the `Variable` object to pull the `datetime` object out of the template context so that it can be rendered with a specific format and returned:

```
class makeFTimeNode(template.Node):
    def __init__(self, aTime):
        self.aTime = template.Variable(aTime)
    def render(self, context):
        aTime = self.aTime.resolve(context)
        return aTime.strftime("%m/%d/%Y %I:%M%p")
```

The `makeFTime` tag could be accessed from the template using the following code:

```
{% makeFTime someTime %}
```

Let's take this a step further. What if you wanted the custom tag to create a new variable with the formatted time as its value so that it could be referenced in several places in the template? Because you have access to the context dictionary from the render function, this is a simple process. The following code shows the `makeFTimeNode` render function, which adds the formatted time to the context as the variable `FTime` and returns an empty string:

```
class makeFTimeNode(template.Node):
    def __init__(self, aTime):
        self.aTime = template.Variable(aTime)
    def render(self, context):
        aTime = self.aTime.resolve(context)
        context['FTime'] = aTime.strftime("%m/%d/%Y %I:%M%p")
        return ''
```

Now you could use the `makeFTime` tag to create a new context variable that could be accessed elsewhere in the template, as shown in the following code:

```
{% makeFTime someTime %
The next meeting will start: {{ FTime }}
```

▼   **Try It Yourself**

Create a Custom Tag That Retrieves and Sets Context Variables

In this section, you will create a custom tag that accepts a list of Blog objects, finds the largest Blog entry, and creates a context variable that contains the largest Blog. Then you will create a home page that uses the custom template tag to display a link to the largest Blog. First, you need to create a custom template tag library.

Follow these steps to create the custom template library, the custom tag, and the home page:

1. Stop the development server.

2. Create and open a file called iFriends/Custom/templatetags/custom_tags.py in an editor.

3. Add the following lines of code to the file to create a template.Library object to tell Django that this is a custom template library:

```
from django import template
register = template.Library()
```

4. Add the following lines of code to the file, as shown in Listing 13.3, to define a renderer object that accepts a Blog list variable name and uses the Variable() function to create a new Variable object:

```
class getLargestBlogNode(template.Node):
    def __init__(self, bList):
        self.bList = template.Variable(bList)
```

5. Add the following lines of code to the renderer object, as shown in Listing 13.3, to define the render() function that uses the resolve() function to obtain the Blog list object from the template context and then find the longest entry:

```
def render(self, context):
    lBlog = None
    longest = 0
    for blog in self.bList.resolve(context):
        if len(blog.text) >= longest:
            longest = len(blog.text)
            lBlog = blog
    context['largestBlog'] = lBlog
    return ''
```

6. Add the following lines of code, as shown in Listing 13.3, to add the largestBlog variable to the context and set it equal to the largest Blog object:

```
context['largestBlog'] = lBlog
return ''
```

▼

7. Add the following lines of code to the file, as shown in Listing 13.3, to define a compilation function that parses the tag contents to retrieve the Blog list object name in bList, handle validation errors, and return the render object you created in steps 4 through 6:

```
def getLargestBlog(parser, token):
    try:
        tag_name, bList = token.split_contents()
    except ValueError:
        raise template.TemplateSyntaxError
    return getLargestBlogNode(bList)
```

8. Add the following line of code, as shown in Listing 13.3, to register the tag in the library:

```
@register.tag(name="getLargestBlog")
```

9. Save the iFriends/Custom/templatetags/custom_tags.py file.

10. Create and open a file called iFriends/templates/Home/homepage.html in an editor.

11. Add the following line of code to the file, as shown in Listing 13.4, to load the custom library you created in step 1:

```
{% load custom_tags %}
```

12. Add the following lines of code to the file, as shown in Listing 13.4, to use the getLargestBlog tag to get the largest Blog from a variable bList. Then use the largestBlog variable that the getLargestBlog tag creates to insert a link to the Blog details web page:

```
{% getLargestBlog bList %}
<a href="/generic/blog_details/{{ largestBlog.id }}">
    {{ largestBlog.title }}</a>
```

13. Add the rest of the supporting HTML that extends the site base file and displays a list of Person objects and the quote of the day, as shown in Listing 13.4.

14. Save the iFriends/templates/Home/homepage.html file.

15. Open the iFriends/Home/views.py file in an editor.

16. Add the following lines of code, shown in Listing 13.5, to import the Person, Blog, and Quote objects:

```
from iFriends.People.models import Person, Blog
from iFriends.Quotes.models import Quote
```

17. Add the following `home_view()` view, as shown in Listing 13.5, to create a list of `Quote`, `Person`, and `Blog` objects and pass them to the `homepage.html` template file:

```
def home_view(request):
    quotes = Quote.objects.all()
    pList = Person.objects.all()
    bList = Blog.objects.all()
    return render_to_response('home/homepage.html', {
        'quotes': quotes, 'pList': pList, 'bList': bList})
```

18. Save the `iFriends/Home/views.py` file.

19. Open the `iFriends/urls.py` file in an editor.

20. Add the following entry to the URL patterns to enable the `home_view()` view:

```
(r'^$', 'iFriends.Home.views.home_view'),
```

21. Save the `iFriends/urls.py` file.

22. Start the development server. It should pick up the new custom tag file.

23. Open the following URL in a web browser to verify that the new home page works correctly and displays a link to the largest blog, as shown in Figure 13.2:

```
http://127.0.0.1:8000/
```

FIGURE 13.2
The home_
view() view in
a web browser
displaying a link
to the largest
Blog entry.

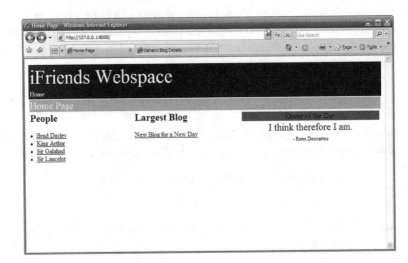

LISTING 13.3 Full Contents of `iFriends/Custom/templatetags/custom_tags.py`

```python
from django import template
register = template.Library()

@register.tag(name="getLargestBlog")
def getLargestBlog(parser, token):
    try:
        tag_name, bList = token.split_contents()
    except ValueError:
        raise template.TemplateSyntaxError
    return getLargestBlogNode(bList)

class getLargestBlogNode(template.Node):
    def __init__(self, bList):
        self.bList = template.Variable(bList)
    def render(self, context):
        lBlog = None
        longest = 0
        for blog in self.bList.resolve(context):
            if len(blog.text) >= longest:
                longest = len(blog.text)
                lBlog = blog
        context['largestBlog'] = lBlog
        return ''
```

LISTING 13.4 Full Contents of `iFriends/templates/Home/homepage.html`

```html
{% extends "iFriends_base.html" %}

{% block title %}Home Page{% endblock %}
{% block content %}
{% load custom_tags %}
<table width=100%>
<tr bgcolor="aabbcc"><td colspan="3">
<font size="5" color="white">Home Page</font>
</td></tr>
<tr valign="top">
<td width="30%">
<h2>People</h2>
{% for p in pList %}
    <li>
    <a href="{% url iFriends.People.views.details p.id %}">
        {{ p.name }}</a>
    </li>
{% endfor %}
</td>
<td width="30%">
<h2>Largest Blog</h2>
    {% getLargestBlog bList %}
    <a href="/generic/blog_details/{{ largestBlog.id }}">
        {{ largestBlog.title }}</a>
</td>
```

LISTING 13.4 continued

```
<td width="40%">
    {% include "quote.html" %}
</td>
</tr>
{% endblock %}
```

LISTING 13.5   Full Contents of `iFriends/Home/views.py`

```python
from django.shortcuts import render_to_response, get_object_or_404
from datetime import datetime
from django import newforms as forms
from iFriends.People.models import Person, Blog
from iFriends.Quotes.models import Quote

class EmailForm(forms.Form):
        title = forms.CharField(max_length=50,
                            widget=forms.TextInput(attrs={'size':'50'}))
        sender = forms.EmailField(max_length=30,
                            widget=forms.TextInput(attrs={'size':'30'}))
        date = forms.DateTimeField()
        text = forms.CharField(widget=forms.Textarea(
                            attrs={'rows':'6','cols':'75'}))

def contact_view(request):
    eForm = EmailForm()
    return render_to_response('home/contact_form.html', { 'eForm':eForm })

def home_view(request):
    quotes = Quote.objects.all()
    pList = Person.objects.all()
    bList = Blog.objects.all()
    return render_to_response('home/homepage.html', {
        'quotes': quotes, 'pList': pList, 'bList': bList})
```

Inclusion Tags

Another useful custom tag is the inclusion tag. Inclusion tags are different from normal tags in a couple of ways.

First, you do not need to define a renderer object. Instead, you register an HTML template file that will be used to render the data. The following line of code registers an `inclusion_tag` with the library that calls the `quote.html` template file using the QuoteLink compilation function:

```python
register.inclusion_tag('quote.html')(QuoteLink)
```

The second thing that is different in inclusion tags is that if you pass a variable to the function, the actual value gets passed, not just the name. For example, the following code defines a `QuoteLink` inclusion tag function that takes a quote object as its only argument and that can access the quote object directly:

```
def QuoteLink(quote):
    qLink = "<a href=\"quote/%d\"></a>" % (quote.id, quote.by)
    return {'qLink': qLink}
```

If you are passing a lot of arguments and you do not want to put them in the function definition, you can use takes_context=True when registering the node, and then add context as the first argument to the function:

```
def QuoteLink(context):
. . .
register.inclusion_tag('quote.html', takes_context=True)(QuoteLink)
```

You can access the variables in the context using the following dictionary syntax:

```
if context.has_key('quote'):
    quote = (context['quote'])
```

Watch Out!

If you include the takes_context=True argument when registering an inclusion_tag, you need to specify context as the first argument of the compilation function. The name of the context argument must be context for you to be able to access the template context inside the function.

The final thing that is different in inclusion tags is that they return a context dictionary that is passed to the render template instead of a template `Node` object. In the preceding example, the function builds a variable called `qLink` and returns it as part of the context dictionary that is passed to `quote.html`.

To access the inclusion tag from a template, use the following code:

```
{% QuoteLink quote %}
```

Try It Yourself

Create an Inclusion Tag to Generate a Set of Navigation Links

In this section, you will create an inclusion tag that generates a list of links that will be rendered in an HTML template. The template will be used to display navigation links for web pages in the site base HTML template file.

By the Way

You don't need to stop the development server to add the inclusion tag, because you created and opened the library file in the preceding "Try It Yourself" section.

Follow these steps to create the inclusion tag, create the navigation link HTML template file, and enable the tag in the site base HTML template:

1. Open the iFriends/Custom/templatetags/custom_tags.py file in an editor.

2. Add the following navLink() compilation function to the file, shown in Listing 13.6, to create a list of links. First you add a Home link, and then you retrieve the pageLinks variable from the template context and add them to the list. The list is returned by the function and is passed in the context to the HTML template file that is included with the tag:

```
def navLink(context):
    links = []
    link = {'name': 'Home', 'value': '/'}
    links.append(link)
    if context.has_key('pageLinks'):
        links.append(context['pageLinks'])
    return {'navLinks': links}
```

3. Add the following line of code, shown in Listing 13.6, to register the navLink tag and specify the navlink.html template to render the tag contents. You must include takes_context=True in the registration and in the navLink() function definition:

```
register.inclusion_tag('navlink.html', takes_context=True)(navLink)
```

4. Save the iFriends/Custom/templatetags/custom_tags.py file.

5. Create and open the iFriends/templates/navlink.html file in an editor.

6. Add the following lines of code to the file, shown in Listing 13.7, to use the navLinks variable to create navigation links for each link in the list:

```
{% for link in navLinks %}
    <a href="{{ link.value }}">{{ link.name }}</a>
{% endfor %}
```

7. Save the iFriends/templates/navlink.html file.

8. Open the iFriends/templates/iFriends_base.html file in an editor.

9. Add the following line of code, shown in Listing 13.8, to load the custom tag library:

```
{% load custom_tags %}
```

10. Replace the <td> that currently displays the text "Home" with the following lines of code, as shown in Listing 13.8, to use the navLink tag to display navigation links:

```
<td bgcolor="bbbbbbb">
    {% navLink %}
</td></tr>
```

11. Save the `iFriends/templates/iFriends_base.html` file.

12. Open the `iFriends/People/views.py` file in an editor.

13. Add the following lines of code to the `details()` view function of the People application, shown in Listing 13.9, to add a dictionary entry that links the `index()` view of the People application to the `pageLinks` list and adds the list to the dictionary that is passed into the `person_details.html` template:

```
pageLinks = ({'name': 'People', 'value': '/People/'})
rDict['pageLinks'] = pageLinks
```

14. Save the `iFriends/People/views.py` file.

15. Open the following URL in a web browser to bring up the `details()` view, shown in Figure 13.3.

```
http://127.0.0.1:8000/People/Info/1/
```

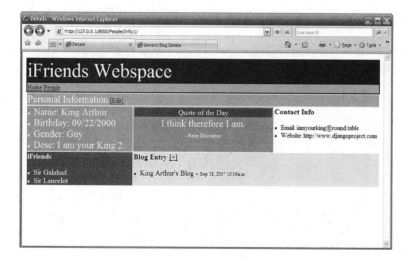

FIGURE 13.3
The Person `details()` view in a web browser displaying a navigation link to the Person `index()` view and a link to the `home_view()` view.

16. Verify that the People link works by clicking it in the new navigation list, shown in Figure 13.3, to bring up the `index()` view, shown in Figure 13.4.

17. Verify that the Home link works by clicking it in the new navigation list, shown in Figure 13.4, to bring up the `home_view()` view, shown in Figure 13.2.

FIGURE 13.4
The Person index() view in a web browser displaying a navigation link to the home_view() view.

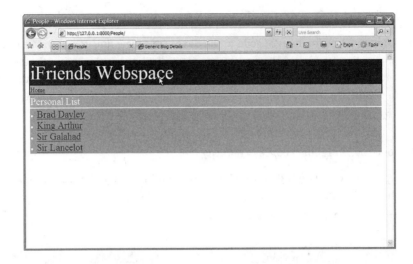

LISTING 13.6   navLink Tag Function and Registration in iFriends/Custom/templatetags/custom_tags.py

```
def navLink(context):
    links = []
    link = {'name': 'Home', 'value': '/'}
    links.append(link)
    if context.has_key('pageLinks'):
        links.append(context['pageLinks'])
    return {'navLinks': links}
register.inclusion_tag('navlink.html', takes_context=True)(navLink)
```

LISTING 13.7   Full Contents of iFriends/templates/navlink.html

```
{% for link in navLinks %}
    <a href="{{ link.value }}">{{ link.name }}</a>
{% endfor %}
```

LISTING 13.8   Full Contents of iFriends/templates/iFriends_base.html

```
<!DOCTYPE html>
<html xmlns="http://www.w3.org/1999/xhtml" lang="en-us" xml:lang="en-us" >
<head>
    <link rel="stylesheet" href="style.css" />
    <title>{% block title %}iFriends{% endblock %}</title>
</head>
<body>
{% load custom_tags %}
<table width=100% bgcolor="111177">
<tr><td>
```

```
<font size="12" color="white">iFriends Webspace</font>
</td></tr>
<tr>
<td bgcolor="bbbbbbb">
    {% navLink %}
</td></tr>
</table>
{% block content %}{% endblock %}
</body>
</html>
```

LISTING 13.9   details() **View Function in** iFriends/People/views.py

```
def details(request, pID='0', opts=()):
    rDict = {}
    p = get_object_or_404(Person, pk=pID)
    rDict['p'] = p
    quotes = Quote.objects.all()
    rDict['quotes'] = quotes
    pageLinks = {'name': 'People', 'value': '/People/'}
    rDict['pageLinks'] = pageLinks
    return render_to_response('people/person_details.html', rDict)
```

Understanding How to Use RequestContexts in Templates

To access information from an HttpRequest object in a template, you need to pass the template a RequestContext object. The django.template.RequestContext is a special template context object that includes the information from the HttpRequest.

The RequestContext requires an HttpRequest object in its constructor when you create an instance. You can also specify an optional dictionary and a list of additional processors that add items to the context.

The following line of code creates a RequestContext object:

```
c = Reqest.context(request, {'aKey': 'aValue'})
```

RequestContext then automatically populates the context with some of the information from the request.

> What information is automatically populated in the RequestContext depends on which context processors are specified by the TEMPLATE_CONTEXTPROCESSORS setting in the settings.py file.
>
> **By the Way**

You can also specify your own processors when creating the `RequestContext` object. For example, the following code snippet defines a processor that gathers the remote hostname in the request and adds it to an instance of a `RequestContext`:

```
def get_host(request):
    return {'remote_host': request.META['REMOTE_HOST']}
. . .
def show_rhost_view(request)
    reqContext = RequestContext(request, {}, [get_host])
```

After you have created the `RequestContext` object, you can pass it as a `context_instance` argument to the `render_to_response()` function. The `HttpRequest` data in the `RequestContext` will be available in the template. The following code snippet shows how to add the `RequestContext` object to a `render_to_response()` function call:

```
return render_to_response('template.html',
        data_dictionary,
        context_instance= reqContext)
```

The following code snippet shows how to access the `User` object in the `HttpRequest` from a template file that was rendered using the `RequestContext`:

```
Hello {{ user.username }}
```

If the user is not logged in, the user object in the `RequestContext` is an `AnonymousUser` object (which is described in Hour 14, "Managing Site Users").

Summary

In this hour, you learned how to create custom tag and filter library files and enable them in your project. You also learned how to create custom filters and use them in your templates.

We also covered creating and using different kinds of custom tags. You also learned how to create `simple_tags` and `inclusion_tags`. We also covered how to access the template context from a tag and use it to retrieve variables from the context and add new variables to the tags.

Using custom tags in Django's template engine really increases the possibilities of what you can do in your templates to quickly generate websites.

Q&A

Q. *Is there a way to use the template system in a stand-alone mode?*

A. Yes, but you must import the pieces you need from the template system and call the `django.conf.settings.configure()` function to configure the system manually. You can find more information about this process in the documentation at www.djangoproject.com.

Q. *Are there other tag and filter libraries bundled in Django?*

A. Yes. Django also bundles the following libraries in `django.contrib`. These libraries can be activated by adding them to the `INSTALLED_APPS` setting in the `settings.py` file.

▶ The `django.contrib.humanize` library contains a set of filters that help in adding a human touch to your templates. For example, the natural-day filter in the humanize library will render a date object in the textual form of yesterday, today, or tomorrow if applicable.

▶ The `django.contrib.markup` library contains a collection of filters that implement common markdown languages. For example, the `textile` filter will implement Textile, `markdown` will implement the Markdown language, and `restructuredtext` will implement the ReST language.

▶ The `django.contrib.webdesign` libraries contain template tags that can be useful while designing a website. Currently, the only tag is the `lorem` tag which will display random "lorem ipsum" Latin text.

Workshop

The workshop consists of a set of questions and answers designed to solidify your understanding of the material covered in this hour. Try answering the questions before looking at the answers.

Quiz

1. Which kind of custom tag would you want to use to retrieve data from the context and then use it to build a large amount of HTML code?

2. Which kind of custom tag would you use to write a simple function to change the case of text?

3. What directory does the template system look in to find filter libraries?

4. What object must be created in a custom library module for Django to recognize it as a valid library?

Quiz Answers

1. An `inclusion_tag`

2. A `simple_tag`

3. The templatetags directory in an installed application

4. A `template.Library` object

Exercises

1. Add some of your own filters to the iFriends/Custom/templatetags/ `custom_filters.py` library.

2. Add some of your own filters to the iFriends/Custom/templatetags/ `custom_tags.py` library.

For these two exercises, just get creative and try different things until you are familiar with creating custom tags and filters.

PART III

Implementing a Full-Featured Website

HOUR 14

Managing Site Users

What You'll Learn in This Hour:

▶ How to create User objects in your views
▶ How to add Group objects to the website and assign them to users
▶ How to create custom permissions in the model
▶ How to assign permissions to users and groups

So far in this book, we have neglected one of the most basic parts of most websites—registration and authentication. Django includes several components that aid in registration and authentication.

This hour discusses getting started with the registration and authentication process. We will cover creating User and Group objects as well as adding custom permissions to your models. We will also discuss setting permissions that allow you to control access to parts of the website.

Django currently provides a whole series of manipulator objects and built-in views to handle user creation, logins, logouts, password changes, and so on. Those manipulators are currently based on the old form framework, so I avoid using them. The examples that I will discuss cover creating your own Forms using the newforms library. I also will show you how to customize the registration and login process.

Adding Users

The first step in adding registration and authentication to the website is to implement some kind of User object so that you can determine who is trying to access the site. Hour 3,

"Adding Models and Objects to Your Website," introduced the admin interface and showed you how to use it to create User objects. Django implements User objects in the admin interface to control access. User objects can also be accessed from your views as part of registration, authentication, and permission control.

The following sections discuss User objects and how to create them from a view function.

Understanding User Objects

Django User objects give you a way to control access to your website by providing a means to force requests to come from authenticated sources. Implementing User objects also allows you to define permissions to specific areas of the website.

The following list describes the fields of a User object:

▶ username is required. It accepts up to 30 alphanumeric and underscore characters.

▶ first_name is optional. It accepts up to 30 characters.

▶ last_name is optional. It accepts up to 30 characters.

▶ email is optional. It accepts a valid email address.

▶ password is required. The password is actually stored as a hash that describes the raw password.

▶ is_staff is Boolean. It defaults to False. It specifies whether the user can access the admin site.

▶ is_active is Boolean. It defaults to True. It specifies whether the user can log into the website.

▶ is_superuser is Boolean. It defaults to False. It specifies whether the user has all permissions to the admin site.

▶ last_login is a datetime object containing the time when the user last logged in.

▶ date_joined is a datetime object containing the time when the User object was created.

▶ groups is a many-to-many field that lists Group objects that the User belongs to.

▶ user_permissions is a many-to-many field that lists permissions assigned to the User.

Anonymous Users

Django implements a special User class to handle anonymous requests. If a request comes from a user who is not currently logged in, the user attribute of the HttpRequest object is a django.contrib.auth.model.AnonymousUser object. The AnonymousUser object is like a normal User object, with the following exceptions:

- ▶ id is always None.

- ▶ is_staff is always False.

- ▶ is_superuser is always False.

- ▶ is_active is always True.

- ▶ groups and user_permissions are always empty.

- ▶ is_anonymous() returns True instead of False.

- ▶ has_perm() always returns False.

- ▶ The set_password(), check_password(), save(), delete(), set_groups(), and set_permission() functions raise a NotImplementedError.

Creating User Objects in Views

The admin interface is an excellent way to create objects. However, you will likely want to automate the creation of User objects by providing a web page that allows people to register with your website. When new users register, they will be able to create their own User objects and immediately access the website using their new account.

You can create User objects from the view function by calling the User.objects create_user(username, email, password=None) function and passing it username, email, and password as arguments.

For example, the following code creates a new User object for a user named Tim:

```
from django.contrib.auth.models import User
user = User.objects.create_user('Tim', 'tim@website.com', 'timspass')
```

Not specifying a password when using the create_user() function is not the same as entering a blank string for the password. An unuseable password is added, and the User object function has_useable_password() returns True. This feature can actually be useful if you are importing User objects from some other source using an automated method and you do not want to give them all the same generic password.

Watch Out!

Changing User Passwords in Views

You can change user passwords in the Django admin interface. However, you may also want to allow users to change their own passwords. To do so, you can create a view that renders a password change form similar to that of a login form. Then, inside the view, use the User.set_password() function on the User object of the request to change the password of the currently logged-in user.

The following code snippet shows the POST handler from a password change view function that sets the password of the current User object:

```
if request.method == 'POST':
    if request.POST['submit'] == 'Change Password':
        newPass = request.POST['password']
        request.user.set_password(newPass)
        request.user.save()
        return HttpResponseRedirect('/home')
```

▼ **Try It Yourself**

Add a User Object from a View Function

This section looks at a practical example of adding a User object to the iFriends website using a custom view. The Person objects are tied to the User objects, so you need to create them at the same time.

You will create a new form template and view function that will allow you to prompt the user for information to use when creating a new User object. You will use the information to create a new Person object and redirect the user to the details page for that object.

Follow these steps to create and enable the new user creation view:

1. Create and open a file called iFriends/templates/registration/ create_user.html in an editor.

2. Add the code shown in Listing 14.1 to the file to extend the site base template and display a form that will be used to create a new user.

3. Save the iFriends/templates/registration/create_user.html file.

4. Open the iFriends/Home/views.py file in an editor.

5. Add the following lines of code, shown in Listing 14.2, to import the User and HttpResponseRedirect objects:

```
from django.http import HttpResponseRedirect
from django.contrib.auth.models import User
```

▼

6. Add the following lines of code, shown in Listing 14.2, to define a
`NewUserForm` class that you will display in the `create_user.html` template
file to collect the information you will need to create the `User` and `Person`
objects. The password field is set to the `PasswordInput` Widget so that the
password is not displayed in the form:

```
gender_list = (('M', 'Male'), ('F', 'Female' ))
class NewUserForm(forms.Form):
        username = forms.CharField(max_length=30)
        password = forms.CharField(max_length=20,
                                   widget=forms.PasswordInput())
        first = forms.CharField(max_length=20)
        last = forms.CharField(max_length=20)
        gender = forms.ChoiceField(choices=gender_list)
        email = forms.EmailField(max_length=30)
```

7. Add the following lines of code, shown in Listing 14.2, to define a
`create_user()` view function that creates an instance of the `NewUserForm`
and renders it using the `create_user.html` template:

```
def create_user(request):
    message = 'Create New User'
    uForm = NewUserForm()
. . .
    return render_to_response('registration/create_user.html',{
                'uForm': uForm,
                'message': message })
```

8. Add the following lines of code to the `create_user()` view, shown in Listing
14.2, to handle a POST request from the form's Create button. This generates
an instance of the `NewUserForm` from the POST data:

```
if request.method == 'POST':
    if request.POST['submit'] == 'Create':
        postDict = request.POST.copy()
        uForm = NewUserForm(postDict)
```

> **Did you Know?**
>
> The reason we build an instance of the `NewUserForm` data is to handle errors in
> the form. If the user creation isn't successful, the form is redisplayed with con-
> tents and any errors that were found during validation.

9. Add the following lines of code to the `create_user()` view, shown in Listing
14.2, to create a new `User` object from the data in the POST request:

```
user = User.objects.create_user(
                        postDict['username'],
                        postDict['email'],
                        'password')
user.last_name = postDict['last']
user.first_name = postDict['first']
user.save()
```

10. Add the following lines of code to the create_user() view, shown in Listing 14.2, to create an instance of a Person form using the name, gender, and email from the POST and the User object that was created in step 9. The favoriteURL and desc Fields need to be filled in with some initial values because they are required in the Person model:

```
perDict = {}
perDict['name'] = "%s %s" % (postDict['first'], postDict['last'])
perDict['email'] = postDict['email']
perDict['gender'] = postDict['gender']
perDict['favoriteURL'] = 'http://www.iFriends.org'
perDict['desc'] = 'New User'
perDict['userID'] = user.id
SaveForm = forms.form_for_model(Person)
pForm = SaveForm(perDict)
```

11. Add the following lines of code to the create_user() view, shown in Listing 14.2, to validate the People form. If an error occurs, delete the User object and set the error message:

```
if pForm.is_valid():
. . .
else:
    message = 'Form Data Error'
    user.delete()
```

12. Add the following lines of code to the create_user() view, shown in Listing 14.2, to save the People form. If an error occurs, delete the User object and set a database error message:

```
try:
    p = pForm.save()
    return HttpResponseRedirect('/People/Info/%d/' % p.id)
except:
    message = 'Database Error.'
    user.delete()
```

13. Save the iFriends/Home/views.py file.

14. Open iFriends/urls.py in an editor.

15. Add the following line of code to enable the create_user() view:

```
(r'^NewUser/$', 'iFriends.Home.views.create_user'),
```

16. Access the following URL in a web browser to verify that the create_user() view, shown in Figure 14.1, correctly displays the creation form:

```
http://127.0.0.1:8000/NewUser/
```

17. Add valid data to the form, and click the Create button to create the new User and Person objects. A Person details() view similar to the one shown in Figure 14.2 should be displayed for the new Person object.

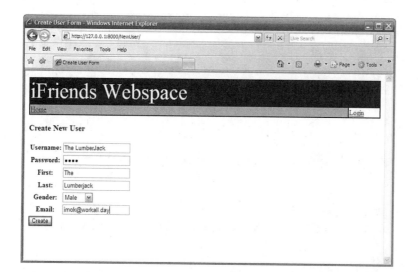

FIGURE 14.1
The create_
user() view dis-
playing the user
creation form.

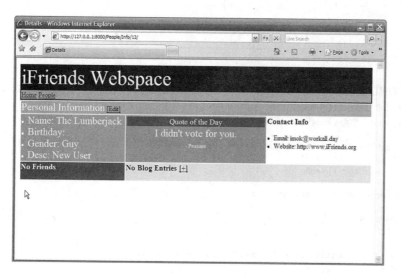

FIGURE 14.2
The Person
details() view
displaying the
newly created
Person object.

18. Verify that the new User object was created in the admin site by accessing the
following URL. Click the new User object you created to bring up the User
object admin page, shown in Figure 14.3:

```
http://127.0.0.1:8000/admin/auth/user/
```

FIGURE 14.3
The User object
view in the
admin site
showing the
newly created
User object.

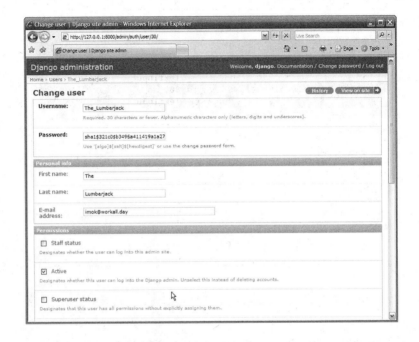

LISTING 14.1 Full Contents of `iFriends/templates/registration/`
`create_user.html`

```
{% extends "iFriends_base.html" %}

{% block title %}Create User Form{% endblock %}
{% block content %}
<h3>{{ message }}</h3>

<form method="post" action=".">
<table>
{{ uForm }}
</table>

<input type="submit" name="submit" value="Create" />
</form>
{% endblock %}
```

LISTING 14.2 Full Contents of `iFriends/Home/views.py`

```
from django.shortcuts import render_to_response, get_object_or_404
from django.http import HttpResponseRedirect
from datetime import datetime
from django import newforms as forms
from iFriends.People.models import Person, Blog
```

LISTING 14.2 Continued

```
from iFriends.Quotes.models import Quote
from django.contrib.auth.models import User

class EmailForm(forms.Form):
        title = forms.CharField(max_length=50,
                        widget=forms.TextInput(attrs={'size':'50'}))
        sender = forms.EmailField(max_length=30,
                        widget=forms.TextInput(attrs={'size':'30'}))
        date = forms.DateTimeField()
        text = forms.CharField(widget=forms.Textarea(
                        attrs={'rows':'6','cols':'75'}))

gender_list = (('M', 'Male'), ('F', 'Female' ))
class NewUserForm(forms.Form):
        username = forms.CharField(max_length=30)
        password = forms.CharField(max_length=20,
                                widget=forms.PasswordInput())
        first = forms.CharField(max_length=20)
        last = forms.CharField(max_length=20)
        gender = forms.ChoiceField(choices=gender_list)
        email = forms.EmailField(max_length=30)

def contact_view(request):
    eForm = EmailForm()
    return render_to_response('home/contact_form.html', { 'eForm':eForm })

def home_view(request):
    quotes = Quote.objects.all()
    pList = Person.objects.all()
    bList = Blog.objects.all()
    return render_to_response('home/homepage.html', {
                            'quotes': quotes,
                            'pList': pList,
                            'bList': bList})

def create_user(request):
    message = 'Create New User'
    uForm = NewUserForm()

    if request.method == 'POST':
        if request.POST['submit'] == 'Create':
            postDict = request.POST.copy()
            uForm = NewUserForm(postDict)
            try:
                #create User object
                user = User.objects.create_user(postDict['username'],
                                        postDict['email'],
                                        postDict['password'])
                user.last_name = postDict['last']
                user.first_name = postDict['first']
                user.save()

                #Create a Person object
                perDict = {}
                perDict['name'] = "%s %s" % (postDict['first'],
➥postDict['last'])
```

LISTING 14.2   Continued

```
                    perDict['email'] = postDict['email']
                    perDict['gender'] = postDict['gender']
                    perDict['favoriteURL'] = 'http://www.iFriends.org'
                    perDict['desc'] = 'New User'
                    perDict['userID'] = user.id
                    SaveForm = forms.form_for_model(Person)
                    pForm = SaveForm(perDict)
                    if pForm.is_valid():
                        try:
                            p = pForm.save()
                            return HttpResponseRedirect('/People/Info/%d/' % p.id)
                        except:
                            message = 'Database Error.'
                            user.delete()
                    else:
                        message = 'Form Data Error'
                        user.delete()
            except:
                message = 'User creation Error'

    return render_to_response('registration/create_user.html',{
                    'uForm': uForm,
                    'message': message })
```

Adding Groups

Django provides a django.contrib.auth.models.Group object that can be added
to the groups field of a User object. The Group object has two fields—name and
permissions. When you set the permissions attribute of the Group object, the permissions flow to each User who is a member of the group.

You can create a Group object using the following code:

```
from django.contrib.auth.models import Group
newGroup = Group()
newGroup.name = 'New Group'
newGroup.save()
```

Group objects can be added to and removed from a User object using the add(),
remove(), and clear() functions. The add() and remove() functions accept one or
more groups and then either add them to or remove them from the User object. The
clear() function removes all the groups from the User object. The following code
shows an example of the add(), remove(), and clear() functions:

```
user.groups.add(groupA, groupB)
user.groups.remove(groupC, groupD)
user.groups.clear()
```

Group objects can also be assigned to User objects in the admin interface. The User object details page lists groups that exist in the site. If you select groups in the groups list, the Group objects are added to the User.

The Group objects that belong to a user can be accessed through the groups attribute of the User object, as shown in the following line of code:

```
userGroups = user.groups
```

Group objects are the best way to assign permissions to several users at the same time. They are also a great way to collect users under a single label.

Try It Yourself ▼

Create a Group and Assign Users to It

In this section, you will create a new Group called iFriends and modify the create_user() view function to automatically assign new users who are created to that group. This allows you to quickly assign permissions to all users who register with the site.

1. Access the Django admin interface using the following URL:

   ```
   http://127.0.0.1:8000/admin/
   ```

2. Click the Groups link to bring up the group list, as shown in Figure 14.4.

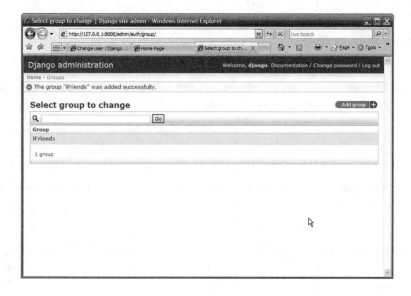

FIGURE 14.4
The Group List view in the admin interface.

3. Click the Add group link, shown in Figure 14.4, to bring up the Add group window, shown in Figure 14.5.

FIGURE 14.5
The Group Add
view in the
admin interface.

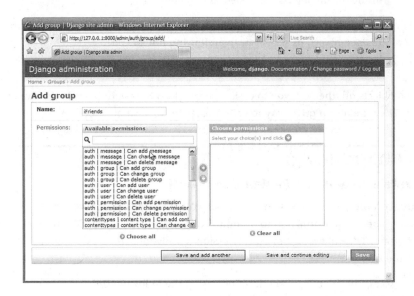

4. Enter the name iFriends into the Name field, and click the Save button. The iFriends group should now appear in the group list.

5. Open the iFriends/Home/views.py file in an editor.

6. Modify the following import statement to include the Group object:

```
from django.contrib.auth.models import User, Group
```

7. Add the following line of code before user.save(), shown in Listing 14.2, to add the iFriends Group object to the User object before saving it:

```
user.groups.add(Group.objects.get(name='iFriends'))
user.save()
```

8. Save the iFriends/Home/views.py file.

9. Create a new User, using the following URL, as discussed in the preceding "Try It Yourself" section:

```
http://127.0.0.1:8000/NewUser/
```

10. Access the User details in the admin interface, as discussed in the preceding section, and verify that the iFriends group is selected in the Groups list for the User object, as shown in Figure 14.6.

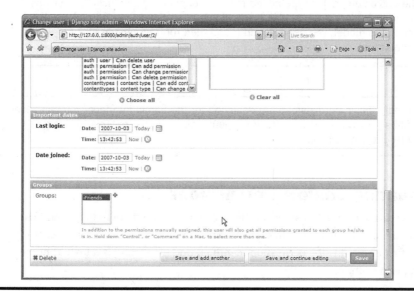

FIGURE 14.6
The User
Details view in
the admin inter-
face, showing
that the iFriends
group was
added to the
new user.

Setting User Permissions

In Django, permissions are basically just a way to set flags for users and groups that
either allow or inhibit them from performing certain actions. Permissions are created at the model object level and can be assigned to either a User or Group object.

> Permissions are set globally per object type. You cannot create permission to con-
> trol a specific instance of the object. For example, you cannot add a permission
> that would apply only to objects that a specific user creates.

Did you Know?

You will work with two different types of permissions. The first type is basic permissions that get assigned to objects automatically. The second type is custom
permissions that you create yourself. The following sections discuss the different
types of permissions.

Basic Permissions

Three types of basic permissions are automatically added to each model. The create,
add, and delete permissions are added to the auth_permission table in the database
for each model. These permissions limit access to the add, change, and delete forms
for the model in the admin interface.

> The basic permissions are added for the model only if you include the class admin definition in the model. If you didn't initially add the class admin definition in the model, you need to add it and then run the syncdb utility to add the permissions.

> Although basic permissions are designed for the admin interface, you can access and use them in your views to verify permissions for users. This is discussed more in the next hour.

Creating Custom Permissions

You create custom permissions in the model by adding them to the permissions attribute of the Meta class. To assign permissions, add them as a two-element list. The first element is the permission identifier, and the second is a textual name for the permission.

For example, the following code adds the custom permissions can_read and can_write to the Student model:

```
class Student(models.Model):
    . . .
    class Meta:
        permissions = (
            ('can_read', 'Reads Well'),
            ('can_write', 'Writes Well'),
        )
```

> After you add the permissions to the Meta class in the model, you need to run the syncdb utility to add the permissions to the database.

Adding Permissions to Users and Groups

You can add permissions to User and Group objects in one of two ways—by using Python code in your views or by using the admin interface.

Permissions objects can also be assigned to User or Group objects in the admin interface. The User and Group object details page lists available user permissions that exist in the site. If you add permissions in the available permissions list to the chosen permissions list, the permissions are available to the user or group.

You can add or remove permissions to and from a User or Group object using the add(), remove(), and clear() functions. The add() and remove() functions accept one or more permissions and then either add them to or remove them from the User or Group object. The clear() function removes all permissions from the User object.

The following code shows an example of the add(), remove(), and clear() functions on a User object:

```
userOBJ.user_permissions.add(permissionA, permissionB)
userOBJ.user_permissions.remove(permissionC, permissionD)
userOBJ.user_permissions.clear()
```

The following code shows an example of the add(), remove(), and clear() functions on a Group object:

```
groupOBJ.permissions.add(permissionA, permissionB)
groupOBJ.permissions.remove(permissionC, permissionD)
groupOBJ.permissions.clear()
```

Try It Yourself
Create and Set Custom Permissions

In this section, you will add a custom permission, can_blog, to the Blog model that will control access to creating blog entries. Then you will assign the can_blog permission to the iFriends group.

1. Stop the development server.

2. Open the iFriends/People/models.py file in an editor.

3. Add the following class definition to the Blog model, shown in Listing 14.3, to add the Meta class and create the can_blog permission in the model:

```
class Meta:
    permissions = (
        ('can_blog', 'Allowed to Blog'),
    )
```

4. Save the iFriends/People/models.py file.

5. From the root directory of the iFriends project, use the following command to synchronize the new permission to the database:

```
python manage.py syncdb
```

6. Start the development server.

7. Access iFriends Group object detail page, shown in Figure 14.7, in the admin interface.

FIGURE 14.7
The iFriends
group Details
view in the
admin interface,
showing the
Allowed
to Blog
permission.

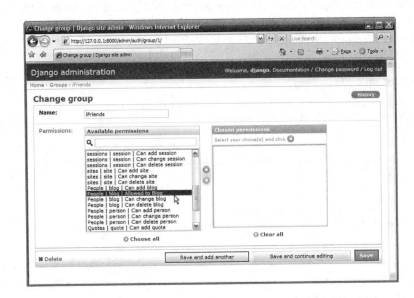

8. Scroll through the list of user permissions until you find the People | blog | Allowed to Blog permission, and select it.

9. Click the right arrow button to add the Allowed to Blog permission to the Chosen permissions list.

10. Click the Save button to update the iFriends group.

LISTING 14.3 Blog Model Definition in the iFriends/People/ models.py File

```python
class Blog(models.Model):
    title = models.CharField('Title', max_length=200)
    text = models.TextField('Text', max_length=2048)
    date = models.DateTimeField('Last Modified')

    def __str__(self):
        return '%s' % (self.title)

    class Admin:
        pass

    class Meta:
        permissions = (
            ('can_blog', 'Allowed to Blog'),
        )
```

Summary

In this hour, we discussed User objects and how to create them using custom forms in a view. We also discussed how to create Group objects. You can assign Group objects to User objects either from the admin interface or from your views. As soon as you have User and Group objects in place, you can add custom permissions to your models and assign them to User and Group objects.

Q&A

Q. *Is there a way to create a Django superuser object without accessing the admin interface or creating a new database?*

A. Yes. A `create_superuser.py` application is located in the following location relative to where you installed Django:

```
django/contrib/auth/create_superuser.py
```

It prompts you for a superuser name and password.

Q. *Is there a way to quickly email the user to let her know that her account has been created?*

A. Yes. The User object includes the function `email_user(subject, message, from_email=None)`. After the User object has been created, call the `email_user()` function with the subject, message, and from address (optional). The user will be notified at the email address she specified when registering the account.

Workshop

The workshop consists of a set of questions and answers designed to solidify your understanding of the material covered in this hour. Try answering the questions before looking at the answers.

Quiz

1. What function can you use to create User objects from a view function?

2. Where do you add custom permission objects?

3. In what format are passwords stored in the database?

4. How do you verify textual passwords against passwords in the database?

Quiz Answers

1. The `User.objects.create_user()` function.

2. Custom permissions are added to the `Meta` attribute of objects in the model.

3. Passwords are stored as a hash inside the database in the format `hashtype$salt$hash`.

4. You use the `User.check_password(textual_password, db_password)` function.

Exercises

1. Create some additional `People` objects and an additional group, Friendly, in the database.

2. Add some of the users in the database to the Friendly group.

3. Create a custom permission in the `Person` class called `can_add_friends`.

4. Add the `can_add_friends` custom permission to the Friendly group.

HOUR 15

Adding Website Security

What You'll Learn in This Hour:

▶ How to add login functionality
▶ How to add logout functionality
▶ How to verify authentication
▶ How to verify permissions
▶ How to limit access to generic views

Hour 14, "Managing Site Users," covered creating users and groups and setting permissions for both. This hour discusses securing the website by forcing users to be authenticated and logged into the site to gain access to certain pages. It also discusses how to use permissions to verify that users can view and change content.

Implementing User Logins

The first step in adding security to the website is creating User objects so that you know who is trying to access the website. The second step is implementing a login to force users to enter a password before they are admitted to the website.

The login process has three steps. The first is to prompt the user for his or her username and password. The next step is to authenticate the user by verifying that the username and password match a User object that exists in the database. The final step is to log the user into the website by adding the authenticated User object to the user's session. (Sessions are discussed more in Hour 16, "Managing Sessions and Cookies.")

Did you Know?

Django provides a simple way to implement logins using the `django.contrib.auth.views.login` view. You add the pattern (`r'^accounts/login/$'`, `login`) to the `URLs.py` file to enable the view and then create a template named `registration/login.html` that creates a form. I won't cover this view in more detail here, because it uses the old forms library and likely will change. (See `www.djangoproject.com` for more details.)

Django provides the `django.contrib.auth.authenticate()` function to help you verify that usernames and passwords match `User` objects in the database. The `authenticate()` function takes the username and password as arguments and then checks them against the database and returns the matching `User` object if one is found. If no match is found, `authenticate()` returns None. For example, the following code tries to authenticate a user named Bill:

```
user = authenticate(username = 'bill', password = 'billPass')
if user is not None:
    #authenticated
else:
    #bad username or password
```

By the Way

You can also manually check the password using the `django.contrib.auth.models.check_password()` function. The `check_password()` function takes a string password as the first argument and the password attribute, containing the password hash, of the `User` object as the second. It returns True if they match and False if they don't. For example:

```
check_password('billPass', user.password)
```

After you use the `authenticate()` function to get a valid user, you can use the `django.contrib.auth.login()` functions to actually log the user into the website. The `login()` function accepts the `HttpRequest` object as the first argument and the `User` object as the second. You also should verify that the `is_active` attribute of the `User` object is true before calling `login()`. The following example shows how to log the `User` object into the session:

```
if user.is_active:
    login(request, user)
else:
    #account has been disabled
```

Try It Yourself ▼

Implement a User Login Page

In this section, you will create a view function and template that prompt users to enter a username and password. The view function checks the username and password against User objects in the system and logs in the user if they match.

Follow these steps to create a user login view and enable it to log in users:

1. Create and open a file called iFriends/templates/registration/login. html in an editor.

2. Add the contents, shown in Listing 15.1, to extend the site base template and display a login form using the variable lForm.

3. Save the iFriends/templates/registration/login.html file.

4. Open the iFriends/Home/views.py file in an editor.

5. Add the following import statement, shown in Listing 15.2, to import the authenticate() and login() functions:

```
from django.contrib.auth import authenticate, login
```

6. Add the following lines of code, shown in Listing 15.2, to define a LoginForm class with username and password Fields that you can use to prompt the user for input and validate:

```
class LoginForm(forms.Form):
    username = forms.CharField(max_length=30)
    password = forms.CharField(max_length=20, widget=forms.PasswordInput())
```

7. Add the following lines of code, shown in Listing 15.2, to define the login_user() view function, accept an optional next argument, create an instance of a LoginForm object, and render the form using the login.html template file:

```
def login_user(request, next= '/'):
    message = 'Login User'
    lForm = LoginForm()
    . . .
    return render_to_response('registration/login.html',{
            'lForm': lForm,
            'message': message })
```

8. Add the following lines of code to see if the GET request included a next key to indicate where to redirect successful logins and to set the next variable accordingly:

```
if request.GET.has_key('next'):
    next = request.GET['next']
```

9. Add the following lines of code, shown in Listing 15.2, to handle the POST request that the user submits to log in to the website:

```
if request.method == 'POST':
    if request.POST['submit'] == 'Login':
```

10. Add the following lines of code, shown in Listing 15.2, to validate the LoginForm. If it's valid, authenticate the user:

```
if lForm.is_valid():
    uName = request.POST['username']
    uPass = request.POST['password']
    user = authenticate(username=uName, password=uPass)
```

11. Add the following lines of code, shown in Listing 15.2, to verify that the user could be authenticated and verify that the account is active. Then use the login() function to log the user into the website and redirect to the URL specified by the next argument:

```
if user is not None:
    if user.is_active:
        login(request, user)
        return HttpResponseRedirect(next)
    else:
        message = 'Account Deactivated'
else:
    message = 'Login Incorrect'
```

12. Save the iFriends/Home/views.py file.

13. Open the iFriends/urls.py file in an editor.

14. Add the following URL pattern to enable the login_user() view:

```
(r'^Login/$', 'iFriends.Home.views.login_user'),
```

15. Save the iFriends/urls.py file.

16. Go to the following URL in a web browser to bring up the login_user() view, as shown in Figure 15.1:

```
http://127.0.0.1:8000/Login/
```

17. Enter a valid username and password for the site, and click the Login button. Verify that the home page comes up.

By the Way

> The admin interface uses the same session that the website does. When you log in as a different user, this affects your rights to the admin interface based on what rights the new user has. If you still want to use the admin interface, you may need to log in again as a user with rights to the admin interface.

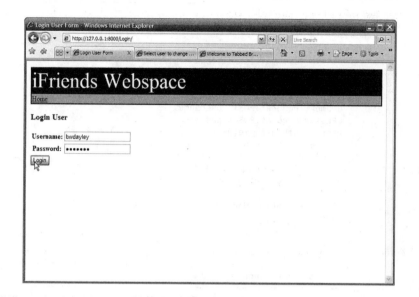

FIGURE 15.1
The user login
form generated
by the user_
login() view.

LISTING 15.1 Full Contents of iFriends/templates/registration/login.html

```
{% extends "iFriends_base.html" %}
{% block title %}Login User Form{% endblock %}
{% block content %}
<h3>{{ message }}</h3>
<form action="" method="post">
<table>
{{ lForm }}
</table>
<input type="submit" name="submit" value="Login" />
</form>
{% endblock %}
```

LISTING 15.2 Imports, LoginForm Definition, and the login_user() Function in the iFriends/Home/views.py File

```
from django.contrib.auth import authenticate, login
. . .
class LoginForm(forms.Form):
      username = forms.CharField(max_length=30)
      password = forms.CharField(max_length=20, widget=forms.PasswordInput())
. . .
def login_user(request, next= '/'):
    message = 'Login User'
    lForm = LoginForm()
```

LISTING 15.2   Continued

```
    if request.GET.has_key('next'):
        next = request.GET['next']

    if request.method == 'POST':
        if request.POST['submit'] == 'Login':
            postDict = request.POST.copy()
            lForm = LoginForm(postDict)
            if lForm.is_valid():
                uName = request.POST['username']
                uPass = request.POST['password']
                user = authenticate(username=uName, password=uPass)
                if user is not None:
                    if user.is_active:
                        login(request, user)
                        return HttpResponseRedirect(next)
                    else:
                        message = 'Account Deactivated'
                else:
                    message = 'Login Incorrect'

    return render_to_response('registration/login.html',{
                    'lForm': lForm,
                    'message': message })
```

Adding Logout Functionality

Now that you have given users a way to log into the website, you likely will want to give them a way to log out. Django provides the `django.contrib.auth.logout()` function to handle removing the logged-in user from the session.

The `logout()` function takes an `HttpRequest` object as its only parameter and decouples the logged-in `User` object from the session. The following example shows how to use the `logout()` function in a view:

```
def logout(request):
    auth.logout(request)
    return HttpResponseRedirect("somelogoutULR")
```

By the Way

The `logout()` function does not raise any errors if the user wasn't logged in, so you don't need to verify that it is being called on a request that has a logged-in user.

Try It Yourself

Add Logout Functionality to Your Website

In this section, you will create a `user_logout()` view function that logs out the current user. Follow these steps to create and enable the logout view so that it redirects the user to the `user_login()` view:

1. Open the `iFriends/Home/views.py` file in an editor.

2. Add `logout` to the following import statement to import the `logout()` function:

   ```
   from django.contrib.auth import authenticate, login, logout
   ```

3. Add the following `logout_user()` function, shown in Listing 15.3, to log out the user and redirect the response to the `user_login()` view:

   ```
   from django.contrib.auth import authenticate, login, logout
   . . .
   def logout_user(request):
       logout(request)
       return HttpResponseRedirect('/Login')
   ```

4. Save the `iFriends/Home/views.py` file.

5. Open the `iFriends/urls.py` file in an editor.

6. Add the following URL pattern to enable the new `logout_user()` view:

   ```
   (r'^Logout/$', 'iFriends.Home.views.logout_user'),
   ```

7. Save the `iFriends/urls.py` file.

8. Access the following URL in a web browser. It should log you out of the website. (You can confirm this by trying to access the admin interface.)

   ```
   http://127.0.0.1:8000/Logout/
   ```

LISTING 15.3 Imports and the Definition of the `logout_user()` Function in the `iFriends/Home/views.py` File

```
from django.contrib.auth import authenticate, login, logout
. . .
def logout_user(request):
    logout(request)
    return HttpResponseRedirect('/Login')
```

Verifying Authentication

Now that you can log users in and out, you can start securing your website by veri-fying that users are authenticated before giving them access to your views. You can verify authentication in both your view functions and template files.

Verifying Authentication in View Functions

You can use the is_authenticated() function of the User object in a view's HttpRequest to determine if the user is authenticated. Then you can modify the view's behavior, depending on whether the user is authenticated. For example, if the user isn't authenticated, you could redirect that person to a login page, render a different view, or render only a portion of the current view.

The following code snippet shows an example of using the is_authenticated() function in a view to redirect unauthenticated users to a login page:

```
def secure_view(request):
    if not request.users.is_authenticated():
        return HttpResponseRedirect('/Login')
```

Django provides a decorator function that simplifies verification of authentication. The login_required() function verifies whether the user is authenticated. If the user isn't authenticated, this function redirects the user to the URL specified in the LOGIN_URL setting in the settings.py file. The login_required() function passes the URL of the current request to the login function as a query string using the next variable name. For example, the following code applies the login_required decorator:

```
@login_required(redirect_field_name='reDir')
def secure_view(request):
. . .
```

If the user is not authenticated, this decorator redirects the browser to the following URL, where LOGIN_URL is set to /Login and the request.get_full_path() for the secure_view() view function is /views/secure_view:

```
/Login?next=/views/secure_view
```

> The login_required() function also accepts an optional argument, redirect_field_name. It allows you to specify the argument name, instead of next, that should be used to pass the redirection URL to your login function:
>
> ```
> @login_required(redirect_field_name='reDir')
> def secure_view(request):
> ```

Verifying Authentication in Templates

You can also verify whether the user has been authenticated in a template by passing in a RequestContext and then accessing the User object. Then you can use the authentication information to determine how to render the template.

For example, the following code snippet verifies whether the user is authenticated before showing a table of data:

```
{% if user.is_authenticated %}
<table>
{{ secure_data }}
</table>
{% endif %}
```

Try It Yourself ▼

Verify Authentication in Templates and Views

In this section, you will modify the base template to display a welcome message if the user is authenticated. You will also add a decorator template to the People details() view function to force users to be authenticated before they view the home page. You will also modify the home_view() function to verify authentication and pass an empty Blog list if the user isn't authenticated so that no blog entries appear on the home page.

1. Open the iFriends/settings.py file in an editor.

2. Add the following line of code to set the LOGIN_URL setting that the login_required() decorator function uses for logins:

   ```
   LOGIN_URL ='/Login'
   ```

3. Save the iFriends/settings.py file.

4. Open the iFriends/People/views.py file in an editor.

5. Add the following import statements to import the RequestContext object and the login_required() decorator function:

   ```
   from django.template import RequestContext
   from django.contrib.auth.decorators import login_required
   ```

6. Add the following decorator function, shown in Listing 15.4, to the details() view function to allow only authenticated users to view the web page:

   ```
   @login_required
   ```

▼

7. Modify the `render_to_response()` call (shown in Listing 15.4) of the `details()` function to include the `context_instance` argument so that the `RequestContext` is available in the `person_details.html` template:

```
return render_to_response('people/person_details.html', rDict,
                    context_instance = RequestContext(request))
```

8. Save the `iFriends/People/views.py` file.

9. Open the `iFriends/Home/views.py` file in an editor.

10. Add the following `import` statements to import the `RequestContext` `login_required()` decorator function:

```
from django.template import RequestContext
```

11. Add the following lines of code, shown in Listing 15.5, to verify that the user is authenticated. If the user isn't authenticated, return an empty `Blog` list so that no blogs are displayed on the home page:

```
if request.user.is_authenticated():
    bList = Blog.objects.all()
else:
    bList = []
```

12. Modify the `render_to_response()` call, shown in Listing 15.5, to include the `context_instance` argument so that the `RequestContext` is available in the `homepage.html` template:

```
context_instance = RequestContext(request))
```

13. Save the `iFriends/Home/views.py` file.

14. Open the `iFriends/templates/iFriends_base.html` file in an editor.

15. Add the following table column entry, as shown in Listing 15.6, to see whether the user is authenticated. If the user is authenticated, a welcome message is displayed. If not, a link to the login page is displayed:

```
<td bgcolor="white"><font size="3">
    {% if user.is_authenticated %}
        Welcome {{ user.username }}.
    {% else %}
        <a href="/Login">Login</a>
    {% endif %}
</font></td>
```

By the Way

All the views that render templates that extend the `iFriends_base.html` file must include the `RequestContext` in the `render_to_response()`. Otherwise, the welcome message is not displayed for authenticated users.

16. Save the `iFriends/templates/iFriends_base.html` file.

17. Access the following URL in a browser to log out of the website:

```
http://127.0.0.1:8000/Logout/
```

Verify that you are redirected to the login page, shown in Figure 15.2.

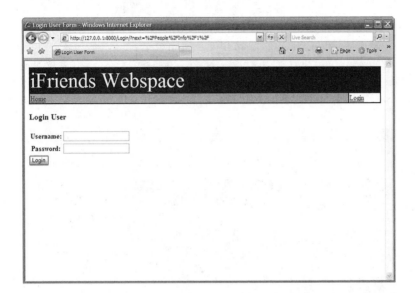

FIGURE 15.2
The web page generated by the login_ user() view function.

18. Click the Home link in the navigation bar to bring up the home page. Verify that no Largest Blog is listed, as shown in Figure 15.3.

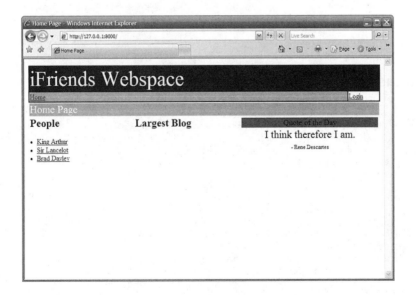

FIGURE 15.3
The home page view for an unauthenticated user, with a Login link and no Largest Blog link.

19. Click one of the people in the list. Authentication should fail, because you have logged out. You should be directed back to the login page, shown in Figure 15.2.

20. Click the Home link again to bring up the home page. Then click the Login link to verify that it links correctly to the login page.

21. From the login page, enter a valid username and password, and verify that you are brought back to the home page. A welcome message should now be displayed instead of the Login link, and the Largest Blog link should also be listed, as shown in Figure 15.4.

FIGURE 15.4
The home page view for an authenticated user, with a welcome message and a Largest Blog link.

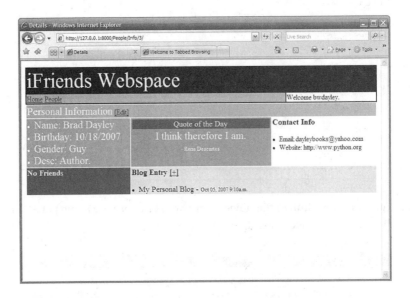

LISTING 15.4   Imports and the `details()` View Function of the `iFriends/People/views.py` File

```
from django.template import RequestContext
from django.contrib.auth.decorators import login_required
. . .
@login_required
def details(request, pID='0', opts=()):
    rDict = {}
    p = get_object_or_404(Person, pk=pID)
    rDict['p'] = p
    quotes = Quote.objects.all()
    rDict['quotes'] = quotes
    pageLinks = ({'name': 'People', 'value': '/People/'})
    rDict['pageLinks'] = pageLinks
    return render_to_response('people/person_details.html', rDict,
                 context_instance = RequestContext(request))
```

LISTING 15.5 Imports and the `home_view()` Function of the
`iFriends/Home/views.py` File

```
from django.template import RequestContext
. . .
def home_view(request):
    quotes = Quote.objects.all()
    pList = Person.objects.all()
    if request.user.is_authenticated():
        bList = Blog.objects.all()
    else:
        bList = []
    return render_to_response('home/homepage.html', {
                              'quotes': quotes,
                              'pList': pList,
                              'bList': bList,},
                              context_instance = RequestContext(request))
```

LISTING 15.6 Table Row Containing the Navigation Link and Login/
Welcome Data in the `iFriends/templates/iFriends_base.html` File

```
. . .
<tr>
<td bgcolor="bbbbbbb">
    {% navLink %}
</td>
<td bgcolor="white"><font size="3">
    {% if user.is_authenticated %}
        Welcome {{ user.username }}.
    {% else %}
        <a href="/Login">Login</a>
    {% endif %}
</font></td>
</tr>
. . .
```

Verifying Permissions

The process of adding code to verify permissions is similar to that of verifying
authentication. Just like authentication, you can verify permissions in both your
view functions and template files. The following sections describe this process.

Verifying Permissions in View Functions

You can use the `User.has_perm()` function of the `User` object in the `HttpRequest`
of a view function to determine if the user has specific permissions. Then you can
modify the view's behavior, depending on what permissions the user has.

The has_perm() function accepts a string representation of the permission in the format *application.permission identifier*. If the User object has the permission specified, the has_perm() function returns True. For example, the following line of code returns True if the user object has the can_modify permission for an application called Report:

```
user.has_perm.('Report.can_modify')
```

The permission identifier comes from the permission definition. In the case of custom permissions, it is the first string specified in the definition. In the case of the default permissions that are automatically created for the admin interface, the value is add_ with the object name appended. For example, if you defined an object named Person in your model, the identifiers for the add, delete, and change permissions would be add_Person, delete_Person, and change_Person, respectively.

> You can also determine if the User object has any permissions in an application by using the User.has_module_perms() function. The has_module_perms() function accepts an application name as an argument and returns True if the User object has any permissions set in the module. The following is an example of using the has_module_perms() function:
>
> ```
> if user.has_module_perms('Report'):
> ```

The following code snippet shows an example of using the has_perm() function in a view to render two completely different templates, depending on what permission the user has:

```
def blog_view(request):
    if request.users.has_perm('Blog.blog_edit'):
        return render_to_response('blog_form.html', {})

    else:
        return render_to_response('blog_form.html', {})
```

Verifying Permissions in Templates

You can also verify user permissions in a template by passing in a RequestContext and then accessing the perms template variable. The perms template variable is an instance of the django.core.context_processors.PermWrapper object, which wraps the permissions together in a template-friendly form.

The permissions can be accessed using the perms variable in two different levels—the module level and the permission level. The module level is equivalent to using the User.has_module_perms() function. For example, to access the permissions for an application named Blog at the module level, you would use the following template code:

```
{{ perms.Blog }}
```

The permission level is equivalent to using the `User.has_perms()` function. For example, to access the `can_edit` permissions for an application named Blog at the permission level, you would use the following template code:

```
{{ perms.Blog.can_edit }}
```

Using the `perms` variable, you can determine in your template what permissions the user has and render the template based on those permissions. For example, the following code snippet determines if the user has the `can_edit` permission for the Report application. It displays editable data if the user has permission and view-only data if he doesn't:

```
{% if perms.Report.can_edit %}
  {{ reportUpdateForm }}
{% else %}
  {{ viewOnlyData }}
{% endif %}
```

Try It Yourself ▼

Use User Permissions to Limit Access in Views and Templates

In this section, you will use the `can_blog` permission that you created in Hour 14 to limit access to the `add_blog()` view. You will first modify the `person_details.html` template to determine if the user has the `can_blog` permission and see whether the request user matches the `userID` of the `Person` object that is being displayed. If those two things don't match, omit the link to the `add_blog()` view. That will stop people who don't have permission from seeing the link.

Next, you will modify the `add_blog()` function directly to verify that the user has the `can_blog` permission. If he doesn't, he is redirected to the home page. This will stop users who try to directly access the `add_blog()` view. You will also modify the `add_blog()` function to use the `User` object from the `HttpRequest` to find the `Person` object that the `Blog` will be added to.

We are using a permission created in the `Blog` class to show that permissions are tied to the module and not the object. The People application has two classes—`Blog` and `Person`. However, to access the `can_blog` permission, you use the People module. Be careful how you name your permissions if the same model has multiple classes so that two classes don't end up with the same permission name.

By the Way ▼

Follow these steps to implement the `can_blog` permission to limit access to the `add_blog()` view:

1. Open the `iFriends/templates/People/person_details.html` file in an editor.

2. Modify the `add_blog()` view link using the following lines of code, shown in Listing 15.7. The link to add `Blog` objects shows up only if the user has the `can_blog` permission and if the `user.id` from the request matches the `userID.id` from the `Person` object passed to the `details()` view:

```
{% if perms.People.can_blog %}
  {% ifequal user p.userID %}
    <a href="{% url iFriends.People.views.add_blog pID=p.id %}">[+]</a>
  {% endifequal %}
{% endif %}
```

3. Save the `iFriends/templates/People/person_details.html` file.

4. Open the `iFriends/People/views.py` file.

5. Add the following lines of code to the beginning of the `add_blog()` function, as shown in Listing 15.8, to see whether the user has the `can_blog` permission. If she doesn't, she is redirected to the home page:

```
if not request.user.has_perm('People.can_blog'):
    return HttpResponseRedirect('/')
```

6. Modify the `get_object_or_404()` function, shown in Listing 15.8, as follows:

```
p = get_object_or_404(Person, userID=request.user)
```

This gets the `Person` object that matches the user from the request by matching the `userID` field to the user object in the request.

7. Save the `iFriends/People/views.py` file.

8. Open the home page in a web browser by accessing the following URL:

```
http://127.0.0.1:8000/
```

9. Click the person you are currently logged in as, and verify that the + link to add a new blog entry is still there (refer to Figure 15.4).

10. Click the Back button in the browser. Access a different user, and verify that the + link is gone, as shown in Figure 15.5.

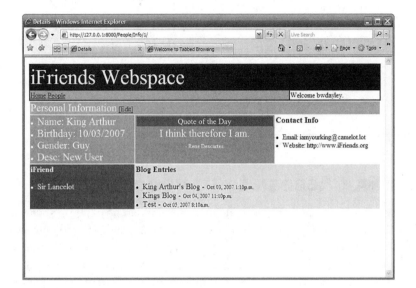

FIGURE 15.5
The People
details() view
for a different
person than the
one who is cur-
rently logged in,
with no + link to
add a new blog.

LISTING 15.7 Table Column Entry That Displays the Blog List in the
`iFriends/templates/People/person_details.html` **File**

```
<td width="70%" bgcolor="eeeeee" colspan="2" valign="top">
    <font size="4">
    {% with p.blogs.all as bl %}
    <h3>
        {{ bl|length|yesno:"Blog,No Blog"}}
        Entr{{ bl|length|pluralize:"y,ies"}}
        {% if perms.People.can_blog %}
          {% ifequal user.id p.userID.id %}
            <a href="{% url iFriends.People.views.add_blog pID=p.id %}">[+]</a>
          {% endifequal %}
        {% endif %}
    </h3>
    {% for b in bl %}
    <li>{{ b.title }} -
        <font size="2"> {{ b.date|date:"M d, Y g:ma" }}</font>
    </li>
    {% endfor %}
    {% endwith %}
    </font>
</td>
```

▼

LISTING 15.8   Beginning of the `add_blog()` View Function in the `iFriends/People/views.py` File

```
def add_blog(request, pID='0'):
    if not request.user.has_perm('People.can_blog'):
        return HttpResponseRedirect('/')

    BlogForm = forms.form_for_model(Blog, fields=('title', 'text'))
    bf = BlogForm()
    message = 'Unknown Request'
    p = get_object_or_404(Person, userID=request.user)
. . .
```

▲

Limiting Access to Generic Views

Limiting access to generic views is a bit different from limiting access to your own views, because there is no view code in which to verify permissions and authentication. Generic views do use a `RequestObject`, so you can access authentication and permissions in the template file of the generic view. However, if you want to limit access before the template gets called, you must create your own wrapper view that handles authentication and password verification.

To create a wrapper, you modify the `URLconf` file and add another pattern to the wrapper view function. Then you create the wrapper view function in the application's `views.py` file. The wrapper view function only needs to verify the permissions and/or authentication and then return the generic view function with arguments and keywords passed through. For example, the following URL pattern links to a generic `object_details` view:

```
(r'^/obj_details/(?P<object_id>\d+)/$', object_detail, obj_info),
```

To implement a wrapper function called `secure_object_detail()`, modify the entry as shown in the following URL pattern:

```
(r'^/obj_details/(?P<object_id>\d+)/$', site.Obj.secure_object_detail,
➥obj_info),
```

You then add the following code snippet to the application's `views.py` file. This code imports the `object_detail()` generic view and defines a wrapper view, `secure_object_detail()`, that verifies that the user is logged in before calling the generic `object_view()` function:

```
from django.views.generic.list_detail import object_detail
@login_required
def secure_object_detail(*args, **kwargs):
    return object_detail(*args, **kwargs)
```

Summary

In this hour, we covered the basics of verifying authentication and permissions. You learned how to verify login status in both view functions and templates. You also learned how to modify the view functions and templates to behave differently for logged-in users than for unauthenticated users.

We also covered how to access the permissions assigned to the user. You learned how to modify the behavior of view functions and templates based on the user's permissions.

Q&A

Q. Is there a way to retrieve all of a user's permissions?

A. Yes. The `User.get_all_permissions()` function returns a list of permission strings that represent the user's permissions.

Q. Is there a way to control what happens during authentication to customize verification?

A. Yes. You can specify your own authentication backend by adding it to the `AUTHENTICATION_BACKENDS` setting in the `settings.py` file. Django applies the backends in the order they are listed in the setting. The backend must be in the Python path. The backend needs to define an `authenticate()` function that checks the credentials and returns a `User` object on success and `None` on failure. For example:

```
from django.contrib.auth.models import User, check_password
class custBackend:
    def authenticate(self, username, password):
        #validation code
        . . .
        if authenticated:
            return user
        else:
        return None
```

Workshop

The workshop consists of a set of questions and answers designed to solidify your understanding of the material covered in this hour. Try answering the questions before looking at the answers.

Quiz

1. Which function verifies that a username and password match a `User` object in the database?

2. Which function adds the `User` object to the current session?

3. Which variable do you use inside a template to access user permissions?

4. What type of context object must be added to the `render_to_response()` call to allow you to access authentication and permission information?

Quiz Answers

1. The `django.contrib.auth.authenticate()` function

2. The `django.contrib.auth.login()` function

3. The `perms` variable

4. A `RequestContext` object

Exercises

1. Create a view function called `add_friends()` in the `iFriends/People/views.py` file, and enable it in the URLconf file. Have the `add_friends()` function accept the `id` of the `Person` object currently logged in as the first parameter after the request, and the `id` of the `Person` object you want to add as a friend as the second.

2. Add code in the `add_friends()` view to verify that the user is logged in and has the `can_add_friends` permission you created in the exercises in Hour 14.

3. Add code to the `add_friends()` view to add the `Person` object specified as a friend to the `friends` Field of the currently logged-in `Person` object.

4. Add an invite link to the Person list on the home page that links to the `add_friends()` view. It should pass in the `id` of the currently logged-in user and the `id` of the `Person` object in the list.

HOUR 16

Managing Sessions and Cookies

What You'll Learn in This Hour:

▶ How Django's session framework works
▶ How to configure the session manager
▶ How to use Django's test cookies to verify that the browser supports cookies
▶ How to add and retrieve session data using the `session` attribute of the `HttpRequest` object
▶ How to set and retrieve cookies using the `HttpRequest` object

In the past couple of hours, we have covered implementing users and authentication. Now it is time to discuss implementing a session framework that will allow you to provide a persistent state for user data.

As a user browses the website and does various activities, you may want to retain certain data about that user's activities. Generally this is accomplished by setting cookies in the web browser. Storing data in cookies has definite advantages and disadvantages.

Django provides a session framework that abstracts cookies and provides a better form of persistent session data.

The following sections discuss Django's session framework and how to configure the session manager. They also cover using the session manager to add and retrieve data about the session. In addition, we will cover using the `HttpRequest` object to set and retrieve cookies from the browser.

Understanding Django's Session Framework

A cookie is simply a piece of data stored on the user's computer by the web browser. The biggest problem with cookies is that they are not secure. The data in the cookie can be modified by the user, an application, or another website. Another problem with cookies is that users can set their browsers to reject cookies, effectively disabling any control you might try to provide using cookies. Cookies are also only sent to the server when a request is made on the same domain that the cookie was created on. Therefore, cookies cannot be accessed across multiple domains.

The Django session framework solves some of the problems with cookies by storing only a hashed session ID on the browser side and the actual user data on the server side. The session framework allows you to store and retrieve data about a specific site user. The session data is stored in a table in the database by default.

Configuring the Session Manager

Django's session framework is provided in two pieces—a middleware application and a Django model. Middleware applications are applications that run between the Django framework and your own custom website code. The session framework should be enabled by default. However, we will cover the steps to enable it anyway.

To enable the session framework, you need to modify the `MIDDLEWARE_CLASSES` setting in the `settings.py` file to include the following class:

```
'django.contrib.sessions.middleware.SessionMiddleware',
```

You also need to add the following model to the `INSTALLED_APPS` setting in the `settings.py` file:

```
'django.contrib.sessions',
```

> If `django.contrib.sessions` wasn't already listed in the installed application, run the `syncdb` application to create the session table in the database.

Django stores session data in a table in the database by default. However, you can also configure the session manager to store the data in the file system or in cached memory. Storing session data in the file system or cache may improve site performance in some instances. To change the session backend, set the `SESSION_ENGINE` setting in the `sessions.py` file to one of the following:

▶ `django.contrib.sessions.backends.db`

▶ `django.contrib.sessions.backends.file`

▶ `django.contrib.sessions.backends.cache`

If you want to use the cache backend, be sure that you have configured your cache. Also, you should use the `cache` session backend only if you are using the `memcached` cache backend.

Watch Out!

If you decide to use the `file` backend for sessions, you can configure the location where the session data is stored by adding the `SESSION_FILE_PATH` setting to the `settings.py` file. The `SESSION_FILE_PATH` setting defaults to the `/tmp` directory.

By the Way

You can use the following settings in the `settings.py` file to configure the session manager:

▶ `SESSION_COOKIE_AGE`: The default is 1209600 (two weeks). Specifies the age of session cookies in seconds.

▶ `SESSION_COOKIE_DOMAIN`: The default is `None`. Specifies the domain string to use for cross-domain cookies.

▶ `SESSION_COOKIE_NAME`: The default is `sessionid`. Specifies the cookie name for sessions.

▶ `SESSION_COOKIE_SECURE`: The default is `False`. If it's set to `True`, the cookie is marked as secure, and the browser should ensure that it will be sent only over an HTTPS connection.

▶ `SESSION_EXPIRE_AT_BROWSER_CLOSE`: The default is `False`. If it's set to `True`, the session expires when the user closes the browser window.

▶ `SESSION_SAVE_EVERY_REQUEST`: The default is `False`. If it's set to `False`, the session is saved only if the data actually changes. If it's set to `True`, the session is saved after every request.

▼ **Try It Yourself**

Configure the Session Manager

In this section, you will verify that the session manager is installed. You also will configure the session to expire the cookie in one week instead of the default two weeks. Follow these steps to modify the settings.py file to configure the session manager:

1. Open the iFriends/settings.py file in an editor.

2. Verify that the following line exists in the MIDDLEWARE_CLASSES setting to enable the session middleware application:

   ```
   'django.contrib.sessions.middleware.SessionMiddleware',
   ```

3. Verify that the following line exists in the INSTALLED_APPS setting to verify that the session framework model is installed:

   ```
   'django.contrib.sessions',
   ```

4. Add the following line to the file to configure the session to expire when the user closes the browser window:

   ```
   SESSION_EXPIRE_AT_BROWSER_CLOSE = True
   ```

5. Save the iFriends/settings.py file.   ▲

Using Django's Test Cookies

Another problem with cookies is that you are not guaranteed that the browser will accept cookies. Some browsers disable cookies as a security precaution. If your website requires access to cookies or to the session framework cookie, you may want to add code to your login to verify that cookies are enabled.

Django provides the set_test_cookie(), test_cookie_worked(), and delete_test_cookie() functions to the HttpRequest.session object to aid in this task. The set_test_cookie() function attempts to set a test cookie in the browser. The test_cookie_worked() function attempts to retrieve the test cookie, and the delete_test_cookie() function deletes the cookie.

> The test_cookie_worked() function needs to be used in a different request than the set_test_cookie() function, because the cookie typically isn't saved until after the request is finished.

Try It Yourself

Implement Test Cookies to Verify That the Browser Will Support Cookies

In this section, you will modify the login_user() view function to have it set a test cookie during the GET request and verify that the cookie is set in the POST request before logging in the user.

Follow these steps to modify the GET and POST handlers of the login_user() view function to implement a test cookie:

1. Open the iFriends/Home/views.py file in an editor.

2. Add the following get handler, shown in Listing 16.1, to set the test cookie on a GET request:

```
if request.method == 'GET':
    request.session.set_test_cookie()
```

3. Add the following check to the POST handler, shown in Listing 16.1, to verify that the test cookie was set. If it was, delete it and continue with the login. If the test cookie was not set, set the message to instruct the user to enable cookies before logging in:

```
if request.session.test_cookie_worked():
    request.session.delete_test_cookie()
. . .
else:
    message = "Please enable cookies and try again."
```

4. Save the iFriends/Home/views.py file.

5. Test that the handlers are working properly by logging out of the website using the following URL:

```
http://127.0.0.1:8000/Logout/
```

6. Disable the cookies in the browser.

7. Try logging in using the following URL:

```
http://127.0.0.1:8000/Login/
```

You should see the message shown in Figure 16.1.

FIGURE 16.1
The user login form generated by the `user_login()` view when a test cookie cannot be set in the browser.

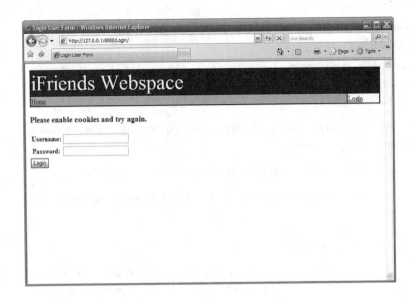

LISTING 16.1   The `login_user()` Function in the `iFriends/Home/views.py` File

```
def login_user(request, next='/'):
    message = 'Login User'
    lForm = LoginForm()

    if request.method == 'GET':
        request.session.set_test_cookie()

    if request.method == 'POST':
        if request.session.test_cookie_worked():
            request.session.delete_test_cookie()

            if request.GET.has_key('next'):
                next = request.GET['next']
            if request.POST['submit'] == 'Login':
                postDict = request.POST.copy()
                lForm = LoginForm(postDict)
                if lForm.is_valid():
                    uName = request.POST['username']
                    uPass = request.POST['password']
                    user = authenticate(username=uName, password=uPass)
                    if user is not None:
                        if user.is_active:
                            login(request, user)
                            return HttpResponseRedirect(next)
                        else:
                            message = 'Account Deactivated'
                    else:
                        message = 'Login Incorrect'
```

LISTING 16.1   Continued

```
        else:
             message = "Please enable cookies and try again."

     return render_to_response('registration/login.html',{
                   'lForm': lForm,
                   'message': message})
```

Setting and Retrieving Session Data

You can access the Django session framework from the browser by accessing the session attribute of the HttpRequest object in a view function. The session attribute acts like a standard Python dictionary. You add items to and get items from the session using standard dictionary syntax.

> The session dictionary accepts any pickleable Python object. This functionality allows you to store a variety of data in the session.

By the Way

For example, the following code snippet creates, retrieves, and deletes a key named i_feel in the session:

```
request.session['i_feel'] = 'happy'
mood = request.session['i_feel']
del request.session['i_feel']
```

> When you define names for entries in the session store, avoid using names that begin with the underscore character. Names beginning with an underscore are reserved for Django.

By the Way

The following line of code checks to see if the i_feel key exists in the session:

```
if 'i_feel' in request.session:
. . .
```

You can also use the get(key, default=None), keys(), and items() dictionary functions on the session attribute.

Setting values in the session attribute stores them in the session, where they can be accessed by other view functions that the user accesses.

▼

Try It Yourself

Set and Retrieve Session Data

In this section, you will modify the add_blog() function to add a session_blog key to the session when the user creates a new blog. Then you will add a check to the add_blog() function to determine if the user has already added a blog entry. Finally, you will redirect the add_blog request to the generic blog_details view of the blog that was already created.

Follow these steps to make the changes to the add_blog() view function:

1. Open the iFriends/People/views.py file in an editor.

2. Modify the following import statement to include the HttpResponseRedirect() function:

```
from django.http import HttpResponse, HttpResponseRedirect
```

3. Add the update_blog() view function, shown in Listing 16.2, to the file that will build a blog update form that includes data from an existing blog. This form will handle the POST request and will redirect the browser to the blog details page.

4. Save the iFriends/People/views.py file in an editor.

5. Create and open a file named iFriends/templates/People/update_blog_ form.html in an editor.

6. Add the contents shown in Listing 16.3 to extend the base site template and display a blog update form.

7. Save the iFriends/templates/People/update_blog_form.html file.

8. Open the iFriends/People/views.py file in an editor.

9. Add the following line of code, shown in Listing 16.4, to set the session_blog value in the session data when the user adds a new Blog object:

```
request.session['session_blog'] = bObj.id
```

10. Add the following check at the beginning of the add_blog() function, shown in Listing 16.4, to determine if a blog has already been added to the session. If it has, redirect the browser to the update page for that Blog object:

```
if 'session_blog' in request.session:
    return HttpResponseRedirect("/generic/blog_details/%d" %
                    request.session['session_blog'])
```

▼

11. Save the iFriends/People/views.py file.

12. Open the iFriends/People/urls.py file in an editor.

13. Add the following URL pattern to enable the update_blog() view:

    ```
    (r'^UpdateBlog/(?P<bID>\d+)/$', 'update_blog'),
    ```

14. Save the iFriends/People/urls.py file.

15. Log in to the website as a user, and access that user's details page.

16. Click the + link above the blog list to bring up the add_blog() view, shown in Figure 16.2.

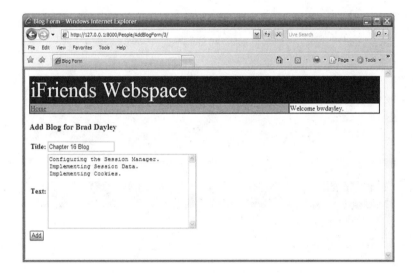

FIGURE 16.2
The blog form generated by the add_blog() view.

17. Add valid blog data to the form, and click the Add button.

18. Access the user page again, and click the + link again. This time you should be redirected to the update_blog() view for the last blog entry you created, shown in Figure 16.3.

19. Click the Update button. You should be redirected to the details view of the updated blog, shown in Figure 16.4.

FIGURE 16.3
The update_
blog() view
generated when
the session
already has a
session_blog
defined.

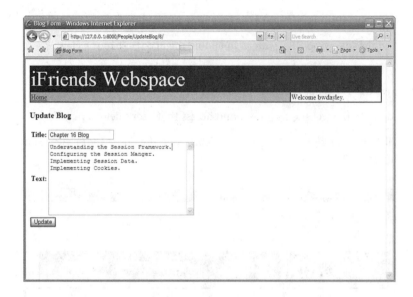

FIGURE 16.4
The generic
details view of
the updated
Blog object.

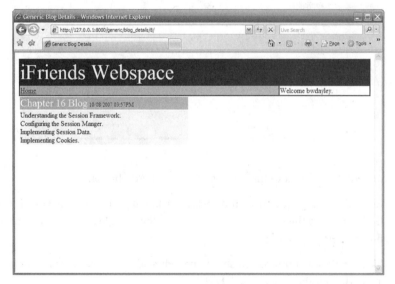

LISTING 16.2   The `update_blog()` Function in the `iFriends/People/`
`views.py` File

```
def update_blog(request, bID='0'):
    blog = get_object_or_404(Blog, pk=bID)
    BlogForm = forms.form_for_instance(blog, fields=('title', 'text'))
    bf = BlogForm()
```

LISTING 16.2   Continued

```
message = 'Update Blog'

if request.method == 'POST':
    if request.POST['submit'] == 'Update':
        blog.title = request.POST['title']
        blog.text = request.POST['text']
        blog.date = datetime.now()
        try:
            blog.save()
            return HttpResponseRedirect("/generic/blog_details/%d" %
blog.id)
        except:
            message = 'Database Error.'

return render_to_response('People/update_blog_form.html',
    {'bForm':bf, 'message': message},
    context_instance = RequestContext(request))
```

LISTING 16.3   Full Contents of the iFriends/templates/People/
update_blog_form.html **Template File**

```
{% extends "iFriends_base.html" %}

{% block title %}Blog Form{% endblock %}
{% block content %}
<h3>{{ message }}</h3>

<form method="post" action=".">
<table>
{{ bForm }}
</table>
<input type="submit" name="submit" value="Update" />
</form>
{% endblock %}
```

LISTING 16.4   A Portion of the add_blog() **Function in the**
iFriends/People/views.py **File**

```
def add_blog(request, pID='0'):
    if not request.user.has_perm('People.can_blog'):
        return HttpResponseRedirect('/')

    if 'session_blog' in request.session:
        return HttpResponseRedirect("/generic/blog_details/%d" %
                    request.session['session_blog'])

. . .

            try:
                bObj = save_bf.save()
                p.blogs.add(bObj)
                p.save()
                message = 'Blog added to %s.' % p.name
                request.session['session_blog'] = bObj.id
. . .
```

Setting and Retrieving Cookies

Setting data in the user's session typically is the best way to keep persistent data. However, sometimes you'll want to add cookies to the browser to store data. Django provides the COOKIES attribute and the set_cookie() function to the HttpRequest object of the view functions to facilitate this.

The COOKIES attribute acts like a dictionary inside the request and includes the cookies sent in the request from the browser. For example, if you wanted to access the sessionid cookie created by Django, you could use the following line of code:

```
sessionID = request.COOKIES['sessionid']
```

Setting cookies requires using the set_cookies() function and passing it the cookie's identifier and value. For example, you could use the following code snippet to set in the browser a cookie named last_login with the current time value:

```
time = "%s" % datetime.now()
response.set_cookie('last_login', time)
```

> Never store important data in cookies. The data is accessible to just about every-one. If you do store values in cookies, make certain that the data is cleaned before you import it into your system.

The set_cookie() function also accepts the following parameters to configure the cookie:

- ▶ max_age: The default is None. Sets the maximum age in seconds that the cookie should last. If it's None, the cookie expires when the browser is closed.

- ▶ expires: The default is None. Specifies the date and time when the cookie will expire. Format is Wdy, DD-MM-YY HH:MM:SS GMT.

- ▶ path: The default is /. Specifies a path prefix where the cookie is valid. The cookie is sent only to requests that begin with the path prefix.

- ▶ domain: The default is None. Specifies the domain in which this cookie is valid.

- ▶ secure: The default is False. If it's set to True, the browser should return the cookie only over HTTPS requests.

Summary

In this hour, we discussed the Django session framework. You learned how Django's session framework differs from simply using cookies. We discussed how to configure the session manager and how to use it to add and retrieve data about the session. In addition, you learned how to use the `HttpRequest` object that is passed to view functions to set cookies in and retrieve cookies from the browser.

Q&A

Q. Is there a way to implement the session framework in stand-alone applications?

A. Yes. You can access `django.contrib.sessions.backends.db.SessionStore` to access the `SessionStore` data. The following code creates a session store, adds a value to it, and then saves it:

```
from django.contrib.sessions.backends.db import SessionStore
s = SessionStore(session_key='123abc321cba1234567890abcdef1234')
s['session_name'] = 'My Session'
s.save()
```

If you are using the db backend, you can access the `session` model directly. However, you need to call the `get_decoded()` function to access the dictionary, because the dictionary is stored in an encoded format. For example:

```
from django.contrib.sessions.models import Session
s = Session.objects.get(pk='123abc321cba1234567890abcdef1234')
s = s.get_decoded()
print 'Session %s' % s.['session_name']
```

Q. Is there a way add the session to the URL like PHP does?

A. No. Django's session framework is entirely cookie-based. Not only is putting the session ID in the URL as a last-resort backup ugly, it also makes the site vulnerable to session ID theft.

Workshop

The workshop consists of a set of questions and answers designed to solidify your understanding of the material covered in this hour. Try answering the questions before looking at the answers.

Quiz

1. How do you test the browser to verify that it will accept cookies before allowing a web page to be displayed?

2. How do you access session data from a view function?

3. How can you request that the browser return only the sessionid cookie on an HTTPS connection?

Quiz Answers

1. Use the set_test_cookie() function to write a cookie to the browser. Then, in a subsequent request, use the test_cookie_worked() function to verify that the cookie was written.

2. Access the session attribute in the HttpRequest object passed to the view function.

3. Set the SESSION_COOKIE_SECURE setting to True in the settings.py file.

Exercises

1. Add a radio button to the login template labeled Show Quotes.

2. Add supporting code to the login_user() function to check the value of the radio button, and set a session variable with the user's preference.

3. Add code to the details() view function to add the session variable to the dictionary passed to the template.

4. Add code to the template to check the variable to determine whether the quote.html template should be loaded.

HOUR 17

Customizing Models in the Admin Interface

What You'll Learn in This Hour:

▶ How to customize fields displayed in the model change list

▶ How to add search functionality to the model change list

▶ How to filter objects in the model change list

▶ How to implement a date hierarchy to navigate model change lists

▶ How to customize model add and create forms so that they are easier to use

▶ How to configure models that are linked by a foreign key so that they can be edited together inline in the admin interface

Until now we have neglected one of the shining features of Django, the admin interface. So far you have used the admin interface to create only users, permissions, and some objects. The admin interface is pretty intuitive right out of the box. However, you can customize it to make it better suit your needs.

In this hour, we will discuss customizing models in the admin interface. When you defined some models in Hour 3, "Adding Models and Objects to Your Website," you added a blank Admin class to enable the model in the admin interface. Django provides several attributes to the Admin class that help you customize module change list and form views. Also, you can modify Field definitions in models to edit two models in the same admin view.

Customizing the Model Change List

As you begin to add numerous objects to your models, it will get more difficult to manage them using the admin interface. The admin interface has some great features to help organize the change list view for your models.

Django provides several attributes to the `Admin` class that enable you to modify object fields, add filters, select ordering, and add searching to the change list views in the admin interface. Because these features will be added to the `Admin` class, each model can be customized to best fit its own data.

Setting Fields to Display

The first customization that you will likely want to do is to define which fields you want to appear in the change list view. Currently Django displays only whatever the output of the `__str__()` function of the model returns. However, you can set the `list_display` attribute of the `Admin` class to define a list of `Fields` to display in the change list view. For example:

```
class Admin:
    list_display = ('name', 'email',)
```

You can also add to the display list a function that is a member of the model. The output of the function is displayed in the change list view.

▼   **Try It Yourself**

Configure the List Display for a Model in the Admin Interface

In this section, you will add the `list_display` attribute to the `Blog` and `Person` models to include specific `Field` objects in the list display. You will also add a new `blog_size()` function to the `Blog` model that returns the size of the `text` field in the `Blog` so that you can add that to the change list view of the `Blog` model.

Follow these steps to make the change:

1. Open the `iFriends/People/models.py` file in an editor.

2. Add the following function to the `Blog` model, shown in Listing 17.1, that returns the length of the `text` Field:

```
def blog_size (self):
    return len(self.text)
```

3. Add the following `list_display` attribute to the `Admin` class of the `Blog` model, shown in Listing 17.1, so that the change list view displays the `title` and `date` fields and the size of the `Blog` using the `blog_size()` function you created in step 2:

```
list_display = ('title', 'date', 'blog_size',)
```

▼

4. Add the following `list_display` attribute to the `Admin` class of the `Person` model, shown in Listing 17.2, so that the change list view displays the `name`, `email`, and `desc` fields:

```
`list_display = ('name', 'email', 'desc')
```

5. Save the `iFriends/People/models.py` file.

6. View the Blog change list, shown in Figure 17.1, to view the list with the title, date, and blog size details.

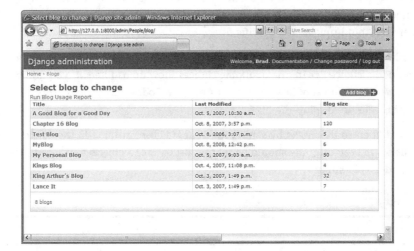

FIGURE 17.1
The Blog change list view in the admin interface with the title, date, and blog size details.

7. View the Person change list, shown in Figure 17.2, to view the list with the name, email, and description details.

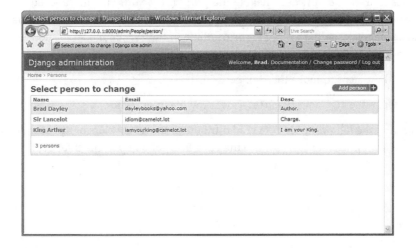

FIGURE 17.2
The Person change list view in the admin interface with the name, email, and description details.

By the Way

> Listings 17.1 and 17.2 are used in the first four "Try It Yourself" sections in this hour. To reduce redundancy and make this hour more readable, they are placed at the end of the fourth "Try It Yourself" section.

Adding Filters

Django also allows you to add filters to limit the objects that are displayed in the change list view. Filters appear on the right side of the screen with a header and a list of links that implement a specific filter.

The filter's behavior depends on the Field type you are using to filter. For example, if you add a choice Field, the available choices show up as filters. If you add a datetime Field, a list of links including Any date, Today, Past 7 days, This month, and This year are displayed.

You add filters to the model by setting the list_filter attribute in the Admin class. The list_filter attribute should be set to a list of Field objects to use as filters for the model. For example:

```
class Admin:
    list_filter = ('zipcode', 'date',)
```

Try It Yourself

Configure the List Filters for a Model in the Admin Interface

In this section, you will add the list_filter attribute to the Blog and Person models. You will add the date field to the list_filter attribute in the Blog model to show how date fields appear in the filter list. You will add the friends and gender fields to the list_filter attribute in the Person model to show how choice and many-to-many fields show up as filters.

Follow these steps to make the change:

1. Open the iFriends/People/models.py file in an editor.

2. Add the following list_filter attribute to the Admin class of the Blog model, shown in Listing 17.1, so that the date field shows up in the filter list:

   ```
   list_filter = ('date',)
   ```

3. Add the following `list_filter` attribute to the Admin class of the Person model, shown in Listing 17.2, so that the gender and friends fields show up in the filter list:

```
list_filter = ('gender', 'friends',)
```

4. Save the iFriends/People/models.py file.

5. View the Blog change list, shown in Figure 17.3, to view the list with the date filter. Try filtering the date using some of the date filters, such as Today or Past 7 days.

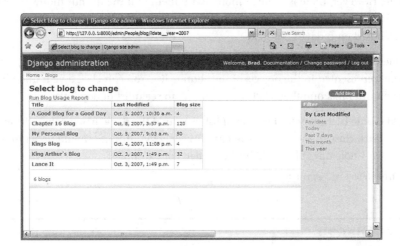

FIGURE 17.3
The Blog change list view in the admin interface with the date filter.

6. View the Person change list, shown in Figure 17.4, to view the list with the gender and friends filters. Try filtering using different genders or people.

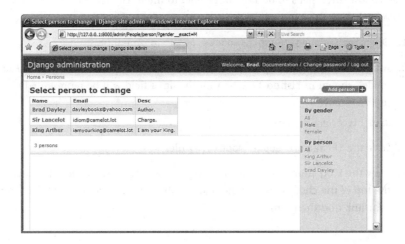

FIGURE 17.4
The Person change list view in the admin interface with the gender and friends filters.

By the Way

> Listings 17.1 and 17.2 are used in the first four "Try It Yourself" sections in this hour. To reduce redundancy and make the hour more readable, they are placed at the end of the fourth "Try It Yourself" section.

Adding a Date Hierarchy

Using a datetime field in the list_filter attribute is a useful way to filter objects by date. However, there is a much more useful method if the list has many objects. The admin interface provides a date hierarchy application that builds a hierarchy of objects based on a datetime field.

The hierarchy appears at the top of the change list and initially includes the years that are represented in the objects of the change list. You can click a year and see a list of month links and then click a month link to see a list of day links.

To add a date hierarchy to the change list view, add the date_hierarchy attribute to the Admin class in the model. The date_hierarchy attribute should be set to the name of a single datetime field in the model. For example:

```
date_hierarchy = 'login_date'
```

Try It Yourself

Configure Date Hierarchy Navigation for a Model in the Admin Interface

In this section, you will add date hierarchy navigation to the change list of the Blog model. Follow these steps to add the date field to the date_hierarchy attribute of the Admin class in the Blog model to implement a date hierarchy:

1. Open the iFriends/People/models.py file in an editor.

2. Add the following date_hierarchy attribute to the Admin class of the Blog model, shown in Listing 17.1, so that the date field will be represented in the hierarchy:

   ```
   date_hierarchy = 'date'
   ```

3. Save the iFriends/People/models.py file.

4. View the Blog change list, shown in Figure 17.5, to view the date hierarchy at the top of the change list. Try navigating through the hierarchy by clicking a year link and then a month link.

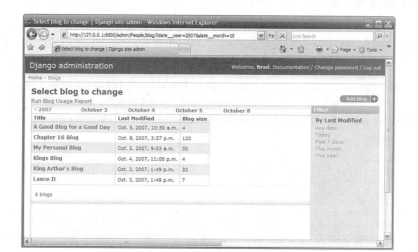

FIGURE 17.5
The date hierar-
chy in the Blog
change list view
in the admin
interface.

Listings 17.1 and 17.2 are used in the first four "Try It Yourself" sections in this
hour. To reduce redundancy and make the hour more readable, they are placed at
the end of the fourth "Try It Yourself" section.

**By the
Way**

Ordering Objects in the Change List

As you may have discovered, if you click the headers in the change list, the list is
ordered based on the values in that column. If you click the header again, it reverses
the ordering of the list.

Django also allows you to set the initial ordering using the `ordering` attribute of the
`Admin` class. To configure the ordering, set the `ordering` attribute to a list of fields in
the model. The list is ordered by the fields in the order in which they appear in the
list. For example:

```
class Admin:
    ordering = ('lastname', 'firstname',)
```

If you put a minus sign in front of the field name, the list is sorted in reverse
order for that field.

**Did you
Know?**

Adding Search Fields

Another useful feature of the admin interface is the ability to search specific Fields in the model and then limit the change list to objects that are found in the search. This feature becomes useful as the number of objects in a model increases.

To implement a search in the change list, add the search_fields attribute to the Admin class. The search_fields attribute should be set to a list of Fields in the object that you want the admin interface to search when building the change list. For example:

```
class Admin:
    search_fields = ('title', 'text',)
```

By the Way

Because the search searches through the objects in the order in which they appear in the list, you should order the list so that entries can be found as quickly as possible.

▼ **Try It Yourself**

Configure a List Search for a Model in the Admin Interface

In this section, you will add search capability to the change list of the Blog model. Follow these steps to add the title and text fields to the search_fields attribute of the Admin class in the Blog model to enable searching:

1. Open the iFriends/People/models.py file in an editor.

2. Add the following search_fields attribute to the Admin class of the Blog model, shown in Listing 17.1, so that the title and text fields will be searched:

   ```
   search_fields = ('title', 'text',)
   ```

3. Save the iFriends/People/models.py file.

4. View the Blog change list, shown in Figure 17.6, to view the list with the search box. Try adding text to the search box and clicking the Go button to reduce the change list to objects matching the search.

▼

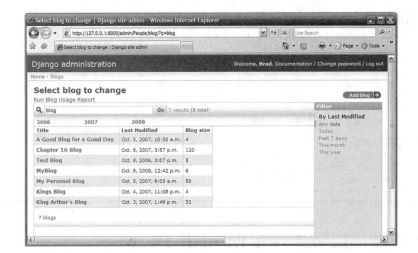

FIGURE 17.6
The Blog
change list view
in the admin
interface with
the search_
fields attribute
enabled.

LISTING 17.1 The Blog **Model Definition in the** iFriends/People/
models.py **File**

```
gender_list = (('M', 'Male'), ('F', 'Female' ))
class Blog(models.Model):
    title = models.CharField('Title', max_length=200)
    text = models.TextField('Text', max_length=2048)
    date = models.DateTimeField('Last Modified')

    def __str__(self):
        return '%s' % (self.title)

    def blog_size (self):
        return len(self.text)

    class Admin:
        list_display = ('title', 'date', 'blog_size',)
        list_filter = ('date',)
        date_hierarchy = 'date'
        search_fields = ('title', 'text',)

    class Meta:
        permissions = (
            ('can_blog', 'Allowed to Blog'),
        )
```

LISTING 17.2 The Person **Model Definition in the** iFriends/People/
models.py **File**

```
class Person(models.Model):
    userID = models.ForeignKey(User, unique=True)
    name = models.CharField('name', max_length=200)
    birthday = models.DateField('Birthday', blank=True, null=True)
    gender = models.CharField(max_length=1, choices=gender_list)
```

LISTING 17.2   Continued

```
email = models.EmailField('Email', max_length=100, unique=True)
favoriteURL = models.URLField('myURL', verify_exists=False)
desc = models.TextField('Desc', max_length=500, null=True)
friends = models.ManyToManyField('self', blank=True)
blogs = models.ManyToManyField(Blog, blank=True)

def __str__(self):
    return '%s' % (self.name)

class Admin:
    list_display = ('name', 'email', 'desc')
    list_filter = ('gender', 'friends',)
    ordering    = ('-name',)
```

Customizing the Model Form

The preceding section covered how to customize the change list of a model in the admin interface. Django also allows you to customize how the add and update forms for the model appear in the admin interface.

You might have noticed when editing Person objects in the iFriends project that the default object forms in the admin interface can become a bit clunky as you add more fields to the model.

Django gives you at least some control in the model over how add and update forms will appear in the admin interface: You use the fields attribute in the Admin class. The fields attribute gets set to a list of field groups that allow you to group and display fields under a label.

To group a model's fields, add the fields attribute to the model's Admin class, and add the fields in groups using the following syntax:

```
fields = ((<name>,  {'fields': (<field list>)}),)
```

The following lines of code show an example of defining the fields attribute of the Admin class:

```
class Admin:
    fields = (
            ('Info', {'fields':('name', 'number')}),
            ('Location', {'fields':('addr', 'city', 'state', 'zip')}),
        )
```

The fields attribute also includes a collapse class that initially displays only the label for the group of fields with a link that expands the fields to a visible state.

The following lines of code show an example of implementing the collapse class:

```
('Blogs', {'fields':('addr', 'city', 'state', 'zip'), 'classes':
  'collapse'}),
```

Try It Yourself ▼

Configure Add and Update Forms for a Model in the Admin Interface

In this section, you will modify the look of the People model in the admin interface to make it a bit more user-friendly. You will add the fields attribute to the Admin class of the People model and define labels for different groups of fields. You will also set the blogs and friends fields to initially be collapsed.

Follow these steps to make the changes:

1. Open the iFriends/Person/models.py file in an editor.

2. Add the following fields attribute, shown in Listing 17.3, to the Admin class of the People model:

   ```
       fields = (
   . . .
             )
   ```

3. Add the following lines of code to the fields attribute, shown in Listing 17.3, to create User, Info, and Contact groups that include pertinent fields:

   ```
   ('User', {'fields':('userID', 'name')}),
   ('Info', {'fields':('birthday', 'gender', 'desc')}),
   ('Contact', {'fields':('email', 'favoriteURL')}),
   ```

4. Add the following lines of code to the fields attribute, shown in Listing 17.3, to create Friends and Blogs groups that implement the collapse class so that they are not initially displayed:

   ```
   ('Friends', {'fields':('friends',), 'classes': 'collapse'}),
   ('Blogs', {'fields':('blogs',), 'classes': 'collapse'}),
   ```

5. Save the iFriends/Person/models.py file.

6. View the update page for a Person object, shown in Figure 17.7, to view the Person object with the new groups. Try expanding and collapsing the Friends and Blogs groups using the Show and Hide links.

FIGURE 17.7
The Person
update view in
the admin
interface
organized using
the fields
attribute.

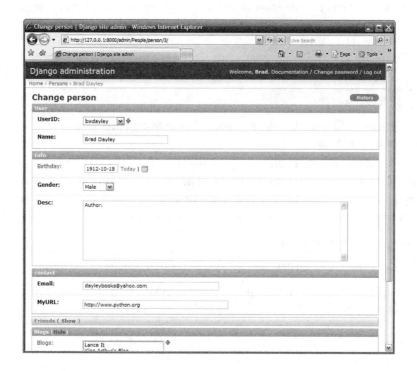

LISTING 17.3   The Person Model Definition in the iFriends/People/
models.py File

```
class Person(models.Model):
    userID = models.ForeignKey(User, unique=True)
    name = models.CharField('name', max_length=200)
    birthday = models.DateField('Birthday', blank=True, null=True)
    gender = models.CharField(max_length=1, choices=gender_list)
    email = models.EmailField('Email', max_length=100, unique=True)
    favoriteURL = models.URLField('myURL', verify_exists=False)
    desc = models.TextField('Desc', max_length=500, null=True)
    friends = models.ManyToManyField('self', blank=True)
    blogs = models.ManyToManyField(Blog, blank=True)

    def __str__(self):
        return '%s' % (self.name)

    class Admin:
        fields = (
                ('User', {'fields':('userID', 'name')}),
                ('Info', {'fields':('birthday', 'gender', 'desc')}),
                ('Contact', {'fields':('email', 'favoriteURL')}),
                ('Friends', {'fields':('friends',), 'classes': 'collapse'}),
                ('Blogs', {'fields':('blogs',), 'classes': 'collapse'}),
            )
```

LISTING 17.3 Continued

```
list_display = ('name', 'email', 'desc')
list_filter = ('gender', 'friends',)
ordering     = ('-name',)
```

Viewing Multiple Models Inline

Another useful model customization of the admin interface is to display in the same form multiple models that link to each other. In the add and update forms in the admin interface, you can configure models with a ForeignKey field link to another model to be displayed with that model.

To view multiple models inline in the admin interface, add the edit_inline argument to the ForeignKey definition. The edit_inline argument can be set to models.TABULAR or models.STACKED.

The models.STACKED option displays the fields stacked on top of each other in the form. The models.TABULAR option displays the fields next to each other in a single table row. Which option you use depends on what fields exist in the model.

You can define the number of instances of the model to be included in the form by setting the num_in_admin argument. You also need to add the core=true attribute to the other fields in the model.

The following example shows how to implement the edit_inline argument to display a model inline with another model:

```
class Quote(models.Model):
    text = models.TextField('text', max_length=200, core=True)
    by = models.CharField('by', max_length=50, core=True)
    person = models.ForeignKey(Person, edit_inline=models.TABULAR)
```

Try It Yourself

Configure an Inline Model in the Admin Interface

In this section, you will create a new Poll application that will include UserPoll and Opinion models. You will define the models so that they can be edited inline in the admin interface.

Follow these steps to create the Poll application and define the models:

1. Stop the development server.

2. Use the following command from the root of the iFriends project to create a Poll application:

   ```
   python manage.py startapp Poll
   ```

3. Create and open the iFriends/Poll/models.py file in an editor.

4. Add the following import statement, shown in Listing 17.4, to import the Person model:

```
from iFriends.People.models import Person
```

5. Add the following lines of code to define the UserPoll model, shown in Listing 17.4, with question, date, and person fields:

```
class UserPoll(models.Model):
    question = models.CharField('Question', max_length=100)
    date = models.DateTimeField('Creation Date')
    person = models.ForeignKey(Person)

    def __str__(self):
        return '%s' % (self.question)
    class Admin:
        pass
```

6. Add the following lines of code to define the Opinion model, shown in Listing 17.4:

```
class Opinion(models.Model):
    . . .
    def __str__(self):
        return '%s' % (self.opinion)
```

By the Way

> We do not include the Admin class in the Opinion model because it will be displayed in the Admin class of the UserPoll object. We do not want it to be displayed on its own in the admin interface, because Opinion objects are always added with the UserPoll objects.

7. Add the following lines of code that add the poll field to the Opinion model, as shown in Listing 17.4. The poll field links the Opinion model to the UserPoll model as a foreign key. The edit_inline option is set to TABULAR so that this model is displayed as a table in UserPoll model forms. The num_in_admin option is set to 4, so four instances are automatically added to the UserPoll forms:

```
poll = models.ForeignKey(UserPoll, edit_inline=models.TABULAR,
  num_in_admin=4)
```

8. Add the following fields to the Opinion model to define the opinion and vote count:

```
opinion = models.CharField('Opinion', max_length=50, core=True)
votes = models.IntegerField('Vote Count', core=True)
```

9. Save the iFriends/Poll/models.py file.

10. Open the iFriends/settings.py file in an editor.

11. Add the following line to the INSTALLED_APPS setting to enable the Poll application:

    ```
    'iFriends.Poll',
    ```

12. Save the iFriends/settings.py file.

13. Use the following command at the root of the iFriends project to synchronize the database:

    ```
    python manage.py syncdb
    ```

14. Start the development server.

15. Access the add form for a UserPoll object in the admin interface, as shown in Figure 17.8, to see the inline Opinion model as well.

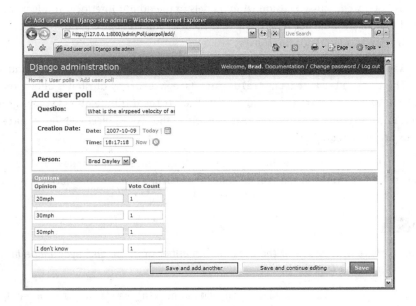

FIGURE 17.8
The UserPoll add view in the admin interface with four instances of the Opinion model displayed inline.

LISTING 17.4   Full Contents of the iFriends/Poll/models.py File

```
from django.db import models
from iFriends.People.models import Person

class UserPoll(models.Model):
    question = models.CharField('Question', max_length=100)
    date = models.DateTimeField('Creation Date')
    person = models.ForeignKey(Person)
```

LISTING 17.4   Continued

```
    def __str__(self):
        return '%s' % (self.question)

    class Admin:
        pass

class Opinion(models.Model):
    poll = models.ForeignKey(UserPoll, edit_inline=models.TABULAR,
        num_in_admin=4)
    opinion = models.CharField('Opinion', max_length=50, core=True)
    votes = models.IntegerField('Vote Count', core=True)

    def __str__(self):
        return '%s' % (self.opinion)
```

Summary

In this hour, we discussed customizing models in the admin interface. You learned that by modifying the Admin class in your models, you can change how they look and behave in the admin interface.

The list_display attribute allows you to define what fields to display in a change list. The list_filter, search_fields, and date_hierarchy attributes allow you to limit the objects displayed in a change list. The fields attribute allows you to group fields under expandable and collapsible labels so that your object add and create forms are more readable.

You also learned how to use the edit_inline argument in ForeignKey field definitions so that multiple objects can be edited in the same form in the admin interface.

Q&A

Q. *Is there a way to limit the maximum number of items displayed inline in the admin interface?*

A. Yes. You can add the max_num_in_admin and min_num_in_admin arguments to the model definition to limit the maximum and minimum number of objects that will be displayed inline in the admin interface.

Q. *If I have a choice element that contains too many items to make a drop down box feasible, is there a way to set up the admin interface to request an* int *value representing object IDs?*

A. Yes. You can add the raw_id_admin argument to the model definition to display an integer field requesting an object ID rather than a choice field.

Workshop

The workshop consists of a set of questions and answers designed to solidify your understanding of the material covered in this hour. Try answering the questions before looking at the answers.

Quiz

1. How can you limit the objects that are displayed in the change list by a word or phrase in the content of one or more fields?

2. How do you enable a group of object fields to be expanded or collapsed in the admin interface?

3. Is there a way to display information other than just the field data in the change list?

Quiz Answers

1. Add the `search_fields` attribute to the `Admin` class in the model.

2. Add the `collapse` class to the dictionary of the group defined in the `fields` attribute of the `Admin` class:

   ```
   ('Blogs', {'fields':('blogs',), 'classes': 'collapse'}),
   ```

3. Yes. You can define a function as a member of the model and then add the function to the `list_display` attribute of the `Admin` class for that model. The function's output is displayed in the change list.

Exercises

1. Add a `search_fields` attribute to the `Admin` class in the `Person` model that searches the `name`, `email`, and `desc` fields.

2. Add a `search_fields` attribute to the `Admin` class in the `Quote` model that searches the `text` field.

3. Add a `list_filter` attribute to the `Admin` class in the `Quote` model that allows you to filter the list using the `by` field.

HOUR 18

Customizing the Admin Interface

What You'll Learn in This Hour:

▶ How to override admin templates at the site level

▶ How to create your own custom admin views

▶ How to override admin templates at the application level

▶ How to override admin templates at the object level

▶ How to override admin templates at the block level

▶ How to override the built-in admin views

The preceding hour discussed how to customize the look of models in the admin inter-face. This hour discusses how to customize the look, feel, and behavior of the admin interface.

The admin interface is made up of URL patterns that link to view functions that render template files. The URL patterns, views, and templates aren't any different from what you have used so far. They include a large amount of code and CSS formatting, but they are still just URL patterns, view functions, and templates.

The admin templates are stored in the following location relative to the root of the Django installation:

```
django/contrib/admin/templates/admin/
```

The admin URL patterns are defined in the following URLconf file relative to the root of the Django installation:

```
django/contrib/admin/urls.py
```

The admin views are located in several Python modules in the following location relative to the root of the Django installation:

`django/contrib/admin/views/`

This hour discusses some of the ways you can modify the look and feel of the admin interface by creating your own custom admin code to either add or override existing admin views.

By the Way

> The information in this hour is not meant to be inclusive. It barely scratches the surface. It is designed to give you some starting points for customizing the admin interface. There is just so much you can do in so many ways. The best documentation available for understanding how to customize the admin interface is the code itself.

Overriding Admin Templates at the Site Level

The most common type of customization that you will likely want to perform in the admin interface is to alter or replace the admin HTML template files. This can present a problem.

If you modify the admin templates in the Django installation, you customize the admin interface. The problem is that you customize the admin interface for all sites on that installation, and if you update Django, your customizations are overwritten.

The Django template loaders solve this problem. If you have added a directory to the `TEMPLATE_DIRS` setting in the site's `settings.py` file, the template loaders look there first to load template files. You can override any admin template at the site level by creating a template there using the same name.

By the Way

> Instead of creating your own custom templates, you can copy the admin template from the Django installation to your own template admin directory and then make the modifications you need to make.

For example, if you wanted to override the `base_site.html` admin template, you could just create a file named `admin/base_site.html` in your template directory.

The following are the most common admin templates that you might want to override:

▶ `admin/base.html` contains most of the base HTML code for the rest of the admin templates.

▶ `admin/base_site.html` extends the `base.html` file and includes the window and banner titles for the site.

▶ `admin/login.html` displays the admin login page.

▶ `admin/index.html` displays the index page of models in the admin interface.

▶ `admin/change_list.html` displays the change list for a model.

▶ `admin/change_form.html` displays the add and update forms for an object in a model.

▶ `admin/object_history.html` displays a history of operations performed on the object.

▶ `admin/delete_confirmation.html` displays a confirmation page when deleting an application.

Try It Yourself

Override the `base_site.html` Template

In this section, you will override the `base_site.html` template to add the iFriends name to the window title and banner for the admin interface. Follow these steps to make the change:

1. Create a directory called iFriends/templates/admin. Any admin templates in this directory are loaded before the ones in the Django installation, because you have already added this directory to your TEMPLATE_DIRS setting.

2. Copy the following file from the Django installation to the admin directory you just created:

   `django/contrib/admin/templates/admin/base_site.html`

3. Open the `iFriends/templates/base_site.html` file in an editor.

4. Modify the following lines of code, shown in Listing 18.1, to add the iFriends name to the window title and banner in the admin interface:

   ```
   {% block title %}{{ title|escape }} | {% trans 'iFriends site admin' %}
     {% endblock %}
   . . .
   <h1 id="site-name">{% trans 'iFriends administration' %}</h1>
   ```

▼

5. Save the `iFriends/templates/base_site.html` file.

6. Go to the following URL in a browser to see the changes shown in Figure 18.1:

`http://127.0.0.1:8000/admin/`

The changes show up on all admin pages that extend the `base_site.html` template.

FIGURE 18.1
The admin inter-
face showing
the modified
window and
banner titles.

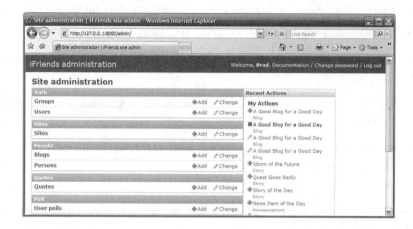

LISTING 18.1   Full Contents of the `iFriends/templates/`
`base_site.html` **File**

```
{% extends "admin/base.html" %}
{% load i18n %}

{% block title %}{{ title|escape }} | {% trans 'iFriends site admin' %}
  {% endblock %}
{% block branding %}
<h1 id="site-name">{% trans 'iFriends administration' %}</h1>
{% endblock %}
{% block nav-global %}{% endblock %}
```

▲

Creating Custom Admin Views

Another way to customize the admin interface for your website is to create your own
custom views to be displayed in the admin interface. You can create your own custom view function and template file and then specify an admin path in the `URLconf`
file when enabling it.

Creating custom views for the admin interface involves the same steps as creating a
normal view. The view function can live in any application, and the template file
can reside anywhere in the template path. The only real differences are that the URL

to access the view begins with admin, and the view function should make certain that the user has staff privileges before allowing him or her to access the view.

The admin URL patterns match just about every URL path you might try to use. So you need to add URL patterns for your custom views before including the django.contrib.admin.urls URLconf file in your own URLconf file.

You can use the staff_member_required decorator function to verify whether the user has staff privileges before giving him or her access to the view:

```
from django.contrib.admin.views.decorators import staff_member_required
@staff_member_required
def custom_admin_view(request):
. . .
```

Try It Yourself

Create a Custom Admin View

In this section, you will create a custom admin view function and template that render usage information about each user's blogs. You will define an URL pattern so that the view can be accessed as an admin URL. You will also add the staff_member_required decorator function to ensure that only users with admin privileges can access the view.

Follow these steps to create and enable the custom admin view:

1. Create a directory called iFriends/templates/Custom in which to store the custom admin template.

2. Create and open a template file called iFriends/templates/Custom/blog_usage.html in an editor.

3. Add the following lines of code, shown in Listing 18.2, to extend the admin/base_site.html template and define the title block that the base_site.html template will render:

   ```
   {% extends "admin/base_site.html" %}
   {% block title %}Blog Usage Report{% endblock %}
   ```

4. Add the full contents of the content block, shown in Listing 18.2, to generate the usage report.

5. Save the iFriends/templates/Custom/blog_usage.html file.

6. Open the iFriends/Custom/views.py file in an editor.

7. Add the following import statements, shown in Listing 18.3. They will give you access to the render_to_response, Person, RequestContext, and staff_member_required functions and objects in the custom view function:

```
from django.shortcuts import render_to_response
from iFriends.People.models import Person
from django.template import RequestContext
from django.contrib.admin.views.decorators import staff_member_required
```

8. Add the following code that defines the blog_usage() view function, shown in Listing 18.3. This generates a list containing the blog usage for each Person object in the database:

```
def blog_usage(request):
    pList = Person.objects.all()
    uList = []
    for p in pList:
        size = 0
        for b in p.blogs.all():
            size += b.blog_size()
        uList.append({'person': p,
                      'count': len(p.blogs.all()),
                      'size': size})
```

9. Add the following render_to_response() return statement to the blog_usage() view function, shown in Listing 18.3. It renders the custom template created in steps 1 through 5:

```
return render_to_response('Custom/blog_usage.html',
                {'uList': uList},
                context_instance = RequestContext(request))
```

By the Way

> You need to add RequestContext to the render_to_response() call so that the admin templates will have access to the User object in the request.

10. Add the following decorator function the blog_usage() view function, listed in Listing 18.3, to ensure that the user is logged in and has staff privileges:

```
@staff_member_required
```

11. Save the iFriends/Custom/views.py file.

12. Open the iFriends/urls.py file in an editor.

13. Add the following URL pattern, before you include django.contrib.admin. urls, to enable the blog_usage() function as an admin URL:

```
(r'^admin/blog_usage/$', 'iFriends.Custom.views.blog_usage'),
```

14. Save the `iFriends/urls.py` file.

15. Access the following URL in a browser to verify that the `blog_usage()` view function works, as shown in Figure 18.2:

```
http://127.0.0.1:8000/admin/blog_usage/
```

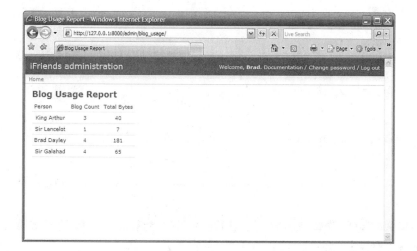

FIGURE 18.2
The custom `blog_usage()` function in the admin interface.

LISTING 18.2   Full Contents of the `iFriends/templates/Custom/blog_usage.html` File

```
{% extends "admin/base_site.html" %}
{% block title %}Blog Usage Report{% endblock %}

{% block content %}
<h1>Blog Usage Report</h1>
<table>
<tr>
  <td>Person</td>
  <td>Blog Count</td>
  <td>Total Bytes</td>
</tr>
{% for item in uList %}
  <tr align="center">
    <td>{{ item.person.name }}</td>
    <td>{{ item.count }}</td>
    <td>{{ item.size }}</td>
  </tr>
{% endfor %}
</table>
{% endblock %}
```

LISTING 18.3   Full Contents of the `iFriends/Custom/views.py` File

```
from django.shortcuts import render_to_response
from iFriends.People.models import Person
from django.template import RequestContext
from django.contrib.admin.views.decorators import staff_member_required

@staff_member_required
def blog_usage(request):
    pList = Person.objects.all()
    uList = []
    for p in pList:
        size = 0
        for b in p.blogs.all():
            size += b.blog_size()
        uList.append({'person': p,
                      'count': len(p.blogs.all()),
                      'size': size})

    return render_to_response('Custom/blog_usage.html',
                    {'uList': uList},
                    context_instance = RequestContext(request))
```

Overriding the Admin Templates at the Application or Object Level

Earlier in this hour, we discussed overriding the admin templates by creating an admin folder in your own template directory. When you put customized templates, using the same name as the admin template files, in that directory, the template loader loads the custom template instead of the one in the Django installation.

That method can create problems. If you modify templates at the admin folder level, the effects are global. For example, if you create a custom `admin/change_form.html` file in your template directory, those same changes are seen in the change view for every model and object in your project.

More often than not, you will want to apply changes to a single model or application. Fortunately, there is a simple solution because of how Django's template system works.

You can put a custom template in the admin/*application* or admin/*application*/*object* folders for specific applications and objects. The custom changes are applied only to that specific application or object.

For example, if you wanted to modify the `change_form.html` template file for an application named Blog, you would put the custom template in the following location in your site template directory:

```
admin/Blog/change_form.html
```

The custom changes would be seen if you tried to access the add or update forms for any objects in the Blog application. However, if you wanted to use the custom forms for only the Entry object in the Blog application, you would put the template in the following location in your site template directory:

```
admin/Blog/Entry/change_form.html
```

The priority in the template loader when loading template files is object, application, and then site. So you could put a different custom template at more than one level so that the entire site can use a custom template. However, a specific object may use a different custom template.

You can modify the following admin templates at the application or object level:

- ▶ admin/change_list.html displays the change list for a model.

- ▶ admin/change_form.html displays the add and update forms for an object in a model.

- ▶ admin/object_history.html displays a history of operations performed on the object.

- ▶ admin/delete_confirmation.html displays a confirmation page when you delete an application.

Overriding Block Tags in a Custom Admin Template

So far we have discussed customizing entire template files by replacing them with either modified copies or completely new ones. You can also customize at a block level inside the template file.

You can extend the original template at the beginning of a custom template using the extend tag. Then you only need to add the custom block tags in the custom template that need to be customized.

For example, if you only wanted to override the extrahead block tag in the change_form.html template file, you could use the following contents in the customized template:

```
{% extends "admin/change_form.html" %}
{% block extrahead %}
    <your custom code>
{% endblock %}
```

You can override any `block` tag in the original template with your own custom code this way. It is not always convenient to override an existing `block` tag.

Another way you can add different code to different applications or objects using this method is to override the full template at the site level with a customized template that includes your own custom `block` tags. Then you can include custom templates at the application or object level that override your custom `block` tags with code specific to that application.

▼ **Try It Yourself**

Override Admin Templates at the Application and Object Level

In this section, you will override the `change_form.html` template for the `Person` object in the People application to include a link to the `person_form()` view. To add the link, you will override the `form_top` block in the original template.

You will also override the `change_list.html` template at the People application level to include a link to the `blog_usage()` view. You need to override the `change_list.html` template at the site level first to add a new custom block that can be overridden at the People application level.

Use the following steps to override the `change_list.html` and `change_form.html` templates:

1. Create the iFriends/admin/People/person directory structure.

2. Create and open the `iFriends/templates/admin/People/person/change_form.html` file in an editor.

3. Add the following line of code, shown in Listing 18.4, to extend the original `change_form.html` template:

   ```
   {% extends "admin/change_form.html" %}
   ```

4. Add the following `block` tag, shown in Listing 18.4, to override the `form_top` block in the original template and render a link to the `person_form()` view for the person being displayed:

   ```
   {% block form_top %}
       <a href="/People/Form/{{ form.data.id }}">
           Edit Person {{ form.data.name }}</a>
   {% endblock %}
   ```

▼

> To get the `Person.id` value used in the link, you access the data dictionary in the
> form object in the template. The best documentation about how to access this
> type of data is the code itself.

By the Way

5. Save the `iFriends/templates/admin/People/person/change_form.html`
   file.

6. Copy the following file from the Django installation to the iFriends/templates/
   admin directory so that you can customize it at the site level:

   `django/contrib/admin/templates/admin/ change_list.html`

7. Open the `iFriends/templates/admin/change_list.html` file in an editor.

8. Modify the content `block` line to include a new custom block named
   `blog_usage`:

   ```
   {% block content %}{% block blog_usage %}{% endblock %}
   ```

9. Save the `iFriends/templates/admin/change_list.html` file.

10. Create and open the `iFriends/templates/admin/People/change_list.html`
    file in an editor.

11. Add the following line of code, shown in Listing 18.5, to extend the
    `change_list.html` template you modified in steps 7 through 10:

    ```
    {% extends "admin/change_list.html" %}
    ```

12. Add the following block tag, shown in Listing 18.5. It overrides the custom
    `blog_usage` block tag you added to the site-level custom template and ren-
    ders a link to the `blog_usage()` view:

    ```
    {% block blog_usage %}
       <a href="/admin/blog_usage">Run Blog Usage Report</a>
    {% endblock %}
    ```

13. Save the `iFriends/templates/admin/People/change_list.html` file.

14. Access the change form view for a `Person` object, shown in Figure 18.3, in the
    admin interface to verify that the Edit Person link appears at the top of the
    change form.

15. Click the Edit Person link to verify that the `person_form()` view is displayed.

FIGURE 18.3
The custom
admin change
form view for a
Person object
displaying the
Edit Person link.

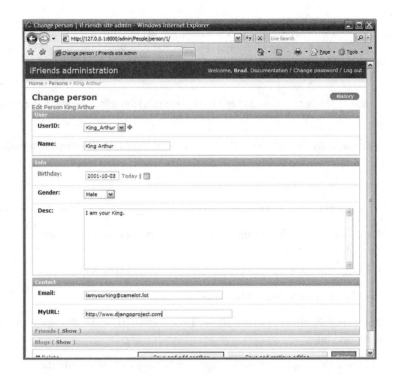

16. Access the change list view for both the Person objects, shown in Figure 18.4, and the Blog objects, shown in Figure 18.5, in the admin interface. Verify that the Run Blog Usage Report link is displayed above the list.

FIGURE 18.4
The custom
admin change
list view for
Person objects
displaying the
Run Blog Usage
Report link.

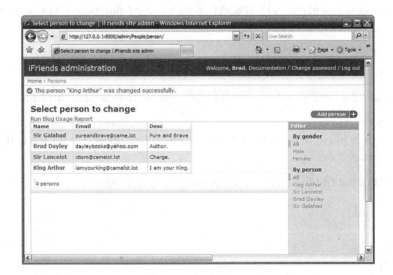

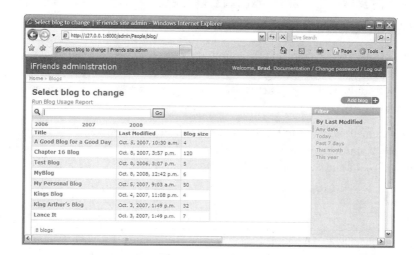

FIGURE 18.5
The custom admin change list view for Blog objects displaying the Run Blog Usage Report link.

17. Click the Run Blog Usage Report link to verify that the blog_usage() view is displayed.

The Run Blog Usage Report link is displayed in both the Person and Blog change lists because the custom template resides at the People application level. The Edit Person link does not show up on the Blog change form views because the custom template resides at the Person object level.

By the Way

LISTING 18.4 Full Contents of the iFriends/templates/admin/People/person/change_form.html **File**

```
{% extends "admin/change_form.html" %}

{% block form_top %}
    <a href="/People/Form/{{ form.data.id }}">
        Edit Person {{ form.data.name }}</a>
{% endblock %}
```

LISTING 18.5 Full Contents of the iFriends/templates/admin/People/change_list.html **File**

```
{% extends "admin/change_list.html" %}

{% block blog_usage %}
    <a href="/admin/blog_usage">Run Blog Usage Report</a>
{% endblock %}
```

Overriding the Built-in Admin Views in the URLconf File

Another option for customizing the admin interface is to simply override the admin URL patterns with your own. You can override patterns that normally link to admin views by adding your own patterns before including the django.contrib.admin. urls URLconf file.

Using this method, you can have admin URLs access your own custom views. For example, if you wanted to override the admin index view with a custom view function, you could add the following URL pattern:

```
(r'^admin/$', 'mySite.CustomViews.views.site_index'),
```

> You can actually do some processing in your view function and then call the admin view function to render the view. However, you must know exactly what you are doing.

▼ Try It Yourself

Override the Admin Logout URL

In this section, you will override the admin/logout URL to link to the iFriends. Home.views.logout_user view function. Follow these steps to override the URL:

1. Open the iFriends/urls.py file in an editor.

2. Add the following URL pattern, before you include django.contrib.admin. urls, to override the admin/logout URL:

   ```
   (r'^admin/logout/$', 'iFriends.Home.views.logout_user'),
   ```

3. Save the iFriends/urls.py file.

4. Access any page in the admin interface, and click the Logout link in the browser. You should be redirected to the login page, shown in Figure 18.6, instead of the normal Django admin page.

▼

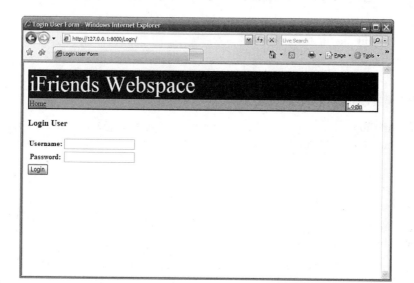

FIGURE 18.6
The iFriends custom Login page for the admin interface.

Summary

In this hour, you learned that you can override the admin templates. Overriding the admin templates allows you to customize the look and feel of the admin interface with your own code.

If you override templates at the site level, the customization affects views at the site, application, and object level. You can narrow down the customization to an application and object level so that only certain applications or object views are affected.

We also covered creating your own custom admin views and overriding them by using your own URL patterns.

Q&A

Q. *Is there a way to customize the index view?*

A. Yes. You can copy the index.html file from the Django distribution into the admin subdirectory of your site template directory and make changes there. You can remove the following code that generates the list in the index and insert your own code to display your own links:

```
{% get_admin_app_list as app_list %}
```

Q. *Is there a way to add custom JavaScript to the admin templates?*

A. Yes. Add the custom JavaScript to the custom templates that you create or copy in the site template directory.

Workshop

The workshop consists of a set of questions and answers designed to solidify your understanding of the material covered in this hour. Try answering the questions before looking at the answers.

Quiz

1. What template would you customize if you wanted to change the behavior of object lists in the admin interface?

2. Where would you put custom template files to customize only the Quote application in a site?

3. Should you put your own custom URLs before or after the `django.contrib.admin.urls` URLconf file in your site URLconf?

4. If you have the same template at the site, application, and object level in your custom admin templates, which file overrides the others?

Quiz Answers

1. The `change_list.html` template file.

2. In the admin/Quote subdirectory of your site template directory.

3. Definitely before.

4. The template located at the object level overrides the others, and then the application, and then the site.

Exercises

The best exercise you can do for this hour is to look at the URLconf, template files, and view functions listed at the beginning of this hour. If you get a feel for how the Django admin is coded, you will be more easily able to customize it.

PART IV

Implementing Advanced Website Components

Implementing Middleware

What You'll Learn in This Hour:

▶ How to install middleware applications
▶ How to use middleware applications
▶ How to implement a request preprocessor
▶ How to implement a view preprocessor
▶ How to implement a response postprocessor
▶ How to implement an exception postprocessor
▶ What built-in middleware comes with Django

So far, all the code that we have written to manipulate views has been in the view functions and templates. Django provides a simple-to-use framework, called middleware, that allows you to manipulate the behavior of views at the request and response level.

Using the middleware framework, you can write your own custom functions that hook into the request and response engine. These custom functions can be used to log information about the request or response, alter the request or response, or perform any number of other operations.

Django itself implements middleware for several things such as providing `request. session` and `request.user` information to the view functions. Several other middleware applications can be installed into Django.

This hour discusses how to install middleware applications and how to build your own custom middleware applications. You'll also learn about some of the middleware applications that are built into Django.

Installing Middleware

You install middleware applications using the MIDDLEWARE_CLASSES setting in the project's settings.py file. Each line in the MIDDLEWARE_CLASSES setting is a string representing the full Python path to a class in the middleware application.

For example, the following middleware applications are automatically installed when you create a new project:

```
MIDDLEWARE_CLASSES = (
    'django.middleware.common.CommonMiddleware',
    'django.contrib.sessions.middleware.SessionMiddleware',
    'django.contrib.auth.middleware.AuthenticationMiddleware',
    'django.middleware.doc.XViewMiddleware',
)
```

To install a middleware application, make certain that it is installed somewhere in the Python path, and then add the middleware application to the MIDDLEWARE_CLASSES setting.

The order in which applications appear in the MIDDLEWARE_CLASSES setting is important. Middleware is applied in the order in which it appears in the setting. For prerequest and preview hooks, the first item in the setting is applied first. For postresponse and postexception hooks, the first item in the setting is applied last.

Implementing Middleware Applications

Implementing a middleware application is not difficult. A middleware application is a basic Python class that defines one or more functions that conform to a specific API. The class does not need to inherit from any other class. However, it does need to define one or more of the following middleware API functions:

▶ process_request(self, request) runs before processing the request.

▶ process_view(self, request, view, args, kwargs) runs before calling the view function.

▶ process_response(self, request, response) runs after the response has been generated.

▶ process_exception(self, request, exception) runs when an exception has been raised and not handled.

To implement a middleware application, simply create a Python class and add a definition to one or more of these functions. Then place the module somewhere in the Python path and add an entry for it in the MIDDLEWARE_CLASSES setting.

You can also define an __init__(self) function in the middleware class. The __init__() function should take no arguments except self. You can use the __init__() function to perform some operations whenever the middleware object is instantiated.

> For long-running server processes, the middleware class is instantiated only once. Therefore, you cannot be certain that the __init__() function will be run every time a request runs.

Watch Out!

Implementing a Request Preprocessor

You implement a request preprocessor by defining a process_request(self, request) function in the middleware class. The process_request() function is called after the request has been received but before the URL gets resolved to determine which view function to run.

The process_request() function is passed the HttpRequest object of the request. Any changes you make to the HttpRequest object are also passed down to the view function.

The process_request() function can return either None or an HttpResponse object. If None is returned, Django continues processing the request. However, if you return an HttpResponse object, the request immediately returns that response.

> No other middleware applications or view functions run if an HttpResponse is returned.

Watch Out!

The SetRemoteAddrFromForwardedFor application uses the following code snippet to replace the REMOTE_ADDR attribute of the request with the HTTP_X_FORWARDED_FOR attribute for requests coming through a proxy:

```
def process_request(self, request):
    try:
        real_ip = request.META['HTTP_X_FORWARDED_FOR']
    except KeyError:
        pass
    else:
        real_ip = real_ip.split(",")[0]
        request.META[REMOTE_ADDR'] = real_ip
```

▼

Try It Yourself

Create and Install a Request Preprocessor Middleware Application

In this section, you will create and install a view preprocessor application, called `CustomViewLogger`, that logs information about view functions before they are run. You will also create a new application called Log in the database, and then you will define a new `RequestEvent` model in the Log application to store information about requests. You will also implement a new `view_log()` view function and template that will render the `RequestEvent` objects.

By the Way

> The examples in this hour are just meant to illustrate data that can be accessed in the middleware. If you want to implement a logging system for a large website that has numerous requests, you will probably want to use another method, such as a buffered file, for storage than the site database.

Follow these steps to implement a request preprocessor middleware application:

1. Stop the development server.

2. Use the following command at the root of the iFriends project to create a new application called Log:

   ```
   python manage.py startapp Log
   ```

3. Open the `iFriends/Log/models.py` file in an editor.

4. Add the following `import` statement to the file, shown in Listing 19.1, to import the User object so that you can use it in your models:

   ```
   from django.contrib.auth.models import User
   ```

5. Add the `RequestEvent` model to the file, shown in Listing 19.1, to define a `RequestEvent` object that can store information about the request.

6. Save the `iFriends/Log/models.py` file.

7. Synchronize the database using the `manage.py syncdb` command from the root of the iFriends project.

8. Create a file named `django/middleware/custom.py` in your Django installation.

▼

> The built-in middleware is installed in the django/middleware directory. However, you can put your middleware applications anywhere Python can find them.

By the Way

9. Add the following imports to the file, shown in Listing 19.2, to import the RequestEvent object you defined in step 5 and the datetime class that you will use to record the time of the request:

```
from iFriends.Log.models import RequestEvent
from datetime import datetime
```

10. Add the CustomRequestLogger middleware class definition to the file and define the process_request() function, shown in Listing 19.2, that collects information about the request and stores it in a RequestEvent in the database.

11. Save the django/middleware/custom.py file.

12. Create and open a file called iFriends/templates/Custom/view_request_log.html in an editor.

13. Add the contents shown in Listing 19.3 to the file.

14. Save the iFriends/templates/Custom/view_request_log.html file.

15. Open the iFriends/Custom/views.py file in an editor.

16. Add the view_log() view function, shown in Listing 19.4, to the file. The evType='request' argument is needed for later examples, as is using the lTemplate variable to define the template file to render.

17. Save the iFriends/Custom/views.py file.

18. Open the iFriends/urls.py file in an editor.

19. Add the following URL pattern to enable the view_log() function and collect the evType argument from the URL:

```
(r'^admin/view_log/(?P<evType>\w+)/$', 'iFriends.Custom.views.view_log'),
```

20. Save the iFriends/urls.py file.

21. Open the iFriends/settings.py file in an editor.

22. Add the following line to the MIDDLEWARE_CLASSES setting to install the CustomRequestLogger application:

```
'django.middleware.custom.CustomRequestLogger',
```

23. Save the iFriends/settings.py file.

24. Start the development server.

25. Access several nonadmin web pages in the iFriends site. Access the following URL to view the request log generated by the CustomRequestLogger application, shown in Figure 19.1:

```
http://127.0.0.1:8000/admin/view_log/request/
```

FIGURE 19.1
The view_log() function displaying the RequestEvent log.

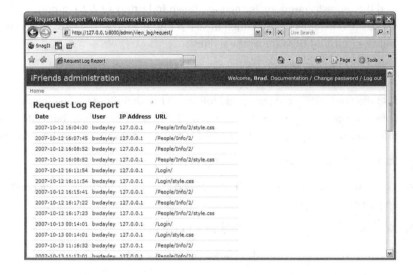

LISTING 19.1 The Imports and RequestEvent Definition of the iFriends/Log/models.py File

```python
from django.db import models
from django.contrib.auth.models import User

class RequestEvent(models.Model):
    event = models.CharField('Event', max_length=30)
    date = models.DateTimeField('Date')
    user = models.ForeignKey(User)
    addr = models.CharField('IP Address', max_length=20)
    url = models.CharField('Url', max_length=80)

    def __str__(self):
        return '%s - %s' % (self.event, self.date)

    class Admin:
        pass
```

LISTING 19.2 The Imports and CustomRequestLogger Definition of the django/middleware/custom.py File

```python
from iFriends.Log.models import RequestEvent
from datetime import datetime

class CustomRequestLogger(object):
```

LISTING 19.2 Continued

```
def process_request(self, request):
    try:
        if not request.META['PATH_INFO'].startswith('/admin'):
            event = RequestEvent()
            event.event = "Request"
            event.user = request.user
            event.addr = request.META['REMOTE_ADDR']
            event.date = datetime.now()
            event.url = request.META['PATH_INFO']
            event.save()
    except KeyError:
        pass
    return None
```

LISTING 19.3 Full Contents of the iFriends/templates/Custom/ view_request_log.py File

```
{% extends "admin/base_site.html" %}
{% block title %}Request Log Report{% endblock %}

{% block content %}
<h1>Request Log Report</h1>
<table>
<tr>
<th>Date</th><th>User</th><th>IP Address</th><th>URL</th>
</tr>
{% for entry in logList %}
    <tr>
        <td>{{ entry.date }}</td>
        <td>{{ entry.user }}</td>
        <td>{{ entry.addr }}</td>
        <td>{{ entry.url }}</td>
    </tr>
{% endfor %}
</table>
{% endblock %}
```

LISTING 19.4 The view_log() View Function of the iFriends/Custom/views.py File

```
@staff_member_required
def view_log(request, evType='request'):
    lTemplate = 'Custom/view_request_log.html'
    logList = RequestEvent.objects.all()

    return render_to_response(lTemplate, {'logList': logList})
```

Implementing a View Preprocessor

You implement a view preprocessor by defining a process_view(self, request, view, args, kwargs) function in the middleware class. The process_view() function is called after the URL has been resolved to determine which view function and arguments to run, but before the view function is called.

The process_view() function is passed the HttpRequest object, view function, positional arguments, and keyword arguments. Any changes you make to the HttpRequest object also are passed down to the view function. The process_view() function is an excellent way to make modifications globally to define specific arguments to all view functions.

The process_view() function can also return either None or an HttpResponse object. If None is returned, Django continues processing the request and calls the view function. However, if you return an HttpResponse object, the request immediately returns that response.

> No other middleware applications or view functions will run if an HttpResponse is returned.

The following code snippet sets the Logging argument to True for all view functions' proxies:

```
class ViewLogging(object):
    def process_view(self, request, view, args, kwargs):
        try:
            kwargs['Logging'] = True
        except KeyError:
            pass

        return None
```

▼   **Try It Yourself**

Create and Install a View Preprocessor Middleware Application

In this section, you will create and install a view preprocessor application called CustomViewLogger that logs information about view functions before they are run. You will define a new ViewEvent model in the Log application to store information about view functions that are called. You will also create a template that the view_log() view function will use to render the ViewEvent objects:

▼

Follow these steps to implement a view preprocessor middleware application:

1. Stop the development server.

2. Open the `iFriends/Log/models.py` file in an editor.

3. Add the `ViewEvent` model to the file, as shown in Listing 19.5, to define a `ViewEvent` object that can store information about the view that is being rendered.

4. Save the `iFriends/Log/models.py` file.

5. Synchronize the database using the `manage.py syncdb` command from the root of the iFriends project.

6. Open the `django/middleware/custom.py` file in your Django installation.

7. Add the following import to the file, as shown in Listing 19.6, to import the `ViewEvent` object you defined in step 3:

```
from iFriends.Log.models import ViewEvent
```

8. Add the `CustomViewLogger` middleware class definition to the file and define the `process_view()` function, as shown in Listing 19.6. This will collect information about the view request and store it in a `ViewEvent` object in the database.

9. Save the `django/middleware/custom.py` file.

10. Create and open a file called `iFriends/templates/Custom/view_view_log.html` in an editor.

11. Add the contents shown in Listing 19.7 to the file.

12. Save the `iFriends/templates/Custom/view_view_log.html` file.

13. Open the `iFriends/Custom/views.py` file in an editor.

14. Add the following code to the `view_log()` view function, shown in Listing 19.8. It sets `lTemplate` to the `view_view_log.html` file and `logList` to the `ViewEvent` objects if `evType` is set to `view`:

```
if evType == "view":
    lTemplate = 'Custom/view_view_log.html'
    logList = ViewEvent.objects.all()
else:
```

15. Save the `iFriends/Custom/views.py` file.

16. Open the `iFriends/settings.py` file in an editor.

17. Add the following line to the MIDDLEWARE_CLASSES setting to install the CustomViewLogger application:

    ```
    'django.middleware.custom.CustomViewLogger',
    ```

18. Save the iFriends/settings.py file.

19. Start the development server.

20. Access several nonadmin web pages in the iFriends site, and then access the following URL to view the log report, as shown in Figure 19.2, generated by the CustomViewLogger application:

    ```
    http://127.0.0.1:8000/admin/view_log/view/
    ```

FIGURE 19.2
The view_log() function displaying the ViewEvent log.

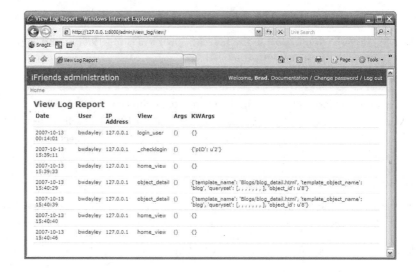

LISTING 19.5   The ViewEvent Definition of the iFriends/Log/models.py File

```
class ViewEvent(models.Model):
    event = models.CharField('Event', max_length=30)
    date = models.DateTimeField('Date')
    user = models.ForeignKey(User)
    addr = models.CharField('IP Address', max_length=20)
    view = models.CharField('View', max_length=80)
    args = models.TextField('Args', max_length=200)
    kwargs = models.TextField('KWArgs', max_length=400)

    def __str__(self):
        return '%s - %s' % (self.event, self.date)

    class Admin:
        pass
```

LISTING 19.6 The Imports and `CustomViewLogger` Definition of the `django/middleware/custom.py` File

```
from iFriends.Log.models import ViewEvent
. . .
class CustomViewLogger(object):
    def process_view(self, request, view, args, kwargs):
        try:
            if not request.META['PATH_INFO'].startswith('/admin'):
                event = ViewEvent()
                event.event = "View"
                event.user = request.user
                event.addr = request.META['REMOTE_ADDR']
                event.date = datetime.now()
                event.view = view.__name__
                event.args = str(args)
                event.kwargs = str(kwargs)
                event.save()
        except KeyError:
            pass
        return None
```

LISTING 19.7 Full Contents of the `iFriends/templates/Custom/view_view_log.py` File

```
{% extends "admin/base_site.html" %}
{% block title %}View Log Report{% endblock %}

{% block content %}
<h1>View Log Report</h1>
<table>
<tr>
<th>Date</th><th>User</th><th>IP Address</th><th>View</th><th>Args</th>
  <th>KWArgs</th>
</tr>
{% for entry in logList %}
    <tr>
        <td>{{ entry.date }}</td>
        <td>{{ entry.user }}</td>
        <td>{{ entry.addr }}</td>
        <td>{{ entry.view }}</td>
        <td>{{ entry.args }}</td>
        <td>{{ entry.kwargs }}</td>
    </tr>
{% endfor %}
</table>
{% endblock %}
```

LISTING 19.8 The `view_log()` View Function of the `iFriends/Custom/views.py` File

```
@staff_member_required
def view_log(request, evType='request'):
    if evType == "view":
        lTemplate = 'Custom/view_view_log.html'
```

▼

LISTING 19.8   Continued

```
        logList = ViewEvent.objects.all()
    else:
        lTemplate = 'Custom/view_request_log.html'
        logList = RequestEvent.objects.all()

    return render_to_response(lTemplate, {'logList': logList})
```

▲

Implementing a Response Postprocessor

You implement a response postprocessor by defining a process_response(self, request, response) function in the middleware class. The process_response() function is called after the HttpResponse has been created but before it is returned to the browser.

The process_response() function is passed the HttpRequest and HttpResponse objects as arguments. Any changes you make to the HttpResponse object also are passed back to the browser. The process_response() function is an excellent way to make modifications globally to verify responses and make changes to them before they are passed back to the browser.

The process_response() function must return only an HttpResponse object. You can pass back the HttpResponse that was passed in, or you can pass back an entirely different one. For example, the following code snippet globally modifies all responses to include footers at the bottom of the HTML document:

```
class AddFooter(object):
    def process_response(self, request, response):
        footer = "<HR>This page was generated by iFriends /
                  \n</body>\n</html>"
        contents = response.content
        contents = contents.replace('</body>\n</html>', footer)

        return None
```

▼

Try It Yourself

Create and Install a Response Postprocessor Middleware Application

In this section, you will create and install a response postprocessor application called CustomResponseLogger that logs information about responses before they are sent to the browser. You will also define a new ResponseEvent model in the Log application to store information about the response before it is sent back to the

▼

browser. You will also create a template that the view_log() view function will use to render the ResponseEvent objects.

Follow these steps to implement a response postprocessor middleware application:

1. Stop the development server.

2. Open the iFriends/Log/models.py file in an editor.

3. Add the ResponseEvent model to the file, as shown in Listing 19.9, to define a ResponseEvent object that can store information about the response.

4. Save the iFriends/Log/models.py file.

5. Synchronize the database using the manage.py syncdb command from the root of the iFriends project.

6. Open the django/middleware/custom.py file in your Django installation.

7. Add the following import to the file, as shown in Listing 19.10, to import the ResponseEvent object you defined in step 3:

```
from iFriends.Log.models import ResponseEvent
```

8. Add the CustomResponseLogger middleware class definition to the file and define the process_response() function, as shown in Listing 19.10. This will collect information about the view request and store it in a ResponseEvent object in the database.

9. Save the django/middleware/custom.py file.

10. Create and open a file called iFriends/templates/Custom/view_response_log.html in an editor.

11. Add the contents shown in Listing 19.11 to the file.

12. Save the iFriends/templates/Custom/view_response_log.html file.

13. Open the iFriends/Custom/views.py file in an editor.

14. Add the following code to the view_log() view function, as shown in Listing 19.12. It sets lTemplate to the view_response_log.html file and logList to the ResponseEvent objects if evType is set to response:

```
elif evType == "response":
    lTemplate = 'Custom/view_response_log.html'
    logList = ViewResponse.objects.all()
```

15. Save the iFriends/Custom/views.py file.

16. Open the iFriends/settings.py file in an editor.

17. Add the following line to the `MIDDLEWARE_CLASSES` setting to install the `CustomResponseLogger` application:

```
'django.middleware.custom.CustomResponseLogger',
```

18. Save the `iFriends/settings.py` file.

19. Start the development server.

20. Access several nonadmin web pages in the iFriends site. Access the following URL to view the log report, as shown in Figure 19.3, generated by the `CustomResponseLogger` application:

```
http://127.0.0.1:8000/admin/view_log/response/
```

FIGURE 19.3
The `view_log()` function displaying the `ResponseEvent` log.

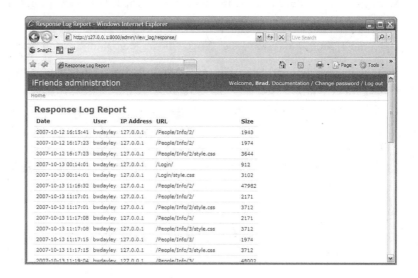

LISTING 19.9   The `ResponseEvent` **Definition of the** `iFriends/Log/models.py` **File**

```
class ResponseEvent(models.Model):
    event = models.CharField('Event', max_length=30)
    date = models.DateTimeField('Date')
    user = models.ForeignKey(User, blank=True, null=True)
    addr = models.CharField('IP Address', max_length=20)
    url = models.CharField('Url', max_length=80)
    size = models.IntegerField('Size')

    def __str__(self):
        return '%s - %s' % (self.event, self.date)

    class Admin:
        pass
```

LISTING 19.10   The Imports and `CustomResponseLogger` **Definition of** the `django/middleware/custom.py` **File**

```
from iFriends.Log.models import ResponseEvent
. . .
class CustomResponseLogger(object):
    def process_response(self, request, response):
        try:
            if not request.META['PATH_INFO'].startswith('/admin'):
                event = ResponseEvent()
                event.event = "Response"
                event.user = request.user
                event.addr = request.META['REMOTE_ADDR']
                event.date = datetime.now()
                event.url = request.META['PATH_INFO']
                event.size = len(response.content)
                event.save()
        except KeyError:
            pass
        return response
```

LISTING 19.11   Full Contents of the `iFriends/templates/Custom/` `view_response_log.py` **File**

```
{% extends "admin/base_site.html" %}
{% block title %}Response Log Report{% endblock %}

{% block content %}
<h1>Response Log Report</h1>
<table>
<tr>
<th>Date</th><th>User</th><th>IP Address</th><th>URL</th><th>Size</th>
</tr>
{% for entry in logList %}
    <tr>
        <td>{{ entry.date }}</td>
        <td>{{ entry.user }}</td>
        <td>{{ entry.addr }}</td>
        <td>{{ entry.url }}</td>
        <td>{{ entry.size }}</td>
    </tr>
{% endfor %}
</table>
{% endblock %}
```

LISTING 19.12   The `view_log()` **View Function of the** `iFriends/` `Custom/views.py` **File**

```
@staff_member_required
def view_log(request, evType='request'):
    if evType == "view":
        lTemplate = 'Custom/view_view_log.html'
        logList = ViewEvent.objects.all()
    elif evType == "response":
```

▼

LISTING 19.12   Continued

```
        lTemplate = 'Custom/view_response_log.html'
        logList = ResponseEvent.objects.all()
    else:
        lTemplate = 'Custom/view_request_log.html'
        logList = RequestEvent.objects.all()

    return render_to_response(lTemplate, {'logList': logList})
```

▲

Implementing an Exception Postprocessor

You implement an exception postprocessor by defining a process_exception (self, request, exception) function in the middleware class. The process_ exception() function is called if an exception was raised by the view and was not handled.

By the Way

> The process_exception() function is not called on Http404 exceptions.

The process_exception() function is passed the HttpRequest object and an Exception object arguments. Using the process_exception() function, you may be able to handle some exceptions and recover so that the browser doesn't receive an error. You can also use the process_exception() function to log and debug errors on the website.

The process_response() function can return None or an HttpResponse object. If None is returned, Django continues processing the exception using its built-in exception handling. If you pass back an HttpResponse object, the browser receives that response instead of an error.

For example, the following code snippet intercepts any unhandled exceptions and calls a HandleErrors() view function that returns some kind of HttpResponse:

```
from mySite.custom.views import HandleErrors
class AddFooter(object):
    def process_exception(self, request, exception):
        return HandleErrors(request, exception)
```

Create and Install an Exception Postprocessor Middleware Application

In this section, you will create and install an exception postprocessor application called `CustomExceptionLogger`. It will log information about exceptions that are not handled and, therefore, are sent to the browser. You will also define a new `ExceptionEvent` model in the Log application to store information about the exception before an error is sent back to the browser. You will also create a template that the `view_log()` view function will use to render the `ExceptionEvent` objects:

Follow these steps to implement the exception postprocessor middleware application:

1. Stop the development server.

2. Open the `iFriends/Log/models.py` file in an editor.

3. Add the `ExceptionEvent` model to the file, as shown in Listing 19.13, to define an `ExceptionEvent` object that can store information about the exception.

4. Save the `iFriends/Log/models.py` file.

5. Synchronize the database using the `manage.py syncdb` command from the root of the iFriends project.

6. Open the `django/middleware/custom.py` file in your Django installation.

7. Add the following import to the file, as shown in Listing 19.14, to import the `ExceptionEvent` object you defined in step 3:

   ```
   from iFriends.Log.models import ExceptionEvent
   ```

8. Add the `CustomExceptionLogger` middleware class definition to the file, and define the `process_exception()` function, as shown in Listing 19.14. It collects information about the view request and stores it in an `ExceptionEvent` object in the database.

9. Save the `django/middleware/custom.py` file.

10. Create and open a file called `iFriends/templates/Custom/view_event_log.html` in an editor.

11. Add the contents shown in Listing 19.15 to the file. ▼

12. Save the `iFriends/templates/Custom/view_event_log.html` file.

13. Open the `iFriends/Custom/views.py` file in an editor.

14. Add the following code to the `view_log()` view function, as shown in Listing 19.16, to set `lTemplate` to the `view_exception_log.html` file and `logList` to the `ExceptionEvent` objects if `evType` is set to exception:

```
elif evType == "response":
    lTemplate = 'Custom/view_response_log.html'
    logList = ViewResponse.objects.all()
```

15. Save the `iFriends/Custom/views.py` file.

16. Open the `iFriends/settings.py` file in an editor.

17. Add the following line to the `MIDDLEWARE_CLASSES` setting to install the `CustomExceptionLogger` application:

```
'django.middleware.custom.CustomExceptionLogger',
```

18. Save the `iFriends/settings.py` file.

19. Start the development server.

20. You need to access URLs that generate exceptions in the iFriends site (you can also force exceptions in your view code). Then access the following URL to view the exception log report, as shown in Figure 19.4, generated by the `CustomExceptionLogger` application:

```
http://127.0.0.1:8000/admin/view_log/exception/
```

FIGURE 19.4
The `view_log()` function displaying the `ExceptionEvent` log.

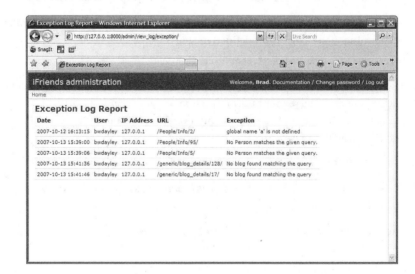

LISTING 19.13 The `ExceptionEvent` **Definition of the** `iFriends/`
`Log/models.py` **File**

```python
class ExceptionEvent(models.Model):
    event = models.CharField('Event', max_length=30)
    date = models.DateTimeField('Date')
    user = models.ForeignKey(User)
    addr = models.CharField('IP Address', max_length=20)
    url = models.CharField('Url', max_length=80)
    exception = models.CharField('Exception', max_length=100)

    def __str__(self):
        return '%s - %s' % (self.event, self.date)

    class Admin:
        pass
```

LISTING 19.14 The Imports and `CustomExceptionLogger` **Definition**
of the `django/middleware/custom.py` **File**

```python
from iFriends.Log.models import ExceptionEvent
. . .
class CustomExceptionLogger(object):
    def process_exception(self, request, exception):
        try:
            if not request.META['PATH_INFO'].startswith('/admin'):
                event = ExceptionEvent()
                event.event = "Exception"
                event.user = request.user
                event.addr = request.META['REMOTE_ADDR']
                event.date = datetime.now()
                event.url = request.META['PATH_INFO']
                event.exception = exception
                event.save()
        except KeyError:
            pass
        return None
```

LISTING 19.15 Full Contents of the `iFriends/templates/Custom/`
`view_exception_log.py` **File**

```
{% extends "admin/base_site.html" %}
{% block title %}Exception Log Report{% endblock %}

{% block content %}
<h1>Exception Log Report</h1>
<table>
<tr>
<th>Date</th><th>User</th><th>IP Address</th><th>URL</th><th>Exception</th>
</tr>
{% for entry in logList %}
    <tr>
        <td>{{ entry.date }}</td>
        <td>{{ entry.user }}</td>
        <td>{{ entry.addr }}</td>
```

LISTING 19.15   Continued

```
        <td>{{ entry.url }}</td>
        <td>{{ entry.exception }}</td>
    </tr>
{% endfor %}
</table>
{% endblock %}
```

LISTING 19.16   The `view_log()` **View Function of the** `iFriends/`
`Custom/views.py` **File**

```
@staff_member_required
def view_log(request, evType='request'):
    if evType == "view":
        lTemplate = 'Custom/view_view_log.html'
        logList = ViewEvent.objects.all()
    elif evType == "response":
        lTemplate = 'Custom/view_response_log.html'
        logList = ResponseEvent.objects.all()
    elif evType == "exception":
        lTemplate = 'Custom/view_exception_log.html'
        logList = ExceptionEvent.objects.all()
    else:
        lTemplate = 'Custom/view_request_log.html'
        logList = RequestEvent.objects.all()

    return render_to_response(lTemplate, {'logList': logList})
```

Django's Built-in Middleware

Django includes several built-in middleware applications, some of which you have already been using. You can install each one by adding it to the `MIDDLEWARE_CLASSES` setting in the `settings.py` file.

The following sections briefly discuss some of the built-in middleware applications. For more information about these and other built-in middleware applications, check out the source at the following location relative to the Django installation directory:

`django/middleware`

`django.middleware.common.CommonMiddleware`

The `CommonMiddleware` application provides some basic functionality to the website. It forbids access to user agents that are listed in the `DISALLOWED_USER_AGENTS` setting of the `settings.py` file.

CommonMiddleware also allows you to implement the APPEND_SLASH and PREPEND_WWW settings to add trailing slashes to the end and prefix a www to URLs. These options help you normalize URLs to match expected behavior.

CommonMiddleware also allows you to set USE_ETAGS=True in the settings.py file. If USE_ETAGS is True, Django calculates an ETag for each request using an MD5 hashing of the page content.

django.contrib.sessions.middleware.SessionMiddleware

The SessionMiddleware application enables session support in requests. It provides the request.session attribute that you have already been using to the request object that is passed to view functions.

django.contrib.auth.middleware.AuthenticationMiddleware

The AuthenticationMiddleware application provides authentication support to requests. It provides the request.user attribute that you have already been using to the request object that is passed to view functions.

django.middleware.cache.CacheMiddleware

The CacheMiddleware application enables site-wide caching. You can set the CACHE_MIDDLEWARE_SECONDS setting in the settings.py file to define how long the Django web pages are cached.

django.middleware.gzip.GZipMiddleware

The GZipMiddleware application allows you to reduce the impact of traffic by compressing content that is sent to browsers that support gzip compression.

> Django recommends that you put this in the first place in the MIDDLEWARE_CLASSES setting so that compression is the last thing that is performed in the postresponse handlers.

By the Way

django.middleware.locale.LocaleMiddleware

The LocaleMiddleware application allows you to select language based on the data provided in the request. Thus, the web content can be customized on a per-user basis.

Examples of how to implement the built-in middleware applications are contained
in the sections of this book where they are used. For example, an example of
implementing the caching middleware is located in Hour 23, "Configuring
Caching."

Summary

In this hour, you learned how to install and implement your own custom middleware. We discussed how middleware applications are basically just hooks into the
request and response processors. You learned that you can define four types of functions in a middleware application.

The process_request() and process_view() functions are prehooks that are run
before the URL is processed and the view functions are called, respectively. The
process_response() and process_exception() functions are posthooks that are
run just before the response is sent to the browser.

Implementing middleware allows you to customize the request and response handling in a variety of ways. For instance, you can make global changes to all requests
and responses.

Q&A

Q. Is it possible to use middleware to redirect web pages?

A. Yes. Instead of returning None from the process_request() function, return a
call to the function that renders an HttpResponse.

Q. Is it possible to conditionally enable middleware?

A. Yes. You can define an __init__(self) function in the middleware application. Put in your code to determine if the application should be enabled or dis-
abled. Then, if the determination is made to disable the middleware, raise a
django.exceptions.MiddlewareNotUsed exception. For example:

```
from django.exceptions import MiddlewareNotUsed
class CustomViewMiddleware(object):
    def __init__(self):
        if <your condition code>:
            raise MiddlewareNotUsed
```

Workshop

The workshop consists of a set of questions and answers designed to solidify your understanding of the material covered in this hour. Try answering the questions before looking at the answers.

Quiz

1. What setting needs to be modified to enable middleware applications?

2. Where in a middleware application would you put code to modify the arguments that will be passed to the view function?

3. Where in a middleware application would you put code to track the size of responses?

4. Which built-in middleware application enables you to access the user object in the view function?

Quiz Answers

1. The `MIDDLEWARE_CLASSES` setting in `settings.py`

2. In the `process_view()` function

3. In the `process_response()` function

4. The `django.contrib.auth.middleware.AuthenticationMiddleware` application

Exercises

1. Add a new middleware application to the `django.middleware.custom.py` file that appends footers with some kind of copyright or information string to every response.

2. Add another new middleware application with a request preprocessor function that determines which `Person` object matches the user in the request. Then modify the `desc` field of the `Person` object that matches the one in the request to include a string noting which IP address they are using.

HOUR 20

Internationalization and Localization

What You'll Learn in This Hour:

- ▶ How to localize strings in Python code
- ▶ How to localize strings in templates
- ▶ How to create language files
- ▶ Where to set language preference
- ▶ How to enable languages at the session level

Django provides full support for internationalization by allowing you to define localized strings in your Python code and template files. Using localized strings allows you to build a website that can be displayed in several different languages.

Internationalizing your website is a three-step process. First, you define which strings should be localized in different languages. Next, you build message files that contain the translated strings for each language. Finally, you configure a way to determine what language should be displayed.

The following sections discuss how to define localized strings, build the message files, and activate languages.

Localizing Strings in Python

The first step in internationalizing your website is to define the strings that need to be translated. In your Python code, strings are identified as being localized by wrapping them in a translation function. The following sections describe how to identify strings for translation using the standard, lazy, and no-op translation methods.

Standard Translation

The standard translation method involves using the `django.utils.translation.gettext()` function. The `gettext()` function accepts a Python string as its only argument. The string that is specified in the `gettext()` function is added to the message file.

For example, the following code enables a direct string and a string variable for translation:

```
from django.utils.translation import gettext
def myView(request):
    rawText = 'Welcome to iFriends'
    transText = gettext(rawText)
    loginText = gettext('Please Login')
    . . .
```

By the Way

> If you have a lot of strings that you would like to be localized, you might want to import the `gettext()` function as a shorter name, as in the following example:
>
> ```
> from django.utils.translation import gettext as _
> . . .
>     transText = _('Please Login')
> ```

You should be mindful when adding variable placeholders to localized strings that you may need to use named-string syntax. That way, when the strings are translated, the variable placeholder can move position in the translation as necessary. For example, the string `Tim is my name.` would be translated to `Ich heisse Tim`. The following code shows an example of using a named variable placeholder:

```
text = gettext('%(name)s is my name.')  % {'name': name}
```

Lazy Translation

The lazy translation method involves using the `django.utils.translation.gettext_lazy()` function. The `gettext_lazy()` function accepts a Python string as its only argument. The `gettext_lazy()` function stores a lazy reference to the string and translates the string only if it is used in a string context.

For example, the following model definition uses the `gettext_lazy()` function:

```
from django.utils.translation import gettext_lazy as _
class Contact(models.Model):
    name = models.CharField(_('Name'), max_length=80)
    location = models.CharField(_('Location', help_text=_('Your city.'))
```

You should always use `gettext_lazy()` to identify strings for translation in your Django models. You can alias `gettext_lazy()` to reduce the amount of text you need to type when identifying strings for translation. For example, the following code aliases `gettext_lazy()` as the _ character:

```
from django.utils.translation import gettext_lazy as _
. . .
    title = models.CharField(_('Title'), help_text=_('Enter a Title Here.'))
```

Watch Out!

No-op String Translation

Django provides the `django.utils.translation.gettext_no-op()` function to identify strings as translation strings. However, they are not actually translated yet. They are translated later as a variable at the last possible point before they are rendered to the user.

You can use no-op strings for things such as constant strings, or strings stored in the database. Django will not translate a no-op strings until the last possible moment.

Try It Yourself   ▼

Add a Localized String to a Python View Function

In this section, you will modify the `login_user()` view function to localize the heading text. Follow these steps to do so:

1. Open the `iFriends/Home/views.py` file in an editor.

2. Add the following import setting to the beginning of the file to import the `gettext()` function:

   ```
   from django.utils.translation import gettext
   ```

3. Modify the following line of code, shown in Listing 20.2, that defines the message variable to use the `gettext()` function to localize the message string:

   ```
   message = gettext('Login User')
   ```

4. Save the `iFriends/Home/views.py` file.

Several of the "Try it Yourself" sections in this hour add small amounts of code to Listing 20.2. Rather than listing the full contents in each "Try It Yourself" section, the full code listing is added in the final section to reduce redundancy.

By the Way

Localizing Strings in Templates

You can also identify strings in template files that should be translated. Strings are localized in the template files the same way they are localized in Python code. However, you need to load the i18n template file into your own template first. Use the following code in your template to do so:

```
{% load i18n %}
```

The following sections discuss the different template tags and variables that you can use when localizing your templates.

The trans Tag

The simplest way to localize a string in a template is to use the trans template tag. The trans template tag works the same way that the gettext() function does; it accepts a string and identifies that string as localized. The following is an example of using the trans template tag:

```
{% trans "Web Search Results" %}
```

> You can also use the noop argument in the trans tag to mark the string for trans-lation but to translate it later from a variable:
>
> ```
> {% trans "title" noop %}
> ```

The blocktrans Tag

The trans tag accepts only constant strings; it cannot accept variables. To localize string variables, you need to use the blocktrans tag. It identifies a block of text, including variables, as localized. The following example shows how to use the blocktrans tag:

```
{% blocktrans %}Title: {{ title }} {% endblocktrans %}
```

If you need to use some kind of template expression on a variable, such as a template filter, you need to bind the expression to a local variable to be used in the block. For example:

```
{% blocktrans with title|CAPFIRST as ctitle %}
    Title: {{ ctitle }}
{% endblocktrans %}
```

Using Translation Hooks in Tags

The i18n template file also provides translation hooks within any template that accepts constant strings. To use those template hooks, use the _() syntax, as shown in the following example:

```
{% CustomTag _("Translation String") %}
```

When you use these translation hooks, the tag sees the translated string and is unaware of the translation.

Accessing Languages in a Template

RequestContext has access to the following translation-specific variables that you can use when designing your templates:

- ► LANGUAGES is a list of two element tuples in which the first element is the language code and the second is the language name.

- ► LANGUAGE_CODE is a string containing the preferred language code for the current user.

- ► LANGUAGE_BIDI is Boolean. If it is True, the current language is one that is read right to left (such as Arabic or Japanese). If it is False, the current language is a left-to-right language (such as English, Spanish, or German).

For example, the following template code uses the LANGUAGE_CODE variable to display English-only code if the user's language is English:

```
{% ifequal LANGUAGE_CODE 'en' %}
    English Elements
    . . .
{% endifequal %}
```

If you are not using the RequestContext extension in the view, you can also assign the translation-specific variables using the following template tag code:

```
{% get_available_languages as LANGUAGES %}
{% get_current_language as LANGUAGE_CODE %}
{% get_current_language_bidi as LANGUAGE_BIDI %}
```

▼ **Try It Yourself**

Add a Localized String to an HTML Template File

In this section, you will modify the `iFriends_base.html` template file to localize the Welcome string that is displayed before the username. Follow these steps to localize the string:

1. Open the `iFriends/templates/iFriends_base.html` file in an editor.

2. Add the following line of code, shown in Listing 20.1, to the head of the file to load the i18n template file:

   ```
   {% load i18n %}
   ```

3. Modify the Welcome string with the following `trans` tag, shown in Listing 20.1, to localize the string:

   ```
   {% trans "Welcome" %}
   ```

4. Save the `iFriends/templates/iFriends_base.html` file.

LISTING 20.1   The `load` `i18n` Block and the Welcome Message Cell Entry in the `iFriends/templates/iFriends_base.html` File

```
{% load i18n %}
. . .
<td bgcolor="white"><font size="3">
    {% if user.is_authenticated %}
        {% trans "Welcome" %} {{ user.username }}.
    {% else %}
        <a href="/Login">Login</a>
    {% endif %}
</font></td>
. . .
```

▲

Creating Language Files

After you have identified all your localized strings in the Python and template code, you need to build message files that Django can use when rendering localized strings. Creating the language files is a three-step process.

The first step is to use the make-messages application to build message files for each language that will be localized. The next step is to add the translation strings to each language message file. The final step is to compile the message files into a binary form that Django can consume.

The following sections describe the process of creating language files. Before proceeding, download the Gnu `gettext` package from the following location, install it, and make certain that the bin directory is in the path:

```
www.gnu.org/software/gettext/gettext.html
```

Using make-messages

The first step in creating language files is to build the message files. A message file is a text file that contains entries that include a message ID and translation string for that particular language. Each language has one message file.

Django provides the `django/bin/make-messages.py` utility to create and update message files. You can also build the message file for a specific language using the `-l language-code` parameter. The following example shows how to build the German message file:

```
message-make.py -l de
```

You need to run the `message-make.py` utility for each language you want to add to your project. However, after you have added the language files, you can use the `-a` parameter to update all the existing message files:

```
message-make.py -a
```

The `message-make.py` file is not automatically added to your PATH. You need to either copy it to a location that is in your path or add the full path to the django/bin/ directory in your Django installation to the PATH setting.

Watch
Out!

Message files can be built at three different levels—the Django installation, the project, and the application.

Django already comes with its own message files built and compiled. You would need to build the message file at the Django installation level only if you modified a string in the Django code or if you wanted to add a language that Django currently doesn't support. To build the message files for the Django installation, run the `make-messages.py` utility at the root of the Django installation. The messages are stored in the following file in the Django installation path:

```
django/confg/locale/language-code/LC_MESSAGES/django.po
```

Typically you will want to build message files for just your project. To do so, create a locale directory in the root of your project in which to store the message files. The message-make.py utility stores the message files in the following location in the project directory. However, it does not create the locale directory if it doesn't exist:

locale/*language-code*/LC_MESSAGES/django.po

The message-make.py utility then searches through the .py and .html files in your project and builds the message files.

You can also build message files for only one application by creating a locale directory in the application directory and then running the messages-make.py application from the application directory.

Translating Messages

The django.po files store localized messages using the following entries for each string:

▶ #: specifies the relative path and line numbers to the source file(s) containing the localized string.

▶ msgid specifies the translation string as it appears in the source. You should not change this value. Django uses it to identify the string.

▶ msgstr specifies the translated string to use for this language. It starts out empty, and you insert the translated string.

Initially the translated strings are blank. You need to add translated strings to each message file you create. To do so, open the django.po file in an editor, and add the strings.

> Make certain that you are using the appropriate character set for the language you are adding translations to.

Using compile-messages

After your have added the translated strings to the message files, you need to compile the message files into a binary file that can be consumed by gettext. Django provides the django/bin/compile-messages.py utility to compile the message files. The compile-messages.py file parses the django.po files and creates django.mo language files.

The `compile-messages.py` file must be run from the same location that the `make-messages.py` utility was run. After you have compiled the message file, you are ready to implement languages in your project.

Try It Yourself ▼

Create a Language File

In this section, you will create a German-language file in the iFriends project. You will add translations for the localized strings that you created in the two preceding "Try It Yourself" sections. Follow these steps to create the language file:

1. Create a directory called iFriends/locale.

2. From the root of the iFriends folder, use the following command to create the iFriends/locale/de/LC_MESSAGES/django.po message file:

```
make-messages.py -l de
```

3. Open the iFriends/locale/de/LC_MESSAGES/django.po message file in an editor.

4. Modify the following `msgstr` entry for the Welcome `msgid` to include the German translation:

```
msgid "Welcome"
msgstr "Willkommen"
```

5. Modify the following `msgstr` entry for the Login User `msgid` to include the German translation:

```
msgid "Login User"
msgstr "Anmeldung"
```

6. Save the iFriends/locale/de/LC_MESSAGES/django.po message file.

7. From the root of the iFriends folder, use the following command to create the iFriends/locale/de/LC_MESSAGES/django.po language file:

```
compile-messages.py
```

Several of the "Try it Yourself" sections in this hour add small amounts of code to Listing 20.2. Rather than listing the full contents in each "Try It Yourself" section, the full code listing is added in the final section to reduce redundancy.

By the Way ▲

Setting Language Preference

Languages can be set at either the site level or session level. The best way to understand how language preferences work is to understand how Django determines the language preference.

Django looks in the following four places to find the language preference:

1. First, Django looks for the django_language key in the current user's session.

2. If Django cannot find the django_language key, it looks for a cookie called django_language in the request.

3. If Django cannot find the django_language cookie, it looks at the HTTP_ACCEPT_LANGUAGE header in the request. The browser sends this header to tell the server which language(s) the user prefers, ordered by priority. Django tries each setting in the list until it finds one that is supported.

4. If Django cannot find a language in the header, it uses the LANGUAGE_CODE setting in the settings.py file.

To set the language at the site level, all you need to do is add the LANGUAGE_CODE setting to the settings.py file. For example, to set the site language to Spanish, you would use the following setting:

```
LANGUAGE_CODE = 'es'
```

If you want to set the language on a per-user basis, you must enable the django. middleware.locale.LocaleMiddleware framework. The LocaleMiddleware framework provides access to the language settings in the session, cookies, and HTTP headers. To enable the LocaleMiddleware framework, add the following entry to the MIDDLEWARE_CLASSES setting in the settings.py file:

```
'django.middleware.locale.LocaleMiddleware',
```

> The LocaleMiddleware framework needs to be installed after SessionMiddleware, but before any other django.middleware frameworks.

After the LocaleMiddleware framework is enabled, your view functions and templates try to determine the language settings for each user in the session, cookies, and HTTP headers.

You can allow the user's browser to specify the preferred language, or you can set the language in the user's session. The language can be set for the user either in the session or by setting a cookie in the user's browser.

The best place to set the language is in the session, because that is the first place the LocaleMiddleware framework looks. For example, the following code sets the language for the session to English. As long as the session is active, the language is English:

```
def myView(request):
    request.session['django_language'] = 'en'
```

Try It Yourself ▼

Set Language Preference in a Session

In this section, you will enable the LocaleMiddleware framework. Then you will modify the login_user() function to allow the user to set his or her preferred language. You will modify the LoginForm to add a language choice field that you can use to set the django_language key in the user's session. Follow these steps to make the changes:

1. Stop the development server.

2. Open the iFriends/settings.py file in an editor.

3. Add the following setting to set the default language for the site to English:

   ```
   LANGUAGE_CODE = 'en-us'
   ```

4. Add the following entry to the MIDDLEWARE_CLASSES setting to enable the LocaleMiddleware framework:

   ```
   'django.middleware.locale.LocaleMiddleware',
   ```

5. Save the iFriends/settings.py file.

6. Open the iFriends/Home/views.py file in an editor.

7. Add the following line of code, shown in Listing 20.2, to define the siteLanguages tuple that contains language names and codes:

   ```
   siteLanguages = (('en', 'English'), ('de', 'German' ))
   ```

8. Add the following ChoiceField, shown in Listing 20.2, to add a list of languages to the LoginForm:

   ```
   Language = forms.ChoiceField(choices=siteLanguages)
   ```
   ▼

9. Add the following line of code, shown in Listing 20.2, to set the `django_` language key in the user's session:

   ```
   request.session['django_language'] = request.POST['Language']
   ```

10. Save the `iFriends/Home/views.py` file.

11. Start the development server.

12. Access the following URL in a web browser to access the login page, shown in Figure 20.1:

    ```
    http://127.0.0.1:8000/Login/
    ```

    The message should be in English, because the language hasn't been set for the session.

FIGURE 20.1
The `login_user()` form with a language option for the iFriends site, displaying an English login message.

13. Enter a valid username and password, and select German from the Language drop-down menu.

14. Click the Login button. You should be redirected to a home page similar to the one shown in Figure 20.2. The welcome message in the upper-right corner should be in German.

15. Access the following URL again in a web browser to go to the login page:

    ```
    http://127.0.0.1:8000/Login/
    ```

    As shown in Figure 20.3, the message should now be in German.

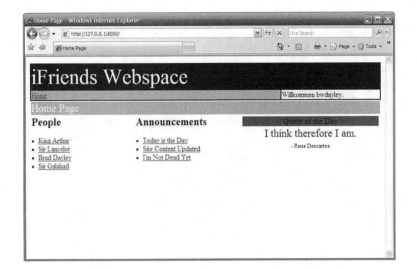

FIGURE 20.2
The home_
view() web
page for the
iFriends site
with a German
welcome
message.

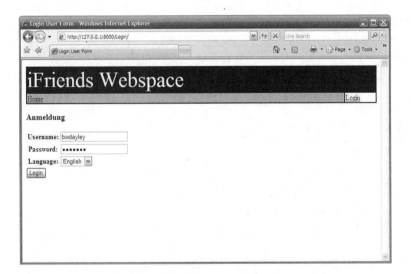

FIGURE 20.3
The login_
user() form
with a language
option for the
iFriends site,
displaying a
German login
message.

16. Enter a valid username and password. This time, select English from the
Language drop-down menu.

17. Click the Login button. You should be redirected to a home page similar to the
one shown in Figure 20.4. The welcome message should be in English.

FIGURE 20.4
The home_
view() web
page for the
iFriends site
with an English
welcome
message.

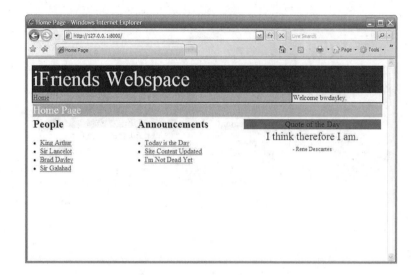

LISTING 20.2   The `LoginForm` and `login_user()` View Function
Definitions in the `iFriends/Home/views.py` File

```
siteLanguages = (('en', 'English'), ('de', 'German' ))
class LoginForm(forms.Form):
        username = forms.CharField(max_length=30)
        password = forms.CharField(max_length=20, widget=forms.PasswordInput())
        Language = forms.ChoiceField(choices=siteLanguages)

def login_user(request, next='/'):
    message = gettext('Login User')
    lForm = LoginForm()

    if request.method == 'GET':
        request.session.set_test_cookie()

    if request.method == 'POST':
        if request.session.test_cookie_worked():
            request.session.delete_test_cookie()

            if request.GET.has_key('next'):
                next = request.GET['next']
            if request.POST['submit'] == 'Login':
                postDict = request.POST.copy()
                lForm = LoginForm(postDict)
                if lForm.is_valid():
                    uName = request.POST['username']
                    uPass = request.POST['password']
                    user = authenticate(username=uName, password=uPass)
                    if user is not None:
                        if user.is_active:
                            login(request, user)
```

LISTING 20.2   Continued

```
                        request.session['django_language'] =
                        request.POST['Language']
                        return HttpResponseRedirect(next)
                    else:
                        message = 'Account Deactivated'
                else:
                    message = 'Login Incorrect'
        else:
            message = "Please enable cookies and try again."

    return render_to_response('registration/login.html',{
                'lForm': lForm,
                'message': message})
```

▲

Summary

In this hour, we discussed the process of internationalizing your website by defining
which strings should be localized, building message files that contain the translated
strings, and setting preferred languages. You learned that strings can be localized in
Python code as well as in template files. We also covered using LocaleMiddleware
to allow different users to use separate languages.

Q&A

Q. Is there a way to add translations to JavaScript in the templates?

A. Yes. Django provides a javascript_catalog view that outputs a JavaScript
code library with functions that mimic the gettext interface as well as translation strings. You can use the javascript_catalog view to dynamically
generate translated JavaScript to use in your views.

Q. Is there a way to restrict the languages that can be used on the website?

A. Yes. You can specify a subset of languages in the LANGUAGES setting of the
settings.py file. For example, the following setting restricts the languages to
English and Spanish:

```
LANGUAGES = (
    ('en', 'English'),
    ('es', 'Spanish'),
)
```

Q. *Is there a way to turn off internationalization if I don't need it?*

A. Yes. If you do not need internationalization, you can turn it off by setting USE_I18N to False in the settings.py file:

```
USE_I18N=False
```

Workshop

The workshop consists of a set of questions and answers designed to solidify your understanding of the material covered in this hour. Try answering the questions before looking at the answers.

Quiz

1. How do you mark a string for translation in Python code?

2. How do you mark a string for translation in a template file?

3. What key in the session does the LocaleMiddleware framework look at to determine the preferred language?

4. Where are localized messages stored if you use the make-messages.py utility at the project level?

Quiz Answers

1. Pass the string to the gettext() function.

2. Add the string to a trans or blocktrans tag in the template.

3. The django_language key.

4. In the locale/*language-code*/LC_MESSAGES/django.po file.

Exercises

1. Create a Spanish-language file.

2. Add Spanish to the list of languages that users can select when they log in.

3. Add more localized strings for headings and messages that are used in the template files and view function.

Creating Sitemaps

What You'll Learn in This Hour:

▶ How to create and enable a sitemap

▶ How to create a sitemap for generic views

▶ How to create a sitemap index

▶ How to notify Google that your website content has changed

Sitemaps are a great way for web developers to inform search engines about pages on their websites.

> Search engines that use a crawling method to index content can use sitemaps to determine information about the URLs on the website. (For more information about sitemaps, see www.sitemaps.org.)

A sitemap is an XML file that includes the URLs in a website. It also includes information about each web page, such as the last update date, change frequency, and relative importance to other pages on the website.

Django provides the `django.contrib.sitemaps` framework, which allows you to quickly and easily create sitemaps for web crawlers. You install the `sitemaps` and `sites` frameworks by adding the following lines to the INSTALLED_APPS setting in the `settings.py` file:

```
'django.contrib.sites',
'django.contrib.sitemaps',
```

You also need to make certain that the `'django.template.loaders.app_`
`directories.load_template_source'`, line is included in the TEMPLATE_
LOADERS setting of the `settings.py` file. It should be there by default.

The following sections describe how to create sitemaps for your website views as well
as for generic views. They also discuss how to create an index for sitemaps and how
to ping Google to notify it that the site has changed.

Creating a Sitemap

Creating a sitemap is a simple two-step process. First you create sitemap classes that
define the URLs to include in the sitemap, and then you enable the sitemap in the
URLconf file. The following sections discuss this process.

Creating a Sitemap Class

Django uses classes to define sitemaps. Each class includes information about sections of entries in the sitemap. For example, you could use one class to define the
blog pages that are available at the website.

`Sitemap` classes extend the `django.contrib.sitemaps.Sitemap` object and include
the following attributes and methods:

- `items()` is required. The `items()` method should return a list of objects that
  will be used to build this section of the sitemap. The `items()` function also is
  used to build a list of objects that are passed to the `location`, `lastmod`,
  `changefreq`, and `priority` members of the class if they are defined as
  functions.

The sitemaps framework doesn't require the objects returned by `items()` to be
objects in the Django model. You could return your own list of objects to customize the sitemap even further.

- `location` is optional. The `location` member can be defined as an attribute or
  function. As a function, `location` should return a string representation of the
  absolute URL of the object that is passed into it from the `items()` list. As an
  attribute, `location` should be set to the URL for all objects in the `items()` list.
  If `location` is not specified in the class, the framework calls the
  `get_absolute_url()` method on the object to obtain the URL.

▶ lastmod is optional. The lastmod member can be defined as an attribute or function. As a function, lastmod should return a Python datetime object representing the last modification date of the object that is passed into it from the items() list. As an attribute, lastmod should be set to the last modified date for all objects in the items() list.

▶ priority is optional. The priority member can be defined as an attribute or function. As a function, priority should return a string or float representing the priority of the object that is passed into it from the items() list. As an attribute, priority should be set to a string or float representing the priority for all objects in the items() list. Valid values are from 0.0 to 1.0. The default value is .5.

▶ changefreq is optional. The changefreq member can be defined as an attribute or function. As a function, changefreq should return a string representing the change frequency of the object that is passed into it from the items() list. As an attribute, changefreq should be set to a string representing the change frequency for all objects in the items() list. Valid strings are always, hourly, daily, weekly, monthly, yearly, and never.

The following code snippet shows an example of a sitemap class definition:

```
from django.contrib.sitemaps import Sitemap
from mySite.data.models import report

class ReportSitemap(Sitemap):
    changefreq = "yearly"
    priority = 0.7
    def items(self):
        return report.objects.all()
    def location(self, obj):
        return '/datea/report/%d' % obj.id
```

Enabling the Sitemap

After you have defined your Sitemap classes, you can make them run by adding an entry for the django.contrib.sitemaps.views.sitemap view to the URLconf file. The sitemap view requires an extra argument called sitemaps. The sitemaps argument should be a dictionary that contains entries for each Sitemap class that you want to include in the sitemap.

For example, to enable the class defined in the preceding section, you would need to add the following code to the URLconf file:

```
sitemaps = { 'report': ReportSitemap, }
urlpatterns += patterns('',
```

```
(r'^sitemap.xml$', 'django.contrib.sitemaps.views.sitemap',
    {'sitemaps': sitemaps}),
)
```

> Search engines search websites only at the level of the sitemap and below. If you
> want the search engine to search the entire site, define the sitemap URL as
> /sitemap.xml. If you want the search engine to search only a specific directory
> and below, define the sitemap as /*directory*/sitemap.xml/.

▼ **Try It Yourself**

Create and Enable a Sitemap

In this section, you will install the sitemaps application and then use it to create
and enable a Sitemap class. This class will build a sitemap for the web pages of all
Person objects in the iFriends database.

Follow these steps to create and enable the sitemap:

1. Stop the development server.

2. Open the iFriends/settings.py file in an editor.

3. Add the following lines to the INSTALLED_APPS setting if they are not already
   there:

   ```
   'django.contrib.sites',
   'django.contrib.sitemaps',
   ```

4. Save the iFriends/settings.py file.

5. Create and open a file called iFriends/sitemaps.py in an editor.

6. Add the following imports, shown in Listing 21.1, to import the Sitemap and
   Person classes:

   ```
   from django.contrib.sitemaps import Sitemap
   from iFriends.People.models import Person
   ```

7. Add the following class definition, shown in Listing 21.1, to define a Sitemap
   class named PersonSitemap and to set the changefreq and priority values
   for all objects in the class:

   ```
   class PersonSitemap(Sitemap):
       changefreq = "Yearly"
       priority = 0.7
   ```

▼

8. Add the following `items()` function, shown in Listing 21.1, to set the `Sitemap` class to pick up all objects in the `Person` table:

```
def items(self):
    return Person.objects.all()
```

9. Add the following `location()` function, shown in Listing 21.1, so that the Sitemap class returns the /Person/info/ URL with the object id appended:

```
def location(self, obj):
    return '/Person/info/%d' % obj.id
```

10. Save the `iFriends/sitemaps.py` file.

11. Open the `iFriends/urls.py` file in an editor.

12. Add the following line of code, shown in Listing 21.2, to import the `PersonSitemap` class you just created:

```
from iFriends.sitemaps import PersonSitemap
```

13. Add the following lines of code, shown in Listing 21.2, to create the sitemap dictionary that includes the `PersonSitemap` class:

```
sitemaps = {
    'person': PersonSitemap,
}
```

14. Add the following lines of code, shown in Listing 21.2, to extend the URL patterns in the `URLconf` file to enable the sitemap URL:

```
urlpatterns += patterns('',
    (r'^sitemap.xml$', 'django.contrib.sitemaps.views.sitemap',
                        {'sitemaps': sitemaps}),
)
```

15. Save the `iFriends/urls.py` file.

16. Start the development server.

17. Open the following URL in a browser to view the sitemap of the `PersonSitemap` class, as shown in Figure 21.1:

```
http://127.0.0.1:8000/sitemap.xml
```

LISTING 21.1   Full Contents of the `iFriends/sitemaps.py` File

```
from django.contrib.sitemaps import Sitemap
from iFriends.People.models import Person

class PersonSitemap(Sitemap):
    changefreq = "Yearly"
    priority = 0.7
```

LISTING 21.1   Continued

```
def items(self):
    return Person.objects.all()

def location(self, obj):
    return '/Person/info/%d' % obj.id
```

LISTING 21.2   The Sitemap Section of the `iFriends/urls.py` **File**

```
from iFriends.sitemaps import PersonSitemap

sitemaps = {
    'person': PersonSitemap,
}
urlpatterns += patterns('',
    (r'^sitemap.xml$', 'django.contrib.sitemaps.views.sitemap',
                        {'sitemaps': sitemaps}),
)
```

FIGURE 21.1
The sitemap.
xml document
of the iFriends
website gener-
ated from the
PersonSitemap
class.

Creating a Sitemap of Generic Views

Django provides a useful shortcut that allows you to create a sitemap for generic
views without having to define your own `Sitemap` class. Instead, you can use the
`django.contrib.sitemaps.GenericSitemap` class.

The `GenericSitemap` class builds a `Sitemap` class from the same info dictionary
that you pass the generic view. Instead of defining a `list()` function, the info dictionary needs to contain a `queryset` entry containing the list of objects. Instead of

lastmod, GenericSitemap uses the date_field entry if one is defined in the dictionary. The priority and changefreq values can be specified as arguments when you create an instance of GenericSitemap.

The following is an example of using the GenericSitemap class to build a sitemap for a generic view:

```
from django.contrib.sitemaps import GenericSitemap
from django.views.generic import date_based
log_info_dict = {
    'queryset' : log.objects.all(),
    'date_field' : 'last_modified',
}
sitemaps = {
    'log': GenericSitemap(log_info_dict, priority=0.2, changefreq='daily'),
}
urlpatterns += patterns('',
    (r'^sitemap.xml$', 'django.contrib.sitemaps.views.sitemap',
    {'sitemaps': sitemaps}),
    (r'^generic/log_arch/$',date_based.archive_index, log_info_dict),
)
```

You can also create sitemaps for flatpages on your website. The location is the only attribute attached to the object in the sitemap. The lastmod, change-freq, and priority attributes are not added. To add flatpages to the sitemap, simply add the django.contrib.sitemaps.FlatPageSitemap class to the sitemaps dictionary:

```
from django.contrib.sitemaps import FlatPageSitemap
sitemaps = { 'flat': FlatPageSitemap, }
```

Did you Know?

Try It Yourself ▼

Create and Enable a Sitemap for Generic Views

In this section, you will create and enable a GenericSitemap class that will generate a sitemap for the blog_details generic view you created in Hour 12, "Utilizing Generic Views." Follow these steps to create and enable the sitemap:

1. Open the iFriends/urls.py file.

2. Add the following import statement, shown in Listing 21.3, to the beginning of the file to import the GenericSitemap class:

   ```
   from django.contrib.sitemaps import GenericSitemap
   ```

▼

3. Add the following line to the `blog_detail_info` dictionary, shown in Listing 21.3, so that the `GenericSitemap` includes the date field as the last modified field in the sitemap:

```
'date_field' : 'date',
```

4. Add the following entry to the `sitemaps` dictionary, shown in Listing 21.3, to add the `GenericSitemap` class for the generic `blog_details` view to the sitemap:

```
'blog': GenericSitemap(blog_detail_info, priority=0.3,
➥changefreq='weekly'),
```

5. Save the `iFriends/urls.py` file.

6. Open the `iFriends/People/models.py` file.

7. Add the following `get_absolute_url()` function to the `Blog` model, as shown in Listing 21.4, so that the `GenericSitemap` can fill in the `location` attribute automatically for each object in the `queryset`:

```
def get_absolute_url(self):
    return '/generic/blog_details/%d' % self.id
```

8. Save the `iFriends/People/models.py` file.

9. Open the following URL in a browser to view the sitemap with the additional entries from the `blog_details` view, as shown in Figure 21.2:

```
http://127.0.0.1:8000/sitemap.xml
```

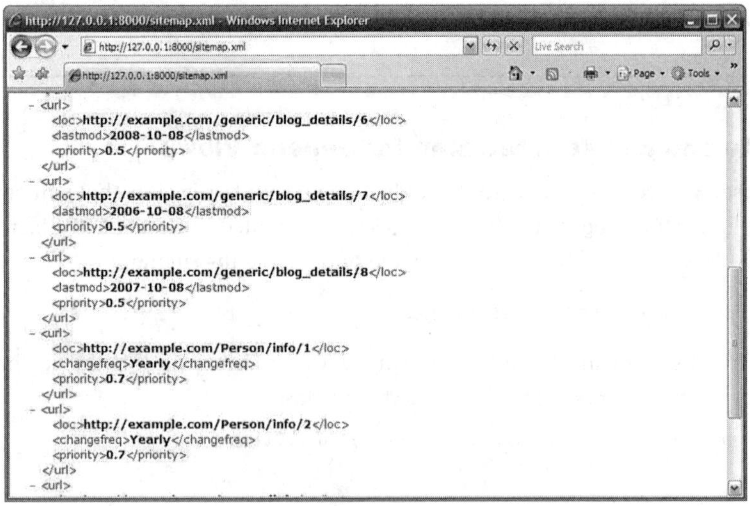

FIGURE 21.2
The sitemap.
xml document
of the iFriends
website, show-
ing additional
entries from the
blog_details
generic view.

LISTING 21.3 The Imports, `blog_detail_info` Dictionary, and Sitemap Sections of the `iFriends/urls.py` File

```
from django.contrib.sitemaps import GenericSitemap
. . .
blog_detail_info = {
    'queryset' : Blog.objects.all(),
    'date_field' : 'date',
    'template_object_name': 'blog',
    'template_name' : 'Blogs/blog_detail.html',
}
. . .
sitemaps = {
    'person': PersonSitemap,
    'blog': GenericSitemap(blog_detail_info, priority=0.3,
                           changefreq='weekly'),
}
urlpatterns += patterns('',
    (r'^sitemap.xml$', 'django.contrib.sitemaps.views.sitemap',
                       {'sitemaps': sitemaps}),
)
```

LISTING 21.4 The `Blog` Class Definition in the `iFriends/People/models.py` File

```
class Blog(models.Model):
    title = models.CharField('Title', max_length=200)
    text = models.TextField('Text', max_length=2048)
    date = models.DateTimeField('Last Modified')

    def __str__(self):
        return '%s' % (self.title)

    def blog_size(self):
        return len(self.text)

    def get_absolute_url(self):
        return '/generic/blog_details/%d' % self.id

    class Admin:
        list_display = ('title', 'date', 'blog_size',)
        list_filter = ('date',)
        date_hierarchy = 'date'
        search_fields = ('title', 'text',)

    class Meta:
        permissions = (
            ('can_blog', 'Allowed to Blog'),
        )
```

Creating a Sitemap Index

As you add more and more `Sitemap` classes to your sitemap, you may find the need to index them individually. Django provides a simple solution for indexing the `Sitemap` classes.

The `django.contrib.sitemaps.views.sitemap` view function accepts a `section` argument that is the string value of one of the keys in the `sitemaps` dictionary.

For example, the following code snippet defines a sitemap with two `Sitemap` classes, `report` and `log`:

```
sitemaps = {
    'report': ReportSitemap,
    'log': GenericSitemap(log_info_dict, priority=0.2, changefreq='daily'),
}
```

The following URL pattern displays sitemaps for both the /sitemap-report.xml and /sitemap-log.xml URLs:

```
(r'^sitemap-(?P<section>.+).xml$', 'django.contrib.sitemaps.views.sitemap',
                    {'sitemaps': sitemaps}),
```

▼   **Try It Yourself**

Implement a Sitemap Index

In this section, you will add a sitemap index that will index both the person and blog sitemaps that you created in the previous sections. Follow these steps to implement the sitemap index:

1. Open the `iFriends/urls.py` file.

2. Add the following pattern to the URL patterns for sitemaps, as shown in Listing 21.5, to implement a sitemap index that allows URL patterns that include the `Sitemap` class key name:

   ```
   (r'^sitemap-(?P<section>.+).xml$', 'django.contrib.sitemaps.views.sitemap',
                       {'sitemaps': sitemaps}),
   ```

3. Open the following URL in a browser to view the sitemap of the `PersonSitemap` class, as shown in Figure 21.3:

   ```
   http://127.0.0.1:8000/sitemap-person.xml
   ```

4. Open the following URL in a browser to view the sitemap with the entries from the `blog_details` view, as shown in Figure 21.4:

   ```
   http://127.0.0.1:8000/sitemap-blog.xml
   ```

▼

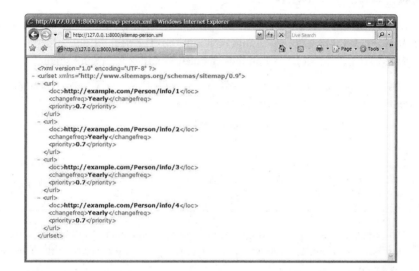

FIGURE 21.3
The sitemap-
person.xml
document of the
iFriends web-
site, showing
the entries from
the Person
details view.

FIGURE 21.4
The sitemap-
blog.xml
document of
the iFriends
website, show-
ing the entries
from the Blog
blog_details
view.

LISTING 21.5   The URL Patterns Section for Sitemaps in the
`iFriends/urls.py` File

```
urlpatterns += patterns('',
    (r'^sitemap.xml$', 'django.contrib.sitemaps.views.sitemap',
                       {'sitemaps': sitemaps}),
    (r'^sitemap-(?P<section>.+).xml$',
    'django.contrib.sitemaps.views.sitemap',
                       {'sitemaps': sitemaps}),
)
```

Pinging Google

Django also provides a simple way to ping Google to notify it that your web content has changed and that your site should be reindexed. The `django.contrib.sitemaps.ping_google()` function tells Google to reindex your site's sitemap.

The default value for the sitemap is `'/sitemap.xml'`. However, you can specify a different value by using the `sitemap_url` argument. For example:

```
ping_google(sitemap_url='/sitemap-report.xml')
```

> The `ping_google()` function raises the `django.contrib.sitemaps.SitemapNotFound` exception if it cannot determine the website.

Using the `ping_google()` function, you can notify Google every time the data in your database changes. The following example pings Google every time the `report` object is saved:

```
from django.contrib.sitemaps import ping_google
class report(models.Model):
    . . .
    def save(self):
        super(report, self).save()
        try:
            ping_google(sitemap_url='/sitemap-report.xml')
        except Exception:
            pass
```

> If objects are being saved frequently, you may not want to add the extra cycles that the `ping_google()` function generates. Pick objects that do not get updated as frequently, or add a timed function that runs periodically to ping Google.

Summary

In this hour, you learned how to create `Sitemap` classes of the different views on your website. You learned how to enable the sitemaps so that a `sitemap.xml` document is created. You also learned how to create an index for sitemaps and how to ping Google to notify it that the site has changed.

Q&A

Q. *Is there a way to ping another search site besides Google?*

A. Not built into Django. However, nothing is stopping you from implementing your own Python ping application and then importing it into your applications.

Workshop

The workshop consists of a set of questions and answers designed to solidify your understanding of the material covered in this hour. Try answering the questions before looking at the answers.

Quiz

1. What type of sitemap class would you use to build sitemaps for generic views?

2. What argument can you pass to the `django.contrib.sitemaps.views.sitemap` view in the URL pattern to build a sitemap for a specific `Sitemap` class?

3. What attribute would you add to the `Sitemap` class to set the importance of the data in that class compared to other `Sitemap` classes on your own website?

Quiz Answers

1. The `GenericSitemap` class

2. The `section` argument

3. The `priority` attribute

Exercises

1. If you haven't already created a view to display the `iFriends.models.Quote` objects, create one. It can be a generic `object_details` view or your own view function.

2. Add a `Sitemap` class for the `iFriends.models.Quote` objects that includes the location of the view you created in Exercise 1.

HOUR 22

Implementing Multiple Websites

What You'll Learn in This Hour:

▶ How to install the sites framework
▶ How to implement the sites framework
▶ How to limit access to content to one class
▶ How to assign content to multiple sites
▶ How to use the Site object to modify the behavior of a view function
▶ How to use the CurrentSiteManager class to limit access to objects in a view function

The django.contrib.sites framework is a simple framework that provides a basic method of implementing multiple websites in the same Django installation. Using the sites framework, you can control which sites have access to content and also control the behavior of views.

This hour discusses implementing the sites framework and using the CurrentSiteManager class to control access to content.

Implementing the sites Framework

Implementing the sites framework for a website is a simple process of creating a Site object and then setting the SITE_ID setting in the settings.py file to the ID of that object.

The following sections discuss the process of installing the sites framework in a website, and assigning content to multiple or single websites. Then they describe how to access the Site from views to modify behavior.

Installing the `sites` Framework

To install the `sites` framework, first add the following line to the INSTALLED_APPS setting in the `settings.py` file:

```
'django.contrib.sites',
```

The next step is to use the admin interface to create a Site object. The Site object contains only two fields—the name and the domain. The name allows you to set a name that can be used throughout your website. The domain can be used to build URLs for the website. You can create a Site object in the admin interface just like you would a User or Group object.

By the Way

> Django automatically creates a site object named example.com when the project is initially created. If you do not create your own site object, Django uses this one.

After you have created the Site object, you need to assign the SITE_ID setting in the `settings.py` file the id of the new Site object. For example:

```
SITE_ID = 5
```

Did you Know?

> The id of the Site object isn't displayed in the admin interface. However, it is easy to obtain from the shell. The following code snippet, run from the shell, displays the name and id of each Site object:
>
> ```
> >>> from django.contrib.sites.models import Site
> >>> sites = Site.objects.all()
> >>> for s in sites:
> ...     print '%s - %d' % (s.name, s.id)
> ```

▼ **Try It Yourself**

Create Multiple Site Objects

In this section, you will create a site object for the iFriends site and for a site called iNews. You will then assign the iFriends site to the iFriends project in the `settings.py` file.

Follow these steps to create and install the new site objects:

1. In the admin interface, click the Add link next to Sites.

2. Create a new Site object with the name set to iFriends and the domain set to iFriends.test.

▼

3. Create another new Site object with the name set to iNews and the domain set to iNews.test.

4. Open the iFriends.settings.py file in an editor.

5. Make certain that the following line is listed in the INSTALLED_APPS setting:

   ```
   'django.contrib.sites',
   ```

6. Set the SITE_ID setting to the id of the iFriends Site object you created in step 2:

   ```
   SITE_ID = 2
   ```

   If you didn't add any other Site objects previously, the SITE_ID setting will probably be 2. However, you should verify that.

7. Save the iFriends.settings.py file.

Assigning Content to Multiple Sites

To assign content to multiple sites, you need to add a Site object ManyToManyField relation. For example:

```
from django.contrib.sites.models import Site
class myData(models.Model):
    . . .
    sites = models.ManyToManyField(Site)
```

Then, when you create objects, you can assign them to the Site object(s) that they should relate to. This allows you to define content that can appear in more than one site. If.you have several sites, you can limit which sites can use the content by limiting which Site objects are included in the object's ManyToManyField.

Try It Yourself

Define a Model That Allows Access from Multiple Sites

In this section, you will create a new application called News. You will define a model in the application called Announcement that includes a ManyToManyField relation to the Site object. This will allow you to define multiple sites that the content can be viewed on.

Follow these steps to define the multisite model:

1. Stop the development server.

2. From the root of the iFriends project, use the following command to create a new application called News:

   ```
   python manage.py startapp News
   ```

3. Open the iFriends/News/models.py file in an editor.

4. Add the following imports, shown in Listing 22.1, to import the User and Site models:

```
from django.contrib.auth.models import User
from django.contrib.sites.models import Site
```

5. Add the Announcement class definition, shown in Listing 22.1, with the following field. This will enable content generated for the class to be accessible from multiple sites:

```
sites = models.ManyToManyField(Site)
```

6. Add the __str__ and Admin definitions shown in Listing 22.1.

7. Save the iFriends/News/models.py file.

Watch Out!

> Don't synchronize the database just yet. You will do that later.

LISTING 22.1   **Full Contents of the** iFriends/News/models.py **File**

```
from django.db import models
from django.contrib.auth.models import User
from django.contrib.sites.models import Site

class Announcement(models.Model):
    userID = models.ForeignKey(User)
    title = models.CharField('Title', max_length=200)
    text = models.TextField('Text', max_length=1024)
    date = models.DateTimeField('Published')
    sites = models.ManyToManyField(Site)

    def __str__(self):
        return '%s' % (self.title)

    class Admin:
        pass
```

Assigning Content to a Single Site

To limit content to a single site, you can add a Site ForeignKey field to the model. For example:

```
from django.contrib.sites.models import Site
class myData(models.Model):
    . . .
    site = models.ForeignKey (Site)
```

Then, when you create objects, you can assign them to the one Site object that they should be linked to. This allows you to define content that can appear in only one site.

Try It Yourself

Define a Model That Limits Access to One Site

In this section, you will define a new model in the News application called Story. It will include a ForeignKey relation to the Site object so that you can define a single site that the content can be viewed on.

Follow these steps to define the single-site model:

1. Open the iFriends/News/models.py file in an editor.

2. Add the Story class definition, shown in Listing 22.2, with the following field to enable content generated for the class to be accessible from only one site:

   ```
   sites = models.ManyToManyField(Site)
   ```

3. Add the __str__ and Admin definitions shown in Listing 22.2.

4. Save the iFriends/News/models.py file.

5. Create some Story objects using the admin interface. Assign some of them to the iFriends site and some to the iNews site.

> Don't synchronize the database just yet. You will do that later.

LISTING 22.2 The Story Class Definition in the iFriends/News/ models.py File

```
class Story(models.Model):
    userID = models.ForeignKey(User)
    title = models.CharField('Title', max_length=200)
    text = models.TextField('Text', max_length=1024)
    date = models.DateTimeField('Published')
    site = models.ForeignKey(Site)
    on_site = CurrentSiteManager()

    def __str__(self):
        return '%s' % (self.title)

    class Admin:
        pass
```

Accessing the Site from Views

So far you have learned how to define models so that they can be assigned to a single site or multiple sites. However, that doesn't stop the other sites from accessing the data. You need to do that in your view functions.

To limit content in your views, you need to match the site that is implementing the view function with the site(s) listed in the objects. Django gives you a simple way to determine which site is currently active for the view.

The `Site.objects.get_current()` function returns the `Site` object that is defined in the `SITE_ID` setting of the `settings.py` file. You can then use that `Site` object to modify the behavior of the view function. For example, the following code snippet gets the current site. Based on the site name, it builds the view differently:

```
from django.contrib.sites.models import Site
def viewMovies(request):
    currentSite = Site.objects.get_current()
    if currentSite.name == 'SalesSite':
        #Build sales page
    elif currentSite.name == 'ReviewSite':
        #Build review page
```

The initial call to `Site.objects.get_current()` results in a database query. To reduce overhead, Django caches the `Site` object from that initial query so that subsequent requests do not perform unneeded lookups. If you need to force the site to be queried from the database again, you can use the following line of code to clear the cached `Site` object:

```
Site.objects.clear_cache()
```

Using the CurrentSiteManager Class

The preceding section discussed how to determine the current `Site` object inside a view function. Using the `Site` object, you can easily alter the view's behavior. You can also alter what data is displayed in the view if the model implements a `ManyToManyField` or `ForeignKey` field linked to the `Site` class.

For example, the `Story` model you created earlier includes the `site` field. You could use the following code in a view function to limit the `Story` objects to the current site:

```
from django.contrib.sites.models import Site
from iFriends.News.models import Story
def viewStories(request):
    currentSite = Site.objects.get_current()
    stories = Story.objects.filter(site=currentSite)
```

Django also provides the django.contrib.sites.managers.CurrentSiteManager class to provide a shortcut to limit content to the current class. The CurrentSiteManager class is a model manager that automatically filters queries to include only objects that are associated with the current Site.

You implement the CurrentSiteManager class by adding it to the on_site field of the model using the following syntax:

```
from django.contrib.sites.managers import CurrentSiteManager
class Story(models.Model):
    . . .
    site = models.ForiegnKey(Site)
    on_site = CurrentSiteManager()
```

If you still want to be able to perform queries that are not filtered on the site first, add your own objects model manager:

```
from django.contrib.sites.managers import CurrentSiteManager
class Story(models.Model):
    . . .
    site = models.ForiegnKey(Site)
    objects = models.Manager()
    on_site = CurrentSiteManager()
```

By the Way

The CurrentSiteManager class looks for a ManyToManyField or ForeignKey field called site. If you name the field that relates to the Site object something different, pass the name of the field into the CurrentSiteManager() function:

```
pubSite = models.ForiegnKey(Site)
on_site = CurrentSiteManager('pubSite')
```

Try It Yourself ▼

Modify a View's Behavior and Content Based on the Site

In this section, you will add a CurrentSiteManager to the Story and Announcement models you created earlier in this hour. You will also modify the home_view() view function to render two different templates with different data depending on what the current site is.

Follow these steps to make the changes:

1. Open the iFriends/News/models.py file in an editor.

2. Add the following lines, shown in Listing 22.3, to the Announcement class to implement the unfiltered manager object and the CurrentSiteManager on_site:

```
objects = models.Manager()
on_site = CurrentSiteManager('sites')
```

▼

3. Add the following lines, shown in Listing 22.3, to the Story class to implement the unfiltered manager object and the CurrentSiteManager on_site:

```
objects = models.Manager()
on_site = CurrentSiteManager()
```

4. Save the iFriends/News/models.py file.

5. Open the iFriends/News/models.py file in an editor.

6. Add the following import statements, as shown in Listing 22.4, to import the Site, Story, and Announcement classes:

```
from django.contrib.sites.models import Site
from iFriends.News.models import Story, Announcement
```

7. Modify the following render statement, as shown in Listing 22.4, to use the hpTemplate and rDict variables for the template name and context:

```
return render_to_response(hpTemplate, rDict,
                          context_instance = RequestContext(request))
```

8. Add the following lines of code, as shown in Listing 22.4, to use the on_site field of the Story and Announcement objects. This builds lists of objects based on the current site:

```
    rDict['announceList'] = Announcement.on_site.all()
 . . .
        rDict['storyList'] = Story.on_site.all()
```

9. Add the following lines of code, as shown in Listing 22.4, to use Site.objects.get_current() to get the current site object and use it to determine which template to render:

```
currentSite = Site.objects.get_current()
if (currentSite.domain == 'iFriends.test'):
        hpTemplate = 'home/homepage.html'
 . . .
    elif (currentSite.domain == 'iNews.test'):
        hpTemplate = 'home/newshomepage.html'
 . . .
```

10. Add the rest of the code shown in Listing 22.4.

11. Save the iFriends/News/models.py file.

12. Open the iFriends/templates/Home/homepage.html file in an editor.

13. Find the table cell entry that displays the Largest Blog, and replace it with the contents of Listing 22.5, which display a list of Announcement objects for the current site.

14. Save the iFriends/templates/Home/homepage.html file.

15. Create and open a file called iFriends/templates/Home/newshomepage.html in an editor.

16. Add the contents of Listing 22.6 to the file that renders a home page for the People, Announcement, and Story objects.

17. Save the iFriends/templates/Home/newshomepage.html file.

18. Synchronize the database by issuing the syncdb command at the root of the iFriends project.

19. Start the development server.

20. Create some Announcement and Story objects using the admin interface.

21. Assign some of objects you just created to the iFriends site and some to the iNews site. Also assign some of the Announcement objects to both sites.

22. Access the following URL in a browser to display the home_view() view. The SITE_ID should still be set to the iFriends site, so the view should display the rendered homepage.html, as shown in Figure 22.1:

```
http://127.0.0.1:8000/
```

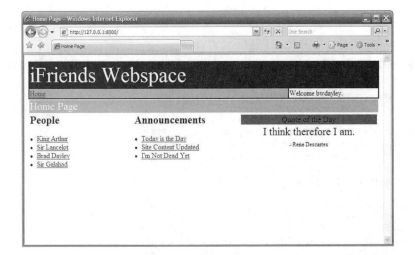

FIGURE 22.1
The home_view() web page that is rendered for the iFriends site.

23. Open the iFriends/settings.py file in an editor.

24. Modify the SITE_ID setting to the id attribute of the iNews Site object. For example:

```
SITE_ID = 3
```

25. Save the iFriends/settings.py file.

26. Access the following URL again in a browser to display the home_view() view:

http://127.0.0.1:8000/

This time the view should display the rendered newshomepage.html, as shown in Figure 22.2. Only the Story and Announcement objects that were assigned to the iNews site should be displayed.

FIGURE 22.2
The home_
view() web
page that is
rendered for the
iNews site.

LISTING 22.3   The Announcement and Story Class Definitions in the iFriends/News/models.py File

```
class Announcement(models.Model):
    userID = models.ForeignKey(User)
    title = models.CharField('Title', max_length=200)
    text = models.TextField('Text', max_length=1024)
    date = models.DateTimeField('Published')
    sites = models.ManyToManyField(Site)
    objects = models.Manager()
    on_site = CurrentSiteManager('sites')
. . .
class Story(models.Model):
    userID = models.ForeignKey(User)
    title = models.CharField('Title', max_length=200)
    text = models.TextField('Text', max_length=1024)
    date = models.DateTimeField('Published')
    site = models.ForeignKey(Site)
    objects = models.Manager()
    on_site = CurrentSiteManager()
```

LISTING 22.4   The Additional Imports and the `home_view()` View
Function in the `iFriends/News/models.py` File

```
from django.contrib.sites.models import Site
from iFriends.News.models import Story, Announcement
. . .
def home_view(request):
    rDict = {}
    rDict['pList'] = Person.objects.all()
    rDict['announceList'] = Announcement.on_site.all()

    currentSite = Site.objects.get_current()
    if (currentSite.domain == 'iFriends.test'):
        hpTemplate = 'home/homepage.html'
        rDict['quotes'] = Quote.objects.all()
    elif (currentSite.domain == 'iNews.test'):
        hpTemplate = 'home/newshomepage.html'
        rDict['storyList'] = Story.on_site.all()

    return render_to_response(hpTemplate, rDict,
                        context_instance = RequestContext(request))
```

LISTING 22.5   The Table Cell Code for Announcements That Replaces
the Largest Blog Table Cell in the `iFriends/templates/Home/`
`homepage.html` File

```
. . .
<td width="30%">
<h2>Announcements</h2>
{% for a in announceList %}
    <li>
    <a href="{% url iFriends.News.views.announce_detail a.id %}">
        {{ a.title }}</a>
    </li>
{% endfor %}
</td>
. . .
```

LISTING 22.6   Full Contents of the `iFriends/templates/Home/`
`newshomepage.html` File

```
{% extends "iFriends_base.html" %}

{% block title %}News Home Page{% endblock %}
{% block content %}
{% load custom_tags %}
<table width=100%>
<tr bgcolor="aabbcc"><td colspan="3">
<font size="5" color="white">News Home Page</font>
</td></tr>
<tr valign="top">
<td width="30%">
<h2>People</h2>
{% for p in pList %}
```

LISTING 22.6   Continued

```
    <li>
    <a href="{% url iFriends.People.views.details p.id %}">
        {{ p.name }}</a>
    </li>
{% endfor %}
</td>
<td width="30%">
<h2>Announcements</h2>
{% for a in announceList %}
    <li>
    <a href="{% url iFriends.News.views.announce_detail a.id %}">
        {{ a.title }}</a>
    </li>
{% endfor %}
</td>
<td width="40%">
<h2>News Stories</h2>
{% for s in storyList %}
    <li>
    <a href="{% url iFriends.News.views.story_detail s.id %}">
        {{ s.title }}</a>
    </li>
{% endfor %}
</td>
</tr>
{% endblock %}
```

Summary

In this hour, you learned how to implement the django.contrib.sites framework to control content that is shared across multiple sites. You learned how to use the sites framework and the CurrentSiteManager class to determine which sites have access to content. Using the sites framework, you can also control the behavior of view functions.

Q&A

Q. *Does Django use the* sites *framework internally?*

A. Yes. The following list describes some of the ways Django uses the sites framework:

▶ The redirects framework associates a redirect object to a particular site. Django uses the SITE_ID setting when searching for redirects.

▶ The authentication framework passes the Site object name to the django.contrib.auth.views.login view as the variable {{ site_name }}.

▶ The sitemaps framework uses the domain from the current Site object to fill in the location attributes in the sitemap.

▶ The admin framework uses the current Site object to determine which domain the view or site link is redirected to.

▶ The comments framework uses the sites framework to tie comments to the current SITE_ID setting.

▶ The flatpages framework links the flatpage to specific sites and then uses the SITE_ID setting when displaying the flatpages.

▶ The django.views.defaults.shortcut view uses the domain of the current Site object to calculate the object's URL.

▶ The syndication framework gives the title and description templates access to the current Site object using the variable {{ site }}.

Workshop

The workshop consists of a set of questions and answers designed to solidify your understanding of the material covered in this hour. Try answering the questions before looking at the answers.

Quiz

1. How do you access the current site object from a view?

2. How do you limit a model to being accessed in only one site?

3. How do you control access of a model in multiple views?

4. How do you get the domain name for a site?

Quiz Answers

1. Call the Site.objects.get_current() function.

2. Add a ForeignKey field that links to the django.contrib.sites.models. Site object.

3. Add a ManyToMany field that links to the django.contrib.sites.models. Site object.

4. Access the domain attribute of the Site object.

Exercises

1. Create a details view function and template that render the details Announcement objects.

2. Create a details view function and template that render the details Story objects.

3. Add code to the details view functions you just created to determine if the object is available for the current site. If it isn't, redirect to another page.

HOUR 23

Configuring Caching

What You'll Learn in This Hour:

▶ How to configure cache backends
▶ How to implement a per-site cache
▶ How to implement a per-view cache
▶ How to manage access to cached pages

One of Django's best features is that it lets you easily generate web pages on-the-fly. It saves you a lot of development and maintenance time. However, this advantage comes at a price. Each time a request comes in, Django spends many cycles in database queries and page generation. On small to medium websites, this isn't much of a problem. However, on large sites that receive several requests per second, this can quickly become a problem.

Django's caching framework solves this problem nicely. Using the cache framework, you can cache web pages and objects so that subsequent requests for the same data can quickly be drawn from the cache rather than performing the resource-intensive query and processing again.

In this hour, we will discuss configuring caching and the different types of backends that are available. We will then discuss how to implement cache at the site, view, and object levels. Finally, we will cover how to use the response headers to manage caching in upstream caches.

Configuring Caching Backends

Django's caching system is easy to implement. The only thing you need to do is define in the settings.py file which backend you want Django to use for caching. Django includes several backends that you can use depending on your particular needs. To enable a caching backend, set the `CACHE_BACKEND` setting in the `settings.py` file. For example, to enable local memory caching, you would use the following setting in the `settings.py` file:

```
CACHE_BACKEND = 'locmem:///'
```

You can also configure how long Django caches data. You can add the following arguments to the `CACHE_BACKEND` setting:

- ▶ `timeout` is the amount of time in seconds that the data is cached. The default is 300.

- ▶ `max_entries` is the maximum number of entries allowed in the cache before old values are removed. The default is 300.

- ▶ `cull_percentage` specifies the percentage of entries that are removed from the cache when the `max_entries` limit is reached. The default is 3, meaning that one in three entries are removed. If you specify a value of `0`, the entire cache is emptied.

For example, the following setting keeps data in the cache for 2 minutes and allows 200 cached entries:

```
CACHE_BACKEND = 'locmem:///?timeout=120&max_entries=200'
```

The following sections describe each of the available backends you can configure for your website.

Database Backend

The database backend allows you to create a table in the database that can then be used to store and retrieve cached data. An advantage of using the database backend is that the cached data is persistently stored and is available even after a server reboot.

Before you can enable the database backend, you need to create a table in the database to store the cache using Python's `createcachetable` application at the root of your project. The table can be given any valid table name as long as the database doesn't already have a table with that name. For example, the following command creates a database backend table called mysitecache:

```
python manage.py createcachetable mysitecache
```

To enable the database backend in the `settings.py` file, set the `CACHE_BACKEND` to the `db://` backend and provide the name of the cache table. For example, to enable the database backend using the table just listed, you would use the following setting:

```
CACHE_BACKEND = 'db://mysitecache'
```

File System Backend

The file system backend allows you to define a directory in which Django stores and retrieves cached data. An advantage of using the file system backend is that the cached data is stored persistently in the file system and is available even after a server reboot.

Before you can enable the file system backend, you need to create a directory in which to store the cached data.

To enable the file system backend in the settings.py file, you should set the CACHE_BACKEND to the file:// backend and provide the full path to the directory. For example, if you create a directory called /var/temp/mysitecache on a Linux system, you would use the following setting to the settings.py file:

```
CACHE_BACKEND = 'db:///mysitecache'
```

As another example, if you create a directory called c:\temp\mysitecache on a Windows system, you would use the following setting to the settings.py file:

```
CACHE_BACKEND = 'db://c:/temp/mysitecache'
```

Local Memory Backend

The local memory backend uses the system memory to store and retrieve cached data. An advantage of using the local memory backend is that the cached data is stored in memory, which is extremely quick to access. The local memory backend uses locking to ensure that it is multiprocess and thread-safe.

> Cached data that is stored in the local memory backend is lost if the server crashes. You should not rely on items in the local memory cache as any kind of data storage.

To enable the local memory backend in the settings.py file, set the CACHE_BACK-END to the locmem:/// backend:

```
CACHE_BACKEND = 'locmem:///'
```

Simple Backend

The simple backend caches data in memory for a single process. This is useful when you are developing the website and for testing purposes. However, you should not use it in production.

To enable the simple backend in the settings.py file, set the CACHE_BACKEND to the simple:/// backend:

```
CACHE_BACKEND = 'simple:///'
```

Dummy Backend

The dummy backend does not cache any data, but it enables the cache interface. The dummy backend should be used only in development or test websites.

To enable the dummy backend in the settings.py file, set the CACHE_BACKEND to the dummy:/// backend:

```
CACHE_BACKEND = 'dummy:///'
```

> The dummy backend is useful if you need to test or debug a website that has a heavy amount of caching. All you need to do is modify the CACHE_BACKEND setting for the test environment.

Memcached Backend

The fastest and most efficient backend available for Django is the Memcached backend. It runs as a daemon that stores and retrieves data into a memory cache.

The Memcached backend is not distributed with Django; you must obtain it from www.django.com/memcached/. Before you can enable Memcached, you must install it, along with the Memcached Python bindings. The Memcached Python bindings are in the Python module, memcache.py, which you can find at www.djangoproject.com/thirdparty/python-memcached/.

To enable the Memcached backend in the settings.py file, you should set the CACHE_BACKEND to the memcached:// backend and provide the IP address and port that the Memcached daemon is running on. For example, if the Memcached daemon is running on the local host (127.0.0.1) using port 12221, you would use the following setting:

```
CACHE_BACKEND = 'memcached://127.0.0.1:12221'
```

One of the best features of Memcached is that you can distribute the cache over multiple servers by running the Memcached daemon on multiple machines. Memcached treats the servers as a single cache.

Try It Yourself ▼

Enable a Database Backend for Caching

In this section, you will create a table in the database and enable the database backend to use that table for caching in the iFriends project. Follow these steps to enable the database backend:

1. Stop the development server.

2. From the root of the iFriends project, use the following command to create a table named ifriends_cache in the database:

   ```
   python manage.py createcachetable ifriends_cache
   ```

3. Open the iFriends/settings.py file in an editor.

4. Add the following line to enable the database backend using the ifriends_cache table you created in step 2. Specify a timeout of 2 minutes and the maximum number of entries as 200:

   ```
   CACHE_BACKEND = 'db://ifriends_cache?timeout=120&max_entries=200'
   ```

5. Save the iFriends/settings.py file.

6. Start the development server. ▲

Implementing a Per-Site Cache

After you have configured a caching backend, you can implement caching on the website. The easiest way to implement caching is at the site level. Django provides the `django.middleware.cache.CacheMiddleware` middleware framework to cache the entire site. Add the following entry to the `MIDDLEWARE_CLASSES` setting in the `settings.py` file to enable caching for the entire website:

```
' django.middleware.cache.CacheMiddleware',
```

> The `CacheMiddleware` application does not cache pages that have `GET` or `POST`. When you design your website, make certain that pages that need to be cached do not require URLs that contain query strings.

After you enable the `CacheMiddleware` framework, you need to add the following required settings to the `settings.py` file:

- ▶ `CACHE_MIDDLEWARE_SECONDS`: Defines the number of seconds that each page should be kept in the cache.

- ▶ `CACHE_MIDDLEWARE_KEY_PREFIX`: If you are using the same cache for multiple websites, you can use a unique string for this setting to designate which site the object is being cached from to prevent collisions. If you are not worried about collisions, you can use an empty string.

> You can enable the same cache for multiple sites that reside on the same Django installation. Just add the middleware to the `settings.py` file for each site.

The `CacheMiddleware` framework also allows you to restrict caching to requests made by anonymous users. If you set `CACHE_MIDDLEWARE_ANONYMOUS_ONLY` in the `settings.py` file to `True`, requests that come from logged-in users are not cached.

> If you use the `CACHE_MIDDLEWARE_ANONYMOUS_ONLY` option, make certain that `AuthenticationMiddleware` is enabled and is listed earlier in the `MIDDLEWARE_CLASSES` setting.

The CacheMiddleware framework automatically sets the value of some headers in each HttpResponse. The Last-Modified header is set to the current date and time when a fresh version of the page is requested. The Expires header is set to the current date and time plus the value defined in CACHE_MIDDLEWARE_SECONDS. The Cache-Control header is set to the value defined in CACHE_MIDDLEWARE_SECONDS.

Try It Yourself   ▼

Implement Caching at the Site Level

In this section, you will use the CacheMiddleware framework to implement caching at the site level. Follow these steps to enable and configure the CacheMiddleware framework:

1. Stop the development server.

2. Open the iFriends/settings.py file in an editor.

3. Add the following line to the MIDDLEWARE_CLASSES setting:

   ```
   ' django.middleware.cache.CacheMiddleware',
   ```

4. Add the following setting to the file to configure the CacheMiddleware framework to cache data for 2 minutes:

   ```
   CACHE_MIDDLEWARE_SECONDS = 120
   ```

5. Add the following setting to the file to configure the CacheMiddleware framework and to add the iFriends prefix to items cached on this site:

   ```
   CACHE_MIDDLEWARE_KEY_PREFIX = 'iFriends'
   ```

6. Save the iFriends/settings.py file.

7. Start the development server.   ▲

Implementing a Per-View Cache

Django's caching makes it possible to implement the cache at the view level as well. Instead of caching every page in the website, you might want to cache only a few specific views.

Use the django.views.decorators.cache.cache_page decorator function to implement caching for a specific view. The cache_page decorator function caches the web page generated by a view function. The cache_page decorator accepts one argument that specifies how many seconds to keep the web page cached.

The following code shows an example of implementing the `cache_page` decorator function to cache the web page generated by `myView` for 3 minutes:

```
@cache_page(180)
def myView(request):
    . . .
```

The `cache_page` decorator keys of the URL are just like the `CacheMiddleware` framework. Different URLs that point to the same view are cached as different entries.

Implementing a Per-Object Cache

Django provides a low-level cache API that allows you to access the cache from your Python code. Instead of caching entire pages, you may want to cache only specific data that will be used to render the display.

The `django.core.cache.cache.set(key, value, timeout_seconds)` function allows you to store any Python object that can be pickled in the cache. The `set()` function accepts three arguments—key, value, and timeout_seconds. The key argument is a string used to reference the object. The value argument is the object to be cached. The `timeout_seconds` argument specifies the number of seconds to cache the object.

The following code stores a list of `Blog` objects in the cache for 25 seconds:

```
from django.core.cache import cache
blogs = Blog.objects.all()
cache.set('Blog_List', blogs, 25)
```

The `django.core.cache.cache.get(key)` function accesses the cache and returns the value of the entry in the cache. If the entry is not found, `None` is returned. For example, the following code accesses the Blog list stored in the cache using the preceding example:

```
blogs = cache.get('Blog_List')
```

The `get()` function can also accept a second argument that specifies a value to be returned instead of `None` if no entry is found:

```
blogs = cache.get('Blog_List', [])
```

The `django.core.cache.cache.getmany(key_list)` function accesses the cache and returns the values of the multiple cache entries. The `getmany()` function accepts a list of keys as its only argument. It returns a dictionary containing the keys from the arguments and their corresponding values in the cache. If the entry is not found or is expired, it is not included in the dictionary.

For example, the following code returns a dictionary containing the Date and User entries in the cache:

```
from datetime import datetime
from django.core.cache import cache
Date = datetime.now()
cache.set('User', request.User, 60)
cache.set('Date', datetime.now(), 60)
. . .
cache.get_many(['User', 'Date'])
```

The cache API is key-based, so you can store an object in one view function and retrieve it in another.

Did you Know?

The `django.core.cache.cache.delete(key)` function deletes the entry specified by the key argument in the cache. The `delete()` function has no return value and does not raise an error if the key is not found in the cache. The following example deletes the `Blog_List` entry from the cache:

```
cache.delete('Blog_List')
```

Try It Yourself ▼

Cache and Retrieve a Specific Object Using the Cache API

In this section, you will use the low-level cache API to implement caching at the object level. You will modify the `home_view()` view function to store and retrieve a list of `Person` objects using the cache API:

1. Open the `iFriends/Home/views.py` file in an editor.

2. Add the following import statement to import the cache package:

   ```
   from django.core.cache import cache
   ```

3. Add the following line of code, shown in Listing 23.1, to determine if the List of Person objects is already cached:

   ```
   pList = cache.get('PersonList')
   ```

   ▼

4. Add the following lines of code, shown in Listing 23.1, to get a list of `Person` objects and store it in the cache if it isn't already there:

```
if pList == None:
    pList = Person.objects.all()
    cache.set('PersonList', pList, 600)
```

5. Modify the following line of code, shown in Listing 23.1, to set the `pList` entry in the `rDict` dictionary to the value returned from the cache:

```
rDict['pList'] = pList
```

6. Save the `iFriends/Home/views.py` file.

LISTING 23.1 The `home_view()` View Function in the `iFriends/Home/views.py` File

```
def home_view(request):
    rDict = {}
    pList = cache.get('PersonList')
    if pList == None:
        pList = Person.objects.all()
        cache.set('PersonList', pList, 600)
    rDict['pList'] = pList
    rDict['announceList'] = Announcement.on_site.all()

    currentSite = Site.objects.get_current()
    if (currentSite.domain == 'iFriends.test'):
        hpTemplate = 'home/homepage.html'
        rDict['quotes'] = Quote.objects.all()
    elif (currentSite.domain == 'iNews.test'):
        hpTemplate = 'home/newshomepage.html'
        rDict['storyList'] = Story.on_site.all()

    return render_to_response(hpTemplate, rDict,
                          context_instance = RequestContext(request))
```

Managing Upstream Caching

So far in this hour we have discussed how to implement caching on your own website. Web pages are also cached upstream from your website by ISPs, proxies, and even web browsers. Upstream caching provides a major boost to the Internet's efficiency, but it can also pose a couple of problems and security holes. For example, a home page that contains personal data about a user may be cached. A subsequent request to that home page would display that user's information in another user's browser.

The HTTP protocol solves these types of problems using `Vary` and `Cache-Control` headers. They allow websites to define some behavior and access requirements before cached pages are distributed. The following sections discuss how to implement these headers in your view functions.

Allowing Cached Pages to Vary Based on Headers

The Vary header allows you to define headers that an upstream cache engine checks when building its cache key. Then the cached page is used only if the values of headers in the Vary header of the request match those in the database.

The Vary header can be set in several different ways in the view function. The simplest way is to set the header manually in the HttpResponse object using the following syntax:

```
def myView(request):
    . . .
    response = HttpResponse()
    response['Vary'] = 'User-Agent'
```

Setting the Vary header manually in this way can potentially overwrite items that are already there. Django provides the django.views.decorators.vary.vary_on_headers() decorator function so that you can easily add headers to the Vary header for the view function.

The vary_on_headers() decorator function adds headers to the Vary header instead of overwriting headers that are already there. The vary_on_headers() decorator function can accept multiple headers as arguments. For example, the following code adds both the User-Agent and Content-Language headers to the Vary header:

```
from django.views.decorators import vary_on_headers
@vary_on_headers('User-Agent', 'Content-Language')
def myView(request):
    . . .
```

Another useful function to modify the Vary header is the django.utils.cache.patch_vary_headers(response, [headers]) function. The patch_vary_headers() function requires a response object as the first argument and a list of headers as the second. All headers listed in the second argument are added to the Vary header of the response object. For example, the following code adds the User-Agent and Content-Language headers to the Vary header inside the view function:

```
from django.utils.cache import patch_vary_headers
def myView(request):
    . . .
    response = HttpResponse()
    patch_vary_headers(response, ['User-Agent', 'Content-Language'])
```

One of the biggest advantages of using the patch_vary_headers() function is that you can selectively set which headers to add using code inside the view function. For example, you might want to add the Cookie header only if your view function actually sets a cookie.

> The values that get passed to vary_on_headers() and patch_vary_headers() are not case-sensitive. For example, the header user-agent is the same as User-Agent.

One of the most common headers that you will want to add to the Vary header is the Cookie header. For that reason, Django has added the django.views.decorators.vary_on_cookie() decorator function to add just the Cookie header to the Vary header. The vary_on_cookie() decorator function does not accept any parameters and simply adds the Cookie header to Vary:

```
from django.views.decorators import vary_on_cookie
@vary_on_cookie
def myView(request):
    . . .
```

Controlling Cached Pages Using the Cache-Control Header

One of the biggest problems with caching is keeping data that should remain private, private. Users basically use two types of caches—the private cache stored in the user's web browser, and the public cache stored by ISPs or other upstream caches. Private data, such as credit card numbers and account numbers, should only be stored in the private cache.

HTTP handles the issue of keeping data private using the Cache-Control header. The Cache-Control header allows you to define directives that caching engines will use to determine if data is public or private and if it should even be cached.

The following are the currently valid directives for the Cache-Control header:

- public=True
- private=True
- no_cache=True
- no_store=True
- no_transform=True
- must_revalidate=True
- proxy_revalidate=True
- max_age=num_seconds
- s_maxage=num_seconds

Django provides the django.views.decorators.cache.cache_control() decorator function to configure the directives in the Cache-Control header. The cache_control() decorator function accepts any valid Cache-Control directive as an argument. For example, the following code sets the private and max_age directives in the Cache-Control header for a view function:

```
from django.views.decorators.cache import cache_control
@ cache_control(private=True, max_age=600)
def myView(request):
    . . .
```

> The max_age directive in the Cache-Control header is set to the value of CACHE_MIDDLEWARE_SECONDS if it is specified in the settings.py file. The value you add to the max_age directive in the cache_control() decorator function takes precedence.

By the Way

Summary

In this hour, we discussed how to configure caching for your website using different types of backends. You also learned that you can implement caching at the site level using the CacheMiddleware framework. You can implement caching at the view level using the cache_page() decorator function. You also can implement caching at the object level using a low-level API that allows you to get, set, and delete items in the cache.

We also discussed how to use the Vary and Cache-Control headers to manage how upstream caches cache web pages.

Q&A

Q. *Does Django's* CacheMiddleware *framework support the* Vary *and* Cache-Control *headers?*

A. Yes. The CacheMiddleware framework conforms to the Vary and Cache-Control specifications.

Q. *Where can I go to better understand the* Cache-Control *and* Vary *headers?*

A. The header definitions can be found at www.w3.org/Protocols/rfc2616/rfc2616-sec14.html.

Workshop

The workshop consists of a set of questions and answers designed to solidify your understanding of the material covered in this hour. Try answering the questions before looking at the answers.

Quiz

1. What types of caching backends could you use if you wanted the cache to be stored in a persistent state?

2. What type of cache should you use if you want web pages from only two specific views cached?

3. How can you cache an instance of a Django model?

4. What function would you use inside a view function to add the Content-Language header to the Vary header?

Quiz Answers

1. The db and file backends.

2. The view-level cache using the cache_page() decorator function.

3. Use the django.core.cache.cache.set() function.

4. The django.utils.cache.patch_vary_headers() function.

Exercises

1. Use the caching low-level API to modify the index() view function in the iFriends/People/views.py file to use the PersonList key to store and retrieve the current list of Person objects from the cache. That way, the home_view() and index() functions can access the same list from the cache.

2. Use the cache_control() decorator function to add directives to the Cache-Control headers in the response of a view function.

3. Use the vary_on_headers() decorator function to add headers to the Vary header in the response of a view function.

HOUR 24

Deploying Django

What You'll Learn in This Hour:

▶ How to deploy Django on an Apache web server with mod_python
▶ How to use other deployment configurations
▶ How to optimize a Django website

In this book, all the development testing has been done on Django's development server. The development server works well for testing your code as you are developing the website. However, you need to deploy your project to a full web server to put it in production.

This hour discusses how to deploy Django projects to a basic Apache web server with mod_python. The object of this hour is to provide you with enough information so that you can get some of the basic configurations deployed and running. Therefore, we will focus on Django-specific tasks, not on Apache, mod_python, or other components. Much documentation and many resources are available online to guide you in implementing web servers using Apache, MySQL, PostgreSQL, and mod_python on both Linux and Windows servers.

Specifically, we will discuss the steps to deploy a Django project on a basic Apache installation, a few custom configuration options, and some optimizations that you should consider when designing your website implementation.

Deploying Django to Apache with mod_python

This section discusses the components and steps required to deploy a Django project to an Apache server. Deploying your Django project to an Apache server is not too difficult as long as all the pieces are in place. The following sections discuss the components and steps necessary to deploy your projects.

Python, Django, a Database, Apache, and mod_python

The basic components that Django requires are Python 2.3 or later, Django, a supported SQL database, Apache 2.x, and mod_python 3.x. I won't recommend specific versions in this book. You should be able to determine that based on your needs.

> If you are using the same machine that you developed the project on, you should already have Python, Django, and the database installed.

You should refer to the documentation at the project sites for these components (see Appendix A, "Django Resources," for a list of reference sites) to get installation and configuration instructions.

After you have installed Apache and mod_python, make certain that the mod_python module is activated. The mod_python module is active if you find the following entry (not commented) in the Apache http.conf file:

```
LoadModule python_module /usr/lib/apache2/modules/mod_python.so
```

> The path to the mod_python.so file may be different depending on where Apache is installed on your server.

> If you are deploying the project on a different machine than it was developed on, the project needs to be copied to that machine.

Placing the Project in PYTHONPATH

You need to make certain that your project is in the PYTHONPATH. You can accomplish this by either placing the project in a directory that is in the PYTHONPATH or by adding your project directory to the PYTHONPATH environment setting.

Configuring Your Django Project

After you have the Python, Django, SQL database, Apache, and mod_python components installed and configured on your system, you may need to configure your project as well.

If you configured a new or different database on the production server, you need to modify the database settings in the settings.py file (as described in Hour 2, "Creating Your First Website").

You may also want to do the following:

▶ Modify values in the settings.py file for productions. For example, you will want to set the DEBUG and TEMPLATE_DEBUG settings to False.

▶ Add or remove middleware.

▶ Configure languages.

▶ Disable some of the views in the URLconf files by commenting out their URL patterns.

Adding Admin Media Files to the Server

The Django development server automatically serves the admin media files. That is not the case with Apache. You need to either copy the django/contrib/admin/media directory to the Apache document root or at least create a symbolic link there. Using a symbolic link may be the best solution, because the files will need to be updated in only one place.

Setting up the `httpd.conf` File

After the components are all installed and configured and the project is configured, you add a <Location> directive to the httpd.conf file to begin serving your site from Apache.

The following snippet shows a sample <Location> directive for a project called myCoolSite:

```
<Location "/myCoolSite/">
    SetHandler python-program
    PythonHandler django.core.handlers.modpython
    SetEnv DJANGO_SETTINGS_MODULE myCoolSite.settings
    PythonDebug On
</Location>
```

Django's URLconf files will *not* trim the path specified in the <Location> directive. For example, all URLs to the project defined by the sample code just shown will begin with /myCoolSite/. If possible, use the root path in the directive. For example:

```
<Location "/">
```

Watch Out!

Did you Know?

You can add a PythonPath entry in the <Location> directive to add the project directory to the PYTHONPATH if it is not already there. For example:

```
<Location "/myCoolSite/">
    SetHandler python-program
    PythonHandler django.core.handlers.modpython
    SetEnv DJANGO_SETTINGS_MODULE mysite.settings
    PythonDebug On
    PythonPath "['/path/to/myCoolSite'] + sys.path"
</Location>
```

▼   **Try It Yourself**

Deploy a Django Project

In this section, you deploy the iFriends project to an Apache web server that has the mod_python module active. Follow these steps:

1. Stop the development server.

2. Install Apache 2.x.

3. Install mod_python 3.x.

4. Verify that the mod_python module is installed by making certain that the mod_python.so file exists in the Apache modules directory.

5. Open the Apache httpd.conf file in an editor.

6. Verify that the mod_python module is active by making certain that the following line exists and is not commented out in the Apache httpd.conf file:

```
LoadModule python_module modules/mod_python.so
```

7. Add the following <Location> directive to the file to enable the Django project:

```
<Location "/">
    SetHandler python-program
    PythonHandler django.core.handlers.modpython
    SetEnv DJANGO_SETTINGS_MODULE iFriends.settings
    PythonDebug On
</Location>
```

8. Save the httpd.conf file.

9. Add the full path to the iFriends project to the PYTHONPATH environment setting. (Or you can copy the iFriends project to a directory that is in the PYTHONPATH.)

▼

10. Either copy the django/contrib/admin/media directory to the Apache document root, or create a symbolic link there.

11. Stop and restart the Apache web server.

12. Access the root URL of the Apache web server to verify that the home page, shown in Figure 24.1, is displayed.

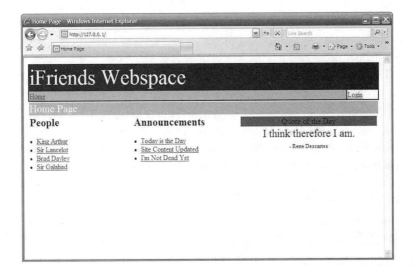

FIGURE 24.1
The home_ view() web page that is rendered for the iFriends site.

Other Deployment Configurations

The preceding section discussed how to deploy a Django project to a basic Apache setup. You may need to configure your Django deployment a bit differently to meet certain needs. The following sections discuss multiple Django installations, media files, and Python eggs.

Implementing Multiple Django Installations in Apache

You can run multiple Django installations on the same Apache instance using <VirtualHost> directives in the Apache httpd.conf file. The following example shows how to use two different <VirtualHost> directives to implement multiple Django installations:

```
NameVirtualHost *
<VirtualHost *>
    ServerName www.myCoolSite.com
```

```
    # ...
    SetEnv DJANGO_SETTINGS_MODULE myCoolSite.settings
</VirtualHost>

<VirtualHost *>
    ServerName www2. myCoolSite.com
    # ...
    SetEnv DJANGO_SETTINGS_MODULE myCoolSite.other_settings
</VirtualHost>
```

By the Way

> Some installations of apache will split the configuration entries into multiple files, so virtual host definitions may be in a different configuration file. For example, `.../apache/conf/extra/httpd-vhosts.conf`.

You can also implement multiple Django installations in a single `<VirtualHost>` directive as long as you include different `<Location>` directives with `PythonInterpreter` directives. The following example shows how to implement multiple Django installations in a single `<VirtualHost>` directive:

```
<VirtualHost *>
    ServerName www. myCoolSite.com
    # ...
    <Location "/myCoolSite/">
        SetEnv DJANGO_SETTINGS_MODULE myCoolSite.settings
        PythonInterpreter myCoolSite
    </Location>

    <Location "/myOtherCoolSite/">
        SetEnv DJANGO_SETTINGS_MODULE myCoolSite.other_settings
        PythonInterpreter myOtherCoolSite
    </Location>
</VirtualHost>
```

Serving Media Files on the Same Server

It is much better to serve media files from a different web server. However, if you absolutely need to serve them from the Django Apache server, turn off mod_python for the media files.

You can turn off mod_python for the media files by specifying a `<Location>` directive with a None handler. For example, the following directive turns off mod_python for files located in the myMedia subdirectory of the Apache root:

```
<Location "/myMedia/">
    SetHandler = None
</Location>
```

Configuring Eggs with mod_python

If you installed Django from a Python egg, or if you are using eggs in your project, you need to create an extra Python file in your project that sets up a directory for the Apache web server process to write to. For example:

```
import os
os.environ['PYTHON_EGG_CACHE'] = '/my/python/egg/directory'
```

You also need to tell mod_python to import this file using the `PythonImport` directive. Be certain that you specify a `PythonInterpreter` directive as well. The following shows an example of importing the Python file:

```
<Location "/myCoolSite/">
    SetHandler python-program
    PythonHandler django.core.handlers.modpython
    SetEnv DJANGO_SETTINGS_MODULE mysite.settings
    PythonDebug OnPythonInterpreter my_django
    PythonImport /path/to/my/project/file.py my_django
</Location>
```

Optimizing Django Deployment

If you are deploying a simple website that will receive only a small amount of traffic, the simple deployment we have discussed so far will suffice. However, as a site receives more and more traffic, you will want to optimize your deployment to make it as efficient as possible.

You can do several things to optimize the Django deployment. The following sections discuss several optimizations that you can use to improve your website's performance.

Database on a Separate Server

One of the best optimizations you can do is move the database to a server separate from the Django deployment. As the website starts being used heavily, a web server and database on the same server will begin to experience resource contention for memory, processes, and file access. Moving the database to a separate server eliminates that contention.

Media on a Separate Server

Another of the best optimizations you can do is move the media to a server separate from the Django deployment. If your website has a large amount of media being served, moving all media that is not being generated by Django views to a separate server results in a big performance boost.

Using Only Necessary Middleware

Installed middleware frameworks are processed for every request that is sent to the server. Even if those frameworks perform only small operations, as the number of requests grows, so does the performance hit incurred by the framework. Removing any unnecessary middleware has a big effect on performance in a heavily used website. For example, if your website doesn't need to use user authentication, the `AuthenticationMiddleware` shouldn't be installed.

Implementing Caching

Caching web pages can provide another boost to web server performance, especially if you use the Memcached backend. Memcached is by far the fastest caching backend.

Hour 23, "Configuring Caching," describes how to configure the caching backends and implement caching in your Django installation. You should optimize caching as much as possible if performance is a must for your website.

Adding RAM

Heavily used websites can never have enough RAM. One of the easiest, and usually most cost-effective, methods of optimizing your web server is adding RAM.

Summary

This hour has discussed the steps to deploy a Django project on a basic Apache installation. We also covered implementing multiple Django installations on a single Apache server, serving media files on the same server, and using Python eggs.

We then covered some important optimizations, such as implementing additional servers and implementing cache, that you should consider when designing your website implementation.

Q&A

Q. *If I decide to do development on an Apache server with mod_python, how do I keep from having to restart the server every time I make a change?*

A. The reason you have to restart the server to apply the updated code is that mod_python caches loaded Python code. If you add the following setting to your Apache `httpd.conf` file, it will force Apache to reload everything for each request. You can use this setting for development, but you should never use it for a production server:

```
MaxRequestPerChild 1
```

Q. *Why can't I see error messages in my Apache error_log?*

A. Django handles errors using its own error-handling system.

Q. *Can I use Django with FastCGI?*

A. Yes. You can use Django with FastCGI, but you need to install the `flup` Python Library to deal with FastCGI. Then you can use the `runfcgi` utility provided with Django. You can find more information about `flup` at `http://trac.saddi.com/flup`. You can find more information about `runfcgi` at `www.djangoproject.com/documentation/fastcgi`.

Workshop

The workshop consists of a set of questions and answers designed to solidify your understanding of the material covered in this hour. Try answering the questions before looking at the answers.

Quiz

1. What type of directive should you add to the Apache `httpd.conf` file to implement a Django project?

2. Is mod_python required to be installed and active in the Apache server in order to deploy a Django project?

3. What type of directive should you add to the Apache `httpd.conf` file to implement multiple Django installations on the same Apache instance?

Quiz Answers

1. The `<location>` directive.

2. Yes. Since Django is written in Python, it requires that mod_python is installed and active on the Apache server.

3. The `<VirtualHost>` directive.

Exercises

1. Check out the iFriends website running on the Apache server. Make sure the web pages load correctly.

2. Access the admin site for the iFriends project, and make certain that the admin media files (buttons and graphics) are displayed in the pages.

3. Use the skills that you have learned in this book to implement another website that implements discussion forums. Allow users to use their same user ID to log in to both websites.

4. Implement a discussion of the day application in the iFriends website that links a discussion from the site created in Exercise 3 to the home page of the iFriends website.

Appendixes

Django Resources

This appendix lists some of the places you can go online to get more information about Django and related products. The following sections list and describe the links.

Django

`http://www.djangoproject.com`

This is the Django project home page. It contains the downloadables, documents, weblog, code, community, and so on for Django. Basically, almost everything you need to know about Django can be found here.

Python

`http://www.python.org`

This is the Python project home page. You can get links and docs for Python here. You can also download the Python modules from here.

Python Imaging Library (PIL)

`http://www.pythonware.com/products/pil/`

This is the Python Imaging Library project home page. You can get links to docs for PIL here. You can also download the PIL modules from here.

Apache

`http://httpd.apache.org/`

This is the Apache web server page. You download the web server and get documentation for installation and configuration here.

mod_python

`http://www.modpython.org`

You download the mod_python and get documentation on how to install it here. mod_python is an Apache HTTP server module that allows you to implement Python code on an Apache server.

flup

http://trac.saddi.com/flup

This is the flup wiki page. You can download flup and get additional information here. flup is a random colleciton of WSGI modules necessary to run Django with FastCGI.

FastCGI

http://www.fastcgi.com

This is the FastCGI web page. You can download FastCGI and access the docs and links here.

http://www.fastcgi.com/mod_fastcgi/docs/mod_fastcgi.html#FastCgiExternalServer

This link contains documentation specific to the FastCGI external server.

PostgreSQL Database

http://www.postgresql.org

This is the PostgreSQL project page. It contains the downloads and docs for the Postgre database.

http://initd.org/projects/psycopg1

You need the psycopg package for PostgreSQL. This page contains information on the psycopg package and a link to download it.

http://stickpeople.com/projects/python/win-psycopg/

This page contains information and a download link for the Windows version of the psycopg package for Postgre.

MySQL

http://www.mysql.com

This is the MySQL project page. You can download MySQL and get all sorts of documentation and other information here.

http://sourceforge.net/projects/mysql-python

You need to install the mysql-python package to access the MySQL database from Python. You can download the mysql-python package and get information here.

SQLite 3

http://www.sqlite.org

This is the SQLite project page. You can download SQLite and get all sorts of documentation and other information here.

http://initd.org/tracker/pysqlite

You need to install the pysqlite package to access the SQLite database from Python. You can download the pysqlite package and get information here.

Microsoft SQL Server

http://www.microsoft.com/sql/

This is the Microsoft SQL database server website. You can find download and support information as well as news and documentation here.

Oracle

http://www.oracle.com/database/

This is the Oracle database website. You can find download and support information as well as news and documentation here.

Subversion

http://subversion.tigris.org/

If you plan to use the development version of Django, you need to install Subversion. This is the Subversion download page.

http://svnbook.red-bean.com/

This page contains documentation on Subversion in case you want to use the development version of Django.

Django Form Field Objects

This appendix is a quick reference for when you add fields to forms. The first section of this appendix discusses the different types of field objects. The second section discusses the Widget objects that translate to HTML elements. The third section discusses form field to model field mapping.

Field Objects

You can add several different types of fields to forms. The advantage of different types of fields is that the form can more closely match the data types that are put into it and validated.

The following sections describe the different types of `Field` objects.

BooleanField

The `BooleanField` is used to display an HTML checkbox input element. The following list describes the `BooleanField`:

- Default Widget: `CheckboxInput`
- Empty value: `None`
- Normalized value: `True` or `False`
- Validation: Does not raise a `ValidationError`
- Optional arguments: None

CharField

The `CharField` is used to display an HTML text input element. The following list describes the `CharField`:

- Default Widget: `TextInput`
- Empty value: Empty string
- Normalized value: Unicode object

- ▶ Validation: Validates `max_length` and `min_length` if they are specified

- ▶ Optional arguments: `max_length`, `min_length`

The `max_length` argument allows you to verify that the string is no longer than the specified value. The `min_length` argument allows you to specify that the string is at least the specified length.

ChoiceField

The `ChoiceField` is used to display an HTML single-select input element. The following list describes the `ChoiceField`:

- ▶ Default Widget: `Select`

- ▶ Empty value: Empty string

- ▶ Normalized value: Unicode object

- ▶ Validation: Validates that the value exists in the list `choices`

- ▶ Required argument: `choices`

The `choices` argument accepts a Python iterable object such as a list or tuple.

DateField

The `DateField` is used to display an HTML text input element for a date. The following list describes the `DateField`:

- ▶ Default Widget: `TextInput`

- ▶ Empty value: `None`

- ▶ Normalized value: Python `datetime.date` object

- ▶ Validation: Validates that the value is a Python `date` or `datetime` or a string formatted in a particular date format

- ▶ Optional argument: `input_formats`

The `input_formats` argument allows you to specify a list of viable formats to use when converting string values to dates.

The `input_formats` argument defaults to the following:

```
'%Y-%m-%d', '%m/%d/%Y',
'%m/%d/%y', '%b %d %Y',
'%b %d, %Y','%d %b %Y',
```

```
'%d %b, %Y', '%B %d %Y',
'%B %d, %Y', '%d %B %Y',
'%d %B, %Y'
```

See Appendix C, "Formatting Dates and Times," for more information about the date format strings.

DateTimeField

The DateTimeField is used to display an HTML text input element for a date. The following list describes the DateTimeField:

▶ Default Widget: TextInput

▶ Empty value: None

▶ Normalized value: Python datetime.datetime object

▶ Validation: Validates that the value is a Python date or datetime or a string formatted in a particular date format

▶ Optional argument: input_formats

The input_formats argument allows you to specify a list of viable formats to use when converting string values to dates and times.

The input_formats argument defaults to the following:

```
'%Y-%m-%d %H:%M:%S',
'%Y-%m-%d %H:%M',
'%Y-%m-%d',
'%m/%d/%Y %H:%M:%S',
'%m/%d/%Y %H:%M',
'%m/%d/%Y',
'%m/%d/%y %H:%M:%S',
'%m/%d/%y %H:%M',
'%m/%d/%y'
```

See Appendix C for more information about the date format strings.

DecimalField

The DecimalField is used to display an HTML text input element for a Python decimal value. The following list describes the DecimalField:

▶ Default Widget: TextInput

▶ Empty value: None

▶ Normalized value: Python decimal

▶ Validation: Validates that the value is decimal (ignores any leading or trailing white spaces)

▶ Optional arguments: `max_value`, `min_value`, `max_digits`, and `decimal_places`

The `max_value` argument allows you to specify a maximum value. The `min_value` argument allows you to specify a minimum value. The `max_digits` argument allows you to specify the total maximum digits, including before and after the decimal point. The `decimal_places` argument allows you to specify the maximum number of digits allowed after the decimal point.

EmailField

The `EmailField` is used to display an HTML text input element for an email address. The following list describes the `EmailField`:

▶ Default Widget: `TextInput`

▶ Empty value: Empty string

▶ Normalized value: Unicode object

▶ Validation: Validates that the value is a valid email address

▶ Optional arguments: `max_length`, `min_length`

The `max_length` argument allows you to verify that the string is no longer than the specified value. The `min_length` argument allows you to specify that the string is at least the specified length.

FileField

The `FileField` is used to display an HTML `FileInput` element for a file upload. The following list describes the `FileField`:

▶ Default Widget: `FileInput`

▶ Empty value: `None`

▶ Normalized value: `UploadFile` object containing the filename and content

▶ Validation: Validates that nonempty file data has been bound to the form

▶ Required arguments: `filename`, `content`

When using file fields in a form, you must remember to bind the file data to the form using the `filename` and `content` arguments.

ImageField

The `ImageField` is used to display an HTML `FileInput` element for an image file upload. The following list describes the `ImageField`:

- ▶ Default Widget: `FileInput`
- ▶ Empty value: `None`
- ▶ Normalized value: `UploadFile` object containing the filename and content
- ▶ Validation: Validates that nonempty file data has been bound to the form
- ▶ Required arguments: `filename, content`

When using file fields in a form, you must remember to bind the file data to the form using the `filename` and `content` arguments.

IntegerField

The `IntegerField` is used to display an HTML text input element for a Python integer value. The following list describes the `IntegerField`:

- ▶ Default Widget: `TextInput`
- ▶ Empty value: `None`
- ▶ Normalized value: Python `integer`
- ▶ Validation: Validates that the value is an integer (ignores any leading or trailing white spaces)
- ▶ Optional arguments: `max_value, min_value`

The `max_value` argument allows you to specify a maximum value. The `min_value` argument allows you to specify a minimum value.

IPAddressField

The `IPAddressField` is used to display an HTML text input element for an IP address. The following list describes the `IPAddressField`:

- ▶ Default Widget: `TextInput`
- ▶ Empty value: Empty string
- ▶ Normalized value: Unicode object
- ▶ Validation: Validates that the value is a valid IPv4 address

MultipleChoiceField

The MultipleChoiceField is used to display an HTML multiple-select input element. The following list describes the MultipleChoiceField:

▶ Default Widget: SelectMultiple

▶ Empty value: An empty Python list ([ ])

▶ Normalized value: A list of Unicode objects

▶ Validation: Validates that each value exists in the list choices

▶ Required arguments: choices

The choices argument is required for the ChoiceField. It accepts a Python iterable object such as a list or tuple.

NullBooleanField

The NullBooleanField is used to display an HTML boolean-select input element. The following list describes the NullBooleanField:

▶ Default Widget: NullBooleanSelect

▶ Empty value: None

▶ Normalized value: True, False, or None

▶ Validation: Does not raise a ValidationError

RegexField

The RegexField is used to display an HTML text input element that contains a regular expression. The following list describes the RegexField:

▶ Default Widget: TextInput

▶ Empty value: Empty string

▶ Normalized value: Unicode object

▶ Validation: Validates that the value matches the regex expression

▶ Required arguments: regex

▶ Optional arguments: max_length, min_length, error_message

The required regex argument allows you to specify a string or a compiled regular expression.

The max_length argument allows you to verify that the string is no longer than the specified value. The min_length argument allows you to specify that the string is at least the specified length. The error_message argument allows you to specify an error message to be returned for failed validation.

TimeField

The TimeField is used to display an HTML text input element for a Python datetime value. The following list describes the TimeField:

- ▶ Default Widget: TextInput
- ▶ Empty value: None
- ▶ Normalized value: Python datetime.time object
- ▶ Validation: Validates that the value is a Python datetime.time or a string formatted in a particular time format
- ▶ Optional arguments: input_formats

The input_formats argument allows you to specify a list of viable formats to use when converting string values to times.

The input_formats argument defaults to the following:

```
'%H:%M:%S',
'%H:%M'
```

URLField

The URLFiels is used to display an HTML text input element for an URL value. The following list describes the URLField:

- ▶ Default Widget: TextInput
- ▶ Empty value: Empty string
- ▶ Normalized value: Unicode object
- ▶ Validation: Validates that the value is a valid URL
- ▶ Optional arguments: max_length, min_length, verify_exists, validator_user_agent

The max_length argument allows you to verify that the string is no longer than the specified value. The min_length argument allows you to specify that the string is at least the specified length. The verify_exists argument allows you to specify a True/False value to turn URL existence validation on or off. The validator_user_agent argument allows you to specify a string to be used as the user agent when validating URL existence. It defaults to URL_VALIDATOR_USER_AGENT.

Widget Objects

The Django forms package uses Widget objects to represent HTML elements. Widget objects are assigned to Form Field objects and provide two services. The first service is to render the Field object as an HTML element. The second service is to extract the data from the HTML elements during a GET/POST request. Table B.1 lists the Widget objects along with their HTML equivalent code.

TABLE B.1   Django Widget Objects and Their HTML Equivalents

Widget	HTML Equivalent
TextInput	<input type='text' ...
PasswordInput	<input type='password' ...
HiddenInput	<input type='hidden' ...
MultipleHiddenInput	Multiple <input type='hidden' ... instances
FileInput	<input type='file' ...
Textarea	<textarea>...</textarea>
CheckboxInput	<input type='checkbox' ...
Select	<select><option ...
NullBooleanSelect	Select widget with options Unknown, Yes, and No
SelectMultiple	<select multiple='multiple'><option ...
RadioSelect	<ul><li><input type='radio' ...
CheckboxSelectMultiple	<ul><li><input type='checkbox' ...
MultiWidget	Wrapper around multiple other widgets
SplitDateTimeWidget	Wrapper around two TextInput widgets: one for the Date and one for the Time

Form Field to Model Field Mapping

Table B.2 shows the mapping of form field objects to model field objects. This mapping is used when you use the form_for_model and form_for_instance helper functions. This table might also help you know which Field objects to use when you create custom forms.

TABLE B.2 Mapping of Form Field Objects to Model Field Objects

Model Field	Form Field
AutoField	Not represented in the form
BooleanField	BooleanField
CharField	CharField with max_length set to the model field's max_length
CommaSeparatedIntegerField	CharField
DateField	DateField
DateTimeField	DateTimeField
DecimalField	DecimalField
EmailField	EmailField
FileField	FileField
FilePathField	CharField
FloatField	FloatField
ForeignKey	ModelChoiceField
ImageField	ImageField
IntegerField	IntegerField
IPAddressField	IPAddressField
ManyToManyField	ModelMultipleChoiceField
NullBooleanField	CharField
PhoneNumberField	USPhoneNumberField
PositiveIntegerField	IntegerField
PositiveSmallIntegerField	IntegerField
SlugField	CharField
SmallIntegerField	IntegerField
TextField	CharField with widget=Textarea
TimeField	TimeField
URLField	URLField with verify_exists set equal to the model field's verify_exists
USStateField	CharField with widget=USStateSelect
XMLField	CharField with widget=Textarea

The USStateSelect and USPhoneNumberField fields are not from the standard set of Widget objects. They are from the django.contrib.localflavor.us package. Watch for additional Widgets and other things as more features are added to Django.

When each form field is generated, Django uses the following rules to set attributes on it:

▶ If the model field has blank=True, required is set to False on the form field. Otherwise, required defaults to True.

▶ The label attribute of the form field is set to the value of the verbose_name attribute of the model field. The first character is uppercase.

▶ The help_text attribute of the form field is set to the value of the help_text attribute of the model field.

▶ The Select and MultiSelect fields of the form have the same choices set as the choices listed in the model.

APPENDIX C

Formatting Dates and Times

This appendix is a quick reference for when you format dates and times in your Django templates. The following tables list the format characters that are available for the now tag and the date and time filters. Table C.1 describes the available format characters for formatting dates. Table C.2 describes the available options for formatting times.

TABLE C.1   Date Format Characters Available for datetime Objects

Character	Description	Example
b	Month, textual, three letters, lowercase.	jan
d	Day of the month, two digits with leading 0s.	01 to 31
D	Day of the week, textual, three letters.	Mon to Sun
F	Month, textual, long.	January
j	Day of the month without leading 0s.	1 to 31
l	Day of the week, textual, long.	Monday
L	Boolean for whether it's a leap year.	True or False
m	Month, two digits with leading 0s.	01 to 12
M	Month, textual, three letters.	Jan to Dec
n	Month, numeric, without leading 0s.	1 to 12
N	Month in Associated Press style. Proprietary extension.	Jan., Feb., March, May
r	RFC 822 formatted date.	Sat, 22 Sep 2007 18:12:05 +0700
S	English ordinal suffix for the day of the month, two characters.	st, nd, rd, th
t	Number of days in the given month.	28 to 31
w	Day of the week, numeric without leading 0s.	0 (Sunday) to 6 (Saturday)
W	ISO-8601 week number in the year, with weeks starting on Monday.	1, 52
y	Year, numeric, two digits.	08
Y	Year, numeric, four digits.	2008
z	Day of the year, numeric.	0 to 365

TABLE C.2 Time Format Characters Available for `datetime` and `time` Objects

Character	Description	Example
a	Lowercase ante meridiem and post meridiem, with periods.	a.m. or p.m.
A	Uppercase ante meridiem and post meridiem.	AM or PM
f	Time, in 12-hour hours and minutes, with minutes omitted if they're 00.	1, 5:30
g	Hour, 12-hour format, without leading 0s.	1 to 12
G	Hour, 24-hour format, without leading 0s.	0 to 23
h	Hour, 12-hour format, with leading 0s.	01 to 12
H	Hour, 24-hour format, with leading 0s.	00 to 23
i	Minutes, with leading 0s.	00 to 59
O	Difference to Greenwich time in hours, four digits.	+0200
P	Time, in 12-hour hours, with minutes and a.m./p.m., with minutes omitted if they're 00, and the special-case strings `midnight` and `noon` if appropriate.	1 a.m., midnight, noon, 12:30 p.m., 5:30 p.m.
r	RFC 822 formatted date.	Sat, 22 Sep 2007 18:12:05 +0700
s	Seconds, two digits with leading 0s.	00 to 59
T	Time zone of this machine.	EST, MDT
Z	Time zone offset in seconds. The offset for time zones west of UTC is always negative, and for those east of UTC, it is always positive.	−43200 to 50400

Index

PostgreSQL project home page, 478

preferences, setting language preferences, 416-421

prefixes, view prefixes, 108-110

prerequisites, installing Django, 14

previous context variable (generic views), 236

previous_day context variable (generic views), 236

previous_month context variable (generic views), 236

primary_key field option, 52

primary keys, updating objects, 90

priority member (sitemap classes), 425

process_exception( ) function, 384, 398

process_request( ) function, 384-385

process_response( ) function, 384, 394

process_view( ) function, 384, 390

program flow. See if logic

projects
  code storage location, 20
  configuring, 466
  creating, 19-21
  defined, 19
  deploying, 468-469
  placing in PYTHONPATH, 466
  synchronizing to database, 26-27

Python
  built-in packages, 20
  as Django prerequisite, 14

Python eggs, loading templates from, 270

Python Imaging Library (PIL) project home page, 477

Python project home page, 477

PYTHONPATH, placing projects in, 466

Q-R

queries, performing in database, 90-97

queryset argument (generic views), 234

QuerySets, 86
  chaining, 93-94
  ordering objects in, 94-95
  retrieving from database, 90-97

raising exceptions from get( ) function, 87

RAM, optimizing Django deployment, 472

random filter, 168-173

randomized QuerySets, 95

range (field lookup type), 93

recursive relationships, 56-57

redirect_to view, 238

referencing objects in templates, 150-151

regex (field lookup type), 93

RegexField object, 187, 486

registration
  custom tags, 276
  filters with decorator functions, 273
  generic views, limiting access to, 330
  groups, creating, 304-307
  login process, 313-318
  logout process, 318-319
  permissions, setting, 307-310
  User objects
    anonymous users, 297
    changing passwords in views, 298
    creating in views, 297-304
    explained, 295-296
    fields of, 296
  verifying authentication
    in templates, 321-325
    in views, 320

verifying permissions
  in templates, 326-330
  in views, 325-326

related_name argument
  ForeignKey field, 56
  ManyToMany field, 57

relationships, adding to models, 55
  many-to-many relationships, 56-60
  many-to-one relationships, 55-60
  one-to-one relationships, 57

released version of Django, installing, 15

remove( ) function, 309

removetags filter, 160

removing HTML tags, 160

render( ) function, 120

render_to_response( ) function, 127-128

renderer objects, creating custom tags, 275

rendering
  forms, 189, 191-194
    as lists, 190-191
    from models, 194-200
    from objects, 195-196
    as paragraphs, 191
    partial forms from models, 196-197
    as tables, 190
  templates as HTTP response, 127-128

REQUEST attribute (HttpRequest class), 65

request preprocessors, implementing, 385-389

RequestContext objects in templates, 289-290

requests, retrieving information from, 64-66

required argument (form fields), 188

requirements. See prerequisites

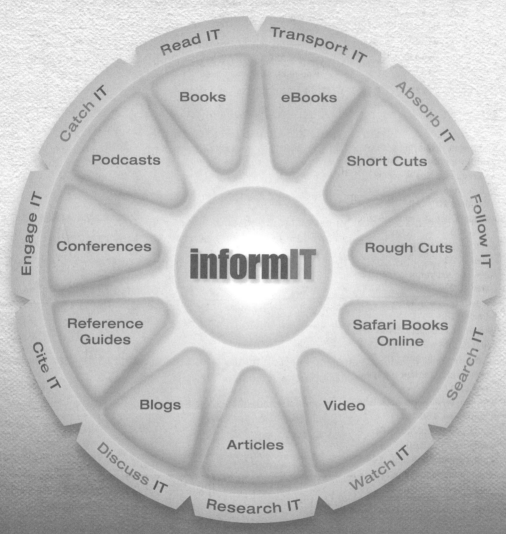

Safari Library
Subscribe Now!
http://safari.informit.com/library

Safari's entire technology collection is now available with no restrictions. Imagine the value of being able to search and access thousands of books, videos and articles from leading technology authors whenever you wish.

EXPLORE TOPICS MORE FULLY

Gain a more robust understanding of related issues by using Safari as your research tool. With Safari Library you can leverage the knowledge of the world's technology gurus. For one flat monthly fee, you'll have unrestricted access to a reference collection offered nowhere else in the world -- all at your fingertips.

With a Safari Library subscription you'll get the following premium services:

- **Immediate access to the newest, cutting-edge books** - Approximately 80 new titles are added per month in conjunction with, or in advance of, their print publication.

- **Chapter downloads** - Download five chapters per month so you can work offline when you need to.

- **Rough Cuts** - A service that provides online access to pre-published information on advanced technologies updated as the author writes the book. You can also download Rough Cuts for offline reference.

- **Videos** - Premier design and development videos from training and e-learning expert lynda.com and other publishers you trust.

- **Cut and paste code** - Cut and paste code directly from Safari. Save time. Eliminate errors.

- **Save up to 35% on print books** - Safari Subscribers receive a discount of up to 35% on publishers' print books.

Safari Books Online

Addison Wesley · Cisco Press · Microsoft Press · Peachpit Press · Redbooks · Adobe Press · FT Press (Financial Times) · New Riders · Prentice Hall · Wharton School Publishing · SAMS · ALPHA · lynda.com · O'REILLY · QUE · IBM Press

BOOKS ONLINE

ENABLED

THIS BOOK IS SAFARI ENABLED

INCLUDES FREE 45-DAY ACCESS TO THE ONLINE EDITION

The Safari® Enabled icon on the cover of your favorite technology book means the book is available through Safari Bookshelf. When you buy this book, you get free access to the online edition for 45 days.

Safari Bookshelf is an electronic reference library that lets you easily search thousands of technical books, find code samples, download chapters, and access technical information whenever and wherever you need it.

TO GAIN 45-DAY SAFARI ENABLED ACCESS TO THIS BOOK:

- Go to **informit.com/safarienabled**
- Complete the brief registration form
- Enter the coupon code found in the front of this book on the "Copyright" page .

If you have difficulty registering on Safari Bookshelf or accessing the online edition, please e-mail customer-service@safaribooksonline.com.